No Justice in Germany
The Breslau Diaries, 1933–1941

STANFORD STUDIES IN JEWISH HISTORY AND CULTURE

EDITED BY *Aron Rodrigue and Steven J. Zipperstein*

No Justice in Germany
The Breslau Diaries, 1933–1941

Willy Cohn

Edited by Norbert Conrads

TRANSLATED BY KENNETH KRONENBERG

STANFORD UNIVERSITY PRESS

STANFORD, CALIFORNIA

Stanford University Press
Stanford, California

English translation ©2012 by the Board of Trustees of the Leland Stanford Junior University. All rights reserved.

No Justice in Germany: The Breslau Diaries, 1933–1941 was originally published in German under the title *Kein Recht, nirgends. Breslauer Tagebücher 1933–1941. Eine Auswahl.* ©2006 by Böhlau Verlag GmbH & Cie, Köln Weimar Wien.

Introduction ©2012 by the Board of Trustees of the Leland Stanford Junior University. All rights reserved.

The translation of this work was funded by Geisteswissenschaften International— Translation Funding for Humanities and Social Sciences from German, a joint initiative of the Fritz Thyssen Foundation, the German Federal Foreign Office, the collecting society VG WORT, and the Börsenverein des Deutschen Buchhandels [German Publishers & Booksellers Association].

Printed in the United States of America on acid-free, archival-quality paper

Library of Congress Cataloging-in-Publication Data

Cohn, Willy, 1888-1941, author.
  [Kein Recht, nirgends. English]
  No justice in Germany : the Breslau diaries, 1933-1941 / Willy Cohn ; edited by Norbert Conrads ; translated by Kenneth Kronenberg.
     pages cm
  Translation of: Kein Recht, nirgends.
  ISBN 978-0-8047-7324-9 (cloth : alk. paper)
  1. Cohn, Willy, 1888-1941—Diaries. 2. Historians—Poland—Wroclaw—Diaries.
  3. Holocaust, Jewish (1939-1945)—Poland—Wroclaw—Personal narratives.
  4. Jews—Persecutions—Poland—Wroclaw. I. Conrads, Norbert, editor. II.
  Kronenberg, Kenneth, 1946- translator. III. Title.
  DS134.72.C64A3 2012
  940.53'15092—dc23

                          2011040725

Typeset by Bruce Lundquist in 10.5/14 Galliard

Contents

Translator's Note

I have spent the past fifteen years of my translation career increasingly focused on diaries and letters. I am fascinated with these documents because they display so clearly the complexity of people's motives and responses to the times in which they live. We may believe that we think one way, but our minds are always battlefields in which contending beliefs and notions struggle interminably. Yet somehow we manage to make our way in the society in which we were born. The writings of diarists, in which they pour out their responses to life, give us a sense after the fact of the contradictory impulses that drove them, and perhaps others, to feel and act the way they did.

Willy Cohn was a complex individual: an Orthodox Jew and a socialist; an ardent Zionist and a staunch German patriot; a democrat but an admirer of Nazi resolve and sometimes even policy; a realist and an idealist often not up to grappling effectively; generous to a fault but also occasionally petty and stubborn. These and other contradictions within his personality, and the wealth of detail that poured from his pen, give us a unique view of a disorienting and frightening time in Germany.

Of course, as always, the editing process—in this case, the selection of one volume's worth of diary entries out of Cohn's opus of years—imposes a perspective, the editor's. But the perspective of the editor of these diaries, Norbert Conrads, has been so capacious that it has permitted the contradictions in Willy Cohn's personality to come to the fore. For a translator, engaged perforce in close reading of Cohn's writings, there can be nothing more fascinating. I hope that my translation will allow his readers to get fully acquainted with this man and his world.

✳

A few comments about vocabulary and footnotes: In general, I have used the most common English spellings for transliterations of Hebrew and Yiddish terms. In this, I was guided by Abraham Ascher, who gave unstintingly of his time. In the case of German words, mostly honorifics and professional titles, I have generally kept the original. But while Direktor can easily be translated as "director," Konsistorialrat (Councilor of the Consistory) and the like convey little to an English-speaking reader and would tend to weigh down the sentence. The same applies to Nazi titles, for which there are no really exact English equivalents. Any possibly unfamiliar terms are defined in the Glossary at the back of the book.

Because of the many Hebrew and Yiddish words that Cohn used freely, we were faced with the problem of which words to italicize. If every non-English word were italicized, the reader might feel swamped. If none, the reader might simply read over them. If some but not others, then on what basis should we decide? I threw up my hands. Richard Gunde, who ably edited the manuscript, distinguished mainly between words that an English-speaking reader might know and those that are perhaps more esoteric. So, words like aliyah or yahrzeit are set in roman, while less common ones like *eruv, teshuva, moire,* and the like are italicized. No doubt, a subjective criterion, but it felt workable to me. I hope the seeming inconsistencies will not annoy the reader.

There are approximately five hundred footnotes in *No Justice in Germany: The Breslau Diaries*. Many of them are references likely to be of interest mainly to specialists. But there are also a very large number of explanatory notes, without which the general reader is likely to have trouble deciphering what is going on. The dirty little secret about endnotes, the usual form of references in scholarly books, is that very few people read them. No reader wants to flip back and forth to references that are hard to locate and too often of little help. That is why I was so delighted when Norris Pope, Director of Scholarly Publishing at Stanford University Press, acceded to my request that footnotes rather than endnotes be used in *The Breslau Diaries*. That makes this contextual material far more accessible, greatly enriching the diaries.

Looking beyond the specific place of footnotes in *The Breslau Diaries*, I have started to wonder whether, in the age of the Internet, the time may have come to rescue references from the nether world of back matter, and restore them to their proper place at the bottom of the page—but now reenvisioned as hypertext. I like the image of the reader "clicking" visually to the bottom of the page and returning with that little piece extra. And perhaps authors will come to see footnotes not merely as necessary scholarly apparatus, but as another opportunity to connect with their readers.

Finally, I cannot imagine a better collaborator in translation than Norbert Conrads. He made himself generously available through all my obsessional questioning, even returning to the archive on occasion to check whether he had transcribed something correctly. His book was wonderful in German, and I hope that this English version does it justice.

KENNETH KRONENBERG
CAMBRIDGE, MASSACHUSETTS
FEBRUARY 15, 2012

Introduction

Prior to the Nazi era, there were three important centers of Jewish life in Germany: Berlin, in Prussia; Frankfurt am Main; and Breslau, in Silesia. The Jewish communities of Frankfurt and Breslau are approximately equally old. But only the Jewish community of Breslau may claim, based on a gravestone from the year 1203, that one of its forebears, Rabbi David, son of Rabbi Sar Schalom, was the very first inhabitant of the city for whom we have a name. Willy Cohn, the author of this diary, made that startling discovery. Over the centuries, the Jewish community of Breslau was subject to alternating periods of recognition, exile, and toleration. Only under Prussian rule were the Jews of Breslau granted permanent settlement rights, and as a result, the Jewish population grew rapidly during and after the nineteenth century. Membership in the synagogues of Breslau totaled 24,503 in 1930.[1] Naturally, this did not include non-observant Jews who did not belong to a synagogue or people of Jewish origin who had converted to Christianity.

Breslau's synagogues, of which only the Zum weissen Storch Synagogue remains, were central to the life of the community. In his diary, Cohn reports the destruction of the magnificent New Synagogue. But the crown jewel of the Jewish community was perhaps its renowned rabbinical school, the Jewish Theological Seminary.[2] Here was devel-

1. Official information, dated August 26, 1930, sent to Willy Cohn by the administrative director of the Breslau Jewish Community, Dr. Ernst Rechnitz. It is housed in the Breslau Community Archive, now the Żydowski Instytut Historyczny [Jewish Historical Institute], in Warsaw.

2. Guido Kisch (ed.), *Das Breslauer Seminar. Jüdisch-Theologisches Seminar "Fraenckelsche Stiftung" in Breslau* (Tübingen: J.C.B. Mohr, 1963).

oped the concept of a "Science of Judaism," which became the model for later rabbinical schools in Berlin, Budapest, and New York. Thanks to the patronage of education-minded philanthropists, Breslau developed a flourishing culture of Jewish schools, evening schools for adults, hospitals, old-age homes, lodges, societies, museums, and foundations.[3] Among other things, this environment provided fertile ground for a number of Nobel Prize winners. This history has been more than well described by others.[4] Nonetheless, it took only a few short years to eradicate this culture. Willy Cohn's diaries describe with incomparable intensity the destruction of Jewish Breslau between 1933 and 1941.

For many years, Willy Cohn (1888–1941) was known only to historians specializing in the Middle Ages or Silesian Jewry. These were both areas in which he published. It had, in fact, long been his dream to become a historian; however, the times in which he came of age were not favorable. Instead, he became one of the most important chroniclers, not only of the history of the Jews of Silesia, but of Germany as a whole. Cohn never sought this role; it was thrust on him by fate and his own intellectual leanings. Cohn was an *homme de lettres* who had kept a diary most of his life. He did it for himself alone, without any view toward later publication. At the same time, he was a sophisticated researcher and scholar who formed independent judgments about his life, his environment, and world events. Only during the last years of his life, as he increasingly came to understand the implications of the Nazi regime's persecution of the Jews, did he become a conscious witness of the terrible times in which he lived. Future generations must be informed about what happened. And so, Cohn's diary entries became increasingly dense and detailed. In the end, he chronicled the mounting evidence that he and the Jewish community as a whole were in mortal danger. This increasing awareness led him to discussions with acquaintances in Berlin, and with the director of the Cathedral Archive, in Breslau, about how his manuscripts, and especially his many diaries, could be saved from destruction by the Nazis in the horrors that were

3. Mirosława Lenarcik, *A Community in Transition: Jewish Welfare in Breslau-Wrocław* (Opladen and Farmington Hills, MI: Barbara Budrich Publishers, 2010).

4. Abraham Ascher, *A Community under Siege: The Jews of Breslau under Nazism* (Stanford, CA: Stanford University Press, 2007).

about to be unleashed. In these plans he succeeded. The rescue of his intellectual legacy may well have been the only consolation that Cohn took with him to his death, in November 1941.

Willy Cohn came from a family of businessmen who moved to Breslau from what was then the Prussian province of Posen. His father, Louis Cohn (1843–1903), worked himself up from modest beginnings, eventually founding a sizable business dealing in textiles and fabric trimmings, in the central business area of Breslau. His mother, Margarete Hainauer, came from a well-known family of music publishers in Breslau. His parents, having become rather well-to-do, visited the World's Fair in Paris in 1889, and in 1902 they constructed a building to house their business, which to this day is impressive for its grandeur and workmanship. They saw themselves as German Jews, and there was little question but that they would name their son, who was born in 1888, the so-called Year of the Three Kaisers, after Kaiser Wilhelm. At Christmastime, they lit both a menorah and a Christmas tree. They were members of the Reform New Synagogue, located in the Schweidnitzer Stadtgraben, and it was here that Willy Cohn celebrated his bar mitzvah, in 1901.

Cohn followed more in the footsteps of his mother when, in 1906, he took up his studies in history. When he sat for his doctoral examination in 1909, in Breslau, he was not yet 21. His dissertation was about the history of the Norman Sicilian fleet.[5] He continued to be interested in Norman and Hohenstaufen history throughout his life, and it was a matter of some pride when he heard colleagues refer to him as "Cohn the Norman." He continued his studies, but ultimately gave up his plans for an academic career when it became clear that, as a Jew, the other historians on the faculty of the University of Breslau rejected him. His attempts to gain a professorship at the Pedagogical Academy of Breslau were also thwarted. Cohn turned to teaching because he had gotten married in 1913 and needed a steady income. When the war broke out, in 1914, Cohn was drafted and sent to the front. He learned about the birth of his first son, Wolfgang (Louis), in 1915, while in France. His second son, Ernst (Abraham), was born during the politically turbulent

---

5. Willy Cohn, *Die Geschichte der normannisch-sicilischen Flotte unter der Regierung Rogers I. und Rogers II. (1060–1154)* (Breslau: M. & H. Marcus, 1910).

year 1919. Cohn was awarded the Iron Cross for his bravery in the field. Never could he have imagined that his services to Germany would one day count for nothing.

Nonetheless, it was sobering to realize that, even during the war, Jewish devotion to duty was valued less than that of other Germans. This increasingly caused him to doubt the wisdom of Jewish assimilation. He began to move away from the Reform Judaism of his parents, turning instead to "positive Judaism," which confirmed him in his Jewish faith. Cohn came to see Zionism and the construction of a Jewish Palestine as the wave of the future. Politically, he became a Social Democrat, joined the party, took part in their associations, and wrote several socialist books for young people. Cohn taught at the Breslau Free Evening School for Adults from its inception, in 1919, to its closure, and he was an engaged member of the Lessing Lodge and other Jewish lodges in Breslau. In 1924 the Lessing Lodge elected him president for a year.

The Johannesgymnasium, in Breslau, remained the center of his teaching activities. What set the school apart from other gymnasiums in Breslau was that it was completely integrated. The faculty was split more or less evenly among Protestants, Catholics, and Jews, and the same held true for the student body. Cohn taught history, German literature, and geography from 1919 to his firing in 1933. By all accounts he was a good and very well-liked teacher. The historian Walter Laqueur was one of his students. Political problems or anti-Semitism had for years been virtually unknown. Christian religious teachers taught alongside rabbis. Cohn continued his scholarly work throughout his career as a teacher. He attended historical conferences and carried on correspondence with other scholars in his fields of interest. A stipend in 1927 allowed him to pursue studies in Sicily, which vastly increased his contacts. When his book about the Hohenstaufens appeared in 1923, in an Italian translation, the Società di Storia Patria per la Sicilia Orientale, in Catania, elected him a member.[6] In early 1933 Cohn's reputation and output were at their height. By this time, he was 44 years old, had married a second time, had two sons from his first marriage and two daughters from

6. Willy Cohn, *L'età degli Hohenstaufen in Sicilia*, translation by Guido Libertini (Catania, 1932).

his second. And he continued to be full of plans for future scholarly work. That came to an end, on January 30, 1933, with Hitler's seizure of power, which cast a dark shadow on everything he had built up.

Nazism not only made anti-Semitism socially acceptable in Germany, it was integral to the movement's program. The Jewish community of Breslau responded to this challenge with a renewed sense of purpose. The synagogues and other community institutions became even more central to Jewish religious, cultural, and economic life. Jewish schools experienced a short-lived renewal, gathering together Jewish students who had been forced out of other schools. The Jewish Museum was reopened with a gala event, and Cohn was a member of the museum board. Jewish journals and newspapers, lodges, and the cultural sphere in general seemed, briefly, to flourish. Cohn, who had been forced into retirement in 1933, was even able to eke out a living for a time on the modest honorariums paid to him on his lecture tours through Silesia and elsewhere in Germany. The crash, however, was rapid. When Cohn was fired from his teaching position, the official reason given was "political unreliability"; not only was he a Jew, he was also an active Social Democrat. As a result of this stigma, not even the Jewish Community, the administrative body of the community as a whole, was willing to put him on the payroll. They were unwilling to risk accusations of harboring the politically suspect. It was not long before Jewish businessmen were forced to sell the fruits of their labors to "Aryans" and the harassment of all Jewish professionals began in earnest. Understandably, Jews throughout Germany sought to emigrate, with almost any country deemed suitable as long as it accepted Jews.

These excerpted diaries leave out much of the daily life of the Cohns, his family, and their relatives in Breslau and Berlin chronicled in his diaries as a whole, although the texture of the diaries is largely intact. We see Cohn's increasing efforts at emigration. Although he initially believed that he could stay in Germany, he made sure that his children got out as soon as they were able. His eldest son fled to Paris immediately after taking his school-leaving examination (Abitur). Ernst and Ruth came to share their father's Zionist dreams, and in March 1935 16-year-old Ernst joined a youth group leaving for Palestine. From there he did all he could to bring his parents over. In 1939 Cohn's second wife, Gertrud (Trudi), enabled her 14-year-old daughter Ruth to go to Denmark on a Youth Aliyah. Even though Denmark was occupied by Germany in April 1940, Ruth nonetheless made her way, hazardous as it was, via Moscow and Istanbul to Palestine.

And in 1937 Cohn and his wife made an exploratory trip to Palestine, where they spent some weeks with Ernst. This "peaceful interlude" in Germany saw a large number of German Jews visiting Mandate Palestine, to explore the possibilities of emigration. To Cohn's amazement, he often ran into old acquaintances from Breslau. And although Cohn would gladly have stayed in Palestine, the couple had two daughters waiting for them back in Breslau. But more than that, Trudi, always more practical and down-to-earth than her idealistic husband, expressed deep misgivings about the regimentation and discomforts of kibbutz life. And it slowly began to dawn on Cohn himself that an aging intellectual of his cut might have a hard time providing for his family in a frontier society. His diary entries from this trip, which are included unabridged, movingly depict his deep attachment to the Promised Land, and the growing realization that his intended emigration was not to be. It was the shattering of his hopes and dreams. Upon his return to Breslau, Cohn plunged into his work, beginning new book projects and plans — all in an effort to numb himself. A sense of resignation becomes evident in his writings.

The *geserah* of November 9, 1938, what we now refer to as Kristallnacht, cleared away any illusions he might have harbored. The New Synagogue was in flames; most synagogues and Jewish institutions, both sacred and profane, were demolished, and many that were not were confiscated. Relatives and friends were dragged off to the concentration camp at Buchenwald, including his own brother and brother-in-law, along with more than two thousand Breslau Jews. Cohn himself avoided arrest, but as he noted, "In my opinion, these days are among the blackest not only in Jewish, but also in German history, and I believe that many Germans are ashamed of what is happening."

Cohn's sense of sitting in a "mouse trap" increased after the pogroms of November 1938, and the outbreak of war, in 1939, as did his realization that he had been too slow to act to get himself and his family out of Germany. One after another, Jewish institutions were confiscated or banned on the flimsiest of pretexts. With Jewish newspapers shuttered, conversations after services at the synagogue became the most important source of information. In some cases, Cohn was extremely well informed about the fate of Polish and other Jews. Despairing, he asked why civilized humanity did not intervene even as Jews in the Warsaw ghetto were dying like flies.

Cohn was able to derive some emotional relief (not to mention needed income) from a scholarly commission that Chief Rabbi Leo Baeck, in Berlin, was able to steer his way, writing articles for *Germania Judaica*, an encyclopedic reference work chronicling Jewish life in Germany up to 1349, the time of the Black Death.[7] This work led to several meetings between Baeck and Cohn in Breslau. But in order to do this work, Cohn would have needed access to the libraries of Breslau, from which Jews were banned by decree, on January 15, 1939. Only the archive and library of the Catholic diocese continued to allow him to work freely. In fact, from May 1939 to his deportation in November 1941, he was an honored guest in that library. This was virtually the only place where he could meet with like-minded scholars, exchange information, and derive some consolation. Among other things, the personnel there had much more detailed information about the crimes committed against Jews in Poland. This is where Cohn learned that some twelve thousand Jews had been shot in Lemberg (now Lviv, in western Ukraine), an unfathomable and extremely ominous piece of news.

In this hopeless situation, Cohn took out his older diaries and began to write his memoirs, something that he had long planned to do. In October 1940 he noted, "It will be a thick book that will bear witness to what German Jewry once was." He finished this project barely a year later. The memoir, published in German under the title *Verwehte Spuren* [Faded Traces], in 1995, runs to 776 pages—thick indeed.[8] Just how this manuscript was salvaged amply demonstrates Willy Cohn's sense of desperation in 1941, and how important it was to him that his testimony be available to future generations. At the time, he kept work on this book, of which he prepared several carbon copies, completely secret. One of these

7. Norbert Conrads, "Die verlorene Germania Judaica. Ein Handbuch- und Autorenschicksal im Dritten Reich," in *Berichte und Forschungen. Jahrbuch des Bundesinstituts für Kultur und Geschichte der Deutschen im östlichen Europa*, vol. 15 (2007), pp. 215–254.

8. Willy Cohn, *Verwehte Spuren. Erinnerungen an das Breslauer Judentum vor seinem Untergang*, ed. Norbert Conrads (Cologne: Böhlau, 1995).

he kept. He gave another copy to the director of the Diocese Archive, in Breslau, and he deposited a third copy in the General Archive of the Jews in Germany, in Berlin. It is not known whether there were other hiding places, but these three manuscripts survived. Willy Cohn, probably the most important witness to the destruction of the Breslau Jewish community, became more widely known only with their publication in 1995.

The deportations of the Breslau Jews were accomplished in accordance with regular bureaucratic protocol. The deportees were informed by mail when they were to vacate their dwellings. Everyone knew that this meant "relocation." Cohn received his notice on November 15, 1941. A year earlier, his family had already prepared an emergency suitcase for this eventuality. Cohn used the time remaining to save his most important manuscripts. He packed up all of his diaries and other writings and sent them to an address in Berlin. On November 21, earlier than expected, Cohn and his family, and about a thousand other Breslau Jews, were rousted out of bed and brought to a prepared assembly place, where they were forced to remain for four days. That is how long it took the Gestapo to record and catalog the assets of the deportees. Everything that remained behind was declared the property of the German Reich. On November 25 these thousand people were led to the nearby Odertor railway station, where a train was waiting to take them to an unknown destination. That destination was Kovno (Kaunas), in Lithuania. We now know much about the terrible events that occurred here and elsewhere. More than 67,000 human beings were murdered in Kovno. At the same time as the train from Breslau arrived in Kovno, another train, again carrying exactly a thousand Jews, from Vienna, arrived as well. Shortly after their arrival, they were taken to a pre-dug pit at Fort Nine, in Kovno, where, on November 29, 1941, they were mowed down by machine gun fire. SS-Standartenführer Karl Jäger oversaw this "action." His written report gave the precise body count: 693 men, 1,155 women, and 152 children, all "resettlers." Willy Cohn, his wife Gertrud, and their daughters Susanne and Tamara were among the victims. Tamara Cohn was barely 3 years old. It comes as a shock to realize that only twelve days elapsed between his last surviving diary entry, on November 17, and the family's grisly murder, on November 29. It is our good fortune that he acted as quickly as he did.

✳

This introduction would be incomplete without some comments about the author's personality and attitudes, and about the manuscript itself. Willy Cohn's diaries are frequently compared to those of his contemporary, Victor Klemperer.[9] Perhaps the greatest difference between the two is in their attitude toward religion. As a young man, Klemperer left Judaism and became an agnostic. Nor did he return to Judaism during the persecutions. Cohn, by contrast, was a faithful and devout Jew for whom regular prayer was a necessity. This is clearly reflected in his diaries, in which the name of God is never spelled out, and which is full of Hebrew words and phrases, sometimes in Hebrew script. He found his religious home in the small Abraham Mugdan Synagogue close to his apartment. He valued its intimacy and the sermons of Rabbi Louis Lewin. Cohn sought to understand the Torah through his own experience. He took Hebrew lessons and began to "study," that is, engage with the text in theological exegesis. He admired the piety and textual knowledge of the eastern Jews, even as he shared with other German Jews certain widely held prejudices against his eastern coreligionists.

Cohn's political judgments are occasionally so self-contradictory that they confound the reader. What must be borne in mind is that Cohn so loved German culture that he was unwilling to relinquish his sense of patriotism and belonging merely because Germany happened to have an anti-Semitic government at the moment. This was the country for which he had risked his life in World War I, and which had awarded him the Iron Cross. Like many Germans, he considered the provisions of the Versailles Treaty to be unjust, and so he agreed with some of the revisionist goals of Hitler's foreign policy. He also applauded the "annexation" of Austria and the end of Czechoslovakia. The latter, he noted, merely reestablished a reality that had existed for centuries. He was also sympathetic to Nazi propaganda about "living space" because as a Zionist he advocated the same for the Jews in Palestine. Even more problematic, however, was when he tried to understand the arguments Hitler used in his incitement speeches. Cohn still viewed Hitler as a

9. Victor Klemperer, *I Will Bear Witness: A Diary of the Nazi Years, 1933–1941*, translated from the German by Martin Chalmers (New York: Random House, 1998).

"head of state" who represented his Fatherland. In 1939, when the Wehrmacht quickly quashed all resistance on the way to victory over Poland, Cohn actually praised Hitler's military success: "We must recognize the greatness of this man, who has given the world a new look." It is difficult to understand such a statement coming from a man who, not a year earlier, had lived through the organized destruction of November 9, 1938. It would have been impermissible to suppress such statements, because they are part and parcel of Cohn's contradictory personality. We can see more from today's perspective than could an observer in 1939, trying to make sense of the welter of confusing and contradictory social and psychological impulses and filtered news reports. Cohn had no idea where events were leading, nor could he have known what happened at Auschwitz. In some sense, Cohn's inner conflict between his sense of injustice and his political sympathies is representative of a certain Jewish mindset of the times, and defines the dilemma facing many of his contemporaries.

Anyone who reads this history as Cohn set it to paper will understand that such statements taken out of context are not what is essential in this book. His subject matter is the fate of the Jews of Breslau, and of their important and rich cultural and intellectual community. No document describes as comprehensively and feelingly the progressive disenfranchisement and despair of the Jewish community in his home city as do these diaries. Within a brief few years that community went from merely being "different" to stigmatization to total elimination. The author and his family shared that fate. Cohn must have recognized that something fundamental was changing when, in 1933, he wrote, "Nowhere in Germany is there justice any longer! Nowhere." The title of the German edition of this book is taken from that quote.

The discovery of Willy Cohn as a chronicler of the Breslau Jewish community began in 1975, when Joseph Walk, in Jerusalem, published excerpts of the diary from the year 1941.[10] A few years later, I got in touch with Walk, and it was through him that I met Cohn's surviving

10. Joseph Walk (ed.), *Als Jude in Breslau, 1941. Aus den Tagebüchern von Studienrat a.D. Dr. Willy Israel Cohn* (Jerusalem: Bar-Ilan University Institute for Research of Diaspora Jewry/Verband ehemaliger Breslauer und Schlesier in Israel, 1975).

children. It took time to gain their confidence, and I only gradually learned about the scope of the manuscripts that had been rescued, his memoirs and his many diaries.[11] In the end we spent very fruitful years collaborating to bring their father's writings to the attention of the public. Just in terms of sheer size, the 1,048 tightly typed pages of his memoir was astonishing. Only after its publication, in 1995, was I shown the entire diaries—all 112 "books" comprising approximately 10,000 pages. For my purposes, I elected to work with the 59 "books" (4,600 pages) covering the years 1933 to 1941. Chronologically, they proceed from the memoir, which stopped in 1933.

The volume of material was so enormous that the loss of a few "books," as Cohn called his diaries, hardly made a difference. The biggest problem was to extract what was essential. I attempted to retain unabridged what is of historical significance in the text, present both politically important and awkward or embarrassing material, but to leave out what I deemed inessential or of a wholly private nature. The large two-volume edition, available only in German, indicates clearly where abridgments were made. The first edition, with its lengthy introduction and personal and place indexes, was very well received.[12] Among other things, the diaries were the subject of a documentary on German television.[13] It also raised the need for a shorter volume, one that would condense the diaries by another two-thirds. Initially, I was less than enthusiastic about shortening the text even more drastically. In any such undertaking, it is unavoidable that certain information, and even persons, must fall by the wayside. I have added chapter headings for the convenience of the reader. These are obviously of an editorial nature and were not in the original because no diarist can know what the next day will bring. They are simply meant as a guide. Legibility has been improved by removing the brackets and ellipses that indicated

11. All of these manuscripts are housed under Signature P 88 in the Central Archives for the History of the Jewish People, in Jerusalem. Recently, Cohn's intellectual legacy has been available on-line. See http://sites.huji.ac.il/cahjp/RP088%20 Cohn.pdf.

12. Willy Cohn, *Kein Recht, nirgends. Tagebuch vom Untergang des Breslauer Judentums 1933–1941*, ed. Norbert Conrads, 2 vols. (Cologne: Böhlau, 2006).

13. The documentary, by Petra Lidschreiber, *Ein Jude, der Deutschland liebte*, was awarded the Bavarian Television Prize in 2009.

abridgments. My primary goal was to concentrate on events within the city of Breslau itself, which largely eliminated Cohn's experiences and observations on his travels. The main exception is his important trip to Palestine, in 1937, which is presented in its totality. But these are mainly "Breslau diaries" as the title indicates. This shortened version again brought Willy Cohn to public attention. Two editions have appeared in Germany, another in the Polish language.[14]

This English-language edition is based on the shortened version of the diaries. It fulfills one of the last wishes of Cohn's son Louis, who died in 2009. Because the relatives of the family have made their lives in all corners of the world, and the younger members of the family do not generally speak German, they may now get to know their grandfather or great-grandfather through this edition of his diaries.

I have many people to thank for this opportunity. First, I wish to thank the historian Abraham Ascher, who put me in touch with Norris Pope, at Stanford University Press. I thank Norris Pope for publishing this book in the respected Stanford Studies in Jewish History and Culture. Gad Freudenthal, in Paris, was good enough to check and improve the Hebrew glossary. My work with my translator, Kenneth Kronenberg, in Cambridge, Massachusetts, proved fortuitous. Whenever there was a lack of clarity in the text, his perceptive questions often led to improvements.

Finally, it should be noted that publication of this edition of the diaries coincides with the seventieth anniversary of the death of their author and his family. In this sense, the book serves as a memorial.

NORBERT CONRADS
STUTTGART, NOVEMBER 29, 2011

14. Willy Cohn, *Żadnego prawa—nigdzie. Dziennik z Breslau 1933–1941*, selected and edited by Norbert Conrads, translated from the German by Viktor Grotowicz (Wrocław: Via Nova, 2010).

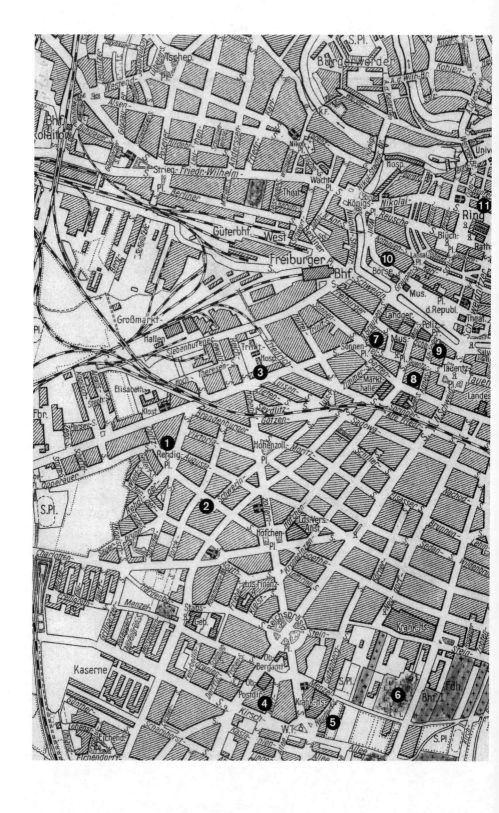

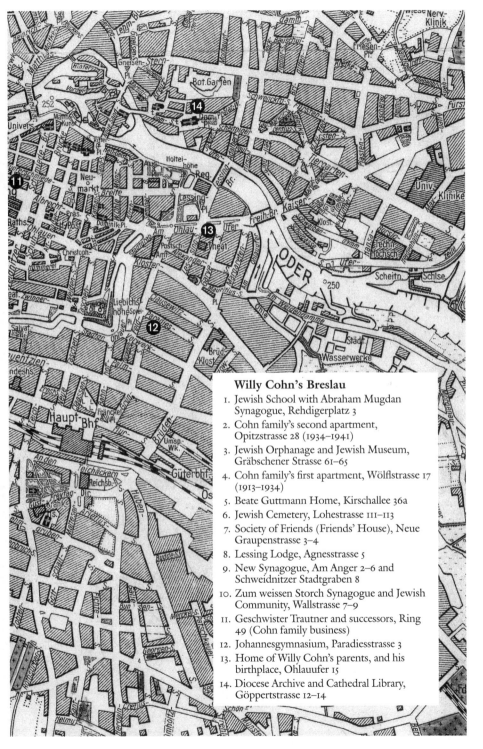

Willy Cohn's Breslau

1. Jewish School with Abraham Mugdan Synagogue, Rehdigerplatz 3
2. Cohn family's second apartment, Opitzstrasse 28 (1934–1941)
3. Jewish Orphanage and Jewish Museum, Gräbschener Strasse 61–65
4. Cohn family's first apartment, Wölflstrasse 17 (1913–1934)
5. Beate Guttmann Home, Kirschallee 36a
6. Jewish Cemetery, Lohestrasse 111–113
7. Society of Friends (Friends' House), Neue Graupenstrasse 3–4
8. Lessing Lodge, Agnesstrasse 5
9. New Synagogue, Am Anger 2–6 and Schweidnitzer Stadtgraben 8
10. Zum weissen Storch Synagogue and Jewish Community, Wallstrasse 7–9
11. Geschwister Trautner and successors, Ring 49 (Cohn family business)
12. Johannesgymnasium, Paradiesstrasse 3
13. Home of Willy Cohn's parents, and his birthplace, Ohlauufer 15
14. Diocese Archive and Cathedral Library, Göppertstrasse 12–14

Map 1. Breslau, 1932. Herder-Institut, Marburg, map collection, K 14 VIII B 33.

The Seizure of Power
and the Abolition of Rights

Monday, January 30, 1933   Breslau

Today is a free day, and I spent a few hours at my desk working on my Norman book. I continue to enjoy it. In the afternoon, I lay down without actually being able to sleep. When I got up, I heard the news that Hitler has been named Reich Chancellor. That had been anticipated over the past several days once Schleicher had been toppled. I fear that this means civil war. Before long, the Right will be victorious, but in the end we will see Communism! And if there's a revolution from the Left, it won't be so benign. But if Hitler sticks to the constitution, he'll be finished as far as his own people are concerned. Troubled times in any case, especially for us Jews. We're sitting in a mouse trap.

Tuesday, January 31, 1933   Breslau

The transition is nasty! They won't shy away from inflationary maneuvers in order to get their SA and SS people into official positions. The boycott against everything intellectual and Jewish will intensify. All we can do is grit our teeth and get through it.

Wednesday, February 1, 1933   Breslau

Yesterday evening a large torch parade. Thank G'd I didn't see any signs of the brown thugs.[1] Now we've got an interim National Socialist com-

---

The dates and days in this edition correspond to those in the original manuscript. We retained the original notation even where dates or days differed by a day. In these few instances the exact date is uncertain but largely inconsequential.

1. As an observant Jew, Cohn never wrote out the German word for God (Gott), but always abbreviated it G'tt. The brown thugs he refers to are members of Ernst Röhm's paramilitary Sturmabteilung (SA).

missarial leader in the Ministry of Culture. If I saw any possible way, I would immediately quit the teaching profession.

Saturday, February 4, 1933   Breslau
Yesterday I did something that I had long intended: I rewrote my will, etc., and wrote a farewell letter to Trudi. All that has to be done too; everyone has to keep their house in order. I am in a rather melancholy mood today and often very much at odds with myself.

Saturday, February 11, 1933   Breslau
We listened to Hitler's speech from the Sportpalast. "A resounding clatter of empty talk," my late teacher Winkler would have said. But Hitler knows how to seduce the dumb masses with his hoopla. He adjusts everything to resonate with the German mentality, even the propaganda about the dead.

Monday, February 20, 1933   Breslau
Today is Trudi's birthday. She is 32 years old. Yesterday evening we spoke frankly about a number of matters, the things that weigh heavily on me, and so it's now easier for me. I told Trudi how unbearable I find things, and how helpless I often feel about the struggle to make a living.

Disgusting Nazi posters with the most grotesque distortions of history have been put up on advertising pillars. The SPD is even being made responsible for inflation. Everything is being turned on its head. One newspaper stated that "all our misfortunes are the fault of the Jews." Repulsive.

Friday, February 24, 1933   Breslau
Yesterday Herr Hitler is supposed to have said that Löbe and his party must be eradicated.[2] I often get the feeling that we are dealing with hysterics who break out in howls whenever they feel emotionally insecure! A person can commit what he thinks about these people only to his diary because any open and public expression of opinion is imme-

---

2. Paul Löbe (1875–1967) was a politician of the Social Democratic Party (SPD). He was editor-in-chief of the *Breslauer Volkswacht* from 1899, and sat on the Breslau city council from 1904 to 1918. Löbe had been a member of the Reichstag since 1920 and was president of the Reichstag from 1920 to 1932.

diately gagged. We have to be prepared for terror of all sorts. Nowhere in Germany is there justice any longer! Nowhere.

I think frequently about Palestine, but I'm sure that if I were there I might well feel homesick for Germany! That is our lot as Jews, but perhaps our children will develop more of an inner consistency in their being. Things don't go the way we intend; we're always somehow dependent on money.

Sunday, February 26, 1933 Breslau
Yesterday Göring apparently gave a speech full of the most hideous insults against Jews. Direct incitement to murder! The passions of the masses are being whipped up to the utmost. Just as in the Middle Ages! In part even worse. One would like not to think about it, but that doesn't work. Even so, it is very difficult to rip my love for Germany completely from my heart.

Tuesday, February 28, 1933 Breslau
The first thing I heard this morning was that the Reichstag is burning. The boys learned about it on the radio. Now it is being claimed that the Communists did it, but surely it must be the work of paid provocateurs. The ugliest terror is being unleashed against the entire Left. Perhaps this battle will at least unite the working classes.

Friday, March 3, 1933 Breslau
During the break, while I was supervising, Vogelstein came up to me and showed me a letter that he had just received from the Jewish Community.[3] An eighth- or ninth-year student's life was being threatened because a National Socialist student had been suspended from school on account of him. I realized immediately that this had to do with the Müller case and was aimed at my son Wölfl. The director called me out of social studies class and took me to his office, where we discussed the entire matter. Until the examinations, Wölfl is not to go out at night, and then he must leave town! In the afternoon, Herr Schwarz, who had learned about the matter by chance, came by.

---

3. Hermann Vogelstein (1870–1942) was a rabbi in Breslau from 1920 to 1938 and one of the leading proponents of Reform Judaism. The Jewish Community was the administrative body of the Jewish community as a whole.

Wednesday, March 8, 1933   Breslau
Wölfl brought home the news that fighting had broken out at union headquarters today; apparently they shot at SA people marching by. There were deaths, and so the union headquarters have been occupied.

Thursday, March 9, 1933   Breslau
Wölfl's Abitur is over! He passed with "good"; in Greek he even got a "very good." His nine years at the Johannesgymnasium flew by; he really made it very easy for us. I must admit I was a bit proud!

The downtown has changed completely as a result of the swastika banners and black-white-red waving from all the public buildings.[4] We see the most unimaginable figures running around, SA people with pistols—people who under normal circumstances would never have been permitted to enlist as soldiers.

Sunday, March 12, 1933   Breslau
The people are as if in a dream from which there will be a terrible awakening. Wertheim is being guarded by SS people after it had previously been closed intermittently. But who is going to shop at department stores when they can count on being beaten? Yesterday, SA hordes invaded a court and yelled "Jews out!" at the judges and lawyers in the bar association room, and they beat attorney Maximilian Weiss bloody. Day before yesterday they dragged the director Barnay into the Oswitzer Forest and knocked him down with rubber truncheons and dog whips.[5] That's the Third Reich.

Wednesday, March 16, 1933   Breslau
All Jewish judges and state prosecutors in Breslau are being fired, even the baptized ones. I have to say, it gives me a certain schadenfreude, but only about the latter. It has been recommended that attorneys not go to court, not even to their offices. Such are the times in which we live.

Friday, March 24, 1933   Breslau
Once again, all sorts of things have been happening. People whom they dragged into brown houses and beat horribly. But it seems to me that

4. The black-white-red flag, which had been the colors of the unified German empire from 1871 to 1918, replaced the black-red-gold flag used by the Weimar republic.
5. Paul Barnay (1884–1960) was the director of the Lobe Theater in Breslau.

the destruction of daily life, the ban on animal slaughter according to Jewish law, and the firings are much worse than even these excesses! How many people now stand before the abyss from one day to the next. And of course, it is all the worse for those who never imagined that their middle-class existences might be upended.

Saturday, March 25, 1933   Breslau
Wölfl just heard on the radio that Heines is going to be chief of police and Brückner Oberpräsident.[6] The former is particularly harsh. They're going to make a clean sweep and bring in all their own people! Nonetheless, I do not think that there will be any more violence. They will try to achieve their ends by peaceful means.

Sunday evening, March 26, 1933   Breslau
Oberbürgermeister Wagner fired, naturally all unpaid SPD city councilors, but also Moering of the public library and Frau Prochownik of the welfare department.[7] But not to worry, everyone in their turn! The march of vengeance.

Thursday, March 30, 1933   Breslau
Spring has arrived in force. That in stark contrast to political matters, which are ever more catastrophic for us Jews. Herr Heines was introduced as police chief today. I happened to see the demonstration from the streetcar. First measure: Under threat of penalty, we Jews must surrender our passports so that their validity outside Germany may be nullified. In other words, measures that have been unthinkable for more than a hundred years. We now have the rights of aliens!

Friday, March 31, 1933   Breslau
In the morning newspapers, the news that the NSDAP has proposed that all Jewish and "bastardized" teachers be removed; only permit one

6. Edmund Heines (1897–1934) was chief of police in Breslau from 1933 to 1934. Gauleiter Helmuth Brückner (1896–1954?) was provincial prefect of Lower Silesia from 1933 to 1934. He died in Russian captivity.

7. Otto Wagner (1877–1962) was lord mayor of Breslau from 1918 to 1933. Protestant pastor Ernst Moering (1886–1973) was a Social Democrat and director of the public library in Breslau. When he was taken to Dürrgoy concentration camp, in 1933, he was forced to wear a dunce's hat. See Walter Tausk, *Breslauer Tagebuch 1933–1940*, ed. Ryszard Kincel (Berlin, 1975; new edition, Berlin: Siedler, 1988), p. 78.

percent Jews at the universities. After school, I took the most humiliating walk of my life to date to the police station to have my passport stamped, making it valid for us Jews for internal purposes only. The official was very nice and friendly while doing the processing, but we had to present ourselves in rows. Degrading, beneath any semblance of human dignity!

Saturday, April 1, 1933   Breslau
I got up early this morning and began working on my book, which is the best diversion because as soon as I glance at the newspaper I'm overcome with rage at how we are being treated. It is the final loss of human dignity. Today they stood out in front of stores with posters bedecked with yellow spots. The words "Jew" and similar things were also evident. The Dark Ages!

I'm rather depressed today. Even when I try to flee into my books, I'm never entirely successful. Any diversion outside the house is out of the question. At the moment I am simply unable and unwilling to think about the future.

Friday, April 14, 1933   Breslau
Many Jewish and leftist university professors have been fired. Marck and Cohn among them.[8] The *numerus clausus* has taken effect at the universities, so that it is clear that Wölfl won't be able to study here. Perhaps we will send him to Paris. All difficult decisions which must be made in the near future. The way we Jews are being treated now, we have never been treated like this before. True, we are not being killed, but we are being tortured mentally, and our ability to make a living is being systematically throttled.

Tuesday, April 18, 1933   Breslau
Wölfl is gone now! It was a very difficult farewell, but a father is not eager to commit to paper or express how he feels at such a moment. Ernst and Trudi were there, as was the Brienitzer family.[9] Wölfl took it

8. The philosopher Siegfried Marck (1889–1957) was a school friend of Willy Cohn's, and jurist Ernst J. Cohn (1904–1976) was one of his early students. In 1932, the latter became a target of the first anti-Semitic campaign at the University of Breslau.

9. Wolfgang Cohn's mother, Ella Brienitzer, was at the station for the farewell along with her family, her second husband, Günther Brienitzer, and her two children from that marriage.

very well and didn't make it too difficult for us; but who knows how he really felt because he is very worried about us. But we must steel ourselves now and make sure that we get through it.

He had gone to the police station this morning at seven, but Police Commissioner Augustini, who has been making Jewish passports valid for travel abroad, only came in at ten. At ten forty-five Wölfl telephoned us with the happy news that he had gotten an exit visa. Such are the times in which we live that even so simple a matter leads to major complications because we really no longer have human rights, but have become second-class citizens.

Saturday, April 29, 1933   Breslau
The *Acht-Uhr Abendblatt* reports that eleven other university professors have been fired, among them Koebner and Waldecker. Koebner is a completely apolitical person who has stood out neither as a Jew nor politically.[10] But he is one of the premier experts in eastern German history! Nonetheless, this "borderland university" must be restructured.

Monday, May 1, 1933   Breslau
Woke up at three in the morning bathed in sweat. I dreamed that I was in protective custody and was put to work painting glass roofs. Then I lay awake in bed for a few hours. Took the 26 with Ernst to the school celebration. Everywhere banners, swastika armbands; at least the weather isn't particularly nice.

Going to the school was especially unsettling for me because I didn't know if I might not immediately be sent home again. However, there was no order to that effect! I'm not being given a full professorship; as a substitute I'll be given one to teach the fourth-year students. I assume that my firing will take place during the week.

At the celebration at the Berlin Lustgarten: the now usual! Goebbels' speech full of anticipatory laurels! Such a thing happens only once every half millennium! The historical verdict is presumed from the outset.

10. Richard Koebner (1885–1958) was a professor of medieval and modern history at the University of Breslau from 1924 until his firing in 1933. He emigrated to Palestine in 1934. A teaching chair was endowed in his name at Hebrew University, in Jerusalem. After retiring in 1954, he moved to London. See the report "Professor Koebner nach Jerusalem berufen," in *Jüdische Zeitung* (for eastern Germany) 40 (1933), no. 48, dated December 8, 1933, p. 4.

Much about overcoming class hatred; as a colleague later quipped in the faculty room, for that they've substituted racial hatred!

Today, after much inner struggle, I stuck the ribbon of my Iron Cross through the buttonhole of my suit jacket and overcoat; perhaps it is a good thing as a Jew to make a show of this right now. We also hung a black-white-red banner in front of the house so they don't demolish it.

Wednesday, May 3, 1933   Breslau

Yesterday all union headquarters and all businesses belonging to the trade unions were occupied for the purpose of *Gleichschaltung*.[11] That's the new byword of our times. – Regarding the session yesterday evening, it should be noted that the Reform Jews are completely unprepared emotionally for this entire turn of events. They are simply stunned. A colleague told me that from one night to the next she had been transformed from a German teacher into a Jewish one!

Ernst told me today that his chaver Bromberger had written him from Palestine. Each newcomer is asked, "Are you here from Germany or out of conviction?" A bitter joke.[12]

Thursday, May 4, 1933   Breslau

I taught for three hours this morning; everything is taking its course, but I no longer feel really free. Each word has to be weighed; as one Jewish student commented, correctly, we feel as if we are just guests. Unfortunately, in these times we have to rid ourselves of all sensitivities! They're not making things easy for us; we have to think about how to feed our families and how to survive the moment.

On the street I read a poster on an advertising pillar about the burning of Jewish and Marxist books that is to take place on May 10. So that's the next *Volksfest*. Didn't say anything about burning the authors.[13] Middle Ages! But they burned the Talmud back then. And it survived.

11. Union headquarters were occupied and unions abolished throughout the Reich on May 2, 1933. *Gleichschaltung*, a term taken from electrical engineering, is usually translated as "coordination" or "forced coordination" in the Nazi context.

12. Walter Laqueur notes this same "bitter joke" in his memoir. See *Thursday's Child Has Far to Go: A Memoir of the Journeying Years* (New York: Macmillan, 1992), p. 105.

13. An allusion to a prophetic line from the German-Jewish poet Heinrich Heine's 1821 play *Almansor*, "Where they burn books, so too will they in the end

Friday, May 5, 1933   Breslau

Apparently I'm no longer to teach the ninth year; the schedule has been changed as of tomorrow and I've been stuck in the first year. I'll just have to endure this insult as well. But perhaps it's in my best interest because the possibility of a clash is more likely in the upper classes, and perhaps it is better to give our little first-year students some emotional support. But what I would really like to do is just give it up, if I didn't have a modicum of a sense of responsibility and weren't thinking of my family, and of the fact that we shouldn't be giving these people something for nothing. Makes me sick! I went to school with Frey, the little second-year student whose father and grandfather are locked up.[14] The little fellow told me that he's been dreaming about it! I feel badly for the little children whose souls are made to suffer so. And this in a time that understands so much about the psyche of the child. Of course, the souls of Jewish or "bastardized" children don't count for anything.

Monday, May 8, 1933   Breslau

Today the commissarial director took me aside and asked whether I would find it awkward to supervise the election of prefects since only Aryan students may be elected. I told him that in these times we are already forced to endure so much that is awkward that it hardly matters. I asked him whether there had been a directive from on high to the effect that I should no longer teach the ninth year. He confirmed this but told me he wasn't at liberty to discuss it. A person of my ability will be permitted to teach only first-year students. But not to get too upset about it; after all I can justify it to myself by saying that I'm merely trying to get whatever I can. But I would like to spew it out that this should be the choice I have to make. Tormented after dinner; no wonder I can't sleep. It's emotional torture—makes me want to puke!

Tuesday, May 9, 1933   Breslau

Barely arrived home when Frau Landau called, completely distraught. She just read in the *Acht-Uhr Abendblatt* that attorney Eckstein has

---

burn human beings." In the play, the line refers to the burning of the Koran during the Spanish Inquisition.

14. Hugo Frey was a Jewish city councilman who was later killed in Gross-Rosen concentration camp.

died. We met in the Kirschallee, and then she came up to our place for a while. Completely shocking. The police report states the cause of death as inflammation of the lungs and kidneys with incipient insanity. The poor man had been in protective custody since February 28 and died because he had ideals other than those that triumphed.[15]

Today I heard that another man in protective custody slit his wrists. It is impossible to set down in writing what one feels and thinks! Poor Eckstein!

Wednesday, May 10, 1933   Breslau
During the last break, a fire truck arrived with an SA car to pick up the books that are to be burned today![16] Yesterday, stickers were affixed to the posters announcing the burning: "Don't forget the Bible. It, too, is Jewish heritage." There's a fine irony in this that was not lost. The Berlin burning will be broadcast on the radio this evening.

Thursday, May 11, 1933   Breslau
Major uproar among those who heard the report from the concentration camp.[17] People like Korn-Steine are incarcerated there, and Erich Landsberg.[18]

School took its usual quiet course today. The director spoke with me at length and turned out to have rather sensible views! Nonetheless, I weigh every word because a person cannot be careful enough. Of course, sometimes I lose my temper in class.

15. Attorney Dr. Ernst Eckstein (1897–1933), founder of the Breslau Socialist Workers Party, was tortured to death in Dürrgoy concentration camp, in Breslau. See Willy Cohn, *Verwehte Spuren. Erinnerungen an das Breslauer Judentum vor seinem Untergang*, ed. Norbert Conrads (Cologne: Böhlau, 1995), p. 606.

16. In his memoirs, Cohn mentions that his biography of Lassalle (and presumably his other socialist biographies) were burned that day. Willy Cohn, *Verwehte Spuren*, p. 89.

17. Apparently a radio report about Dürrgoy concentration camp in Breslau, which is mentioned here for the first time. An external description of the camp may be found in Walter Tausk, *Breslauer Tagebuch*, p. 108.

18. The physician Dr. Hans Alexander Korn-Steine was finally released in the fall of 1933. He committed suicide shortly thereafter.

Tuesday, May 16, 1933   Breslau
The Philology Society has decreed that everyone must immediately read Hitler's *Mein Kampf.* Thank G'd that as members of an alien race we no longer belong to this organization. Today my first-year students wrote, "Welcome, dear Uncle Willy." These are the things that keep my spirits up whenever I feel down.

Wednesday, May 17, 1933   Breslau
During a teacher's conference at the break, we were told to promote two seventh-year students to the eighth year because of their "nationalist activities"! In other words, intellectual achievement now takes a back seat. We just have to sit there and let matters play out. Perhaps things will change.

Thursday, May 18, 1933   Breslau
This morning I taught for four consecutive hours. It takes a lot of energy to teach the little ones; the older ones engage in spying. With them it is very clear how they pay attention to each word. It is very strange, all the brown uniforms at the university. It is sad to see how isolated the Jewish students are. Nonetheless, I believe that these things will go back to normal after the first wave has passed.

Saturday, May 20, 1933   Breslau
I heard this morning that Moering has been arrested. Mache was taken to a concentration camp; he's not a young man either anymore![19] Terrible! Very bad. There is no way to predict how such protective custody will end.

Monday, May 22, 1933   Breslau
Today we had to fill out a form stating whether we are of Aryan or non-Aryan ancestry. If the latter, we had to indicate whether or not we were veterans. I attached a page with a list of all the battles in which I participated, and then I had Grosse certify that it was correct. We also had to state which party we belong to. He asked whether I still belong

19. That is, to Dürrgoy. Karl Mache (1880–1944), a Jewish Social Democrat and provisional mayor of Breslau, was imprisoned along with Paul Löbe, the president of the Reichstag. He later died in Gross-Rosen concentration camp. See Paul Löbe, *Der Weg war lang. Lebenserinnerungen* (Berlin: Arani, 1954).

to the SPD. I told him that this was the case. He said to me, "You know, my friend, you impress them. I know people who have had their backs broken twice, once in 1918 and once now." To which I replied, "My entire life, I have always walked a straight path and worked for an ideal. History will decide who is right."

Today, with the first mail, I received a very respectful offer from Catania for a visiting residency.[20] There is such a disjunction between these two occurrences. And yet, I continue in the firm conviction that the terrible injustice that is being done to us German Jews will eventually be made right. However, our lives go on. We must continually remind ourselves to be strong.

Saturday, May 27, 1933   Breslau
The Schlageter celebration, at which Jaeckel gave a ceremonial speech that struck a tight militaristic note of the sort we haven't heard in 15 years and that "does a man good."[21] As is G'd's will, I shall remain still! Nonetheless, it requires nervous effort to remain silent. For us Jews it is no pleasure to hear the "Horst Wessel Lied." After all, we can't very well raise our Jewish boys to be National Socialists now that we have been declared an alien race.

Whit Monday, June 5, 1933   Breslau
Visited Professor Landsberger for tea. I'm very reluctant to make such visits because not much comes of them; people always talk about the same things, but I couldn't very well turn him down. My, but his wife is nervous! In fact, his income has been greatly reduced as a result of their taking the *Monatshefte* away from him.[22] And it is doubtful whether he will retain his teaching appointment. He will give up his apartment on

20. Apparently a reference to an invitation to Catania, perhaps in preparation for the 500th anniversary of the University of Catania. As he reported on January 10, 1939, Cohn was also supposed to join the board of the local association there. His hopes for Catania were to occupy Cohn's thoughts for a long time.

21. Albert Leo Schlageter (1894–1923) was a member of the right-wing paramilitary Freikorps, initially in Upper Silesia. He was involved in sabotaging the French occupation of the Ruhr, and was arrested and executed by the French. Schlageter became a martyr to the Nazi cause.

22. Art historian Franz Landsberger (1883–1964) had published the respected *Schlesische Monatshefte* since 1927. He emigrated to England in 1938, and was given

July 1, and he plans to wait for half a year to see what happens. But in any case, he does have monetary reserves!

Saturday evening, June 10, 1933   Breslau
Yesterday I took a lovely walk in the beautiful evening air as far as the Rosengarten, where I ran into Bildhauer, who told me a few things about the civil service law.[23] For one thing, when a person retires, in my case only for political reasons, he will not receive his full pension for three months, but only a portion thereof, which in my case would at the most come to 210 marks. This law expires at the end of September, which I knew. So all we can do is wait.

Sunday, June 18, 1933   Breslau
On Friday, while I was lying in bed sweating, the caretaker, Stephan, returned from school to bring me a letter to the effect that I have been dismissed as of immediately. I had been expecting this because they are poking around in people's politics and compensating for all of their foreign policy failures by tightening up domestically. Perhaps my suspension will save me from other conflicts. But it was unpleasant to get this letter at precisely the moment when I was feeling so miserable, and so it really affected me. Any plans for the future are futile at the moment because I have to wait to see how much of a pension they will give me.

Trudi has been absolutely heroic during these times, and she will surely continue to help, even if we have to readjust our lives completely. I can really depend on her! Naturally, I have various plans, but right now all I can do is wait so as not to do the wrong thing. The entire situation would surely have become increasingly untenable, and perhaps it is good that it happened this way so that I am not forced into a continual sacrifice of the intellect.

Monday, June 19, 1933   Breslau
Today is the first day on which I am forced to stay home from school. It is a strange feeling, but I'm sure I'll get over it.

I did a good piece of work this morning; I wrote out a discussion for the *Mitteilungen aus der historischen Literatur* and a longer section

---

an appointment at the Hebrew Union College, in Cincinnati, in 1939. His papers are housed at the Center for Jewish History, in New York.

23. Erich Bildhauer was the editor of the *Breslauer Jüdische Zeitung*.

for the book *Sizilien im Urteil seiner Besucher*.[24] Then Gabriel came to visit.[25] I thought it very attentive of him to come on the first day; he was here for a good hour, and we discussed the entire situation. He thought that I should petition the city and provincial prefect to be hired by the library, but I don't think I'm capable of deciding on such a course.

Tuesday, June 20, 1933   Breslau

I slept for many hours, dreams that are in some way connected to school; but that will work itself out. I worked energetically in the morning, dictated a few letters to Trudi, only the most necessary. A lovely package arrived from Berlin with costly foods, which makes things considerably easier for us at the moment. It was accompanied by a very understanding letter from my mother-in-law, which pleased me greatly.[26] I'm already fairly reconciled to the school matter and am glad to have my freedom.

---

24. In his memoirs, Cohn described his 1927 visit to Sicily as the high point of his life. Since then, he continued to collect material for an intended book titled *Sicily in the Judgment of Its Visitors*. Although he worked intently on this manuscript in 1933, it was probably never completed.

25. Alexis Gabriel (1875–1939) was director of the Johannesgymnasium, in Breslau, until his firing, in 1933.

26. A letter from Berlin from Margarete Rothmann, Trudi's mother.

Looking for Work and Intellectual Diversion

Saturday, June 24, 1933   Breslau

Dictated an application for a Zionist post in Berlin; it feels very strange to have to do such a thing at my age, but in the end it would be a mistake to slight any possibilities. The civil service law has been revised; now any civil servant may be forced to retire.[1]

I went to the synagogue this morning with Ruth. She was very insistent that I accompany her now that I have time. We arrived just in time for the Hallel. Today was Rosh Chodesh; these days, when music is so seldom heard, it made me feel especially good.[2] And it revives me in other respects, too, even though it does not, perhaps, balance all my brooding. I stood with Ruth in front of the old seats that we used to have, and I showed her the old places, just as my father had 30 years ago.[3] So do the generations come and go.

Paul Löbe was arrested; Lüdemann is in the concentration camp here and is said to have been paraded through the streets of the city.[4]

1. According to the revised Law for the Restoration of the Professional Civil Service, of June 23, 1933, officials could be forced to retire even if they were fully capable of performing their duties. See *Reichsgesetzblatt* [Reich Law Gazette], part 1 (1933), published by the Reich Minister of the Interior, Berlin 1933, no. 68, p. 389.

2. The first day of each month in the Jewish calendar is called Rosh Chodesh and is considered a minor holiday.

3. Louis Cohn's seat in the New Synagogue was 156/220. So reads the entry in the synagogue registry, which is housed at the Żydowski Instytut Historyczny, in Warsaw. AZIH 105/189, p. 28.

4. In his memoirs, Paul Löbe describes "welcoming" his old party friend Hermann Lüdemann (1880–1959) to Dürrgoy. See Paul Löbe, *Der Weg war lang. Lebenserinnerungen* (Berlin: Arani, 1954), p. 222f.

Who knows what the next days will bring in terms of arrests of SPD members!

Sunday, June 25, 1933   Breslau
Dreamed a lot about the school; it is strange that I have been dreaming so much about it since my firing. It never used to enter my thoughts that much before. Ernst met with his Jewish youth fellowship to sing; they will hold a memorial service this afternoon for the murdered Arlosoroff.[5]

Tuesday, June 27, 1933   Breslau
Trudi is very insistent about emigrating; I don't see any great possibilities for us and for what I am able to do. That is why I am a little tired of this conversation, especially because I think it is best to wait. All these discussions eat terribly at my nerves, and I am always extremely regretful that Trudi and I are of such completely different opinions in this regard. It's very sad. I don't want to start all over again from the beginning. Here I can do something, I am something; it is an open question whether I would ever be able to accomplish anything down there! Some clever people view the prospects here as very dark, but still, I feel so deeply rooted here. Very turbulent internal struggles; it requires all my nervous energy to get through. Trudi, who most certainly means well, and who may perhaps even be correct from her perspective, wears me down more than the firing.

Wednesday, July 5, 1933   Breslau
The feeling I have about the extent to which we Jews in Germany have become expendable and how difficult it would be to separate myself is becoming ever stronger. There is an endless split, and then again there is the material question, because otherwise we would be able to reconcile the emotional one. But we are stuck here!

Friday, July 7, 1933   Breslau
Yesterday morning I finished a lengthy book review for the *Mitteilungen aus der historischen Literatur*. Writing still isn't easy, but it was better

---

5. The Zionist Chaim Arlosoroff (1899–1933), a leader of the Labor Zionist movement in Palestine, was murdered in Tel Aviv, on June 16, 1933, shortly after returning from Nazi Germany, where he negotiated a transfer agreement to make it easier for Jews to emigrate.

today! Took a walk at noon, met former students. Heard the new evening prayer: Dear G'd make me mute lest Dürrgoy be my fate.[6] Spent some time in the Südpark. Everything smelled wonderful! I felt like an old pensioner.

Wednesday, September 6, 1933   Breslau
Yesterday went to see Marcus, the publisher, who is most touchingly concerned for my well-being and that I keep up my mental resilience. He has already done a great deal for me. His opinion is that the Sicilians are unlikely to create a paid position for me, but that it might well be possible that if they asked me to do scholarly work for them, my pension might be transferrable to Italy. He thought that it would, of course, be good if I traveled down there to discuss all these matters; however, it was, unfortunately, clear to us that under the prevailing circumstances this should be done only if I received an official request. So, at the moment I can only continue to wait. Marcus has thought through all of the details; I can really depend on him. I spent about an hour there.

The street is full of brown and black uniforms. Once you've spent time in the village, the constant scurrying in the city seems very peculiar, and I'm always happy to get out again.

Thursday, September 7, 1933   Breslau
It is a very strange feeling to watch the children go to school, even though from day to day it becomes increasingly clear that teaching would have been emotionally unbearable for me. Many of the students who used to attend Johannesgymnasium now go to the Jewish school.[7]

Went to the Jewish Community to exchange my seat card. I have to go to the Hermann Lodge this time because no service is taking place at the *Vorwärts*. Waiting there, not pleasant. To the city library. Had a brief

6. Reference to the Breslau-Dürrgoy concentration camp. Cf. diary entry of May 20, 1933. Walter Tausk also knew this verse; see his *Breslauer Tagebuch 1933–1940*, ed. Ryszard Kincel (Berlin, 1975; new edition, Berlin: Siedler, 1988), p. 87.

7. The Jewish Reform Realgymnasium at Rehdigerplatz 3. See also Abraham Ascher, *A Community under Siege: The Jews of Breslau under Nazism* (Stanford, CA: Stanford University Press, 2007), pp. 98–108.

conversation there with a former colleague, Fräulein Dr. Goldmann, who was dismissed because of the Aryan paragraphs.[8]

Wednesday, September 13, 1933   Breslau
To the Jewish Community, where I was able to sell mother's synagogue card for ten marks. From there to the *Jüdische Zeitung*, where I copied the addresses of the Jewish newspapers published in Germany. In the process, I discovered an unauthorized second printing; will try to get remuneration. In these times, one can't let anything pass.

Friday, September 14, 1933   Breslau
Spoke on the phone with Lewkowitz. The Jewish Evening School for adults will be initiated this winter.[9] Very good news. I am convinced that people will attend my courses. On the way into the city, naturally spoke with a lot of people, even though I kept it as brief as possible, among others Dr. Schäffer, who is very well-intentioned.

Saturday, September 16, 1933   Breslau
Sat with Perle in the president's room at the lodge and informed him of the status of the matter.[10] He thinks that everything has been appropriately set in motion, and that I should now wait for an official invitation to go to Italy. The discussion between Marcus and the consul is taking place today; I'm very curious about the outcome!

Then to the New Synagogue; these days I often feel the need to go and pray. G'd's house is the best place to collect oneself emotionally, and I am especially partial to services on Friday evening. In addition to Trudi, I met my former student Pulvermacher and two young girls at Frau Conberti's. Frau Conberti, whose beauty is still evident, speaks a marvelous Italian that I can easily understand.

---

8. Paragraph 3 of the Law for the Restoration of the Professional Civil Service provided for the discharge of officials for reasons of "non-Aryan ancestry."

9. After 1935, the Jewish Evening School [Jüdische Volkshochschule] was forced to change its name to Jewish House of Teaching [Jüdische Lehrhaus].

10. The businessman Felix Perle (1875–1940) advised the family on financial matters and, in his capacity as president of the lodge and member of the board of the Jewish Museum, was also a friend of Cohn's. His name is mentioned frequently in the diaries.

Monday, September 18, 1933   Breslau

Spoke with Ernst Hainauer; consulted about various matters concerning the Jewish Cultural Association. It seems that here, too, the organization is not working out. Ernst Hainauer intends to sell his inventory and move his music publishing house abroad. It would mean that this old company would be transferred from our family into Aryan hands. He wants to be with his sister. Overall, our young people want to get out completely. In the Gartenstrasse I observed an SA man apparently escorting two prisoners in protective custody carrying pails; they were probably being forced to wash off graffiti!

Tuesday, September 19, 1933   Breslau

To the Jewish school, where I had a conversation with Feuchtwanger, the director. I liked him very much. As far as my being hired at that school is concerned, the course schedule for the winter remains as is, and then he would first have to inquire with the authorities whether it is even possible to hire me in view of Paragraph 4.[11] I at least wanted to leave this door open.

Friday evening, September 22, 1933   Breslau

I had an appointment at six to see Marcus, who reported to me about his meeting with the Italian consul. He pointed out a way in which a temporary stay in Italy might be arranged. I will go and see the consul tomorrow to discuss a few matters with him! The outcome is very questionable because if it is going to cost the Italians anything, they naturally won't want to do it. The consul recommended that I ask the German government through an attorney whether they would transfer

---

11. The purpose of the Law for the Restoration of the Professional Civil Service, decreed by the Nazis on April 7, 1933, was to remove all Jews and political opponents from the civil service. According to §3, all civil servants of "non-Aryan ancestry" were to be fired, including, of course, all Jews. §4 dealt in like manner with all civil servants who were suspect because of their "previous political activities." Active membership in the Social Democratic Party sufficed to be included under this paragraph. According to §6, people could be fired without reason, "to simplify administration." To be fired under §4 was tantamount to a complete ban on employment because no one would hire the politically suspect. Even the Jewish Community of Breslau feared problems if they hired such a person. As a left-wing Social Democrat, Cohn had been fired under §4.

my pay abroad, that is, a portion of my pension. The entire conversation upset me because I see over and over again just how rooted I am in Germany.

Saturday, September 23, 1933   Breslau
Went to the Italian consulate. Had a lengthy conversation with the consul and gave him a copy of the Italian edition of my Hohenstaufen book. He will contact my publisher and again confirm in writing the interest that the Italian government takes in the continuation of my work.

Tuesday, September 26, 1933   Breslau
Yesterday, Professor Guido Kisch from Halle called, a visit that pleased me greatly.[12] Even though he has lived in Germany for a long time, his entire manner is that of a typical Prague Jew, very charming. He has also been suspended for the past half year, but as he tells me, he has, unlike me, not been able to do any proper work. And so the matter has taken a considerable toll on him. He had not counted on being discharged. He has gained more of an understanding of human beings! Herr Aubin told him that the Jews had penetrated too deeply into German legal history.[13] Kisch then asked him why it should have taken centuries for a Jew, Kisch, to be first to publish an edition of the Kulmer Handfeste.[14] They don't like it when Jews engage with East Prussian history. Kisch had a few gracious comments about my work; it is always nice to hear such things from an authority. We then spoke about the possibility of reorganizing German-Jewish historical research, but he foresees great

12. Guido Kisch (1889–1985) was a Prague-born jurist and legal historian. He briefly taught at the Jewish Theological Seminary in Breslau, eventually emigrating to the United States, in 1935, where he taught for a time at Hebrew Union College. One of his scholarly interests was the legal history of German Jews. His papers are held at the Center for Jewish History, in New York.

13. For more on the attitude of the leading Breslau historian Hermann Aubin (1885–1969), which oscillated between inaction and bystanderism, see Eduard Mühle, *Für Volk und deutschen Osten. Der Historiker Hermann Aubin und die deutsche Ostforschung* (Düsseldorf: Droste, 2005).

14. Guido Kisch, *Die Kulmer Handfeste* (Stuttgart: W. Kohlhammer, 1931). The Kulmer Handfeste was an important medieval privilege for the city of Kulm. It became the model for similar privileges for other cities.

difficulties there as well because the funds are lacking, though the task is certainly urgent. In contrast to me, he is pessimistic about the situation for us Jews.

Wednesday, September 27, 1933   Breslau
An ever widening divergence is becoming evident between me and Trudi in our entire reading of the current situation. I love Germany so much that this love cannot be shaken by the unpleasantries that we are now experiencing. It is the country whose language we speak and whose good days we have also experienced! We have to be loyal enough to submit even to a government that comes from an entirely different camp. In that respect, I know that I am free of all feelings of hatred. Emotionally, however, Trudi wants out of Germany; I feel subjected to a pressure that perhaps is not overtly expressed in words. I am continuing to work on my plans regarding Catania, but I would much rather remain here where the roots of my strength are.

Went to see Marcus, who has not yet received the letter from the consul. We have decided not to involve an attorney yet. Marcus has some pending business before the Reich Propaganda Ministry. He has been summoned there along with the large Munich publisher Oldenbourg and will be asked how best to counter the boycott of German scholarly works abroad. He intends to raise the matter on this occasion and try to obtain a one-year stay in Catania for the purpose of study. I told him that for the foreseeable future I would prefer outright rejection to my current uncertainty.

Spent a wonderful hour with Dr. Aronades. I accompanied him to the train; it is no small matter to go to Palestine like that. At the end, I called out, *Chasak!* He is very pessimistic about the future of German Jews. He believes that within a few years no German Jews will be involved in economic life; there will be only pensioners and old people. The Aronadeses are going to Haifa, where they plan to start a pediatric practice. However, they have enough to live on for two years, so they aren't risking much.

Monday, October 2, 1933   Breslau
At the city office building at Theaterstrasse, I took the opportunity to ask about my pension. With child allowances I get 366.15 marks, from which a number of deductions are made. To live as we are accustomed it isn't

much. – Nonetheless, I now know where I stand. Then to Wertheim, from where I telephoned Trudi about the results. Bought a diary there. Went to see Hainauer; I had a book to take back there. Ernst Hainauer showed me some very interesting family papers belonging to my grandfather and great-grandfather Hainauer. Eventually, I want to write a family history!

Tuesday, October 3, 1933   Breslau

Tomorrow we will have been married for ten years. To celebrate the day we plan an excursion to Zobten. The ten years have passed like a day; we have become very happy with each other, even though we have sometimes had differences. But, after all, that happens in any good marriage.

Friday, October 6, 1933   Breslau

These times are very interesting. The Reichstag fire trial, the Geneva minorities debate. A resolution for approval, according to which no one is to be disadvantaged as a result of their race, will be put forward very energetically! But will it also be carried out? I am awaiting my former student Feibusch, who is in the process of going to Erez. He will be leaving for Erez with courage and spirit to work there as a chalutz. He is, it should be said, taking money with him in reserve. In the meantime, Trudi went to see Sophie Kaim, who leads the Youth Aliyah. We got the forms. I decided quickly and filled out the forms; registration can be withdrawn at any time, but it keeps the door open. I would find separation from this son very difficult as well, but in these times we must not be egoistic but think only of the future of our children.

Tuesday, October 17, 1933   Breslau

There were barely a hundred people in attendance yesterday evening at the opening of the evening school; and when we arrived not a single ticket had yet been sold. A shameful showing at a time when one would think that people would be eager to learn something.

Monday, October 23, 1933   Breslau

Telephoned Marcus, my publisher; he hasn't heard anything from Italy, but very little mail is coming from there right now. I sometimes have the feeling these days that nothing much will come of the matter, and that in the final analysis we will have to make do with the pension I receive. As Lao Tse says, "Non-action is best."

My former student Pax came to visit at four in the afternoon.[15] He stayed for over an hour, and we talked about scholarship and its current state in Germany. He told me that Bibliotheksrat Honigmann had been discharged without any pension; the director of the zoological garden here expects the same fate at Easter.[16]

Wednesday, October 25, 1933   Breslau
If I let my beard go for two days, it is completely gray! If I allowed my beard to grow out, I'd look like a tired old Jew.

Nothing came of my course at the Jewish Evening School; not a single person registered. I've been teaching at the evening school for 14 years now. I thought that this winter people would be thronging; the reason may partly lie with poor advertising, partly because now that I have no position, I am without influence.

Thursday, October 26, 1933   Breslau
Had a long telephone call with Vogelstein regarding talks at Jewish communities around Breslau; the intent at the moment is to have only rabbis speak. They have their reasons. He informed me toward evening that perhaps my turn would come in January. Naturally, one has to take advantage of every opportunity to earn. I don't like it, but it can't be helped.

Today, the *Hamburger Familienblatt* carried an article of mine about cultural work in the countryside, publication of which I have been awaiting for a long time, and which is very important for me.[17] It turned out rather long. People read the *Jüdische Blätter* very carefully! Goebbels will be speaking in Breslau this evening.

Friday, October 27, 1933   Breslau
Ernst informed me that my former colleague Jaroschek, that fervent member of the Center Party and opponent of National Socialism, has

15. Wolfgang Pax (1912–1993) converted to Catholicism after World War II, living in Jerusalem as a Franciscan monk and scholar after 1973. By his own account, Pax was heavily influenced by Willy Cohn.

16. Zoo director Hans Honigmann (1891–1943) and Bibliotheksrat Ernst Honigmann (1892–1954) were brothers. The former emigrated to England in 1935; his brother to Belgium in 1933, and from there to the United States.

17. See Willy Cohn, "Jüdische Kulturarbeit in der Provinz," in *Israelitisches Familienblatt* (Hamburg) 35 (1933), no. 43, dated October 26, 1933, p. 13.

joined the SA. Apparently he is out to further his career. Received a very detailed airmail letter from Wölfl filled with enthusiasm for his studies. I am very happy that he is so contented, and even though I am infinitely fearful for him, I am nonetheless happy that he is doing so well. He has made a connection with a Sephardic family with whom he went on a driving tour.

Saturday, October 28, 1933   Breslau
I went for a bit of a walk; first I ran into Ludwig Ittmann, who looks older and tired; emotionally he is very stressed by the situation. Then I fell into the hands of Frau Professor Landsberger, who is completely despairing because, contrary to his expectations, her husband lost his *Venia legendi*.[18] The woman was completely beside herself and wept. Hönigswald, in Munich, has lost his position as well.[19]

Monday, October 30, 1933   Breslau
Frau Felicia Bab set up a "small house of conviviality" in her apartment, where in these times "non-Aryans," who also need such things, can hear a little art.[20] Lotte Schöps (piano) and Max Frenkel (violin) played, and for an hour and a half people were transported to another world. I don't understand much about music, but hearing the works of Brahms, Mozart, and Wieniawski was a great joy. Intermittently I spoke with Martin Bab, who will be going to Erez as a chalutz this week. He thinks that the last Arab uprisings cost us 3,000 certificates!

Saturday, November 11, 1933   Breslau
A nice letter from Wölfl on Ruth's birthday with letters for Freund and Mittelhaus. The boy is very enthusiastic about his studies; then went to synagogue with Ruth. She already knows quite a bit of Hebrew. It was the bar mitzvah of a former student of mine, Röthler, who did his piece very nicely.

---

18. Teaching credentials.

19. Philosopher Richard Hönigswald (1875–1947) taught at the University of Breslau from 1916 to 1930. His son was a schoolmate of Wolfgang Cohn's at the Johannesgymnasium. Hönigswald emigrated to the United States in 1939.

20. According to the Breslau address book of 1928, Felicia Bab, widow of a Justizrat, lived at Moritzstrasse 3.5.

Sunday, November 12, 1933   Breslau

Trudi prepared a package with cake for Wölfl, which I sent off as a sample without value. At least he should get greetings from Ruth's birthday. The election is today; we went to cast our vote shortly after nine in the morning and had to wait in a long line.[21] But it went without a hitch. Naturally, the picture was completely different: no one wore party insignias, only Hitler Youth and SA people. You had to buy a pin with "yes" for five pfennigs, and they kept a special check-off list to make sure that everyone voted. I didn't find it difficult to vote "yes" for the government's foreign policy!

Monday, November 13, 1933   Breslau

The election turned out much as had been expected. I never believed that there would be many no-votes in the plebiscite. I hope that there will be a certain reconciliation, even toward former opponents of the government! However, whether we Jews will ever be reintegrated into German life remains questionable.

It is already mid-November, and still no word about my pension; nor has there been any final decision on the matter of our apartment.

21. On November 12, 1933, Hitler instituted elections for a new, purely National Socialist Reichstag, at the same time holding a plebiscite on his policies. In the Reichstag election, 92.1 percent voted National Socialist, while 95.1 percent voted "yes" in the plebiscite.

The Jewish Museum

Wednesday, November 15, 1933   Breslau

I had an appointment at quarter to ten with Felix Perle to look at the new Jewish Museum that has been established in the Jewish Orphanage.[1] The gentlemen have truly accomplished something grand, beautiful, and lasting. Saturday evening is the preview, Sunday the official opening. I will do the publicity.

When I returned home at quarter to two, Felix Lyon was there to make me an offer on the Ring property, which is for sale. This put me in a difficult situation because if I sell the property, the new owner will naturally want the store, which would mean the end of Trautner.[2] This means that Rudolf would lose his livelihood, and it would be my fault.

Friday, November 17, 1933   Breslau

I had an appointment with Fräulein Cohn at the Jewish Museum to make a few notes for the article that I plan to write. There I had conversations with a number of people. Perle with his wife, Silberberg with wife and son, Dr. Frank, who spoke here yesterday for the Jewish Agency about the Arab question.[3] He came to ask Silberberg for a do-

1. The Jewish Museum of Breslau opened in 1929 with a much commented on exhibition in rooms provided by the Silesian Museum of Decorative Arts and Antiquities. It did not yet have space of its own. This is why the opening of the Jewish Museum in the Jewish Orphanage, on November 19, 1933, was viewed as an important event. Cohn was very attached to the museum and conducted many of its tours.

2. Geschwister Trautner (Geschwister means "siblings," in this case two sisters: Sisters Trautner) was the large Breslau textile business owned by the Cohn family.

3. Max Silberberg was the chairman of the Jewish Museum Society, which was founded in 1929.

nation for Keren Hayesod.[4] Spitz reported something that my brother Rudolf had said, namely that it makes no difference what happens—the future belongs to the Naumanns.[5]

Saturday, November 18, 1933   Breslau
Went with Trudi to the preview of the Jewish Museum. A large number of people were there: Rosenberg from the *Neue Breslauer Zeitung*, Dr. Bruck representing the *Israelitische Familienblatt*, Schwerin representing the *CV Zeitung*, the same Schwerin whom I know from the historical studies series, Andreae's former assistant.[6] Schwerin told me that Dersch, at the Society for Silesian History, got into trouble with Brückner on my account because he allowed me to speak before the Society for Silesian History.[7] Because of that, the society was to lose its subsidy. Schwerin said that Andreae's behavior is exemplary; his wife is also a "non-Aryan." Silberberg presided over the preview, very matter of fact, but without heart. Had a longer conversation with Kommerzienrat Pinkus from Neustadt, a magnificent old gentleman.[8]

Sunday, November 19, 1933   Breslau
Schwerin came at one o'clock; we spoke about several matters concerning Jewish journalism. He went to see *Jud Süss* yesterday at the Lobe Theater.[9] Went to the opening of the Jewish Museum. It was a lovely ceremony. Silberberg spoke much more warmly than usual; in my

4. Keren Hayesod, the Palestine Foundation Fund, or United Israel Appeal, was established in 1920 at the World Zionist Conference.

5. Max Naumann (1875–1939) founded the League of National German Jews, the goal of which was the complete assimilation of Jews into German society.

6. The *CV Zeitung* was the newspaper of the Centralverein deutscher Staatsbürger jüdischen Glaubens [Central Association of German Citizens of Jewish Faith]. After his emigration, Kurt Schwerin (1902–1995) became a respected legal scholar and social scientist in the United States. The Leo Baeck Institute, in New York, has his voluminous papers. The finding aid to his papers is online at http://findingaids.cjh.org/?pID=475276.

7. See Willy Cohn, *Verwehte Spuren. Erinnerungen an das Breslauer Judentum vor seinem Untergang*, ed. Norbert Conrads (Cologne: Böhlau, 1995), p. 665f.

8. Max Pinkus (1857–1934) was one of the leading textile manufacturers in eastern Germany. He was a major benefactor of Silesian historiography.

9. Schwerin saw the premiere of the theatrical version of the Jud Süss story by Eugen Ortner (1890–1947).

opinion; Heinemann did not speak especially skillfully. Lotte Schoeps played the piano, Mirjam Lewin the cello. Spoke with old Frau Marck, heard some things about what her son is doing.

Walked part of the way home with Lewkowitz; Koebner has now been called to Hebrew University, in Jerusalem, after all, and he is only now beginning to learn Hebrew. How grotesque! Koebner always rejected any connection with Judaism, even refusing to attend lectures by the Jewish section at the Historians Congress, in Warsaw, ostensibly because he had no time. Such a man without any relation to the Jewish milieu gets called to Jerusalem!

Thursday, November 23, 1933   Breslau
The concert at the synagogue yesterday evening was very uplifting.[10] The most beautiful part was the Hebrew Psalm "Min hammeitzar," but the bass arias from *Judas Maccabeus* were marvelous as well.[11] I'm not especially musical, but this most noble music speaks to the heart. We had the cheapest seats, each costing 50 pfennigs in the first balcony behind a heavy pillar. It was well attended, even though the enormous synagogue was not completely full. The times draw people together.

Friday, December 1, 1933   Breslau
Dr. Werner Milch came by. He is working on a family history at the behest of his uncle.[12] I had been helpful in preparing the material. He is one of those people who is dyed in the wool and naturally feels very unhappy these days because as a "non-Aryan" he doesn't know where he belongs! He has returned to Judaism through his involvement with his family history.

In the evening, good mail; a lecture will probably be organized in Nuremberg; I got a very nice letter. The Petrarca House, in Cologne, has asked me for a list of my published works. I am happy that I have gained a new contact there. So today was a full and satisfactory day.

10. For more about this concert in the New Synagogue, see Hff. [= Ernst Hoffmann], "3. Konzert in der neuen Synagoge," in *Jüdische Zeitung* (for eastern Germany) 40 (1933), no. 46, dated November 24, 1933, p. 4.

11. Psalm 118:5.

12. The German scholar Werner Milch (1903–1950) received his first professorship in 1947, in Marburg.

Saturday, December 2, 1933   Breslau
To the savings bank, where I for the first time picked up my decreased pension; still, we should be pleased that the matter turned out this way and that we are not left destitute.

Saturday, December 9, 1933   Breslau
I had various business to conduct at a number of city offices. I am very reluctant to enter an office, but I had to ask about the deductions, and particularly to inquire whether my health insurance had been properly paid. The officials were all very nice and wanted to be helpful in decreasing my poll tax. I also asked whether I would be able to enroll Ernst in the free school, but they told me that this is completely out of the question for Jewish students, even for the sons of war veterans. It was humiliating even having to ask!

Tuesday, December 12, 1933   Breslau
Ruth painted a lovely bookmark for my birthday today; she also crocheted a kippah for me, partly by herself. I was very pleased by the attention. Today I am 45 years old, a nice round number. Actually, I am still at the height of my powers, as they say. But, I have been through more than a few storms. I am still full of ideas, even though I sometimes feel very tired.

Ella called as we were praying in the afternoon to congratulate me, and to make inquiries; then a Herr Grosch, who is interested in the rooms in the building on the Ring and made me a ridiculous offer of 200 marks for the third floor, which I rejected. In addition, he wanted to move in no earlier than July 1, 1934. Today in particular I was not in the mood for such negotiations.

Saturday, December 16, 1933   Breslau
Went downtown at twelve thirty, for the first time for 10 pfennigs. I hope it will stick because there is a nice little sign in the streetcar warning about fare dodgers. A black man is sitting among the other passengers, who move away from him!

Ran into probationary teacher Freudenthal on the streetcar, a strict Catholic. Nonetheless he was fired because of his non-Aryan ancestry, and he will be going abroad to attend a missionary school. At the city library met Wiese, the former director of the Fine Arts Museum; for a moment I didn't even recognize him.[13]

Saturday, December 22, 1933   Breslau
Ernst and Ruth both brought home good grades; Ernst actually did quite nicely for a fifth-year student. To the bank, the savings bank, where I spoke with my colleague Lebek, whom I hadn't seen in half a year. Went to police headquarters, where I asked whether the notation "For domestic use only" could be deleted. Very badly treated by an official in the visa office.

Wednesday, December 27, 1933   Breslau
Yesterday evening read through old diaries; re-experienced our entire winter trip through East Prussia last year! Irritated by a remark by Mother because I told her that we wanted to send Ernst to Erez, and she said, "You're sending all the children away." If only she had an inkling of how difficult the separation from Wölfl is for me! This evening, I will be speaking at the Society for Jewish History and Literature about the Jews in Silesia up to the beginning of the nineteenth century.[14]

Saturday, December 29, 1933   Breslau
Had to fill out a lengthy questionnaire from the Reich League of German Writers, with whom I have to register—and pay dues. The details cost me a great deal of effort, and it is awkward, particularly now, to respond to such things. There is something shaming in all of it.

Sunday, December 31, 1933   Breslau
New Year's Eve. The German newspapers, and even the printed solicitations from the newspaper lady, all tell us that this year was a year of fulfillment. I'm not willing to take a position on that; in any case, for us German Jews this was no year of fulfillment. It may well be that in the end this development will redound to the good of us Jews because our young people may be nudged in a healthier direction, entering more

---

13. Director Erich Wiese (1891–1979) was discharged from his position in 1933 on racial grounds. After the war he directed the Hessian State Museum, in Darmstadt, from 1950 to 1958.

14. See "Vortrag von Studienrat a.D. Dr. Willy Cohn," in *Jüdische Zeitung* (for eastern Germany) 40 (1933), no. 51, dated December 29, 1933, p. 2.

normal professions; however, this year, 1933, has destroyed countless Jewish lives and torn apart families, and for me personally it was very painful to separate from my eldest son.

This year has surely robbed us older German Jews of the heimat for which we fought and in which we did *not* feel ourselves to be guests![15] We will never forget the year 1933! Nor will we celebrate the New Year this evening. German Jewry is in mourning.

Saturday, January 6, 1934   Breslau
This morning I read in the newspaper that Heines received the Honor Dagger of the SA from Chief of Staff Röhm. Heines is supposedly on Capri at the moment. Went to the Society of Friends to register in their books, which had actually already been done by the director.[16] Met Uncle Perls, who, unexpectedly, still looks rather spry. Took the 14 to the university library, where I met Mann, the former director of the evening school, who is in financial difficulty. Various officials were very amiable, Bibliotheksrat Hübner, Schneider, Deputy Director Gruhn, Dr. Gaebel, the head of the Manuscript Department. And this evening the commemoration of the founding of the Society of Friends.

Sunday, January 7, 1934   Breslau
The gentlemen's dinner took on the ritualistic forms characteristic of these affairs. The dinner was excellent, but other than that these affairs are stupefying. I sat between Dr. Treitel, an old AMVer, and a Herr Hoff.[17] The former hasn't gotten any wiser over the years. Tarnowski gave a witty speech for the ladies, and not indecent the way he used to like them. The speech by the first director was well intentioned but provided no new thoughts about the future. Emil Kaim was very solicitous when he inquired about me; otherwise, one is so often subjected to childish questions. Still, the old halls, which I have not entered in a long time, have something homey about them.

15. *Heimat* is an untranslatable word sometimes rendered as "homeland." However, it is far more local and particularistic, comprising notions of history and the landscape as a living force shaping the people of a region.

16. The Gesellschaft der Freunde [Society of Friends] was a Jewish social service organization founded in 1792 in Berlin. It had a chapter in Breslau.

17. Member of the AMV, the Akademisch-Medizinischer Verein [Academic-Medical Association].

Wednesday, January 10, 1934   Breslau
Walked into the city yesterday evening; nice, clear winter air. Picked up Rabbi Dr. Wahrmann after his lecture at the Jewish Evening School, then went to the Lessing Lodge and had a cup of coffee! There talked about the entire situation out in the small communities. Recently, everyone in Militsch was arrested because they got together for a Hebrew course, which was interpreted as a banned secret meeting. Everywhere people are scared and hardly dare to congregate.

Monday, January 15, 1934   Breslau
Grzesik just telephoned to say that he wants to rent both stories that are still empty in the Ring building. It's a big jump from Faust to business matters. But that's what life is about, and everything must be dealt with. In the afternoon, I was able to rent the third and fourth floors, and this evening I concluded a rental agreement with Paul Grzesik at Polke's office.[18] I hope it is for the best, and I think that we may gain something from it.

Tuesday, January 23, 1934   Breslau
Yesterday evening, walked at the double as far as Tauentzienplatz and back. The cold evening air did me good. Regierungsrat Muhr rang and asked me to speak in Haynau and Guhrau. I immediately contacted both communities; I am tirelessly on the lookout for any new possibilities for earning money. I am leaving no avenue untried.

To the Community Library. On the way there, I met Davidsohn, the religion teacher, who upset me with something he said about Wölfl. He told me that someone who had spoken with him there had said that Wölfl spoke to the effect that he is slogging his way through, but that he would never blame his parents and is always contented with whatever he gets. Unfortunately, there is nothing I can do to help the boy. But it is certainly a shock for a father's heart, and in any case it was stupid of Davidsohn, who is no great light, to tell me such a thing.

---

18. This enabled the businessman Paul Grzesik to gain a foothold in the Cohn family's building at Ring 49. In July 1939, he acquired the entire building and property, thus concluding the Aryanization of Geschwister Trautner.

Saturday, January 27, 1934   Breslau

At dinner, I received a letter from our landlord, Obst, saying that he had rented the apartment to someone else. This was a great shock for me because I am so attached to the apartment and would have liked to stay here. Even though Obst sent what was basically a nice note, he could have inquired ahead of time before he rented the apartment to someone else. I'm sure there are other reasons for his behavior. It made me feel very bad! Just as I thought I was getting my finances under control again! Must try to get over it.

Tuesday, January 30, 1934   Breslau

Went looking for an apartment with Trudi, and after we inspected various apartments, we rented the one at Opitzstrasse 28. We saw a nicer apartment in the Schwerinstrasse, but it was beyond our means; the new apartment costs 95 marks, and that is much more affordable. It was a strain, but there was no way around it; Uncle Perls accompanied us part of the way! I hope that we will experience happy hours in the new apartment and have some peace.[19]

19. There is a gap in the diaries between February 6 and June 29, 1934.

The Röhm Putsch

Saturday, June 30, 1934   Breslau

I read in the *Nationalsozialistische Schlesische Tageszeitung* today that the *CV Zeitung* has been expropriated![1] We are again approaching a very sharply anti-Jewish time. In a response to the German transfer provisions, the United States has stated that Germany is making trouble for itself in the world by its policies.

All sorts of rumors have been circulating throughout the city today, but it is a good idea not to believe them!! We are told that Röhm has been removed, that the SA and SS are on an emergency footing.[2] Toward evening, an SS motorcycle squadron raced up the Kirschallee.

Sunday, July 1, 1934   Breslau

Yesterday evening I bought an extra edition that confirmed officially the removal of Chief of Staff Röhm. His homosexual misconduct has now been openly admitted; almost surely some others had been accused of this earlier. Today's morning newspaper contains much important news, even though we as yet have no clear overview of the events of the past few days. A putsch by higher SA leaders, Schleicher, connections abroad, this is the confusion of news that we are currently getting.

1. Cohn often abbreviates the name as *Schlesische Tageszeitung* or simply *Tageszeitung*.

2. Between June 30 and July 2, 1934, Hitler carried out the so-called Night of the Long Knives, or Röhm putsch, in which he had murdered many members of the SA, or Sturmabteilung, including Ernst Röhm, a potential rival. Although weakened, the SA was never dissolved. These political killings extended beyond the SA and included even conservative opponents of the Nazis such as Kurt von Schleicher, the last Weimar-era chancellor of Germany.

The fact is that Schleicher has been shot dead; in addition, a number of Gruppenführer and Obergruppenführer have been shot dead, among them "our" Heines, who was caught in bed with his catamite at the Röhm villa. The typical end of a mercenary: the higher they rise, the farther they fall! He tormented us Breslau Jews no end. In the long run, however, his anti-Jewish speeches and his latest song availed him not at all. Now, more than one Heinesstrasse will have to be renamed. Today's newspaper also noted that all streets in Breslau that were named for a Jew will be renamed, among them Fraenckelplatz.[3] Another piece of Jewish fate.

Monday, July 2, 1934   Breslau
The most beautiful thing is to walk beside the ripening grain, and to breathe in its aroma. I now sometimes have a great yearning for a few weeks in the country and a complete lack of noise.

Tuesday, July 3, 1934   Breslau
A big NSDAP gathering in the Südpark! We could hear loudspeakers! – This morning I read that Heines's adjutant is being sought by the state police. This Herr Schmidt was the catamite of the dead Obergruppenführer. He had, as I probably noted once before, demolished Liebich's dance hall while in a state of inebriation. Sic transit gloria mundi.

Contemplating the events of the past several days, it is certainly not for us Jews to take a position on them. But what is evident is that people were shot dead without a trial. Revolutionary times rapidly lift people to the heights and smash them to the depths. One has a sense that the world has not yet recovered from the chaos that was created 20 years ago, and that all relations between peoples are in a state of flux! Many rumors are circulating around the city. We no longer see SA uniforms, only SS. What will prove decisive is whether they are able to reestablish commerce with the outside world. In any case, it is impossible to know whether the crisis has been surmounted. To the outsider, everything is opaque.

---

3. Named after Jonas Fraenckel (1773–1846), the Jewish philanthropist and founder of the Jewish Theological Seminary, this plaza was renamed Fontaneplatz in 1934.

Wednesday, July 4, 1934   Breslau

Went with Ruth to a lecture yesterday evening; she was, I think, very proud to have been taken along. The large Lessing Hall was filled to overflowing, and the temperature really became unbearable. Speyer introduced the program, then came Hebrew songs, after which I spoke for about fifty minutes! I think I spoke well, and to the heart. It came from the soul, and I was able to say a few things about the people who claim to have no opinions.

Everything is still unclear. It is unbelievable, such a strange feeling; we know that a great many things are happening, but we cannot conjure up any sort of picture, at least not without great difficulty. The most senseless rumors are whirring about: Heines was supposedly being bribed by the Jews. Papen is in custody.[4] It appears that the Jewish question has largely receded into the background. It is to be hoped that any possibility of civil war has been quashed because *bellum civile* is the greatest of horrors.

Thursday, July 5, 1934   Breslau

Today is the last day of school, and in the past, we would have already been making plans to go to our beloved Hohndorf.[5] This time, we have to stay home. Five Jews are said to have been shot dead in Hirschberg, among them a businessman named Charig, an attorney named Förster, the son-in-law of Justizrat Siegmund Cohn. One can't even imagine; one can only hope that it isn't true! It has, however, really affected me!

The streets here are calm; every once in a while we see armed military police units, but only in small groups. Apparently, Papen is no longer vice-chancellor.

Saturday, July 7, 1934   Breslau

Yesterday I heard that Heines's brother, Oberregierungsrat Engel, has also turned up in the morgue. Sic transit gloria mundi. We still have no

---

4. Franz von Papen (1879–1969) was a politician and member of the Catholic Center Party. He was briefly German chancellor in 1932. Papen believed that Hitler could be held in check once he was in office. He was placed under house arrest for a short time as a result of statements about the Röhm putsch, but was later named ambassador to Austria.

5. The family had spent their vacations for many years in Hohndorf, in the county of Glatz.

clear overview of the situation, and it seems likely that the entire matter has not yet come to a head. There is next to nothing in the newspapers! Hints that the SA is to be reorganized.

Sunday, July 8, 1934   Breslau
I cannot get out of my head the notion that I have become a burden to Trudi, who is, after all, much younger than I. My life force has diminished more than a little. Yesterday, I asked Hanna Widawski for a small package of Palestinian soil from Jerusalem. An observant Jew wants at least to be buried with it. I think that I personally will have to give up any plans for Erez Israel that I still harbor. I have become very tired.

Monday, July 9, 1934   Breslau
Thinking about the world war on the occasion of the twentieth anniversary of its outbreak! Regarding the shooting of the Jews in Hirschberg, I have also heard a version in which it was an attack carried out prematurely by the rebels. Supposedly, they were trying to take hostages in exchange for Jewish fortunes. What is true is of course unknown, and those poor people aren't going to be brought back to life. Both Dr. Zweige and his wife seem to have paid the price because she wouldn't let him go out alone.

Friday, July 20, 1934   Breslau
Yesterday morning, spent several hours on my book about the fleet. This is really enjoyable because it is an area of history that I so love. Rode to the Jewish Community reading room, where I spoke with Rabbi Jünger. Read the Jewish newspapers, borrowed a few books, among them an edition of Benjamin of Tudela.

Yesterday evening, I got upset about an item from the newspaper *Der Deutsche* that was reprinted in the *Jüdische Rundschau*. Now they are apparently even commenting unfavorably about the pain of Jewish parents whose children are moving to Erez. It is ugly. One must armor one's heart, but unfortunately that is something I cannot do! Such things really reverberate in me.

Lectures

Monday, July 25, 1934   Breslau
In the morning, I will go to the training course sponsored by the Zionist Groups of Lower and Upper Silesia, in St. Annaberg, near Deschowitz. I am very glad to get away for a few days. Such trips always give a person new impetus.

Friday, July 27, 1934   St. Annaberg
Yesterday afternoon, I opened my seminar, lecturing for two hours out in the open. Spoke about Jewish works of history and approaches to Jewish history.[1] This morning, two hours about the fundamentals of the Emancipation period. The seminar participants understood what I was saying.

Full moon tonight; a beautiful view this morning of the Upper Silesian countryside from this volcanic mountain in Chelm—yesterday over the lit villages! The atmosphere here is very agreeable! On the Annaberg heard mostly Polish yesterday. Beautiful white costumes worn by the girls carrying their icons. I noted the names of several participants who interested me. Attorney Schlossberg, Landgerichtsrat Schlesinger, from Oppeln, the husband of Betty Braun, Landgerichtsrat and judge Pierkowski was especially nice; Dr. Prinz from Breslau. Attorney Fritz Cohn, from Breslau, Dr. Unger and son, from Gross Strehlitz.

Thursday, August 2, 1934   Breslau
Hindenburg died this morning, just twenty years after the outbreak of the war. A life fully lived! In his entire manner, a model of duty per-

---

1. See "Schulungslager der zionistischen Gruppenverbände Nieder- und Oberschlesien in Sankt Annaberg O-S," in *Jüdische Zeitung* (for eastern Germany) 41 (1934), no. 30, dated August 3, 1934, p. 2.

formed, especially the way he led the troops back after the war! We still recall his beautiful letter to Friedrich Ebert.[2] But, we must also recall his words that the war had become him like a molten cauldron of steel. An entire era dies with him! Germany's future is even darker as a result, but we feel ourselves so excluded.

Rabbi Nellhaus from Pirmasens, an old acquaintance of mine, was here in the afternoon. Perhaps I will be able to give a few lectures after all. We spoke a great deal about Jewish people who don't want to hear a word about *teshuva*. Trudi brought home an *Abendblatt*. Hitler has been named Reich President.[3] This was to be expected. Ernst will be attending the preparatory camp at Gut Winkel on August 9.

Friday, August 17, 1934   Breslau
Met Dr. Eisner, who is president of the Zacharias Frankel Lodge.[4] Materially he is well off; he has been a Zionist since March 1933, but he seems to have come by this change in worldview honestly. Went to the editorial office of the *Jüdische Zeitung*, where I heard that Schatsky has laid off all of his employees. This great press now also appears to be approaching the end. And so, one Jewish concern after another goes down the drain. Then to the Palestine Office again, where I spoke with Fräulein Levy, Fräulein David, and Dr. Prinz. Fräulein Levy told me that the membership of the local group is shrinking because so many people are leaving. The urge to emigrate is now very strong; the situation for German Jews, especially for young people, is less and less hopeful. In the end, only the elderly will remain.

2. Friedrich Ebert (1871–1925) was a Social Democratic Party politician. He served as the first president of Germany, from 1919 to 1925.

3. On August 1, the Nazis decreed the following law, effectively elevating Hitler to a position of absolute power:

> Section 1. The office of Reich President will be combined with that of Reich Chancellor. The existing authority of the Reich President will consequently be transferred to the Führer and Reich Chancellor, Adolf Hitler. He will select his deputy.
>
> Section 2. This law is effective as of the time of the death of Reich President von Hindenburg.

4. Eisner wrote about his time as lodge president and director of Jewish social services. Louis Eisner, "Erfahrungen als ehrenamtlicher Wohlfahrtsdirektor in Breslau," in *Mitteilungen des Verbandes ehemaliger Breslauer und Schlesier in Israel*, no. 48/49 (1981), p. 17.

My separation from Wölfl weighs heavily upon me, as does the shrinking prospect of my seeing him again in the foreseeable future! This feeling overwhelms me at night in particular; but none of this is of any help, and we must simply endure it!

Ruth is sometimes so hard to control! She is already in need as a tutor. Today she is with a young school friend; she gets transportation costs in exchange for helping her with her Hebrew.

Saturday, August 18, 1934   Breslau

Yesterday, I heard that they were playing concentration camp at the Gerhart Hauptmann School, and naturally they dragged the Jewish students to the "camp." When one of the fathers complained, the director shrugged his shoulders, only after which he withdrew his daughter. Eventually, Jewish parents will come to understand that the atmosphere in German schools is not conducive to their children's well-being.

Sunday, August 19, 1934   Breslau

Yesterday, when I went down to the mailbox, I saw an edition of the *Stürmer* with the headline, "Ritual Murder in Breslau." It's an old criminal case, the unsolved murder of the Fehse children, from 1926, that is now being dredged up again for the purpose of blaming the Jews.[5] This on the day before the so-called election. If only we saw a way to continue our lives elsewhere, because living amid constant vituperation is unbearable over the long term. This morning we were awakened at six o'clock by sloganeering and drumming. They shouted, "Wake up—go to the polls." But really, there are so many sick and suffering people here!

Tuesday, August 21, 1934   Breslau

To a meeting of the humanistic committee at the Lessing Lodge with Grotte and Heinemann. Also discussed the question of the adult evening school with Grotte. Guido Kisch will apparently receive a professorship in Prague. Grotte is of the opinion that I should go over to the seminary; however, I don't want to, out of principle.

---

5. See the article, "Der Ritualmord zu Breslau—Was die Mutter zweier geschächteter Kinder berichtet," in *Der Stürmer* no. 32 (1934).

Sunday, August 26, 1934   Breslau

Got on the 18 with Trudi and rode to Scheitniger Park; sat on a bench in the Japanese Garden there and had dinner. Afterwards, took a nice walk; first looked at the dahlia garden, which is magnificent, a symphony of colors, then through the old park, then walked via Leerbeutel and Wilhelmsruh along the Grossschiffahrtsweg as far as the end of the 24 line. Evening illuminated by the moon, though somewhat cool. Rode home.

Got up early. Music in the streets early; the parade by the Labor Front in Rosenthal starts early in the morning.[6] Supposed to draw a million people. Cui bono? Felix Perle invited us to the lodge house in Krummhübel for Rosh Hashanah. I don't really want to go because I don't like to be given things! Trudi doesn't share my concerns, and so she is somewhat annoyed with me!

Tuesday, September 4, 1934   Breslau

Yesterday visited Theodor Marcus. We spoke about various publishing matters; he sold the *Wirtschafts- und verkehrsgeographischer Atlas von Schlesien* to the Ministry of Propaganda.[7] It was no longer convenient to have the Marcus name on the cover as the party was using the book for propaganda purposes.

He recommended me to Professor Brackmann for a paper to appear in the *Jahresberichte für deutsche Geschichte*.[8] I want to talk to Dr. Friedeberg, one of the curators at the Jewish Theological Seminary, about an appointment there. I think the matter is completely hopeless because they are of the opinion that I am a "marked man"! I also no longer believe that my fate will be changed by some external circumstance. The main thing is just to get by somehow.

Wednesday, September 5, 1934   Breslau

Went to Ruth's school garden, where we bought a few things. I also consulted with her teacher, Fräulein Daniel. Ruth's grades have really

6. The German Labor Front replaced the trade unions and professional organizations and was supposed to galvanize all German employees into an effective force for the Nazi state.

7. The Marcus publishing house had previously published Walter Geisler's work, the *Comprehensive Economic Atlas of Silesia* (Breslau, 1932).

8. The historian Albert Brackmann (1871–1952) had, since 1929, been director general of the Prussian State Archive.

suffered recently; we are very concerned because she is so distracted and jumpy. Perhaps she is suffering from the times as well.

In the evening, sat back in my easy chair and talked with Trudi; went for a walk in the lovely evening air of early fall. Magnificent flowers in the dahlia gardens! To Leedeborntrift with its new settlements. That was my dream once too, but not any longer, not in this country. I've become like an alien.

Thursday, September 6, 1934   Breslau
Ernst Centawer visited early today; he is traveling back to Paris day after tomorrow, and thank G'd he was able to bring us good news about our boy, except that he seems to be too diligent. There is nothing we can do about that; it's a family weakness. I've always been the same way. He says that Wölfl looks good and has enough to live on. On the one hand, our conversation pleased me, but it upset me, too, because it rekindled all of the pain of separation.

There was another unbelievable anti-Jewish speech at the Nurem-berg Party Congress! "Those who constantly agitate for war, always profit from war, but never fight a war themselves!" Eventually they will tone things down, or they should; it is difficult to breathe this air!

Sunday, September 9, 1934   Breslau
Today is the end of the year 5694. A difficult year for us German Jews, a difficult year for me as well, but we should be grateful to have survived it! Life, in the sense of feeling comfortable, is no longer possible in this country that doesn't want us! Today I read in the newspaper that the Führer spoke to the women in Nuremberg in a denigrating way about Jewish intellectuals.

With Trudi to the cemetery; endless numbers of people today, the last day of Elul, in the house of eternity. Met Frau Proskauer, who spoke with Ernst in Berlin on Friday.[9] – He looks very good, thank G'd. Made the rounds of all the many people whom we knew and who are already resting beyond. Also visited the grave of Lassalle; this year, too, a few unknown persons placed some flowers on the anniversary of his death!

9. Willy Cohn's mother-in-law from his first marriage, Selma Proskauer.

Tuesday, September 11, 1934   Breslau
The holidays have now concluded! We spent them in the usual manner! I
went to all four religious services at the synagogue and found encourage-
ment and consolation in prayer. I was less enthusiastic about Vogelstein's
sermons! He hasn't learned much in all this time. On the one hand, he
says that our young people are scattered throughout the entire world,
and on the other that our youth should be raised to be loyal to Germany.
This doesn't fit together. If our children have to leave the country, we
cannot demand loyalty of them.

Wednesday, September 12, 1934   Breslau
Submitted to the police my application for the Front Fighter's Cross!
(Overcame my emotional misgivings; let them not draw false conclu-
sions from a small number of Jews.)

Sunday, September 16, 1934   Klein Silsterwitz
At the Proskauer home with the chalutzim. The meeting at the lodge to
mourn departed members was very short yesterday evening, and Posner's
speech only so-so. The individual deceased brothers were merely remembered by name. Among the pictures decorated with mourning bands was
one of Franz. Made me feel very melancholy.

Bus to Klein Silsterwitz. We feel very comfortable here among the
chaverim. The kibbutz currently has twelve people: ten boys and two
girls; however the girls and a few of the boys are not here today! Discussed with them the problems facing them in the world: hachshara; the
sexual question; and their relationship to their surroundings here. Their
windows were recently smashed in, and shots were fired. Problems with
the SA school. Talk centers exclusively on the Jewish farm. But they have
good relations with most of the villagers.

Friday, September 21, 1934   Breslau
The Feigs were here yesterday evening; their aliyah is pending. Both
very smart people firmly anchored in reality; they will make their way in
Erez. They also inquired about our plans for the future, and I laid out
for them the various possibilities that seem plausible. I think that they
will also evince an emotional interest. Pinczower, who was in Catania
on hachshara, came by. He also reported to me about Libertini. So,
they have no intention of letting me go there on such vague terms for

the anniversary of the university; of course I would have gladly gone! Libertini sent his apologies for not writing; things would improve after October 20. Other than that, Libertini was well informed about everything.

Sunday, October 21, 1934   Breslau

At six forty-five to the exhibition of Jewish artists at the orphanage, which I enjoyed immensely! I'm going to write about it for the *Jüdische Zeitung*![10] Spoke to the Perles; Silberberg, who was so good as to inquire about me; Aschheim and wife Lydia Baruchsen; Schwerin from the *CV Zeitung*; Rosenfeld from the *Gemeindeblatt*, who accompanied me part of the way afterwards; Fräulein Cohn, among others.[11]

Then to the lodge, where I drank a cup of coffee to go with the slices that I brought along. Had a conversation with the Perles. Lecture at the lodge; 104 brothers were there, a good turnout. Posner recognized my return to the lodge with a few kind words. I think that I spoke well!

Monday, October 22, 1934   Breslau

Yesterday was very interesting for me, even though somewhat strenuous because I had not yet recovered from the day before! There was a meeting of the Zionist groups of Lower Silesia at which Franz Meyer, the main speaker, spoke very well about the present state of Zionism! Smart, and always proceeding from the realities. Shorter reports about KH and KKL work rounded out the morning.[12] Prinz spoke in the afternoon about the status of work in the provinces. There were about 40 like-minded persons from the provinces in attendance!

Had a conversation with attorney Fritz Cohn, who had also been present at Annaberg. He inquired about a course on the geopolitical situation of Palestine, which he thought I should conduct. Spoke with

10. Willy Cohn, "Ausstellung von Werken jüdischer Künstler in Deutschland aus Vergangenheit und Gegenwart," in *Jüdische Zeitung* (for eastern Germany) 41 (1934), no. 39, dated October 26, 1934, p. 2.

11. The painter Isidor Aschheim (1891–1968) had studied at the Breslau Academy of Art. In 1940, he made his way to Palestine on his own. He died in Jerusalem. Lydia Baruchsen (1902–1943) was Aschheim's wife. She and her mother committed suicide in 1943.

12. *Keren Hayesod*, "Foundation Fund" for Jewish works in Palestine; *Keren Kayemet LeYisrael*, the Jewish National Fund.

Franz Meyer for a few moments alone about personal matters, about why I was not being included in the work of the Zionist Association of Germany. He also recommended that I get in touch with Studienrat Leschnitzer at the Reich Representation of the German Jews about history courses for teachers in training.[13]

Tuesday afternoon, October 23, 1934   Breslau
This morning, a man named Salzmann visited to ask me for advice. A typical Jewish destiny. Born a Russian citizen, that part of the country later went to Poland, so he became a Polish citizen; naturalized in Germany in 1920, now expatriated. In other words, stateless; an artist, which means that he would be able to practice his profession anywhere in the world—if someone let him in. But no one will without a passport. I recommended that he contact the commissioner for refugees, or even better, because he still has money, emigrate to Erez as a capitalist!

Wednesday, October 24, 1934   Breslau
Placards on the advertising pillars with the words "Roma-Judah," slogan for a public meeting. Herr Streicher, Gauleiter of the NSDAP in Franconia, will speak here next Sunday. He is the shrillest inciter against the Jews. They probably deem it necessary again for Breslau; it always draws. Aschheim, who wants me to compose a marketing letter to the lodges for the sale of works of art by Jewish artists, came at eleven thirty.

Placards have been put up, "Avoid the Jews like the plague!" Such are the heralds of Herr Julius Streicher's visit! At a meeting of the NS-Hago, there were protests against a speaker who receives twice as much pay as the former half-Aryan syndic and does nothing for the craftsmen.[14] There is also talk that unemployment will rise! All one can do is let it take its course.

13. Founded on September 17, 1933, the Reich Representation served as an umbrella group for all Jewish organizations in Germany. It was headed by Leo Baeck. After Kristallnacht, on November 9, 1938, it was renamed the Reich Federation of the Jews in Germany, reflecting the reality that Jews were no longer citizens. In 1939, it was renamed the Reich Association of the Jews in Germany.

14. NS-Hago, abbreviation for Nationalsozialistische Handels-, Handwerks-, und Gewerbeorganisation [National Socialist Workers' Commerce and Trade Organization].

Friday, October 26, 1934   Breslau

At noon visited with Ernst and Susanne, whom I found sitting in the sun in the Freundegarten.[15] The noon hours are particularly glorious now. It is so lovely watching Susannchen play! Everyone loves her! Ernst gets along very well with her. To the Rehdigerplatz synagogue. On the way, I got an airmail letter from Wölfl, which pleased me greatly. He is working very hard on his exams right now; I'm sure he works much too hard. But I know how he is. He writes that he is doing all right economically!

Saturday, October 27, 1934   Breslau

As of Monday, I will be holding a lecture almost every day, with the exception of Shabbat; naturally, I am very happy about it because I love to work. I am wrestling with myself about the Shabbat; we preach to others but don't draw the consequences for ourselves! I am currently spending a good deal of time reading the Torah. This not only improves my knowledge of Hebrew, it also does a great deal for my soul, which is very important in these times.

Tuesday, October 30, 1934   Breslau

In the afternoon, I taught Hans Proskauer, whom I have been asked to prepare for the school-leaving examinations in German, history, and geography, and in the evening I gave my first presentation at the Jewish Adult Evening School. More than 30 people attended the presentation. It took place in the Religious Instruction Institute at the Am Anger School. – Afterwards, we got together with the Perles, including Ernst, at Schwarz's restaurant, and after that we walked home together.

Saturday, November 3, 1934   Breslau

Ernst Miodowski came by at noon to say goodbye. He is leaving for Erez tomorrow and will attend Biram's technical school, in Haifa.[16] He is living with the Pragers and will be emigrating on the same ship as the Pragers. I was very pleased about his farewell visit; Ernst will ac-

---

15. The Gesellschaft der Freunde had an elegant house in the Neue Graupen-strasse, in Breslau, called the "Freundehaus," or Friends' House, where the society held meetings. The adjacent garden, the "Freundegarten," was also a popular meeting place.

16. This school, founded in 1913 by Artur Biram (1878–1967), still exists.

company him to the train tomorrow. Shabbat with the children with a fancier dinner. In this way, we are ever more celebratory. Susannchen always eats with us and is scared to death that she won't get her proper share. – Afterwards, I read every word of the Torah portion; I now do this every week, and Trudi has learned Hebrew with Ernst. Thus do the times change!

Tuesday, November 6, 1934   Breslau
Yesterday I spoke about the Jews in Mainz, Trier, and Cologne. There developed a very interesting discussion about the causes of Jewish ex-pulsions during the Middle Ages in which the people soon arrived at the nub of it! The thoughts that I have regarding the connections be-tween economic crises and persecutions of the Jews should be set down in a larger monograph. Unfortunately, I won't be able to do it given all of the work that must be done each day. But another way to look at it is that I should be glad to be permitted to accomplish anything at all, and supporting the Jews is very important as well.

Seven SA automobiles stood in front of the Breslauers' former resi-dence on Hindenburgplatz; there are also offices on the Hohenzollern-strasse. However, the likes of us shouldn't be paying any attention to these things; the best thing is to live out one's life in private. The Saar question has been extremely volatile for the past several days; it would be a terrible thing if the world were to collapse in renewed slaughter.[17]

Thursday, November 8, 1934   Breslau
A very agreeable letter arrived from Dr. Leschnitzer, the head of the school section of the Reich Representation of the German Jews. They will try to make a suitable position for me as they reorganize continuing training for Jewish teachers. Regardless of outcome, the tenor of the letter was extraordinarily nice!

---

17. After World War I, the Saar region was occupied by the French and British under a League of Nations mandate. This made it a major flashpoint for German nationalists. A plebiscite, in 1935, returned the Saar to Germany.

Ernst on His Way to Palestine

Friday, November 9, 1934 Breslau

We received news from the Jewish Youth Assistance Society that Ernst's group will probably leave in December; and so the time draws ever nearer when the pain of separation will be upon me. Nonetheless, I know that the boy will be set free and have a future ahead of him. As a father one may not be selfish in any way.

The Revolution took place in Berlin 16 years ago, and today the swastika flags are at half-mast.[1] We have lived through a good piece of history since then!

Tuesday, November 20, 1934 Breslau

Ran into Waldemar von Grumbkow, who told me that Kühnemann spoke very well at the Schiller celebration![2] "The spirit hovers above all." He even accorded Heine his place in German literature.

Today, the newspapers, and particularly the *Nationalsozialistische Schlesische Tageszeitung*, report that they have proceeded against Jewish profiteers in Westphalia. Naturally, all parasites must be fought, but why must the Jews be singled out for it again? In the process, large in-

1. Swastika flags were placed at half-mast in commemoration of the failed Hitler putsch, in Munich, on November 8–9, 1923.

2. For more on radio journalist Waldemar von Grumbkow (1888–1959), see Willy Cohn, *Verwehte Spuren. Erinnerungen an das Breslauer Judentum vor seinem Untergang*, ed. Norbert Conrads (Cologne: Böhlau, 1995), p. 556f. Until April 1933, Grumbkow had been director of the lecture and press department of the *Schlesische Funkstunde* [Silesian Radio Hour]. The philosopher Eugen Kühnemann (1868–1946) had been a full professor in Breslau, from 1906 to 1909, and again from 1917 to 1935. Since 1928, he was also president of the Gesellschaft für deutsches Schrifttum [Society for German Literature].

ventories of fabrics, etc., were confiscated! If poverty grows worse this winter, we will have to pay for it all the more!

Saturday, November 24, 1934   Breslau
Went to synagogue; on the way back conversed with old Herr Grün-mandel, and then alone with Herr Feuchtwanger, the director of the Jewish school.[3] He told me that it was Vogelstein who barred my involvement in the adult education course in Salzbrunn that was sup-posed to have begun in January. He wants to prevent his teachers in the Reform school from being overly influenced by Zionist and Orthodox ideas! Feuchtwanger was very indignant, and he told me that if things really didn't change, he was going to ask me to teach a special course. Vogelstein remains the same old intriguer; this is how my scope of ac-tion is being limited!

Shabbat! My sweet little thing looked on with critical eyes to make sure she got enough to eat! Sang "Shir HaMaalot." I blessed my little one; the other children didn't want it. – I took a walk with Ernst after dinner, and we discussed various questions regarding his aliyah! He is very sensible and is irrepressibly happy! Even though I am proud to be giving Erez a builder, it is also painful for me.

Sunday, November 25, 1934   Kamenz
It is a strange life that I now lead; I'm often on the train. Soon I will know all of the Silesian train stations, all the waiting rooms, all the hawkers. I feel at home everywhere; I can think and go into myself, and as much as I must speak at the places where I hold lectures, I nonethe-less make every effort to remain silent on the trip, and to be alone with myself! I think a great deal about Ernst's departure; it is not so easy.[4]

---

3. Cohn had an ongoing friendship with businessman Hermann Grünmandel, di-rector of the Abraham Mugdan Synagogue. Grünmandel's many services to the syna-gogue are documented in his thick file, which is today housed in the Jewish Historical Institute in Warsaw. In addition to synagogue financial records, it also contains heart-rending pleas from recently impoverished community members. AZIH 105/1052.

4. Cohn described his feelings in a newspaper article titled, "An meinen Sohn, der nach Erez Israel geht, um Arbeiter zu werden!" [To my son who is going to Erez Israel to be a worker]. It was republished in the same year in *Bayerische Israeli-tische Gemeindezeitung* 11 (1935), no. 8, p. 184, and in *Jüdische Zeitung* (for eastern Germany) 41 (1934), no. 46, dated December 14, 1934, pp. 1–2.

Tuesday, November 27, 1934   Dresden

Yesterday was an enormous success. When I arrived with the Wienskowitzes, the lodge was overflowing with men and women. I spoke for over an hour, after which I spent several hours answering questions about Jewish history, moderated by Rabbi Wolf. At the lodge, spoke with old Professor Winter, who has been a rabbi here since 1886. Brother Leyser, with whom I corresponded, brother Merzsohn, who took care of the money, which was quite decent this time.

This morning, a letter from Trudi; she suggests that I inquire into Kipsdorf for Ruth, but I don't think I will have time for it![5] We will probably have to send the child because Leichtentritt thinks it is a good idea, although I am not well disposed to a Christian home. Went into town, bought the *Jüdische Rundschau*; to the incomparable old quarter of Dresden, a view onto the Elbe from the Brühlsche Terrace, somewhat somber November atmosphere. To the art gallery, where I looked at the Dutch masters. This time, I was especially fascinated by the Rembrandt paintings in which he portrays typical Jewish figures, and the magnificent painting of his wife Saskia, the innumerable smaller Dutch paintings in the side galleries, all of which capture real life so confidently and with such immediacy. Even though I was still somewhat tired from yesterday, it was a lovely and elevating hour. Also sat for a few moments next to the Sistine Madonna, whose motherliness made a completely different impression on me now that I am more mature.

Friday, November 30, 1934   Breslau

I will have to send Ruth to Kipsdorf after all; it is clear to me that the child needs something for her emotional condition. Naturally, it is very difficult to do all that. I hope that I will not collapse again. The newspapers are now full of news from England about German armaments. The world looks very threatening.

Sunday, December 2, 1934   Breslau

Yesterday was the blackest day of my life. In the afternoon, I screamed so horribly on the sofa, and when I tried to walk after taking Eupaco, I fell down.[6] My legs simply gave out. Afterwards, Dr. Schäffer came

5. Kipsdorf, a sanitarium in the Saxony Erzgebirge, south of Dresden.
6. An analgesic.

by, but the attack had subsided. Nonetheless, it left me feeling terribly cold! I have a hard time writing about it. In the evening, we lit the Hanukkah candles and sang "Ma'oz Tzur." Lecture at the "Friends," which went quite well, but with great effort; on the way home talked with Vogelstein, who always asks so warmly about the boys! Went to sleep after taking Phanodorm, but it makes me feel so heavy!

Tuesday, December 4, 1934   Breslau
Yesterday's lecture went as planned, although it started fairly late because of a committee meeting. Approximately 36 brothers were present. The turnout was probably low because the actual meeting day is usually on Wednesday. However, the brothers were fascinated by my topic, dry as it was.

Wednesday, December 5, 1934   Breslau
Oberpräsident and Gauleiter Brückner has been thrown out of the NSDAP and deprived of all his offices. Sic transit gloria mundi. Now, all three of Breslau's leading political figures who were spewed ashore by the waves of the National Socialist revolution are no longer with us, and it is worth considering how quickly people rise and fall in these times! Well, we Jews in Germany are supposed to have no inner connections to all these things, nor do we want them; we are simply to comport ourselves like decent guests.

I am seriously considering meeting Wölfl at Rosette Ruf's at Christmas.[7] Perhaps I'm a bit frivolous risking the money, but I think I will be calmer once I have seen the boy again, and if things work out more or less next quarter, I hope that I will earn it all back!

Thursday, December 6, 1934   Breslau
Yesterday evening took a bath and went to bed early. Trudi got an extra edition of the newspaper in which the new Gauleiter for Silesia, Wagner, was introduced.[8] Lay awake much of the night.

---

7. Rosette Ruf was a childhood friend of Cohn's who had married and moved to St. Gallen, Switzerland. Here, Cohn met with his son Wolfgang in 1934 and again in 1938.

8. Josef Wagner (1899–1945) was Gauleiter and provincial prefect of Silesia from 1934 to 1940. He lost these positions in 1941 as a result of an indiscreet letter sent by

Friday, December 7, 1934   Breslau

Yesterday morning worked on my own things; finally made some headway with my mental stables, then to the barber, Dresdner Bank, where I inquired about where things stand with foreign currency for when I meet Wölfl in Switzerland. I would have to decide within one week at the latest. Ernst accompanied me on my rounds. Went to the WIZO Hanukkah celebration; the main attraction was a recitation by Ludwig Hardt, a man of great artistic power.[9] His reading of the Heine poem "Nicht gedacht soll seiner werden" was especially brilliant.[10]

Saturday, December 8, 1934   Breslau

Yesterday afternoon with Ruth and Ernst to the Rehdigerplatz synagogue. Hanukkah Shabbat. – A Herr Neustadt from Erez, who is visiting here and who belonged to the synagogue, presented the synagogue with a magnificent Hanukkah menorah. He also lit the candles and led the prayer. Unfortunately, Ruth is now no longer religious; perhaps this is Ernst's influence since he is fundamentally hostile to all things religious. In this respect, unfortunately, I have absolutely no influence! Afterwards, we opened Hanukkah presents; it is always wonderful to see the pleasure in the children's eyes!

I was fearful after Wölfl left; it is now almost three-quarters of a year since he has been gone, and unfortunately I will be unable to meet him in St. Gallen at Christmas! I won't have the money together. Trudi may go to Berlin on the 17th for a few days. I may spend a week in Silsterwitz with the chalutzim. This means no additional costs! Ernst may spend a few days away doing winter sports, and Ruth will go to Kipsdorf; thus does the family split apart.

Wednesday, December 12, 1934   Breslau

My birthday. Trudi had the three children photographed, which was a most wonderful birthday surprise. The photo turned out beautifully.[11]

---

his wife, and he was stripped of his Nazi membership in 1942. Wagner was arrested on July 20, 1944, after the assassination attempt on Hitler, and killed in 1945.

9. WIZO, the Women's International Zionist Organization. Ludwig Hardt (1886–1947) was a well-known recitation artist.

10. Roughly, "May his name not be thought!"

11. See Photograph 6.

To the bank, where I ordered 200 Swiss francs; whether they let me have them is another matter!

Tuesday, December 18, 1934   Breslau
I decided to travel to St. Gallen after all since they granted me the necessary foreign currency! Felix Perle was good enough to lend me 200 marks to finance the trip; I hope that I will be able to repay him over the course of January from receipts from my lecture tour. – Exactly how much that will bring in I cannot tell at the moment; nonetheless, a person must be willing to incur risk to see his child again!

Thursday, December 20, 1934   Breslau
Walked to the lodge, where the religious committee was meeting about the program for the next quarter, and about the festschrift commemorating their fiftieth anniversary, which will contain a contribution from me!

Afterwards, went for a walk with Heinemann; I explained to him my entire situation, for which he showed great sympathy. I told him that it had especially pained me that I had not been permitted to do the Jewish work that I had hoped for. He was kind enough to tell me that I hadn't done anything wrong, and that I have always stood by my convictions! Bought Ruth's ticket, met Trudi, Ruth, and Ernst; shipped the baggage. The train was just arriving as we walked onto the platform. Ruth's farewell from Ernst was the most difficult because she doesn't know whether she will ever see him again in Breslau.[12]

Monday, December 24, 1934   St. Gallen, Teufenerstr. 116
Yesterday, thank G'd, I arrived safely at the harbor of Rorschach; the trip over was very pleasant, then immediately the train connection to the city of Rorschach, and there connected with a marvelous electric express train, which got me to St. Gallen in no time. There I was met by Herr Ruf, who recognized me by my description. Wölfl was standing at the far end of the platform. My joy at seeing the boy after such a long time is indescribable, of course. His appearance is unchanged, although his presence is much more self-confident. The Rufs are lovely

12. Cohn's daughter Ruth was sent to a sanatorium in Kipsdorf for several weeks. Her brother Ernst was still at home when she returned.

people; she hasn't changed at all, he is a very quiet man who will soon turn fifty, self-assured; the two of them fit well together.

Wednesday, December 26, 1934   St. Gallen
The return route yesterday was lovely; we first climbed a mountain, which I found somewhat strenuous, but then, finally, an endless panorama opened out over the Alpstein, and occasionally we could see the jagged peaks of the Säntis glinting forth in ice and snow. It was deeply peaceful. The houses of Teufen are widely spread across the countryside; a large broom hangs in front of each one so people can clean their over-clothing when the village is snowed in. Most of the houses have paneled woodwork on the outside! There is a large girl's school and a children's sanatorium at the upper end of the village. We were at almost a thousand meters elevation, about as high as on the Schlingelbaude.[13] The thin pure air did me good. We descended through a forest, and sometimes we saw where the water eats away part of the path each spring. I stayed back a little with Wölfl in order to discuss some matters with him alone. He told me some things about his busy life, which he conducts along certain set lines. He is currently studying linguistics.

Friday evening, December 29, 1934   St. Gallen
Went down to the city; I thought that synagogue services would start at four, but they only start at five, so great is the difference in longitude. A very nice service. Rabbi Schlesinger spoke about the weekly portion, about G'd's appearance in the bush of thorns! Walked slowly home. Yesterday evening said Kiddush; a real Friday evening with fish. It was very cozy.

Monday, December 31, 1934   St. Gallen
Visited the abbey library and looked at the interlinear version of Notker Labeo and studied other manuscripts.[14] I then went to the office and spoke to the very nice librarian, Dr. Müller, and looked through the St. Gallen book of documents at documents relating to Friedrich II.

13. The Schlingelbaude is a large mountain lodge overlooking the village of Krummhübel, in the Riesengebirge.
14. Notker Labeo, also known as Notker the German (ca. 950–1022), was a scholarly monk at the Abbey of St. Gallen.

Later, I packed, then took a nice walk with Wölfl as far as Solitude; from there a view toward Säntis and Lake Constance as far as the other shore, a view of two worlds! We drank deeply of this unique panorama. Full of gratitude for these days.

Tuesday, January 1, 1935   Rorschach
Wölfl left by train for Zürich shortly before ten. Parting was very hard for me! But I have full confidence in the boy; he will make his way. Separating from children seems to be our fate. My train left an hour later. The Rufs also came to the train station; tactfully, they allowed me and Wölfl to say our farewells alone!

Monday, January 14, 1935   Breslau
Today is the anniversary of Martin's death, according to the German calendar. I recall this brother with special affection.[15] The cemetery was snowed in, though not completely; placed flowers on Martin's grave. It has been 13 years since he departed, and I relived the terrible hours at Eberswalde.[16] He has slept through more than a few things! Made the rounds of all those I am in the habit of visiting, including Ferdinand Lassalle.

Saturday, January 19, 1935   Breslau
Yesterday went to the Abraham Mugdan Synagogue; this walk on Friday evening is my favorite of the entire week. Religious life is increasingly my deepest experience, faith my greatest support.

Afterwards, sat with Feuchtwanger in the Jewish Reformgymnasium. First he accompanied me, and then I met up with Trudi, and we accompanied him a piece. I told him that if I received permission to teach at Easter, I would be able to assume responsibility for twelve hours per week. More than that I would not currently be able to do. Nonetheless, it is very doubtful that I will be granted the necessary teaching permit!

Saturday, January 26, 1935   Breslau
Rehdigerplatz synagogue; Rabbi Dr. Lewin asked me to come over to the east wall; however, I didn't want to and remained at my usual seat with the children.

15. Martin Cohn (1873–1922) was Willy Cohn's oldest brother.
16. See Willy Cohn, *Verwehte Spuren*, p. 318f.

We had a date with the Perles after eight o'clock at Seelig's bakery. I had, regretfully, not seen them in a long time. They will be traveling to Palestine as tourists in early February; Perle was very friendly, and he is very understanding of my situation. He was so good as to invite me to spend fourteen days at the recreational home belonging to the lodge, in Krummhübel. It is doubtful that I will be able to. I find it difficult to accept a gift, however well-intentioned.

Dr. Josephtal from the Hechalutz is coming to see me this morning. I like him very much! Ernst will make aliyah at the end of February. The reason for the delay is that Givat Brenner had not yet been able to make all of the preparations necessary for receiving the young people.[17] Dr. Josephtal has been in Erez himself and observed everything. One gets the feeling that the children can be entrusted to the Youth Assistance Society, and that they will be well taken care of. Dr. Josephtal has a good impression of Ernst as well. I then discussed with him a possible role for myself within the Hechalutz. The planned Beth Chalutz for the middle group here in Breslau will probably not come to anything. Supposedly—that is, according to what Philipp Lachi, one of the super-assimilationists, says—there aren't enough young people. But the truth is that assimilationist circles have absolutely no interest in resettling their young people in Palestine because they want to keep them here as apprentices, as convenient objects of exploitation.

Sunday, January 27, 1935   Breslau

In the evening, went to a lecture by Dr. Josephtal that took place in the rooms of the Social Group, which are located above the Gloriapalast.[18] They are really lovely, not at all to be compared to the old rooms in the Karlsstrasse. It was shameful how poorly this meeting was attended, particularly how few parents were present. After all, the Youth Aliyah today represents the sole path to freedom. But the CV people sabotage everything so as not to lose their apprentices. But, thank G'd, young people aren't willing to follow them into the commercial professions.

---

17. Givat Brenner, a largely agricultural settlement south of Jaffa, in Palestine.

18. The "Social Group of Employed Jewish Women and Girls" [Soziale Gruppe für erwerbstätige jüdische Frauen und Mädchen] was an initiative of the Breslau Jewish Community. It sponsored educational evening programs and served as an employment exchange.

Walked home with Ernst. Invited his girlfriend Ilse Miodownik for coffee today; Ernst is one of the loyal types. In everything, his opinions are reasonable and decent!

Ella Brienitzer was here yesterday as well to listen to Josephtal's speech, which I thought was good.[19] Eventually, she, too, will realize that the path that Ernst is taking is the right one!

Tuesday, January 29, 1935   Breslau
Ruth, thank G'd, has returned home revived and fatter; she had a lot to talk about. She had it very good in Kipsdorf, and she also learned a great deal about people!

Thursday, January 31, 1935   Breslau
In the evening, went for a nice walk for an hour and a half in the snow with Ernst and talked about all of his interests. He is really looking forward to his aliyah. I think that we can let him go, reassured that he will do well!

Monday, February 4, 1935   Breslau
I used the afternoon largely to do my income taxes. If you have all of your papers together it is fairly easy and not too much effort. The totals are not all that large. In the afternoon, Frau Dr. Jutkowski, an old friend, came from Militsch. Two of her children are in Erez; the third is getting ready. Of course, given the intense anti-Semitism in Militsch they live in complete isolation. Recently, a group of children passed by shouting slogans like, "The Jews are Germany's misfortune," and the Jews "betrayed the Fatherland."

In the evening, walked with Ernst as far as the Ring; it is too raw outside. One can have a good reasonable conversation with the boy. Much of him is in Erez already. Hopefully he will make a good chalutz.

Tuesday, February 5, 1935   Breslau
Toward seven o'clock yesterday I took part in the teacher's meeting at the Jewish school at Am Anger Street. But then I was irritated with myself for having gone because I allowed myself to express my rather radical opinions about Jewish education, which met with fierce resis-

19. Ella Brienitzer, née Proskauer, was Cohn's first wife and the mother of his sons Wölfl and Ernst.

tance from the strongly assimilationist crowd there. Jacoby started to talk about our sense of heimat and the like, whereas in fact today the most terrible insults are hurled at Jews in Klettendorf and other towns in our "heimat."

Then to the police station to receive the Front Fighter's Cross.[20] I had to sign that I had gotten the passport back. – Then the precinct police chief gave a short speech in which he pointed out that wearing the cross is an honor; he granted it in the name of the Führer and on behalf of the police commissioner. The entire war and everything that I have experienced since appeared before my eyes. The precinct police chief then handed each of us the certificate and shook our hands. Upon being called upon, each of us called out "Present," just as we had in the military, and then we clicked our heels! Those are the things you have to do!

Friday, February 8, 1935   Breslau
My father-in-law sent me 300 marks, and regardless of how difficult it is for me to accept such a loan, it is a great help at the moment because it allows me to take care of some matters, and because my capacity for earning money is currently so limited. So I have to accept it regardless of how difficult.

Sunday, February 10, 1935   Breslau
Went to the former Johannesgymnasium, which is now the Zwinger.[21] Great agitation; the NSDAP has posted the *Stürmer*. Whether Jewish parents will draw the correct conclusions and remove their children? There will be some who just don't learn!

Wednesday, February 13, 1935   Breslau
I had an appointment this afternoon at four thirty with Marcus. Among other things, we talked through my entire situation and came to the conclusion that we must try to obtain a teaching permit. To this end, Trudi is to visit Sthamer and ask him whether he would be willing

20. This honor had been endowed in 1934 by Reich President Hindenburg for participants in World War I. There were three different versions. See also the diary entry of September 12, 1934.

21. The city secondary school which had been located at Am Zwinger had been moved to the building of the former Johannesgymnasium.

to testify today at the ministry that he, Sthamer, considers it important to further my scholarly work. Marcus immediately dictated a letter to Trudi; perhaps she can still see Sthamer today.

Trudi telephoned at noon from Berlin; she spent an hour with Sthamer. However, he rejected her request to testify because he had already done so in two similar cases and was therefore already considered tainted. He furthermore considers the matter hopeless. I didn't want to hear any more details over the telephone! We discussed whether she might not go to see Walter Vogel, but we decided against it. So, she will come home today, and she is probably on the way as I write these lines. Our conversation upset me, of course. Although I was aware that this might be the outcome, a certain portion of me believed that Sthamer would have done this given the decades of scholarly friendship that bound us.[22] But the times are not conducive to personal sacrifice.

Thursday, February 14, 1935 Breslau
There was much to talk about because, after all, Trudi had been away for fourteen days. Her conversation with Professor Sthamer was actually different than I had imagined it from her telephone call. She said that he was very nice and thanked us for entrusting this matter to him. However, at the moment he sees no possibility for expanding my ability to earn a living. Trudi met with him for an hour.[23]

Wednesday, April 17, 1935 Breslau
The evening mail brought me a very nice letter from Ernst; this time we had to wait somewhat longer. But he has a great deal to do, especially because in addition to his work he is active on various committees. He

22. Cohn refers to Eduard Sthamer (1883–1938) as his "oldest scholarly friend" in his memoirs as well. See Willy Cohn, *Verwehte Spuren*, p. 302f, as well as other places. Sthamer's scholarly papers in the Archiv der Monumenta Germaniae Historica, Munich, contain hitherto unevaluated letters from Willy Cohn.

23. There is a gap in the diaries from February 17 to April 12, 1935, comprising an entire notebook. This is all the more regrettable because it includes the time of Ernst's departure for Palestine. According to Gestapo documents, Cohn gave official notice of his son's leaving on February 25, 1935. Shortly thereafter, in March 1935, Ernst sailed from Trieste to Palestine. The Mandowskys accompanied young Breslauers to Givat Brenner, as later photos showed.

writes very vividly. Trudi picked up the Mandowskys at the train and delivered young Gidi safely to his parents. The Mandowskys were very tired from their twenty-four-hour trip from Trieste. So in this short time they have not been able to tell us much. They brought us a magnificent book of pictures of Palestine and a grapefruit and a Jaffa orange.

Berlin or Palestine?

Thursday, April 18, 1935   Breslau

Bernhard Rothmann was our guest. Georg had to stay in bed, which I felt badly about because it was important to me that he experience a real Seder.[11] It was all very comfortable. Susannchen was also there and behaved quite properly; something does remain in the soul of even such a young child after all. The deep symbolism of this evening means a great deal to me in these times and strengthens me emotionally!

Woke up early. Susannchen is always lively, and even though I can't be angry at the child, the morning hours are strenuous nonetheless. Ruth has just gone with her to the Freundegarten. I myself won't attend synagogue today; given the aftereffects of yesterday, I don't feel up to a long stay in closed rooms.

The mail brought the news that the children's allowance for April has already been cut back because of Ernst's aliyah; this decreases my income for May by 50 marks. Even though I expected it, it was nonetheless painful, and I will have to make up the income elsewhere. Still, it has always worked out! I am sometimes very, very tired!

Good Friday, second day of Pesach, April 19, 1935   Breslau

Started the Seder after seven-thirty. This time we set a rather small table. Susannchen had already gone to sleep and Ruth went to bed shortly after dinner. The evening was very pleasurable for me. Slept well!

---

1. After Ernst's departure, the Cohns took in young Georg Rudich as a boarder. He remained with them until his bar mitzvah, on November 23, 1935. Rudich currently lives in Berlin.

Saturday, April 20, 1935   Breslau
Walked with Ruth up the Kaiser Wilhelm Strasse. At Reichspräsiden-
tenplatz I was approached by a Herr Priester, the father of my former
student Harry Priester, who brought me very recent greetings from
Ernst in Givat Brenner. He told me that Enzo Sereni is also at Givat
Brenner.[2] I have been overcome by such a yearning for that land, and
I will do whatever I can to visit sometime. Perhaps Sereni will be able
to help me.

Wednesday, April 24, 1935   Breslau
Went to see Rabbi Dr. Lewin; however he was not in. As I was leaving,
I met him on the street and walked back with him. Lewin has an enormous library, mostly Talmudica and Judaica. Naturally, I am interested
in the Jewish history section. I felt very comfortable in this scientific
and scholarly atmosphere.

Met Mandowsky, who told me a few things about Erez. Discussed
my plan to go to a kwuzah, but larger problems keep arising that I
hadn't foreseen. Because I am not able to work physically, it is questionable whether a kwuzah, each of which is economically independent,
would accept me. All of this needs to be carefully pursued.

Thursday, April 25, 1935   Breslau
The Mandowskys came by in the afternoon and told us a great deal
about Erez! Mandowsky is completely unreligious, and so this part of
the trip made hardly any impression on him. Next to laboring Palestine, this would have been the main point of interest for me. I am very
happy about the photos that they took of Ernst. I let them tell me much
about the kwuzot!

Friday, April 26, 1935   Breslau
I greatly enjoyed the service in the Old Synagogue; once you understand what is going on, you get much more from a religious service
there than in a neological synagogue! Hoffmann spoke plainly and
beautifully about the rules for the year of mourning. The prayers for
the dead just affect one more directly.

2. Enzo Sereni (1905–1944) was an Italian Zionist and one of the founders of
Givat Brenner. As a resistance fighter against the Nazis, he parachuted into Nazi-
occupied Italy, was captured, and shot in Dachau, in 1944.

Rabbi Dr. Lewin came at ten thirty and stayed for an hour; he brought me a few books, which pleased me greatly, among others a history of the Jews of Kattowitz. I gave him a copy of my *Hermann von Salza*.[3] I will, presumably, get other books from him as well. He is a scholarly man from whom one can learn much! He enjoyed browsing my Judaica, not all of which he has.

Sunday, April 28, 1935 Breslau
At nine thirty, I took the streetcar with Trudi and Ruth to Rothkretscham. It was a wonderful spring day. Georg [Rudich] wanted to attend the Keren Kayemet LeYisrael rally. Walked through the Ostpark to Pirscham. Filling and damming have made the Ostpark very beautiful. The Ohle is at high water today! We Jews get a very strange feeling whenever we walk out in the open these days. On the one hand, this is the land in which we were born, whose development we have pursued over the decades; on the other, we have been excluded from it and been made alien. We are completely isolated. The walk was nonetheless lovely, and I tried to push all of that aside.

Thursday, May 2, 1935 Breslau
After dinner, the German seminar in my apartment: the ladies Helft, Foerder, Weingarten; the gentlemen Daniel Czollak, Perle, music teacher Aaron, whom I had not met before. Golinski from Beuthen was here at the beginning, but then he left to talk with Grete Schindler. She told me that both rabbis in Beuthen, his father, Professor Dr. Golinski, and the new rabbi, Dr. Keller, had been thrown in jail. Golinski has apparently been released again. Supposedly a denunciation by a Jew. Of course, I have no way of knowing what is true in the story!

Called Professor Grotte; he told me that he has found the oldest Breslau synagogue, which dates from the thirteenth century.[4] That would be a major find. In addition, Grotte told me over the telephone that Kober has been fired from the New Jewish School Association.

3. Willy Cohn, *Hermann von Salza* (Breslau: M. & H. Marcus, 1930).
4. See Alfred Grotte, *Synagogenspuren in schlesischen Kirchen* (Breslau: M. & H. Marcus, 1937).

Saturday, May 4, 1935   Breslau

We are considering moving out of Breslau; I have been thinking about a suburb of Berlin in order to continue to live on the smallest possible scale, perhaps have Ruth live with my parents-in-law so that she can be sent to the Jewish school from there. I must try to work less for money in order perhaps to prolong my life. Trudi was very reasonable, as in all such discussions; she may well be thinking about my heart!

Wednesday, May 8, 1935   Breslau

Dictated a few things to Trudi yesterday morning, among them an article for the *Dortmunder Gemeindeblatt*.[5] Then to post office 21, after which, because I was feeling fairly weak, only got as far as the first bench at Sauerbrunn. Sat on a bench there in the sun and fell fast asleep. Did me good; then to former Amtsgerichtsrat Selten, who seemed quite broken. Tried to encourage him a little. I am much better able to do that for others. However, he has no desire to live; it is especially hard for the former jurists! Trudi went to see Dr. Hannach in the morning about our plans for Erez. There is no possibility of monetary compensation. However, there is perhaps some prospect of having my pension sent to Erez. He will follow up.

Friday, May 10, 1935   Breslau

Excursion to Dyhernfurth: They are getting so many requests for reservations that not all of them can be met because no further buses are to be had. With this lovely weather that is understandable. In Dyhernfurth, no innkeeper would have taken us anyway, so it is a good thing that we found accommodations on the property of Herr Mendelssohn, in Hennigsdorf. Yes, it isn't all that easy for Jewish people to entertain the desire to get out into the country with a few fellow "racial comrades."

Sunday, May 12, 1935   Hennigsdorf

This morning, left at eight forty-five; I sat on an emergency seat, which was somewhat uncomfortable. Through the city, Odertor, Rosenthal, Leipe, Petersdorf; at Rosenthal enormous barracks being built; Weiden-

---

5. Willy Cohn, "Lag BaOmer," in *Nachrichtenblatt für die jüdische Religions-gemeinde Dortmund* 2 (1935), no. 26, dated May 17, 1935, pp. 1–2.

hof, Schebitz, Haasenau, Kottwitz, Hennigsdorf, Kunzendorf, Liebenau, Obernigk. Turned off along the Wohlauer Chaussee, through wonderful forests, Riemberg, Pathendorf, Seifersdorf, Dyhernfurth; they are close to the park. The Saurma-Hoyms are currently resident in Dyhernfurth.[6] Went to the cemetery; I gave an introductory lecture there. I think that I succeeded in giving the people some sense of the atmosphere of the cemetery and of its Jewish history. Then a visit to the former synagogue, which was founded in 1847 and is currently being used as a storage depot by the fire department.

Monday, May 13, 1935 Breslau
Yesterday afternoon had a conversation with Herr Mendelssohn and his two sons in his office, in Hennigsdorf. Herr Mendelssohn is a Polish citizen who owns the Hennigsdorf estate in Obernigk; his eldest son, also a Polish citizen, owns the Gutow estate in Poland.[7] His second son is a German citizen and wants to go to Palestine. As far as Jewish matters are concerned, the family has changed completely; formerly, they wanted nothing to do with Judaism. This was again a peek into a whole other world! This sort of Silesian manor house is constructed in its own special way. Below there is a large hall with a chimney, polar bear pelt! Adjacent to it, the rooms.

Tuesday, May 14, 1935 Breslau
This morning, to my great pleasure, the morning mail brought a letter from Ernst. He reports that he is completely immersed in his work at Givat Brenner and tells about new purchases of land. I am happy that the boy has grown into his new profession, and is now so rooted with body and soul in Erez. By contrast, I am somewhat worried about Wölfl; both we and the Brienitzers are awaiting news. I hope he is healthy. Whenever one's children are so far away, it is natural to be somewhat concerned. But nonetheless I am happy that they are gone and in freedom where no one is forced to bear pillory boards through

6. The last owner of Dyhernfurth Castle was Thassilo Count Saurma-Hoym (1892–1965).

7. Emil Mendelssohn, the owner of the Hennigsdorf estate, had permitted the socialist Jewish youth organization called Werkleute [Workmen] to use the property to set up camp. Hennigsdorf was Aryanized by the Nazis a few years later.

the street! I also received a very dear letter from Friedrich Bloch; retirement has rendered his life fairly devoid of content.

Monday, May 20, 1935   Breslau
With Trudi and Susanne in the Freundegarten. I discussed our summer plans with Trudi on this occasion. After Hohndorf turned me down, I consider it right and proper to take my long vacation in Kudowa. I couldn't very well leave Breslau for two months.

Wednesday, May 22, 1935   Breslau
Dr. Hannach called; information arrived from the Palestine Office regarding the transfer of my pension, according to which it is not out of the question and could perhaps be done. Of course, there are a few other things to consider, especially whether I am healthy enough to emigrate.

Thursday, May 23, 1935   Breslau
Visited Dr. Hannach regarding our aliyah; he will now go to the municipal administration with the formal application that I drafted. Now as before, he thinks I would have a very difficult time living on this pension; nonetheless, it is worth trying this approach. At the moment, it is especially difficult to transfer pensions because so many people are attempting to do so. For me the whole matter always engenders great inner conflicts: on the one hand, with all my strength I want to get out; on the other hand, I feel increasingly the insufficiency of my heart muscle, which raises the question of whether I even have the right to make fresh plans.

Then went to see Mother. I had hoped for a half hour of relaxation; however, we had only unhappy conversations. Unfortunately, all truly Jewish feeling is foreign to Mother. A great source of pain for me. There are so many Jewish people who lack a sense of dignity: Professor Heymann recently registered his son at the Zwingergymnasium—in spite of the director's warning; then, when a fellow student stuck a picture from the *Stürmer* up on the blackboard with his name on it, he finally removed his son. At the same institution, non-Aryan students are forbidden to come to school on bicycles—ostensibly because there is a lack of space in the bicycle cellar.

Friday, May 24, 1935   Breslau
Yesterday evening took a walk for almost two hours with Trudi; we both spoke our minds about our plans for the future. It is very ques-

tionable whether the two of us are strong enough at the moment to build an entirely new existence in Palestine. First, we will have to recuperate over the summer. Trudi will take her long vacation in Gompersdorf, near Seitenberg! I will probably go to Kudowa!

Monday, May 27, 1935 Breslau
The film I saw yesterday was a great experience; I only see Jewish movies; the others don't interest me anymore. The Jewish people at work; no individual actor was named, and what moved me the most was the large number of images from Givat Brenner. In other words, I was able to see the place where my son is working and is happy. The song "Emek" was deeply moving in its melancholy![8] But over the whole of it, an aura of constructive, joyful work! *Land of Promise*. The Tauentzien movie theater was completely sold out.

After a break for tea, went to the group meeting of the Zionist League of Lower Silesia, less to hear the lectures than to talk with people.[9] On such days that is still a big decision. Rabin from the seminary approached me: he asked me to teach general history for two hours each week in a training course for teachers intending to emigrate to Erez. In other words, adults! In addition, I was asked to work on the Jewish youth calendar which his wife will soon publish.

The meeting was over at seven o'clock! Went to Schwarz's restaurant with Joel and Prinz and Dr. Schlossberg, where I permitted myself a crab soup for 30 pfennigs; this gave me the opportunity to discuss matters in greater detail with Schlossberg. He asked me why I continue to sit around in Breslau and don't just move to Berlin; I told him that I couldn't simply do this out of the blue, with all the uncertainties. Personally, I have a great dislike for Berlin. It would be an opportunity in terms of Jewish politics. But I don't think I can manage it anymore.

8. A song popularized by the 1935 film *The Land of Promise*. See www.youtube .com/watch?v=QDoD6W2zo1s, made available by the Spielberg Jewish Film Archive; last accessed January 15, 2012.

9. See the report, "Schlesiens Zionisten tagten," in the *Jüdische Zeitung* (for eastern Germany), 42 (1935), no. 20, dated May 31, 1935, p. 3.

Wednesday, May 29, 1935   Breslau

Herr Perle would be very pleased if I turned up at his birthday celebration (60th) tomorrow in Krummhübel. I am in a somewhat difficult situation; on the one hand, these mass gatherings rub me the wrong way, on the other hand, I don't want to ruin things for one of the few people who has behaved well and decently toward us. Trudi is for making the trip; I haven't made up my mind yet.

Tomorrow morning we will take the extra train to Krummhübel. Herr Perle paid for the tickets. I am especially happy for Trudi because she will get something out of it! I'm a little anxious about all the people.

Friday, May 31, 1935   Breslau

As a result of electrification, even of the mountain railway, we were able to ride through all the way to Krummhübel, arriving shortly before nine o'clock. The mountains were mostly shrouded in fog, which only cleared up toward evening before we left. And then the mountains looked as if you could touch them. With Trudi, walked very, very slowly up the paved road as far as Logenheim; in spite of that, almost ran out of breath with each step, which is terribly depressing. I so used to love these mountains, and have been rooted in this landscape for decades—I visited Krummhübel for the first time in 1897, and I see clearly before my eyes everything that I experienced back then. And yet we have become strangers because the people around us don't want us anymore. Greeted Frau Perle in the Logenheim; Felix Perle had gone for a walk. Got a second wind.

The celebrants eventually gathered: Rabbi Dr. Langer for the Lodge Association, Dr. Posner, Dr. Schäfer, Dr. Singer for the Lessing Lodge. Falisch for the board of trustees of the convalescent home, Silberberg and his wife. The various members of the Perle family, among them the somewhat eccentric Heinz Perle, whom I have always liked, and with whom I became close friends; a strange man. The meal extended from two to six o'clock, and the table was festively set. I sat between Trudi and Fräulein Leschinsky, Herr Perle's older secretary. There were many speeches, and I was called on to speak as well; I spoke on behalf of the board of the Jewish Museum, to which I now belong.

Monday, June 3, 1935 Breslau

Rode to the offices of Felix Perle to a general meeting of the Jewish Museum.[10] First there was a special meeting and then a regular one; I was elected to the board and will try to turn the Jewish Museum into a real place of cultural interest, about which the members of the Breslau community will be informed. There were relatively few people, among them the son of the late Kommerzienrat Pinkus, from Neustadt, the former theater director Dr. Loewe, Fräulein Dr. Lydia Baruchsen-Aschheim, in full regalia. I find it repulsive when women attend such sober events dressed up like that.[11] Silberberg led the proceedings.

Wednesday, June 5, 1935 Breslau

I wanted to go to the Abraham Mugdan Synagogue to say Kaddish for Franz, but religious services were held at eight forty-five because of Sephira. I couldn't wait that long. Glanced through the newspapers for a while in the reading room at the Community Library. Managed to constitute a minyan at the Lessing Lodge. Herr Perle said Mincha Kaddish, and I said Maariv.

Conversed with Posner; perhaps I will speak again at the Lessing Lodge. Spoke on the subject of "Questions regarding the conduct of Jewish life" at the Frankel Lodge. It was lamentable; only twenty brothers and fifteen sisters were there. A good audience, but nonetheless it always seems like a waste of resources whenever a lecture has so few in attendance.

Thursday, June 6, 1935 Breslau

Yesterday morning at Felix Perle's office, dictated a number of letters about the Jewish Museum to Fräulein Spiro, also a brief article about the general meeting of the Museum Association.

After dinner, the teacher seminar, I largely spoke about questions relating to the German essay. At my suggestion, Fräulein Weingarten spoke in both first-year classes about "What are my hopes for the future."

10. A detailed report about the general meeting of the Jewish Museum Association was published as "Jüdisches Museum e. V. Breslau," in *Jüdische Zeitung* (for eastern Germany) 42 (1935), no. 21, dated June 7, 1935, p. 3.

11. It is interesting that he refers to her as "Fräulein" since Lydia Baruchsen was married to the painter Isidor Aschheim. This may have been Cohn's way of indicating his displeasure at her behavior.

A large percentage of the children—in the first-year classes, over fifty percent—are thinking about Erez; of the children in the Jewish elementary school, almost all.

Saturday, June 8, 1935   Breslau
This morning rode to the Storch Synagogue; there spoke to Rabbi Simonsohn and his wife at the door, and then to attorney Grzebinasch, who will shortly be resettling in Erez Israel. I sent greetings to Ernst through him.

Hoffmann spoke well and said that if people had been placed in the Jewish pillory first, they might never have been placed in the general pillory. I studied Hebrew from four to five; we translated the Torah portion for the first day of the Feast of Weeks. A tremendous power hovers over the pronouncement of the Ten Words.

Youth Work

Whit Monday, June 10, 1935   Breslau

Went to Obernigk yesterday morning; Ruth and her girlfriends got off in Auras-Hennigsdorf. They are going to the Whitsun camp for Habonim on Herr Mendelssohn's estate. There were about 200 young people; a wonderfully lively crowd, except that the girls, when they are not engaged in actual sport, run around in a relatively unclothed state which, I believe, in consideration of the inhabitants of the village who come to watch, is not right, and I expressed this opinion several times. Such things always redound to the detriment of Jews in general.

Everyone sat on the ground at dinner, as did we. There was pudding and slices of cake, of which we got some, too. They sang Hebrew songs beforehand. We arrived too late with Rozniko and Assael for the Hebrew *sicha*.[1] This was a big experience for Ruth; she is filled with thoughts about community.

Ruth came back relatively early this morning. The police broke up the camp. Yesterday evening while they had their campfire, two gendarmes came by and made them put it out, told them to go to sleep, then have breakfast, and disappear from the area. From what Ruth told me, the officials were friendly enough. Ruth was very tired and went to bed right away, but it is very sad for the young people to have their Whitsun outing terminated in such a way. We're not living any sort of life here, we are merely vegetating.

---

1. Assael ben-David (1908–2001) was an agronomist and was born in Palestine. He visited Breslau several times to teach young people about agriculture.

June 11, 1935

I read a good deal yesterday about the history of the Jews in Frankfurt am Main.[2] I would very much like to write something similar for Breslau, but where would I find a publisher? And yet, I would be very capable of writing such a history.

The Werkleute, who were camping near Schedlau, in Falkenberg administrative district, Upper Silesia, had the same experience as the Habonim.[3] Even though the camp was located on the nature preserve of a count who had given consent for it, the police broke it up. The count himself came to apologize.[4] He was obviously embarrassed and said that he was forced to do it in order not to be suspected of friendliness toward the Jews. This is really the worst type of suspicion. This is how things were when the Jewish code of residence was in effect in Frankfurt am Main! I wouldn't have believed that such a thing was possible in Upper Silesia because special provisions obtain there.[5] The community of Oppeln conducted itself very decently, housing the young people in the parish house; one man donated a hundred links of sausage.

Saturday, June 15, 1935   Breslau

On Saturday morning, attachments of rowdy Hitler Youth marched through the streets with marching drums, making a tremendous racket. It is a pleasure to be alive!

My thoughts are now often with Wölfl, who is having a difficult time during these examination weeks. I am very sorry that he must make his studies so much more difficult by giving lessons, but unfortunately it is not possible any other way. In this respect I had things much easier!

2. Isidor Kracauer, *Geschichte der Juden in Frankfurt am Main 1150–1824*, 3 vols. (Frankfurt a. M., 1925–1927).

3. Werkleute [Workmen] was a Jewish socialist youth organization.

4. Schedlau belonged to the Counts von Pückler.

5. These special provisions were the result of a plebiscite mandated by the Versailles Treaty in the highly industrialized border region of Upper Silesia, which was ethnically divided between Poles and Germans. The plebiscite was held in March 1921. According to League of Nations protections, which lapsed in July 1937, the Reich's anti-Jewish laws did not apply in this part of Germany in 1935. Cf. footnote to diary entry of November 19, 1938.

Monday, June 17, 1935   Breslau

Yesterday I pulled myself together after all in order to go to Lessing Lodge for the meeting of the League of Synagogue Communities of Lower Silesia. It is perhaps a good thing to bring myself to do something and give my utmost! For many reasons I have never regretted doing so!

I arrived too late for Vogelstein's lecture; however, I heard the one that Hoffmann gave about the obligations of a Jewish community according to Maimonides; nicely done and spirited, but what he didn't say is that among the obligations of a community is to build Erez Israel.[6] When I later asked him about it, he replied that this is not in Maimonides. But the truth is that Hoffmann does not like to stress his interest in Palestine when Reform Jews are around. He has no backbone. The meeting was skillfully led by Obermagistratsrat Guttmann.

At my urging, Jutkowski-Militsch brought forth a motion to set aside 100 marks for the Palestine Office, whereupon Herr Lachs immediately brought forth a countermotion for a 100 mark donation to the Central Association. However, both motions were withdrawn. Dr. Hirschfeld talked stupid stuff about the fact that Jewish youth no longer wish to become sales apprentices. I thoroughly told him my opinion in private. These people understand nothing of what it means to be a chalutz! I got upset about a tactless remark by Rabbi Hoffmann from the Jewish Community: "For you (i.e., me) scholarship is the foundation for making money" (poor idiot, I gave him a good piece of my mind). Only 420,000 German Jews remain; what is the point of provincial leagues, state leagues, the Reich Representation. The Reich Representation alone costs us 400,000 marks in office and personnel expenses.

Friday, June 21, 1935   Breslau

Our house is now full. Herr Feldstein moved in with us; we rented the half-room for a good price. In addition, Hannelore Alexander lives with us, an 11-year-old girl; the daughter of Trudi's Hebrew teacher; mother and daughter will take care of our apartment during our absence from Breslau.

6. An article by Rabbi Dr. Hermann Vogelstein titled "Maimonides. Zum 800. Geburtstag des Rabbi Mose ben Maimon" had already appeared in the *Breslauer Jüdisches Gemeindeblatt* 12 (1935), no. 7, dated April 15, 1935, pp. 1–3.

Lotte Tichauer told me a few things about her life! She will be making hachshara in August! Today she made a somewhat calmer impression than when she arrived.

Saturday, June 22, 1935   Breslau

Yesterday afternoon, Salo Berliner and Erich Berliner came by to ask my advice. I recommended that they allow their boy to get his ninth-year certificate, and then to attend courses for Hebrew teachers. Joel from the Palestine Office called me about the same matter; half a year ago, Joel was in Bunzlau looking for a contribution for Keren Hayesod. At the time, he had not a pfennig to spare for Erez Israel; now he is taking advantage of it for his son. That's how this Reform Jewish community is.

Later went to the Abraham Mugdan Synagogue, where I was joined by our lodgers Feldstein and Georg Rudich. I have now mounted the photographs of Trudi and the four girls next to each other in an album![7] The only place a Jewish family can be held together is in an album; otherwise, they are strewn far and wide.

---

7. Certainly an error as Cohn had two daughters at the time, a total of four children.

In Bad Kudowa

Sunday, June 30, 1935 Kudowa, Administrative District of Glatz
Good and inexpensive accommodations, 150 marks. I've already un-
packed all my things and put them away. May G'd grant that I recuperate fully here.[1]

Monday, July 1, 1935 Kudowa
Plagued by restlessness; studied some Hebrew! Walked in the forest
above the resort, but climbing was difficult; I got out of breath at the
slightest exertion. Sat down on various benches, later in the reading
room; unfortunately, no Jewish newspaper subscriptions this year.

Tuesday, July 2, 1935 Kudowa
After dinner, I went for a walk; if you walk east from Edenhall you get
to a bench with a broad panoramic view far into Bohemia. I sat there
until the sun went down; then it began to get cool.

Wednesday, July 3, 1935 Kudowa
Yesterday afternoon I was in bad state in every regard! I was thinking
about Wölfl; the boy will be very worried. It would make a difference
if I could talk to him, but the distance is so great.
 In the afternoon, went to Cermna Mala and into the Gute Laune.[2]
Read newspapers, drank coffee. The border is intensely guarded on

1. Willy Cohn frequently visited Bad Kudowa to recuperate because his brother
Franz Cohn (1881–1934) had been a spa physician there. His practice was later continued by his wife, Lotte.
 2. Čermná Malá, a district of Nachod, is located a few kilometers south of
Kudowa, in Czech territory. The Gute Laune [lit. "good mood"] was a small restaurant or café.

both sides; you always have to show identification. You are also asked about the money that you bring along; it is obvious that you have to obey the legal provisions. In the newspapers, read about the big Catholic conference in Prague; there they also drew attention to the importance of the Torah. The negotiations within the Prague Parliament and its position on the Sudeten German party were also interesting. I think that in Prague they do not understand how large a popular movement it really is.

Friday, July 5, 1935   Kudowa
Walked to the spring; Wolff, a lodge brother, spoke to me; later I asked two Chassidim when prayer began today. They asked me whether I, too, prayed, whereupon I replied, "Ivri anochi."[3]

Sunday, July 7, 1935   Kudowa
Walked in the woods part of the way toward Gross Georgsdorf; it was very quiet and peaceful. On the way back, saw the ridge of the Riesengebirge, almost close enough to touch; sat on a bench in the Lindenweg. Toward the town of Lewin everything was dark and oppressive; toward the west the sun peeked through the clouds and illuminated the landscape. I could see all the way into Bohemia! Sitting on this bench I feel closer to nature! The scent of the soil, which I so love. It is my hope that our children will one day be rooted like this in Palestine and live from the soil.

Wednesday, July 17, 1935   Kudowa
Went into a simple inn for a cup of coffee. A group of Jewish young people on a trip came by, and when I greeted them with "shalom," they replied "guten Tag," and when I asked them if they were from the Habonim, they told me they were from BdjJ (Organization of German Jewish Youth; this only for later times when this abbreviation will no longer be understood).[4]

In Tscherbeney, a *Stürmer* bulletin board with the heading "The Jews are our misfortune." This isn't done in Kudowa during the season be-

3. "I am a Hebrew," in Jonah 1:9.
4. Bund deutscher jüdischer Jugend. The explanation in parentheses is in the original. It indicates that at this point Cohn was not merely writing for himself but "for later times."

cause they need the money from the Jews visiting the spa; here they are anti-Semitic only during the winter.

Wednesday, July 24, 1935   Kudowa
I heard that some swimming pools have been completely closed to Jews in Breslau; in others, separate accommodations have been granted by "special courtesy of the police chief." The only thing missing is the head tax in accordance with the value of a Styrian ox, as in the days of Moses Mendelssohn![5] Hopefully, our Breslau Jews will now avoid the swimming pools completely! All this is so beneath human dignity and eats at one's life, which is, after all, probably only a one-time affair.

Wednesday, July 31, 1935   Kudowa
Talked for a time with Spier, the director of the Talmud-Torah School, in Hamburg. Eighty percent of the school costs are paid by the state of Hamburg, and the teachers receive a pension from the state.

Saturday, August 3, 1935   Kudowa
Wrote Trudi a long, somewhat melancholy letter. I plan to go home on Wednesday; I think that I have had enough. Asked whether my mother-in-law is still there; I would like to have Trudi alone for myself. Now I am sorry that I wrote it because it may upset her. Today, two gentlemen with party insignias ostentatiously carrying the *Stürmer*. I heard the following snatch of a conversation. The wife, of an older Aryan couple, "We don't want any struggle against the Jews that will cost Germany." One of the men with the *Stürmer* retorts, "We won't get anywhere with that attitude."

Thursday, August 8, 1935   Breslau
Yesterday, thank G'd, arrived here safely at five forty-five; Trudi was waiting for me at the train. Took the bus and streetcar home. Susanne

---

5. Here, Cohn is playing on an anecdote from the life of the philosopher Moses Mendelssohn. Whenever Jews traveled to Dresden, in Saxony, they had to pay a special duty, or head tax, called the *Leibzoll*. In 1776, when Mendelssohn visited Dresden, the collector asked him for 20 groschen, the same amount demanded for an ox. When it became known in Dresden that the renowned philosopher had been placed at the same level as an ox, the city refunded his money. The head tax for Jews was abolished only at the end of the eighteenth century. In Prussia, the last such tax came to 8 Reichstaler per head per annum.

and Ruth stood sweetly stationed at the entrance to the apartment, and I was happy to see them again.

My mother-in-law was there as well; this morning I had a long talk with her, and I told her everything that is on my chest, that I always have the feeling that they don't think about us much in Berlin. Tears welled up in her eyes.

Wednesday, August 14, 1935   Breslau
Director Krause, who my nephews Paul Proskauer and Gerhart Cohn tell me over and over again is so-o nice, is doing everything he can to get rid of all the Jewish students. Today, Kössling, the supervisory official of the school department on the executive committee, and Schulrätin Lehmann came to the Reformgymnasium to find out whether there is enough space. There are always Jews who get out of the way only *after* they've been kicked, and I am blessed with such people in my own family.

We don't subscribe to any more newspapers. Goes without saying for us Jews! Every other day look in at the barber's. That's enough for me. All over the city there are now NSDAP bulletin boards with the *Stürmer*.

Friday, August 16, 1935   Breslau
Dr. Leschnitzer called this morning. He asked me to meet him at the Hotel Hohenzollernhof at a quarter to nine. I told him how nerve-racking it is to be forced to take on even the lowliest earnings opportunities, and that I didn't understand how the German Jewish Community could simply have passed me over. He told me that the main reason is the *moire* that people feel when burdened with someone with a political history. I pointed out to him that even in Breslau, where people know about these things, no one caused me any difficulties when I taught at the Jewish Evening School for Adults. He outlined the following possibility for potential employment in Jewish schools. If the Jewish schools are to be expanded (which is to be expected because Jewish students everywhere will have to leave the German schools), they might during a discussion with government officials suggest that they should perhaps also make allowances by permitting Paragraph 4 people like me. Of course, these are overtures for the future that cannot be counted on.

Saturday, August 17, 1935   Breslau

The Mandowskys and Frau Abelmann came by after dinner. Mandowsky showed wonderful photographs from Erez, as well as many from Givat Brenner. As I'm writing this, Hitler Youth are marching by with their massive marching drums. A lot of noise is a must; it is part and parcel of the steeling process.

Monday, August 19, 1935   Breslau

I got to know Fräulein Tausk at the Jewish Museum. She supervises there on behalf of the Museum Association. She also teaches applied arts at the Am Anger School![6] Over time, a number of colleagues from both schools gathered, gentlemen and ladies. Most of them want to start next Sunday. I gave a brief introductory talk at the Anstalt Synagogue about the Jews in Silesia, which consisted of the main points; we then had a discussion about Jewish history as a whole.[7]

Went for a walk with Trudi; we looked at the housing settlement on the Kürassierstrasse, which is currently under construction. All the streets there have naval names. The Jewish Community is also using foundation monies to build a housing block for families with many children. At the Gartenschönheit Restaurant, a large and obvious sign: "Jews not wanted." In Germany, cemeteries may soon be the only places where we are wanted! From now on, I plan to record our Jewish fate more intently; perhaps it will be of interest to later generations.

Thursday, August 22, 1935   Breslau

At the SA beer hall at the old Generalkommando there is a sign: "Jews enter these premises at their own risk!" As if a Jew would even think of entering this beer hall. I read a few newspaper headlines as I was transferring at Zwingerplatz. They are currently vying with each other in

---

6. Hertha Tausk was the older sister of sales representative and writer Walter Tausk (1890–1941), who also became a chronicler of these years with his *Breslauer Tagebuch 1933–1940*, ed. Ryszard Kincel (Berlin, 1975; new edition, Berlin: Siedler, 1988). Her deportation file is now housed at Archiwum Państwowe we Wrocławiu. Urząd Skarbowy Prowincji Dolnośląskiej, KMZŻ, no. 3747.

7. The Anstalt Synagogue was a prayer room located in the Am Anger School.

their attacks on us. The German newspaper community seems to have nothing better to write about than us Jews.

While at the barber, looked at Rosenberg's response to attacks on his book *The Myth of the Twentieth Century*. According to this deep oeuvre, Abraham was a pimp! The Torah will survive this too!

Sunday, August 25, 1935   Breslau
Read the *Jüdische Rundschau*. Uplifting, the reports from the Zionist conference. Naturally, there were no German diplomats in attendance at the conference. The speech by the Swiss national council member was especially sympathetic in that he compared the liberation struggle of the Jews with that of the Germans! In screaming contrast to the reports coming out in Germany. Everywhere, fresh abuse heaped on our people and a general throttling of our activities. It would certainly be shameful if there are still Jews in Germany so lacking in a sense of honor that they do not perceive this because they are still making money!

Sat down at the Sauerbrunn, and then met my former colleague Lebek. Because his wife is of Jewish ancestry, he can no longer teach German in the lower classes. He anticipates that as soon as the Jewish students are removed from the school, he, too, will be fired. His children have absolutely no idea where they belong, and they are cut off from any future possibilities. He himself is spied upon from all sides.

Monday, August 26, 1935   Breslau
Georg went on an outing with his youth organization. In the evening, he reported that they had to make a quick getaway from one place—there were only a few of them—because Hitler Youth had surrounded them and were thinking about beating up some Jewish boys. The education that these Aryan offspring are getting is such that this sort of behavior is not surprising. An understanding that our young people must leave this country is increasingly gaining in strength.

Friday, August 30, 1935   Breslau
Trudi may possibly have gotten us in trouble with the so-called Reform school by an ill-considered remark she made while promoting the Jewish School Association. When they asked her about the difference between the two schools, she said that one was a Jewish school and the

other was a school that only Jewish students attend. This way of putting things is assuredly correct; however, her remark was immediately written down and passed along. This matter may have other consequences for us as well because my colleague Schäffer frequently refers private students to me.

The Directorship at the Jewish Gymnasium

Thursday, September 5, 1935   Breslau
Hebrew lesson at Daniel's home, which I always enjoy greatly. I am making good progress. Went for a short walk with Uhu; talked about the possibility of becoming director of the Jewish Gymnasium if Feuchtwanger doesn't return. I told him that I would only do it if I were actually made such an offer; I would then apply for permission from the government.

Yesterday, a Gauleiter declared (in a large meeting at the Jahrhunderthalle) that the Jews are to blame for all the misfortunes that have befallen Germany over the past decades.[1]

Saturday, September 7, 1935   Breslau
Yesterday afternoon was the first time in quite a while that I attended the Abraham Mugdan Synagogue. I was happy that I was able to this time because I feel an inner need. Walked home with Rabbi Dr. Lewin. He recommended that I reconcile with Rudolf on the occasion of Gerhart's impending bar mitzvah; I don't know whether I will be able to see my way clear to that.

The evening mail brought a letter from my mother-in-law. Ernst Rothmann will not go to Palestine if Haifa serves as a port for warships. Better far from the shooting, she writes. My son is also over there. She

---

1. The Jahrhunderthalle [Centennial Hall] was built between 1911 and 1913 to commemorate the 1813 war of liberation against Napoleon. The dome of the main hall was constructed of reinforced concrete, and at the time was the largest such construction in the world. This avant-garde piece of modern architecture was included in the UNESCO World Heritage List in 2006.

doesn't inquire about the boys. I think that we, that is my mother-in-law and I, have become quite estranged.

Monday, September 9, 1935   Breslau
In the morning, I went to the Abraham Mugdan Synagogue in the Rehdigerplatz to purchase a seat card for the high holidays. This synagogue is the most convenient for me. Herr Meisel, the father of a former private student, is organizing the sale!

Wednesday, September 11, 1935   Breslau
Frau Reich showed me the pastoral letter that the Fulda Bishops' Conference addressed to the faithful in the German-Catholic world, which contains sharp attacks against the regime, and against Rosenberg in particular.[2] Among other things, it accuses him of having no understanding of the "sources" of the Christian church.

Thursday, September 12, 1935   Breslau
An unprecedentedly obscene *Stürmer* placard was posted on the advertising pillars: "The murderous people." The Jewish people will survive this insult as well. We stand before history at least as clean as other peoples. What is terrible is that one has to live in an environment that permits such vitriol. Even though I make great efforts not to take notice of these things, I cannot prevent their intruding into my dreams at night.

Naturally, the party rally for "Freedom" that is currently taking place in Nuremberg yields the usual insults against us.[3]

Friday, September 13, 1935   Breslau
The Jewish elementary school students will now have to leave the public schools at Easter. Of course, in certain circles, Jewish parents just had to wait until their children were thrown out. Unfortunately, there are still enough people among us with no sense of honor! Dr. Schäffer

---

2. See *The Bishop of Münster and the Nazis: The Documents in the Case*, translated and edited by Patrick Smith (London: Burns Oates, 1943), and *Hirtenbriefe der deutschen, österreichischen und deutsch-schweizerischen Bischöfe 1935* (Paderborn: Verlag der Junckermannschen Buchhandlung, 1935), pp. 66–72.

3. The so-called Nuremberg Rallies, which were held between 1933 and 1939, were each dedicated to a theme. The "Freedom" rally was held from September 10 to 16, 1935.

told me that my entire life will have to be one of continuous struggle. I know that, of course, and these diary entries testify to my own internal struggles.

Saturday, September 14, 1935   Breslau
I walked home from synagogue yesterday with Rabbi Lewin and Stein, the teacher from the Jewish Gymnasium. The latter told me that the Reform Jewish parents of children in the Zwinger school have appealed to the Ministry of Culture to approve Reform classes in parallel with those in the Jewish Gymnasium. Gross indecency. I must assume that my esteemed siblings Erna and Rudolf also signed this appeal!

Monday, September 16, 1935   Breslau
I have now read the new laws; they are largely things that we already knew: a ban on mixed marriage and no Aryan maids below the age of 45. Reich citizenship; Jews are now merely subjects of the state.[4] Anyone who paid attention to the National Socialist movement would have seen these things coming; here they are systematic. From a Jewish perspective, I am absolutely in favor of the ban on mixed marriages.

Tuesday, September 17, 1935   Breslau
Trudi told me that Rudolf has finally resigned from Naumann's terrible Jewish organization.[5] I will now write him to say that I consider our disagreement of many years duration to be buried. I am happy to provide my elderly mother with this pleasure; before this, my conscience would have stood in the way of reconciliation.

Thursday, September 19, 1935   Breslau
Bought the *Jüdische Rundschau*. It looks as if the laws of the previous Sunday have brought about a certain calm in relations between Ger-

---

4. These were the so-called "The Reich Citizenship Law" and the "The Law for the Protection of German Blood and German Honor" of September 15, 1935 (generally known as the "Nuremberg Laws"), which were set down in the *Reich Law Gazette*, part I (1935), p. 1146f. They forbade marriages and sexual relations between Jews and "Aryans," the employment of "Aryan" domestic servants, and even the flying of the German flag by Jews, among other things.

5. The League of National German Jews, founded in 1921 by the lawyer Max Naumann (1875–1939), was opposed to Zionism; nonetheless, in spite of its stridently German nationalism it was dissolved in 1935 for "anti-state activities."

mans and Jews. The good thing is that Jews are now being viewed as a people. This removes all possibility of assimilation. Hopefully, the assimilationists will learn something from this. Read in the *Tageszeitung* that although the leadership is trying to ensure a tolerable relationship between Germans and Jews, those in lower leadership positions are doing whatever they want. Thus, Jews have now been forbidden to use the playing field in Oswitz; but how can this be reconciled with the assurances made for the Olympic Games?[6]

Sunday, September 22, 1935   Breslau

To the provincial insurance office about Ilse's insurance card! Everything is in good order. Of course, I always greet officials with "Good morning," even though others say "Heil Hitler." I am thinking about how I might earn some money, but unfortunately the possibilities are limited; it is very hard to keep up the household like this. Even our closest relatives make no attempt to alleviate our situation! As long as I can work on my own, I will do so, but how long will my strength hold out? I often reproach myself for not helping Wölfl the way I should!

Monday, September 23, 1935   Breslau

Today I had a strange dream. G'd informed me that I had departed this life. He sent my file card down from heaven and Franz read it to me. He told me, however, that my good deeds were not enough for me to enter Heaven.[7]

Wednesday, September 25, 1935   Breslau

Yesterday morning picked Susannchen up from kindergarten, met Trudi, and ate with Susannchen at the Sauerbrunn. She was so delightful. Of all my children, this is the child from whom I get the most pleasure because I am able to dedicate myself most to her. She is very devoted to me. But not emotionally calm. When I think of Job, I know that I should not complain, but it is difficult, often very, very difficult to endure this life.

6. The playing field in Oswitz had been used by the Jewish Bar Kochba gymnastics and sports club.

7. Willy Cohn's brother Dr. med. Franz Cohn, who practiced in Kudowa, had died a year and a half earlier.

Bought the *Jüdische Rundschau*, which today contains noteworthy announcements from the Reich Representation about the Jewish situation. The Central Association has now also had to change its name.[8] The Reich Representation demands that the defamation and boycott of the Jews must stop, and that the Reich Representation be recognized.

Friday, Rosh Hashanah eve, September 27, 1935   Breslau
Yesterday evening had a Hebrew lesson at Daniel's. Read several pieces in *Hamatchil*, then read and translated in detail the Unetanneh Tokef. Afterward, a discussion with Trudi about religious practices in the house, which went nowhere. These days are always filled with a special aura. This allows me to give to many people, just not to my wife.

The year 5695 comes to a close! What this year brought to us Jews in Germany we know well. In contrast to some people, I am of the opinion that it has brought Jewry a certain renewal! Within my small circle, I must be thankful that it motivated my son Ernst to make aliyah, and that, thank G'd, he feels well there; and also that Wölfl has found his way, and that the little girls are developing nicely. And my relations with Trudi are intimate. I would be very happy if the New Year brought me aliyah as well!

Sunday evening, September 29, 1935   Breslau
The holidays have passed; they have, thank G'd, brought me some quiet and calm. And then I did go to the Abraham Mugdan Synagogue together with our renter, and the old familiar melodies gave me some peace. The evening at home was very pleasant. Frau Reich was here with her 12-year-old daughter. Trudi set the table beautifully. Four candles were lit, which lent the entire evening a very celebratory atmosphere. We had a wonderful holiday meal: the goose sent from Berlin. Afterward, Ruth sang beautifully: "Shir HaMaalot." I said the blessing; afterward, Ruth and Georg each sang the song "Emek." Then the children went off to play in their rooms.

---

8. The Centralverein deutscher Staatsbürger jüdischen Glaubens (CV) [Central Association of German Citizens of Jewish Faith] was founded in 1893, in Berlin. Because this name indicated that Jews were citizens, the Nazis demanded that it be changed to Jewish Central Association.

We had a conversation with Frau Reich. She wants to get out of Germany no matter what; she has no desire to continue to be subject to German laws. Perhaps well-off relatives will make possible a life in Erez. She, a Christian, wants only to go there; she is not interested in resuming a bourgeois existence in England or Holland, something that says a great deal for her.

Wednesday, October 2, 1935   Breslau
The talk yesterday was that all Jewish lawyers who are still notaries will now be denied the office of notary. There are fifty here in Breslau. The war of destruction against the Jews in Germany continues relentlessly; when one part has been done in, they will speak of a tolerable relationship.

Thursday, October 3, 1935   Breslau
Daniel came for my Hebrew lesson after dinner. He told me the following. At a meeting of the board of the local Breslau Zionist group, the chairman, Tauber, raised the question of filling the position of director of the Jewish Gymnasium, and he recommended me. Whereupon my former colleague Alfred Cohn jumped up as if stung by a tarantula and declared that this was not at all proper. People besmirched with Paragraph 4 were out of the question, and so forth; and he declared, confidentially, that an application from me had already been rejected. The great indecency in this is that he was speaking before people who could not have known about the details of what went on; it was an appeal to fear, something which under the present circumstances always has an effect. Motive: fear of competition for the Reform school. Not that I anticipate becoming director of the Rehdigerplatz school, but it is once again a testament to people's lack of character. Bah! Nasty! This Alfred Cohn was always a scoundrel.[9] After all, he always pretended to have the same political orientation, and now he is determined to harm the man who, out of inner consistency, stands up for his own convictions. Nasty!

9. Studienrat Alfred Cohn (1898–1976) had been a rival of Willy Cohn's at the Johannesgymnasium. However, he was well-liked by his students. For more, see Abraham Tobias, "Am Anger und im Fichtenhain. Aus der pädagogischen Provinz des Humanisten Alfred Cohn," in *Mitteilungen des Verbandes ehemaliger Breslauer und Schlesier in Israel*, no. 48/49 (1981), p. 12.

A police official just came by to ask about Wölfl, apparently about military service. Luckily, I was able to present certificates from the German consulate. It is a good thing to have all your papers together.

Friday, October 4, 1935   Breslau
We married twelve years ago today, a dozen years that have not always been easy. But Trudi has stuck by me through thick and thin and raised my children. For this I am deeply grateful, and for everything that she has been to me. Hopefully, we will be granted many more years to fight this battle for existence together, and perhaps to achieve a Palestinian future. To celebrate the day we plan to ride out a bit into the country!

Saturday, October 5, 1935   Breslau
To the synagogue! Spoke with Dr. Sgaller, the physician, about the question of hiring a new director for the Jewish Reformgymnasium. During the night, disturbed twice by wrong telephone calls; I hope this won't be a permanent fixture. Heavy with bad fortune, these days.

Sunday, October 6, 1935   Breslau
Went to Perl's grocery store at noon, where we do most of our shopping now; we Jews must stand together. At the moment, there are butter shortages everywhere, and there isn't enough pork either. Because of the shortage of foreign currency brought about by the lack of exports, nothing is coming in, or very little. The evening of Yom Kippur, always my favorite day of the year! The day of self-examination and peace. This time I am approaching it with some worry because my weak spells will not make fasting easy! I don't want to force it. Emotionally, I have become somewhat calmer, and I hope that the Yom Hakippurim will bring me peace, as its power has through countless generations.

Tuesday, October 8, 1935   Breslau
How superior is such prayer in a small shul like the Abraham Mugdan Synagogue over services in the New Synagogue. Here we really have a large praying community! Of course, it occasionally gets somewhat loud, and the cantor looks around threateningly, but each person is wrestling with his G'd. Rabbi Leeuwen spoke directly and simply, as it came from his heart. The melodies that Herr Grünmandel played

sometimes carried a hint of gaiety, but no sentimentality despite Yom Kippur, only the conviction that the old G'd of the Jews, who has helped us up to now, will continue to help us.

Wednesday, October 9, 1935   Breslau
Spoke with Frau Landau and Fräulein Silberstein. The latter was let go in April from Bielschowsky's, the Aryanized linen store. That was to be anticipated, but as far as I am concerned what is worse is the fact that the former owner, Bielschowsky, who left the company a rich man, did nothing to take care of his older Jewish employees who, in the final analysis, worked themselves to the bone to build his fortune. Typical capitalist mentality! Frau Bielschowsky stated that she was willing to hire one girl to work in her villa. Previously, she would have paid 40 marks; but because the girls don't know anything, she wants to pay only 20 marks!

Friday, October 11, 1935   Breslau
Herr Tauber, the chairman of the assembly representatives faction, was here; he plans to do all he can to ensure that I get a teaching permit so that I may become director of the Jewish Reformgymnasium. I like Tauber very much; he is an energetic man. Went to synagogue with him and afterwards spoke with Golinski and held his errors up to him! He was very reasonable.

Saturday, October 12, 1935   Breslau
Went to the New Synagogue for Gerhart's bar mitzvah. I finally de-cided to go after a long inner struggle. Trudi also went with the two children. This made Rudolf very happy.[10] Gerhart did his piece quite nicely. Mother was also there, and I'm sure that she was very happy to have experienced it. This was the first time in over a year that I had been to the New Synagogue, the first time since the renovations. Once you have become used to services at the Abraham Mugdan Synagogue, you don't like these much! I left before the sermon.

10. Once Willy Cohn's brother Rudolf had left the League of National German Jews, the most important barrier to reconciliation between the brothers was gone. Willy Cohn's participation in his nephew Gerhart's bar mitzvah was the outward signal of this reconciliation.

Thursday, October 24, 1935   Breslau
After the lecture, spoke with Simonsohn, who broached the subject of my possible hiring by the Jewish Reformgymnasium. I told him about what had recently been going on in this matter, and that I personally was not willing to do anything more. Before the lecture, discussed lodge matters with Posner. Posner now takes care of the finances himself after Felix Perle's megalomaniacal plans. Among other things, Posner petitioned the authorities to expand the concession, whereupon it was restricted.[11] Posner, however, successfully petitioned the municipal committee to restore matters to their former state by referring to the Nuremberg Laws, and hence to the limitations on our present lives. He was able to press his position even against the opposition of the representative of the Gestapo; a Baron von Richthofen chaired the proceedings.

Saturday, October 26, 1935   Breslau
Minister President Göring is to be in Breslau today; the streets are decorated, but the weather is very bad for the district party rally. Well, we need not pay any attention to these matters, just live our lives and keep to ourselves. If only the lives of so many of us were not made so difficult and bitter; there is little consolation for all of the many Jewish employees who are being denied their incomes because the businesses have been transferred to Aryan hands.

Monday, October 28, 1935   Breslau
Friedrich Meinecke has stepped down as head of the *Historische Zeitschrift*, which he headed for 35 years; he is being replaced by a Herr von Müller, from Munich, who probably toes the new line.[12] His scholarly works are unknown to me. Hermann Oncken had to step down not long ago.[13] Paul Kehr felt obliged to write a posthumous attack on Harry Bresslau in an *Abhandlung der Akademie der Wissenschaften*,

11. Apparently, the lodge served food, for which they required a food concession.

12. The historian Karl Alexander von Müller (1882–1964) forced the much-respected Friedrich Meinecke (1862–1954) from the editorship of the *Historische Zeitschrift*, and was responsible, between 1936 and 1945, for the forced coordination of this leading German historical journal. Müller was forced to retire in 1945.

13. Hermann Oncken (1869–1945) was coeditor of the *Historische Zeitschrift* until 1935.

accusing him of philo-Semitic tendencies, never bothering to mention that Harry Bresslau was a Jew.[14]

Tuesday, October 29, 1935   Breslau
Read very nasty things in the Jta about us![15] A Silesian mayor compared us to lice; it doesn't pay to get upset about these people, and the name of the Jews will be celebrated long after such people are forgotten.

Wednesday, October 30, 1935   Breslau
Spoke with Regierungsrat Mandowsky; discussed matters relating to the Jewish school. The Reform parents in the community are attempting to use the Jewish Community to obtain a concession from the government for another Jewish secondary school. They will undoubtedly not succeed. Our Jewish Reformgymnasium will have no trouble absorbing the students who are leaving the public secondary schools.

Thursday, October 31, 1935   Breslau
In all probability, I will not be made director of the Jewish Reformgymnasium. Went to the university. Not a single Jewish face there. Professor Löwi, the last Jew, at least on the philosophy faculty, has now been fired; severe war injuries, upper thigh amputation.[16] The principle must be implemented with the utmost consistency.

Saturday, November 2, 1935   Breslau
I sometimes worry when I work on Shabbat, but I have to do as my body permits. I am so dependent on my sense of general well-being. Dictated the usual number of letters; over and above that, a lecture about "World culture and Jewish education," which I hope to give, G'd willing, in Neisse next week. In addition, an introductory speech for the installation of officials! Both of these gave me great pleasure.

14. The medievalist Paul Fridolin Kehr (1860–1944) was, until 1936, director of the Prussian Historical Institute, in Rome. He rebuked his late colleague Harry Bresslau (1848–1926) for his "philo-Semitic tendencies," stating that they were the result of his "reform confession of faith." In addition, Bresslau's work was of "only conditional value."

15. Jta, abbreviation of the Jewish Telegraphic Agency. It was published between 1927 and 1939.

16. The philosopher Moritz Löwi (1891–1942) was a student of Richard Hönigswald. Löwi later emigrated to the United States.

Sunday, November 3, 1935   Breslau

At the lodge just managed to catch Josephtal, to whom I confided my aliyah worries. He will write to Kibbutz Hameuchad to see whether they might not take me![17] That is probably the only possibility for us to settle there. There is much about the kibbutz that I find attractive; my only worry is that I will not be able to lead an intellectual life and do my own work. Nonetheless, we will try this path.

This morning went to the Jewish Museum to guide a tour cosponsored by the Cultural Association.[18] Only one person had bought a ticket, which was probably because the announcement had come out too late. Nonetheless, it gave me great pleasure to conduct this tour with this single participant, the long-time organist, or better said chorus director, of the New Synagogue, Herr Pulvermacher.

Monday, November 4, 1935   Breslau

Daniel reported the following: in the executive committee, Oberschulrätin Frau Lehmann has been replaced by Studienrat Bahr. The latter summoned Director Feuchtwanger and Frau Bluhm and inquired as to who Feuchtwanger's successor would be. He had heard that it was someone who is politically not completely unimpeachable, which could harm the school. In other words, Schäffer or Alfred Cohn must have said something to him about me, which would certainly be a great indecency—but something that Alfred Cohn would surely be capable of.

Tuesday evening, November 5, 1935   Breslau

First evening of the Jewish Evening School for Adults, or the Jewish House of Teaching, as it is now called.[19] In the group, I discussed the

17. Kibbutz Hameuchad was one of the three large kibbutz associations in Palestine.

18. Willy Cohn's tour of the Jewish Museum on October 27 was announced in the *Jüdische Zeitung*, no. 40, dated October 18, 1935, p. 4.

19. The idea for the Jewish House of Teaching originated in Frankfurt am Main after World War I. Many such houses were founded in German cities based on the Frankfurt model. The name "House of Teaching" [Lehrhaus] is a translation from the Hebrew of Beit HaMidrash. Breslau, like some other cities, instead had a Jewish Evening School for Adults [Jüdische Volkshochschule], a more secular notion. After 1933, many Jews became more conscious of their Jewishness; the change in

beginnings of the Jewish presence in Germany; there were more than thirty people in attendance, and they were able to follow along. Hans Proskauer, who knows a great deal, participated very actively.

Tuesday, November 12, 1935   Breslau
Director Feuchtwanger called to discuss the directorship of the Jewish Gymnasium with me. I presented my perspective, namely that I would do nothing myself, that those who are interested in having me have a responsibility to apply in Berlin.

Wednesday, November 13, 1935   Breslau
Leschnitzer is coming to Breslau tomorrow to intervene at the Am Anger School. I plan to take no notice of his presence; I do not wish to be drawn further into the question of the director position, which I consider hopeless.

I now get the Jta daily, the reports of the Jewish Telegraphic Agency. Sales of Jewish businesses continue unabated. Jewish employees are let go; they lodge an appeal, receive a month's salary, and then they're finished. Generally, the bosses have managed to feather their own nests. These appeals before the labor court are supposed to give the appearance of justice; the *Times* calls it a cold pogrom![20] It is increasingly reminiscent of the expulsion of the Jews from Spain. We are supposed to get out, too; however, we are not allowed to take money with us, and there is no opportunity to make a living domestically.

Thursday, November 14, 1935   Breslau
Frau Pinczower rang up this morning to tell me about all of the things that the Reform people are putting out about me to make it impossible for me to be appointed director of the Jewish Gymnasium. There is no point in listing everything. Leschnitzer from the Reich Representation is in Breslau today. I am awaiting Daniel for a Hebrew lesson, and in the evening I will travel out to Oels, to talk about Jewish life in the Middle Ages.

---

name seems not to have been mandated by the Nazis, but was rather a conscious return to Jewish roots.

20. "A cold pogrom," *London Times*, November 8, 1935.

Saturday, November 16, 1935 Breslau
The implementing statutes to the Nuremberg Jewish laws have now been announced. Aryan domestic servants may remain if there is no male Jew in the house. This includes Fräulein Grete at Mother's! It is so beneath all dignity. *Quidquid id est, timeo Danaos et dona ferentes!*[21] Some relief has been granted, but will the rest of the Jews in Germany be given the necessary space, or will their livelihoods continue to be undermined? At the end of the year, the last Jewish officials will have retired; if they were front-line soldiers they will receive their entire last salary in pension.

Saturday, November 23, 1935 Breslau
Accompanied Georg to the Abraham Mugdan Synagogue.[22] The boy was very anxious, but then did his piece quite well. Rabbi Lewin gave a lovely speech in which he pointed out the obligations that Georg had taken on as a Jew. Lewin preached on the Torah portion about Sarah's death and said that all the things that Jews are now experiencing may prove to be a blessing if they are understood as a sign of the times— which is my opinion as well. But there are some who do not wish to see it. Several visitors came: Rabbi Lewin, Uhu, Czollak, Sklarz and wife. After the meal, the Schüftans as well. The boy also invited some of his friends for tea. And so he will remember this day for his entire life; I am only sorry that we must give the boy up now.

Thursday, November 28, 1935 Breslau
Yesterday afternoon, a seminar with the teachers at the Jewish Reformgymnasium. At Martin Perle's urging we talked about the geography curriculum. I recommended that they compile an archive of newspaper clippings!

Went to see attorney Lux, who asked me to come in regarding the directorship at the Jewish Reformgymnasium. He wanted me to submit an application to the authorities in this matter, which I rejected. In this whole matter, I have been consistent in my position, which I will not relinquish under any circumstances: I never applied. If they want

---

21. Laocoön's famous warning about the Trojan horse: "Whatever it is, I fear the Greeks, even those bearing gifts."

22. This was the day of Georg Rudich's bar mitzvah.

me, they will have to make the effort on my behalf. If I were called, I would not withdraw from a challenge to serve the Jewish community. I had the impression that Lux was uncomfortable with my position, but I can't change that! I am staying true to myself, which is what I really owe myself. I will not be subjected to criticism by the gentlemen of the school committee. Dictated to Trudi a Hanukkah article that came from the depths of my soul for the *Bayerische Israelitische Gemeindezeitung*.[23]

Friday, November 29, 1935   Breslau
The League of National German Jews has been disbanded for anti-state tendencies, and its assets confiscated. I don't even feel sorry about it. How these people attacked positive Judaism.

Tuesday, December 3, 1935   Breslau
Final evening at the Jewish House of Teaching, very high attendance: "The inner life of Jews in the German Middle Ages." The inner equilibrium that I sought to portray made a visible impression. There were three Proskauers in attendance. Spoke to the daughter of Schlesinger, the eye doctor. He is very happy in Erez, and there has been no trouble getting his pension transferred.

Friday, December 6, 1935   Breslau
Yesterday evening, a lecture at the Eintracht Lodge, "The dawning of a new age." Perhaps not as full as usual when it is held on Saturday, but still quite well attended. An official of the Gestapo was present. I think that I spoke quite well. Trudi was at her WIZO training course, which was hosted by Rabbi Wassermann's wife at the same time.[24] I am very pleased that my wife is also so intellectually active.

Friday, December 6, 1935   Breslau
I am happy that today is Shabbat. To synagogue at four o'clock. On the way back, spoke with Dr. Sgaller again about the directorship of the Jewish Gymnasium. I told him what I thought.

---

23. Willy Cohn, "Die jüdische Jugend und das Chanukkafest," in *Bayerische Israelitische Gemeindezeitung* 11 (1935), no. 24, pp. 535–536.

24. In the *Jüdische Zeitung* (for eastern Germany) 42 (1935), no. 46, dated November 29, 1935, there is an announcement of a lecture on December 2, 1935, given by Gertrud Cohn titled "Living Judaism in poetic creation."

Sunday, December 8, 1935   Breslau

Yesterday evening, a lecture at the Lessing Lodge: "Impressions of Jewish communities." Closed lodge meeting that was extraordinarily well attended. First, Posner, the president, gave a speech in which he talked about my 25 years of membership in the Lessing Lodge; perhaps not always completely tactfully, but well-intended nonetheless.

In his talk, Posner claimed that I had over the course of these 25 years perhaps not been able to establish personal contact with the brothers; I don't feel that he is right in this. But some of the other lodge brothers said the same to me afterward! Of course, I am not a skat player or smoker, nor am I a Ressource type; that is simply not who I am.[25] But given the responses that I got yesterday, I could see that I have gained at least a few supporters over the course of those 25 years.

Tuesday, December 10, 1935   Breslau

To my great joy, the evening mail brought me a very detailed letter from Ernst, along with a birthday letter. He had started it on November 29, and it was stamped December 4, so it arrived here very quickly. The letter shows great maturity and cordiality; it is the loveliest of anticipatory pleasures of my birthday, and I can read it over and over again. I am again more at peace. I send greetings to you, my beloved child, so far away.

Thursday, December 12, 1935   Breslau

Yesterday evening discussed various matters with Trudi. Thank G'd, everything is settled between us. This morning, the first day without domestic help. Trudi prepared everything well, and so it worked out nicely. Ruth embroidered a lovely little kippah for me. At eight o'clock went to my course and spoke about the Jews of Cologne. Method for evaluating sources; by streetcar to see Mother to pick up my birthday wishes. Received a package from my in-laws with two shirts and a tie, and cheese biscuits from Ella. Trudi had already given me a pair of warm house shoes. It is lovely on one's birthday to be surrounded by those for whom one lives, and to be shown such love; I do not value conventional conviviality.

25. The Ressource, also called the Zwinger, was an exclusive Christian business club.

Friday, December 13, 1935   Breslau
At our building, the following negotiations: first with Grzesik, who would take the second floor when Ring, Gerber, and Rother leave. Second, with Ring and Rother from their company. The latter very disagreeable. Anti-Semite! And Ring is a Jew. No final decision made. Third, Wartenberger from Singer & Co.; informed him of the status of the negotiations. Fourth, ditto Rudolf. I hope that Grzesik buys this building, and that we get out of this thing.

Sunday, December 15, 1935   Breslau
Yesterday evening, as a conclusion to my lecture cycle at the Eintracht Lodge, talked about "Herzl and his work." It was well attended again, if not quite as well as the last time because a community evening was scheduled at the same time in the New Synagogue. A Schupo came before the lecture and asked about how many people were expected and how long it would last.[26] An official from the Gestapo was also present.[27]

Monday, March 16, 1936   Breslau
I like Director Abt very much, and even though he is an Agudist, he is a man with a broad perspective.[28] We discussed the entire problem resulting from the Am Anger School's nonsensical demand that it be turned into a Reich gymnasium. I initiated him into the web of small and petty intrigues. Horrible, the news that one reads from Poland in the Jta. In one town a real pogrom! It is a relapse into czarist times!

26. Members of the *Schutzpolizei*, the regular German police, were called Schupos.

27. Unfortunately, the notebook chronicling the time between December 29, 1935, and March 10, 1936, is missing. The directorship of the Jewish Reformgymnasium was decided during this time. Dr. Harry Abt, not Willy Cohn, was named director. This lost notebook also probably contained more about Cohn's planned trip to Paris, which he undertook in April 1936.

28. Abt was a member of the organization Agudat Israel, a world federation of observant Jews, founded in Kattowitz in 1912, which often held aloof from Zionism and in some cases was actually hostile to the movement.

Lectures and Publications

Wednesday, March 18, 1936   Breslau
I ran into a former student of mine at the fair; he is now an assistant archivist! He told me a funny story. He spent 12 days in protective custody for photographing a sign at the zoo: "This facility is closed to the German Labor Front" (if it is even true). In any case, it made me laugh.

Friday, March 20, 1936   Breslau
Walked as far as the Ohlau riverfront in the glorious spring sun. A swastika flag was hanging out the window of my boyhood room! Sic transit gloria mundi! The Führer will be speaking at the Jahrhunderthalle on Sunday; they are already beginning to festoon the streets.

Sunday, March 22, 1936   Breslau
The Führer is coming today; the weather is glorious; in earlier days we would have called it Kaiser's weather! Today, to get away from all of the hustle and bustle, I went to the one place where Jews are really welcome, the Lohestrasse cemetery, where I had a silent conversation with my father. It was very peaceful outside, and I could sit down and really sun myself. I wrote down all of birth and death dates on my relatives' gravestones for the family tree.

A lot of traffic on the streets today. SA, HJ, BDM, flags, military units. We live our own private existences.

Monday, March 23, 1936   Breslau
I am told that Jewish families living on the streets through which the Führer passed were forbidden to open their windows. Naturally, I have no idea whether this is true!

Wednesday, March 26, 1936   Breslau
Yesterday evening, a lecture at the Geselligkeitsverein, the former Spinoza Lodge in the Hindenburgplatz.[1] I spoke on the subject of "Tales from the medieval Jewish street," which I have done several times already this winter, and which I very much like to talk about. It was extraordinarily well attended; the large hall was filled to capacity! The Gestapo was also represented!

Saturday evening, March 28, 1936   Breslau
This evening there is supposed to be a great parade involving numerous formations with lighting in the windows. I believe that in overwhelming numbers the German people will demonstrate its faith in the Führer. For the first time, we Jews are denied the right to vote; perhaps it is a good thing that we are now outsiders because we have no further responsibility for whatever the outcome may be!

Sunday, March 29, 1936   Breslau
Beautiful weather out, "election Sunday." Marchers began chanting their slogans early. The streets were full of people hurrying to the polls; those who had already voted wore a shiny gold badge. It was a very strange feeling not taking part in an election for the first time, and I thought about the war and the sacrifices that we made for Germany.

Monday, March 30, 1936   Breslau
The results of yesterday's election were as expected: 98 percent for the Führer! We hope that peace will continue. Perhaps this unified verdict by the German people will maintain the peace.

Friday, May 8, 1936   Breslau
The teachers at the Jewish school are to have their incomes reduced again. I find this incredible, but just as much so as that the Am Anger School has added an eighth year, which is being attended by all of two students—one of them a relative of Schäffer, the other a relative of

---

1. The Spinoza Lodge changed its name to Geselligkeitsverein [lit. Conviviality Society], in 1933. Lectures of interest to a Jewish audience were held there; Cohn spoke there several times.

Jacoby. The Reich Representation wants to freeze subsidies; only in Breslau will two school systems exist in parallel![2]

Sunday, May 10, 1936   Breslau
In the evening, attended the 25th anniversary celebration of the founding of the Jewish Tradesmen's Association to write a report for the Jta. In the rooms of the Eintracht Lodge, unbelievably full and hot. Many speeches: Hugo Spanier did a good job presiding. Among others, Wilhelm Marcus, director of the Central Organization of Jewish Trades, spoke. Then the countless welcoming speeches.

Sunday, May 10, 1936   Zobten am Berge
Left Breslau at 8:33. At the kibbutz almost all new faces. Those arriving today on hachshara are no longer of the top quality. The girls are better because they had to struggle to prevail over their families. At lunch a crowd of people! At my request, all waited until everyone was served their lunch, and then we said *beteavon*.

Monday, May 11, 1936   Breslau
I read the *Schlesische Tageszeitung* yesterday at the Zobten train station. Apparently, the Olympic Games in Berlin were opened with festivities that ended with Beethoven's Ninth and the "Ode to Joy." Of course, it says that all people are brothers. Does that include the Jews? A hideous dishonesty animates these things, and is probably inherent to them.

Tuesday, May 12, 1936   Breslau
I just received the shocking news that Rabbi Simonsohn has died. Abdominal influenza; his heart gave out. Such a Jewish heart cannot long endure; he wore himself out fighting in the Jewish interest. This is an irreplaceable loss for the school association because he was its most courageous advocate. Simonsohn was my age; we knew each other from our school days.[3]

2. The gap between April 6 and May 4, 1936, comprising one entire notebook, is also regrettable because Willy Cohn visited his son Wolfgang in Paris briefly during the first half of April 1936. By the beginning of May, when the diary entries resume, day-to-day life had already crowded out his impressions of Paris.

3. Both the *Breslauer Jüdisches Gemeindeblatt*, vol. 13, no. 9, dated May 15, 1936, and the *Jüdische Zeitung*, vol. 43, no. 19, dated May 15, 1936, carried detailed appreciations on the occasion of his death.

At three forty-five I went to the schoolyard of the Jewish Gymnasium; almost the entire school was gathered there, at least the older classes. At seven thirty, Simonsohn's mortal remains passed by; the hearse halted for a moment at the place that he so loved.

Saturday, May 16, 1936   Breslau
Ruth went to the Pinchas Synagogue with the Schüftans. She also had dinner with them. Kiddush, then the Mandowskys came by. He asked me about the school association! In the so-called family classes at the Am Anger School, there is an O II and a U I, which together have six students.[4] It is scandalous that funds are still approved for such things.

Friday, May 22, 1936   Breslau
Went to a meeting of the editorial committee of the *Gemeindeblatt*, which I recently joined. Its director is old Geheimrat Goldfeld; the editor, the unfortunate Rosenfeld. I livened the proceedings up a little! The *Breslauer Gemeindeblatt* is the most pitiful Jewish community newspaper in all of Germany. Spoke with Joel from the Palestine Office about my aliyah!

Whit Monday, June 1, 1936   Breslau
Yesterday's excursion went very nicely. Franz Centawer was awaiting us at the train station in Obernigk. Without passing through the center of the town, we were able to go directly to the Sonnenschein Children's Home, which belongs to his mother and where we have registered Ruth and Susanne for their long vacation.

The home is beautifully situated right in the forest and is charming in every respect. In addition to Frau Centawer herself, two governesses are also employed, one Jewish, Fräulein Anni Gordon, and one Catholic. But what is completely missing is any sign of Jewishness! The Children's Home also has a large vegetable farm growing the famous Obernigk asparagus. We were shown around and saw the many animals, among them a Palestinian turtle, which Frau Centawer recently brought back from Erez.

4. O II (Obersekunda) was the seventh year of secondary school; U I (Unterprima) was the eighth year.

Sat on a bench with Trudi, got into a conversation with an 83-year-old gentleman, who turned out to be Herr Richter, the former horticultural director in Breslau. He is the man whom Breslau has to thank for its incomparably beautiful park lands of the past several decades. He was very upset when I told him that the placard on the memorial to Ferdinand Cohn had been removed.[5] Richter had known him well. We also talked about Julius Schottländer, who donated the space for the Südpark.[6]

Friday, June 5, 1936   Breslau
Rode to the meeting of the editorial board of the *Gemeindeblatt*. I try as best I can to enliven these meetings. Left together with Lech Joel; he told me a wonderful story about the assimilationists in the Breslau rowing club. One of the boats was named the *Aviv*, whereupon some of the members declared that they would not climb aboard. To which Joel quipped that to save their fortunes they would surely have little trouble getting aboard a steamer named the *Tel Aviv*. Well, there are some odd people among us.

Sunday, June 7, 1936   Breslau
Yesterday morning did some work for myself; read through the Torah portion. This time, the shocking passage in which Israel complains that it no longer receives sustenance from Egypt, and Moses laments to G'd that he must lead this people. It has always been the same story with us, worries about our stomachs are not the least of it, and then they always look back. This is how it is today when they go to South America. Edgar Cohn, the son of Hugo, wants to emigrate to South Africa. Rode with Trudi to see Felix Perle, who told us a few stories about Erez Israel. He looks at things rather soberly, like a merchant.

Then he talked to me about his actual reason for asking me to come, which was a lecture cycle at the Jewish Museum that he wanted me to give in the winter. I suggested a collaboration with the Jewish House of

5. Ferdinand Julius Cohn (1828–1898), botanist at the University of Breslau, earned a reputation as one of the "fathers of bacteriology" because of his pathbreaking research. In 1933, the Nazis stripped him of his honorary citizenship in Breslau.

6. Julius Schottländer (1835–1911), a Jew and owner of a manor, distinguished himself by his numerous charitable works and donations in Breslau. The well-known Breslau park, the Südpark, was carved out of his estates in Krietern, which he bequeathed to the city in 1890.

Teaching. The topic would be the Jews of Silesia, or some such, based on the collections of the Jewish Museum.

Wednesday, June 10, 1936   Breslau
Yesterday afternoon at six o'clock, had a meeting at the departmental office of the synagogue community. In attendance were Rechnitz, Heppner, Brilling, Frau Dr. Pinczower, and I; the topic was the history of the Jews in Breslau. Marcus laid out his ideas: first stringent scholarship, then popular adaptation. I had the impression that I was to be put in charge of this matter, but the question is whether my strength is up to it. If the certificate were to come from Erez Israel, I would leave everything! So, I just have to wait.

Friday, June 19, 1936   Breslau
Yesterday, continuing education course for the Jewish teachers in the Am Anger School, spoke about the beginnings of our people up to the destruction of the Jewish Temple. It was well attended, even if something of a strain because of the heat. But the people paid attention. Then went right to the great hall at the Lessing Lodge: Community meeting for the Youth Aliyah. Think about it, the Jewish Community is now holding such meetings. Dr. Feyken, Vogelstein (sic!), and Alfred Cohn spoke; in addition Fräulein Stein and Fräulein Goldberg from Berlin.[7] Vogelstein declared his full support for the Youth Aliyah; for this we have the Führer to thank!

Saturday, June 20, 1936   Breslau
Yesterday went to synagogue. Susannchen has become unfaithful to me and went with other children from the house to the Pinchas Synagogue. Discussed questions of Jewish economic history with Rabbi Lewin.

This morning read the Torah portion, which is about the Korahites. Unfortunately, Mother hurt me deeply by a remark she made. I showed her a picture of Susanne Becker in my album and told her that she had gone to Palestine, whereupon she remarked, "That's about how she looks!" This seems to me so characteristic of Mother's attitude toward Palestine.

7. The "sic" is in the original. Willy Cohn was apparently quite surprised by Vogelstein's presence. Vogelstein had changed his position as a result of National Socialist policies.

Tuesday, June 23, 1936   Breslau
This morning wrote to the labor office. They had summoned me to pick up my employment book, which I now must have as a lecturer for the Reich Federation of Jewish Cultural Associations. This was the first time I have ever gone to the labor office here.

Thursday, June 25, 1936   Breslau
Wrote Ernst a detailed letter about our aliyah this morning. I hope he can do something; I would like to see the land before I take leave of this world.

Wednesday, July 1, 1936   Breslau
In the evening, had to take part in a meeting in the council hall to which all homeowners and business proprietors on the Ring were summoned. As a Jew, I am not eager to attend such meetings because I don't like to be together with so many "national comrades." In the evening, I asked the official attendant on duty whether my summons might not have been in error. He made inquiry and then told me that other Jews were also coming. – I hadn't been in this hall for more than three years; the last time about the census. The teachers at the Evening School for Adults used to hold meetings here. Now an enormous portrait of the Führer hangs on the wall.

The meeting itself, which was chaired by Mayor Schönwälder, was quite interesting.[8] It revolved around the fact that once City Hall has been restored to its original state, the entire Ring is to get a unified look. A young architect named Stein spoke very competently about the medieval style of architecture, which had led to something unified. I liked the way the mayor spoke; naturally, he had to heap invective upon the previous regime.

Friday, July 3, 1936   Breslau
At eleven thirty at a meeting of the editorial committee of the *Gemeindeblatt*. The editor, Rosenfeld, celebrated his 50th birthday. Stadtrat Less gave a nice speech and presented him with a gift basket. I really enjoy seeing how the committee listens to my expert opinion.

---

8. Josef Schönwälder (1897–1972) was a Nazi politician and mayor of Breslau from 1933 to 1940.

Thursday, July 9, 1936   Breslau

Went to see Marcus, the publisher and bookseller, where I hadn't been in over a year. Discussed with him the history of the Jews in Breslau, although it is doubtful that anything will come of it because the Community authorities will never be able to decide. Then discussed with him the question of whether one could, as a Jew, do German cultural work, to which he answered in the affirmative, but to which I increasingly tend to respond in the negative. He thinks, however, that we have a duty to persist in spite of everything.

Monday, July 13, 1936   Breslau

Went with Ruth into the city yesterday to show her some things relating to Breslau's Jewish history. The child is getting older and is able to understand more about Breslau, art, and history. Met Dr. Lewkowitz and Heinemann; went into Seelig's at Karlsplatz. Walked over the Sandinsel, and then rode home. We had a lovely time.

Terrible, the National Socialist student newspaper at the university here. The fights in the halls of past years and the battle against Professor Ernst Cohn are glorified. Then, another student newspaper that appeared on the occasion of the 550th anniversary of the University of Heidelberg, tuned to the same chord. Not the slightest hint of scholarship. – Brrr.

Wednesday, July 15, 1936   Breslau

When I arrived home, I found that Trudi had bought new accessories for 20 marks for my trip to Kudowa. I got rather upset because, in my opinion, our circumstances do not permit such an expenditure, and I could have gotten along without these things. – Great annoyance. Had to take a lot of Bromural to calm down!

Bought *Le Matin* and read the moving report about the ceremony on the battlefield of Verdun—to commemorate the battle 20 years ago.[9] Tears streamed down my cheeks! Yes, I, too, took part with all my strength, and I do not regret having done so. But now all that is past, and it is almost more than I can do to keep up my strength to stay afloat!

9. "A Verdun, aujourd'hui cent mille anciens combattants de tous pays jureront la paix sur la terre des morts," *Le Matin*, Sunday, July 12, 1936, p. 1.

Thursday, July 16, 1936   Kudowa

So here I am again in Kudowa, in the same house, this time a lovely room, a room with a balcony with a beautiful view. It is as if I'd never been away. May G'd grant that this stay helps me recover my ability to work. And brings me some peace.

Friday, July 17, 1936   Kudowa

My blood pressure is very low, and I have the impression that Lotte was satisfied with my health. I feel it myself. This morning at the fountain, electrical heart massage by Lotte, picked up the bath tickets, went and had an electrocardiogram.

When I sit here in the seclusion of my balcony, thinking about myself, there is really only one thing that bothers me with all my ailments, and that is that I will only be able to complete a fraction of all that I have undertaken, and who knows if I can even accomplish that. How gladly would I have worked to accomplish something in א"י![10] – As things are, I must simply accept what G'd gives me. I hope that I will gradually find my equilibrium here. The only exchange of views that I seek is with this book because I do not wish to encumber Trudi during these weeks!

Sunday, July 19, 1936   Kudowa

Read in the Torah; found Book 5 especially uplifting as it radiates such intense religious power. If only our people had kept to the words of the teachings, how much we would have been spared! – I often have the feeling that there is no helping individuals. And yet, one may not and should not lose one's faith in the people as a whole! – And we have recently experienced another disappointment. We asked Dr. Josephtal from the Hechalutz to work on behalf of our aliyah to Givat Brenner. He rejected my plea, saying that I wouldn't be able to adapt there! What possible idea does a young man like that have about what the likes of us are capable of! Well, we will just have to try to make our way on our own. A small bit of gratitude for all that I have done on behalf of laboring Israel. But of course, I didn't do it for the gratitude.

Tuesday, July 21, 1936   Kudowa

I walked slowly along the Wiesenweg. Ran into the former mayor,

---

10. Cohn writes א"י as an abbreviation for ארץ ישראל, i.e., Erez Israel.

Schindler, who was working in his garden. Materially he is doing poorly; he has to sell his library now. Stepped into the Wiesengrund Café, where I enjoyed sitting last year. It belongs to the sister-in-law of the provincial poet Anna Bernard, whom I have known for a long time. We have spent many a pleasant hour in conversation, and she told me a good deal about the work that she is in the process of creating. She has a wonderful way of portraying typical Glatz characters.[11]

I am slowly starting to get stronger, and I am also quite satisfied with my stay here, except that it is not quiet enough in the house. Too many of my eastern coreligionists are less than agreeable. Their behavior leaves more than a little to be desired. They spoil their children the worst way. Above all, they have no understanding that people should not make themselves conspicuous. Today I told an older woman whom I had gotten to know the previous year that she should not apply make-up to her eyelids. When such people get together in larger groups, I can well imagine that anti-Jewish sentiment grows in places like this. They may well be good people, but others cannot see that, and so they judge them by their manner, which is disagreeable through and through. Sad enough that one even has to make the observation.

Wednesday afternoon, July 22, 1936
Reading room. Things look very bad in Spain; it is not yet clear who will come out on top there. Other than that, everything is full of the Olympics! No word, of course, that Jews, too, are fighting for the German colors; but if there is anything bad to be said about the Jews, it is commented on immediately. Well, it really shouldn't affect me anymore!

Friday noon, July 24, 1936   Kudowa
Briefly noted: Last summer, Café Weber hung out signs saying, "Jews not welcome." They were hanging there until yesterday; today they are gone. Business seems to be that bad! Brr!

Saturday, July 25, 1936   Kudowa
The harvest is in full swing; will we perhaps experience it in Palestine next year? Yesterday, I was already in bed by eight forty-five, and so

11. The writer Anna Bernard (1865–1938) spent most of her life in the Grafschaft (county) of Glatz. Her novels and plays mainly revolve around local characters and issues.

exhausted that I couldn't even say the Friday evening prayer. Got into a conversation with a Frau Holländer. Her name interested me, and I found out that we are related through my grandmother.[12] She herself is a daughter of the rabbi from Nakel.[13] Times long gone.

Monday, July 27, 1936   Kudowa
I'm completely fed up with these reports about the Olympic Games! Such self-admiration. In one article about the Olympics, Schacht writes that all hands in Germany should be able to work.[14] But no one gives work to the Jews.

This evening is Tisha B'Av; I probably won't go to services because I find it very hard to be among so many people. Each year Jerusalem is destroyed for us anew. Although I am in the right mood for Tisha B'Av today, this time I am having a hard time coming to terms with myself and feel very downcast. I believe that I have reached the pinnacle of my literary creativity. This is not something one wishes to admit. – But it is G'd's will. I have written a few things, and the main thing is that the children will bear my name forward.

Sunday, August 2, 1936   Kudowa
Reading room. – Much about the Olympics! "I greet the young people of the world"—Jewish young people, too?

Monday, August 3, 1936   Kudowa
Today, the *Neue Wiener Journal* was on display again for the first time since being approved in Germany. Other than that, things look very bad in Europe, actually worse from day to day. Europe is threatening to splinter into two groups, the Fascist and the Marxist states. All that is needed now is a match, and everything will go up in flames.

Wednesday, August 12, 1936   Kudowa
At the Wiesengrund Café, a Jew from the Abraham Mugdan Synagogue, a translator, and an eastern Jewish woman from Berlin sat at

12. Henriette Cohn (1816–1910), née Holländer, was the author's grandmother.
13. That is, the rabbi from Nakel on the Netze River, in the administrative district of Bromberg.
14. Hjalmar Schacht (1877–1970) was an economist who served as president of the Reichsbank and minister of economics under the Hitler regime.

my table. We talked for a while, and then I took my usual walk along the Wiesengrundweg, and then back via the main road. I got into a conversation with an elderly berry picker. She was coming from Jakobowitz with 13 liters of raspberries, which three families had gathered. She was hoping to get 35 pfennigs per liter so that each family would, perhaps, make a mark and a half. She told me a little about her life. Her husband is old and out of work; he used to work in the forest. Back then she was able to gather firewood in the forest; now they have to pay for everything, and that's what these pfennigs, which she hopes to earn from gathering berries, are for. In the winter their elevated village is completely snowed in; if someone dies he has to be carried to the cemetery at Tscherbeney, or dragged by sled. She told me about the time her daughter got so sick during the night, and the neighbor had to bicycle to get the doctor in Kudowa. Devout Catholics; they prayed and the child was saved from a terrible case of pleurisy. That's how people live up there, and yet the old woman radiated such trust.

How often do we Jews complain about how bad things are for us; we need more often to look below ourselves. Of course, these people are ahead of us *galut* Jews in that they have a spot in which they are deeply rooted; they are at home, impoverished though they may be. I found this conversation very enlightening. I have always had a feel for the people of this county. This woman's mother tongue was Czech. She told me that whenever children are around they now speak German to them in their village; it is better for them, and the teachers don't have such a hard job with them in school.

Wednesday, August 19, 1936   Breslau
I wanted to study the Torah a bit with Trudi yesterday evening. Unfortunately, she didn't want to; at the moment it is very difficult to interest her in my world. Today, a meeting of the editorial committee; it is still possible to accomplish a few good things, even though there is no joy in dealing with people who are mostly in their dotage. Started to read a new book by Martin Buber: *On Zion: The History of an Idea*.[15]

15. Cohn's review of Buber's book, which was published in 1936, is in *Breslauer Jüdisches Gemeindeblatt* 13 (1936), no. 19, p. 14.

Friday, August 21, 1936   Breslau
This morning, I received an inquiry from the Prussian State League of Jewish Communities regarding my willingness to undertake a cultural tour at the end of August, beginning of September. After lengthy consideration and consultation with Trudi, I said yes; I would not gladly give up such a fortuitous source of income. On the other hand, I have worries about my health because, actually, I don't trust my ability to undertake such strenuous activities. Began Hebrew class with Kaleko's textbook; I'm sure I'll learn a great deal from it.[16] Then, to my great joy, Trudi worked with me for a while; I was also able to dictate an article for the *Bayerische Gemeindezeitung*.

Tuesday, August 25, 1936   Breslau
Germany has introduced two-year mandatory military service in response to Russian rearmament, which is ultimately a result of "racial mingling." In other words, the Jews are to blame for this as well. And so these monstrous arms preparations continue and will undoubtedly lead to war.

September 9, 1936   Breslau
The newspapers are now full of the Nuremberg party rally. It is also remarked upon that in the larger political sphere, England has decided to increase its troop strength in Palestine. The Jewish people will not be left hanging by London.

I spoke with Heidenfeld, the cantor from Striegau, on the streetcar today. The synagogue there will be dissolved as of October 1; the ritual objects will be brought here to the Abraham Mugdan Synagogue.[17] And so, for the second time in our history, a Jewish community in Striegau is to be dissolved.[18]

16. Saul Kaleko, *Hebräisch für Jedermann* (Berlin: Verlag Jüdische Rundschau, 1934).

17. This event was also reported in the *Breslauer Jüdisches Gemeindeblatt* 13, dated October 15, 1936, p. 6.

18. There had been a Jewish community in Striegau in the Middle Ages, which was dissolved in 1454 as a result of persecution. The then synagogue was turned into a Christian church. No Jews lived in Striegau again until the nineteenth century. This second community ceased to exist in 1936.

Thursday, September 10, 1936   Breslau
Yesterday afternoon, I had the opportunity to do scholarly work without disturbance for the first time in a long time. I was able to do a good piece of work on my book on lien law.[19] In the evening, Trudi accompanied me to a meeting of the Community representatives, which I always go to because of the Jta reports. Rechnitz spoke with me about my intended history of the Jews in Breslau.[20] The board agreed with my concerns. Perhaps I will be asked to attend a meeting on this matter. The Community representatives' meeting was also interesting because of the 1,000 marks, which had been submitted for approval for a traveling orchestra for the Jewish Cultural Association. It was rejected because Herr Prüwer, who was baptized, was to be its director. I had initiated this matter via the Zionist faction.

Friday, September 11, 1936   Breslau
Went to the bank yesterday morning, where I heard that the director of our bank, Bertharth, is being retired, the last Jew at the Dresdner Bank. In the evening, went for a walk with Trudi and ran into Rabbi Lewin and his wife. They are in deep mourning over the death of their son-in-law in Erez Israel after only five months of marriage.

We were once again unpleasantly insulted in Nuremberg yesterday. Goebbels and Rosenberg went after the Jews; I read only a few details in the posted newspapers; it is best not to take any notice of these things. Our ancient Jewish people is immortal; how much good it has done us to get involved in the politics of other peoples is, however, another question. Zionism is the only appropriate politics for us.

Sunday, September 13, 1936   Breslau
This morning, for the first time in my life I attended synagogue and heard *selichot*, and the way in which old Grünmandel chanted the old prayers made a deep impression on me. Now I even understand most

19. During these years, Cohn was working on a book to be titled *Pfandrecht und Pfandleihe, ihre Einwirkungen auf das Schicksal der Juden im Mittelalter* [Lien law and pawnbroking: Their effects on the fate of the Jews in the Middle Ages]. Here, he took on the question of credit provided by Jews, and how they were secured by liens. The manuscript was largely completed in 1941, but was never published.

20. Another book that Cohn had intended to write, *History of the Jews in Breslau*. Cohn tended to work on several books simultaneously.

of it. It met with some displeasure that I did not put on tefillin, but I just can't do that on demand! Perhaps I will eventually be able to find my way to doing it. Walked home with Rabbi Lewin. The gymnasium held services in the auditorium.

Monday, September 14, 1936   Breslau
Yesterday morning, Susanne and I observed the parade of old cavalrymen wearing the uniforms of the time before the world war. They looked like ghosts; most of them old soldiers. At their vanguard, a mounted band with kettle drum!

Thursday, September 17, 1936   Breslau
The service was very short yesterday evening; I had anticipated that Rabbi Dr. Lewin would give a short sermon. Walked home with him and Professor Kisch. The latter has been living in New York for many years now; I actually can't stand him. Then got into a discussion with him and Lewin about Grau, which I would have preferred not to have happen on a holiday.[21] Then we prayed at home. Trudi prepared everything beautifully; the Seidler children were well-mannered. Benediction. My thoughts were also with my boys far away. When will we be together again? Nonetheless, I am thankful that they are doing more or less well out in the world.

Monday, September 21, 1936   Breslau
Saturday after lunch, with Trudi to the Freiburg train, and from there shortly after four o'clock, via Ruhbank and Liebau, and after brief border controls, arrived in Trautenau. This was the first time since the "national uprising" that Trudi has crossed the border.[22] Shortly before arriving in Trautenau, I had a very interesting conversation with a gentleman who thought I was a "national comrade," who told me that he had 300 photographs with him from the Reich political party rally.

21. Cf. diary entry of September 30, 1936, about the historian Wilhelm Grau. Grau (1910–2000) was an anti-Semite who in his 1934 doctoral dissertation made use, without attribution, of the findings of the Jewish historian Raphael Straus (1887–1947), often distorting the meaning of the documents that Straus had found. Straus fled Germany in 1933.

22. The border with Czechoslovakia. Because of its proximity, this was a day trip. The Czech name for Trautenau is Trutnov.

Professor Stern was waiting for us at the train station; went with him to Hotel Klein, where Trudi changed quickly. We then ate something at the adjacent restaurant, and drove by automobile to the lodge. Because my lecture had been announced neither with my name nor the topic, attendance was not as large as usual. I spoke on the subject of "Tales from the medieval Jewish street," which I have done several times before. After the lecture came the more strenuous part: conversation with the people, who are by and large very nice, but very demanding. They seem to be from a completely different world! They consider certain things to be important that for us Jews in Germany seem absolutely irrelevant, and they ignore other things that are unimaginable for the likes of us. Even though they see the fate of Jews living only a few kilometers away, they have nonetheless changed nothing in their own lives! As a result, this fate will overtake them as well. Most of them are Zionists, but it is a Zionism without consistency. It seems as if our Jewish people can only be awakened by beatings.

Went to the Jewish cemetery; it always interests me to see what these places of repose look like. Here, too, one could observe the march of assimilation: there were even pictures on some of the gravestones. Lippmann Bloch is buried in the Trautenau cemetery; he was a champion of Zionism in Breslau at a time when Zionism was completely taboo in bourgeois circles.[23]

Thursday, September 24, 1936   Breslau
Last night, I dreamed that I was standing in front of a class teaching "national comrades." Good thing this is not the case.

City library, found very nice material for my book on lien law; if only I can find the strength to complete it, but sometimes I have my doubts. Meeting of the editorial committee of the *Gemeindeblatt*; it all went amicably enough, though it stretched on too long, but I was given a number of very interesting Jewish books to take home. In the afternoon, I dictated a Sukkot article to Trudi!

Saturday, September 26, 1936   Breslau
Yom Kippur is now over; it was very hard for me not to fast, but I can-

---

23. The manufacturer Lippmann Bloch had been chairman of the board of the Jewish Community in Breslau.

not go against the expressed concerns of my doctor. Spent an hour and a half at home, and as a result I missed the Avoda, which I so love. Herr Grünmandel chanted Musaf, and Rabbi Lewin Neila! I very much liked the simplicity of his sermons yesterday and today. In my own prayers, I devoted my entire strength to myself and my family in the Neila.

Sunday, September 27, 1936   Breslau
Today is the inauguration of a large stretch of the Reich autobahn, which extends all the way beyond Liegnitz. Accordingly, marching units on the streets at six in the morning. Such things are always done with the greatest pomp and propaganda here in Germany, with an apparatus that is always the same. It is being said that the Führer will be coming to Breslau.

On such days, we Jews avoid the streets on which these festivities are taking place, not so much out of fear but, understandably, to maintain our distance. These things no longer touch us emotionally. It used to be that everything relating to the progress of my home province was of interest to me. Now everything has changed, and the only feeling I have is of being a guest! And as far as these Reich autobahns are concerned, there is the painful realization that they are above all preparations for war, and that the world is hurtling ever faster toward a terrible catastrophe. But the masses do not see that.

Sunday, September 27, 1936   Breslau
Had a not very pleasant talk with Trudi. Yesterday, on Yom Kippur, Trudi wrote a letter to her friend Rose Hoffmann, which I discovered by chance, and about which I was rather unhappy. It seems that I cannot influence my own wife in such matters, and the conversation led nowhere. I won't do it again.

Monday, September 28, 1936   Breslau
I was unable to sleep last night because of all the upheaval yesterday. None of this would have happened if Trudi had not had the effrontery to write a letter on a typewriter on the Day of Atonement.[24] Unfortunately, such upsets are unavoidable in life.

---

24. Gertrud Cohn had violated religious law. Apparently, however, he did not consider writing in his diary to be work. Cf. diary entry of December 9, 1936.

Tuesday, September 29, 1936   Breslau
Fräulein Schwarz lives a strangely split life: on the Day of Atonement she fasted and attended both the new and the old synagogue. And then on Sunday she went to Catholic church. She says that she cannot yet detach herself from there. Naturally, I am very careful, especially about not interrupting such spiritual processes of maturation, but I am trying over time to win her back to Judaism.

September 30, 1936   Breslau
Ludwig Feuchtwanger visited us for coffee yesterday. It was a very stimulating hour; I now so seldom have the opportunity for scholarly discussion. We talked about Wilhelm Grau, who is now acting head of the Reich Institute for Historical Research.[25] Feuchtwanger had, as head of the publishing house Duncker & Humblot, inspired Grau's book about anti-Semitism in the late Middle Ages. Feuchtwanger also showed much interest in my work, about which he proved to be very well informed. He expressed his astonishment that German Jewry had so passed me over. I then went with him to the Jewish Museum, where Perle just happened to be, and I showed him a few things! Perle made his presence felt.

Friday, October 2, 1936   Breslau
Went to the Abraham Mugdan Synagogue with Dr. Wahrmann, the district rabbi. Wahrmann tried to convince me to write the history of the Jews in Breslau; I expressed my reservations, which I have already set down in my diary. For me personally, it is very important that I complete my book on economic history.[26]

---

25. The Reich Institute for the History of the New Germany was founded in 1935 at the behest of Reich Education Minister Bernhard Rust (1883–1945). It was headed by Walter Frank (1905–1945). One of its departments, in Munich, was the "Research Department on the Jewish Question," which was established for the purpose of providing the National Socialists with "scientific" rationales for their "struggle against world Jewry." The president of this enterprise was Karl Alexander von Müller, its director Wilhelm Grau.

26. There is another gap in the diary between October 3 and November 9, 1936, covering the entries in an entire notebook.

Monday, November 30, 1936   Breslau

Had a minor difference of opinion with Trudi; it may be true that I am sometimes a bit oversensitive, perhaps too much so for this world.

Yesterday brought great joy in the form of a letter from Wölfl, who again passed an examination with an *assez bien*. And so he is now approaching the end of his studies. He is going his own way, and for that I am grateful to fate. We also had indirect news from Ernst; he has been able to extend his trip through the country as far as Tel Chai. Givat Brenner sent him as deputy for youth farming in Israel. I have a great desire to see my children.

Tuesday, December 1, 1936   Breslau

I passed my state examination 25 years ago today. Previously, people celebrated their professional jubilee under different circumstances. Today, everything is a bit melancholy! Now I have withdrawn into myself, and there remains only the danger of bitterness to overcome. I increasingly encapsulate myself.

Friday, December 4, 1936   Breslau

Went for a walk with Susanne who, thank G'd, was able to leave the house again for the first time. I hope that she stays healthy for a good long time. The child is so disarming when she chats. For example, today she told me that she doesn't know what she will do when she grows up; I replied, be a farmer in Palestine. I read in the newspaper today that the secondary schools are going to be shortened by a year, and that the eighth-year students will be tested at Easter this year! Is this a harbinger of war next spring?

Teaching Appointment
at the Jewish Theological Seminary

Saturday, December 5, 1936   Breslau

Today I received a letter from the board of the Fraenckel Foundation to the effect that the faculty of the seminary had authorized a lectureship for me in medieval and modern history. They remembered me after all, but belatedly. Now, unfortunately, I have the feeling that I am achieving this appointment at a time when I am feeling rather spent. Life is frequently like that. I am to come in on Wednesday to discuss the matter!

After a long hiatus, went for a walk with Trudi for about an hour; I think it has been almost a month since we went out together. Discussed with her the entire problem resulting from the letter from the Jewish Theological Seminary. If we both simply followed our feelings, I would probably reject the appointment. But of course, considerations of reason are also involved, and so I cannot simply follow my feelings. Perhaps this lectureship will give me the opportunity for more intensive scholarly work. For now, I will wait to see what the gentlemen have to say.

Tuesday, December 8, 1936   Breslau

The menorah is lit while I am writing this! One isn't really supposed to do any work as long as the lights are lit, but I really don't see writing in my beloved diary as a form of work! How often I have lit this old menorah, which I took from my parents' house, and how many memories are attached to it! May this menorah yet experience being lit in celebration of our four children's happy futures!

Thursday, December 10, 1936   Breslau

Had an appointment yesterday at seven in the evening with the faculty of the Fraenckel Foundation regarding the lectureship. Dr. Kober presided. In general, the prospect was not a pleasant one; the compensation I was offered was so stingy that if I were to give up my other sources of employment I would harm my family, and if I did not give them up I would run myself into the ground. Emotionally, I have actually decided to say no; perhaps Trudi will talk to Heinemann beforehand.

Wednesday, December 16, 1936   Breslau
Yesterday afternoon we gave Hanukkah gifts to our two daughters. They were very happy and contented. And what is more beautiful than contentment in a child's eyes. – If only the girls would stay healthy for a while! Where will we light the menorah next year?

Thursday, December 17, 1936   Breslau
Rudolf was informed of Grzesik's offer, and he told him that I would reject it as long as he, Rudolf, is director at Trautner.[1] We are now getting the capital from Reichelt GmbH, and that will perhaps make possible our intended trip to Palestine in the spring. We plan to travel through Paris in order to see Wölfl! Too good to be true!

Friday, December 18, 1936   Breslau
I took part in a meeting of the archive and library committee of the Jewish Community yesterday evening. I had been asked to attend to give my opinion about a possible history of the Jews in Breslau, which may be written. I told them that if such a history were to be written in a scholarly manner, it would take years, and that the results might not match their expectations. It was decided that Frau Pinczower would get in touch with Theodor Marcus, and that the Community as such would not take the lead.

Synagogue; walked home with Rabbi Lewin. I told him about my lectureship at the seminary; he said I was right to accept it and suggested that I build up my position there!

Thursday, December 31, 1936   Landeck
Walked with Trudi through the parks and along the right bank of the Biele, away from the city. We talked about how our lives might be struc-

---

1. This was the first time that the renter, Paul Grzesik, had tendered an offer on the property and the building at Ring 49. The Cohn family business, Trautner, was in the same building.

tured in the future, and I told Trudi how much I needed her intellectual collaboration, and that it was an essential part of our marriage.

In a few hours, 1936 will come to an end, and it is only natural that we Jews should take stock as well. Of course, our account-taking goes back thousands of years, but in the process of writing down dates day in and day out, thoughts arise involuntarily, and so this year, and the years in general, are subjected to review. My memories go back 37 years, to the turn of the century, when I experienced the dawn of the new century from Robert Kaim's balcony.[2] Most of the people with whom I stood on that balcony back then are long dead. And now this year. We must be grateful that it was as it was, that we were able to feed ourselves, and that the children made some progress. Trudi and I totted everything up, the hard and the easy, the beautiful and the ugly, and if we have the strength we intend to carry on.[3]

Thursday, January 14, 1937   Breslau
Gave my lectures at the seminary about Salian historical sources; this work pleases me greatly, as does all intellectual labor that lifts me above the miseries of everyday life. After the lecture, I walked a piece with Dr. Urbach; he is a professor at the seminary, although he is only in his twenties. An eastern Jew.

Thursday, January 21, 1937   Breslau
Max Bermann celebrated his eightieth birthday.[4] I simply cannot understand how one can celebrate such a day with a spectacle like that, but *de gustibus non est disputandum*. Some Jews behave as if nothing has happened. However, I was very happy to see Bruno Schwarz and his wife again after so many years. They always behaved very properly toward me. Paul Mannheim, Agnes Wreschner. Names from decades ago bubbled up again.

2. See Willy Cohn, *Verwehte Spuren. Erinnerungen an das Breslauer Judentum vor seinem Untergang*, ed. Norbert Conrads (Cologne: Böhlau, 1995), p. 59f.

3. There is a gap in the diary covering the period from January 1 to January 13, 1937. This was when Cohn began to teach at the Jewish Theological Seminary.

4. A family celebration. Max Bermann (1857–1939) was a cousin of Cohn's. This occasion was attended by the relatives of Cohn's aunt Marie Schwarz, née Cohn (1847–1936).

Saturday, January 23, 1937   Breslau
In the evening, Gerhart and Werner, Rudolf's boys, came for dinner. The younger one in particular has a certain feel for what it means to be Jewish; perhaps he is compensating for the sins of his father against Judaism!

Wednesday, January 27, 1937   Breslau
Chamisha asar b'Shvat, 15 Shvat, New Year of the Trees. Susannchen celebrated this lovely day in kindergarten yesterday; Ruth has the day off from school. Wilhelm II's birthday. Today he will be 78 years old, and this day always brings up times long gone. Celebrating the Kaiser's birthday in office, celebrating in the field. A nice piece of history we took part in!

Saturday, January 30, 1937   Breslau
Georg Rudich was here in the afternoon asking my advice about his future. He would like to study, but it is very doubtful whether such studies and the time required for the school-leaving exam should now be undertaken using Jewish funds! I assembled a number of my Jewish essays; I think I will try once again to collect my production since 1933 into a small book.

Sunday, January 31, 1937   Breslau
Sat in my armchair by the stove; sometimes my concentration simply gives out. Wrote a few letters. Walked to the seminary to take part in the ceremony for Kommerzienrat Fränckel.[5] Bitter cold; my hands gave out in turns because I had to carry the hatbox. I certainly didn't want to be seen on the streets with this head covering! The ceremony was dignified, although of course uneven in parts. Cantor Wartenberger sang El Male Rachamim magnificently for Kommerzienrat Fränckel! Heinemann spoke very tactfully, whereas Lewkowitz's speech on the concept of humanity really didn't fit in with our times! It was wonderful how Dr. Ochs elaborated on the duties in these times of a rabbi who must again work his way from being a rabbi to becoming a *rav*. The second part of his speech was in Hebrew, which I understood quite well. With a priestly blessing, he dismissed the gentlemen to their various duties. Rabbi Rothschild from Saarbrücken also spoke very well!

5. The annual commemoration of the founder of the seminary, Kommerzienrat Jonas Fraenckel, who died on January 27, 1846.

We then went to have breakfast at Glogowski's kosher restaurant at the Schweidnitzer Stadtgraben. I walked, some of the gentlemen rode in Egon Löwenstein's car. In addition to the faculty, the breakfast included only Kober, the attorney, Dr. Friedeberg, the businessman Herr Peyser, and the professors of the seminary except for Rabbi Wahrmann, from Oels. Dr. Klee from the Prussian State League, a solid Zionist, probably one of the oldest and most vital of the Zionist fighters. Stadtrat Less, the honorary trustee of the seminary, Goldfeld, Director Glaser from the welfare office. Apart from the physical pleasures, there were many useful conversations. Klee spoke very nicely about the necessity of maintaining this particular seminary. Whether it really is a necessity is something I have not yet decided to my complete satisfaction. In a very amiable fashion, Stadtrat Less apostrophized well beyond my modest Jewish knowledge.

Tuesday, February 2, 1937 Breslau
Uncle Perls will give up his medical practice on April 1, after 50 years of service; he will also have to give up his apartment. Financially, he seems to be doing poorly; it is sad if this is what constitutes old age. He also seems to have lost his work at Reichelt's. His daughter Hildegard is still dependent on him for money; too often, improper upbringing seems to be to blame. If I could, I would gladly help him; he did so much for me over the years, but unfortunately I cannot. The travel prospects for Palestine look very favorable. May G'd grant that everything works smoothly! A reunion with my two boys would be too wonderful; Wölfl in particular seems very fearful!

Tuesday, February 9, 1937 Breslau
Walked to the seminary, gave what I hope was a good lecture about Henry IV.[6] Conversed with student teacher Schaal. Meeting of the editorial committee, which resulted in nothing particularly exciting. Dinner alone at Schwarz's; briefly in the Community reading room: lecture in the Jewish House of Teaching about Jews in the eleventh century. The discussion in the working group was occasionally very heated; brakes had to be applied.

---

6. Cohn's lecture was about Henry IV (1050–1106), Holy Roman Emperor from 1084 until 1105. He was the third emperor of the Salian dynasty—one of Cohn's scholarly interests.

Exploratory Trip to Palestine

Thursday, February 11, 1937   Breslau
The details and formalities that must be taken care of for a long trip are endless; visa, currency exchange approvals, and even if Travel Agency Cohn were to take care of all the details, it would still take endless effort to get everything together. Because woe unto him who lacks a particular stamp at a particular border. Nonetheless, there is some pleasure in being permitted to make these preparations, and I just hope that everything goes smoothly.

Friday, February 19, 1937   Breslau
Trudi bought what we need for the trip yesterday. In the afternoon, I went to be fitted by Szczupak, the tailor; then the teacher course, where I spoke about the court Jews and Glückel of Hameln. Walked home with Braun, the painter, who teaches drawing at the Am Anger School.[1] We talked about the terrible things that the New Jewish School Association instigated there. In the school there are now placards that indicate the reorganization, which is to be implemented by our colleague Schäffer.[2]

We have had major difficulties again with getting a visa for Palestine! We had been told that it would be approved without our having to furnish security; now at the last moment the policy has changed, and getting our hands on 1,600 marks is no small matter. It is very hard!

---

1. Willi Braun emigrated to Montevideo, Uruguay, at the end of July 1937. Lydia Baruchsen-Aschheim wrote an appreciation on this occasion in the *Jüdisches Gemeindeblatt*, dated August 26, 1937.

2. This "school struggle" was reported on in the *Jüdische Zeitung* (for eastern Germany), 44 (1937), no. 14, p. 1.

Thursday, February 25, 1937   Breslau
To the *megillah* at the Abraham Mugdan Synagogue. It was very full, and the bad air made it exhausting. Then to the police, where in order to get my pension I had to confirm that I am still among the living. Will that still be necessary next year? But let us not lose heart since this is what I preach to others! – Purim.

Sunday, March 7, 1937   Breslau
Yesterday morning went to visit Mother, whom I hadn't seen in a long time. Intellectually, I found her very active, thank G'd. Of course, she always complains about her symptoms, which she can't seem to get used to—and, unfortunately, I always leave somewhat disillusioned. Her whole way of thinking is so different.

   In the evening went to the main train station to send off letters. Trudi had herself photographed because she needs a picture to disembark in Erez Israel. If everything works out smoothly, we could be in Paris a week from today!

Tuesday, March 9, 1937   Breslau
In the evening, got very upset about Lewkowitz; this little man is absolutely opposed to my getting a position at the Jewish Theological Seminary. There appears to be unrest in Erez Israel again! This time, the Jews appear not to be putting up with it.

March 12, 1937   Breslau
Early in the morning, a difficult farewell from Susanne, that is, I made it difficult for myself. In the afternoon with Ruth, then Mother and Erna. Synagogue, said Kaddish for my father! Walked home with Rabbi Lewin and Alice Friedlaender. Frau Landau will come for a farewell visit; will I ever sit in this room again? I am so happy that I will see my children and our land.

Sunday, March 14, 1937   Paris, 30 Rue St. André des Arts
So, we arrived at Gare du Nord at six forty-five Western European Time after a pleasant trip, and I saw Wölfl standing at the exit, healthy and looking pleased. It is hard to describe such a feeling of joy. During the taxi ride here, he began to tell us about his life, which is taking the usual course. He has a great deal to do at the moment. But how happy

we are to be together again. Talked with Wölfl about his future. I've been lying in bed now for quite a while.

Tuesday, March 16, 1937   Paris
We were unable to spend much time with Wölfl this morning because he had to give several lessons; ate breakfast with him, standing. Walked to the Louvre with Trudi. Bought some flowers for Frau Schwarz, who invited us. Everything was very cordial there, as if we had parted only yesterday. The conversation was largely in French; Trudi was also able to make herself understood. Here, too, we got the impression that the boy is well taken care of. Very reassuring.

Wednesday, March 17, 1937   On the train to Marseille
My farewell from Wölfl was very, very difficult. I should be thankful that he is doing so well; this leave-taking tears at my heart! But I am grateful to fate that I was able to see him like this.

Thursday, March 18, 1937   On board the *Mariette Pasha*
Everything went smoothly in Marseille. Received all necessary papers at the shipping company office. We are now resting on the foredeck. Trudi has wrapped herself in a blanket, and I am going to say the prayer for setting out on a sea voyage. French soldiers of various hue all around us.

Monday, March 22, 1937
I am full of celebratory feelings on this voyage, of the sort that Walther von der Vogelweide, in his faith, expressed in his crusading song.[3] However, one does not encounter much sympathy for such emotions among the more realistically minded people of these times; nonetheless, it is the dream of a lifetime being fulfilled.

Sun and water and sky, and all the many destinies that such a boat ferries with it. Each of the *olim* is full of hope! Not all of them will make their way. Some of them do not appear well prepared. Some of them are probably going only because they lost their positions, but feel no real connection with Erez Israel!

---

3. The crusading song "Vil süeze waere minne" by lyric poet Walther von der Vogelweide (ca. 1170–ca. 1230).

Tuesday, March 23, 1937

After dinner, conversed with the old rabbi on the foredeck about last things. I envy an old, dignified *rav* like this for the certainty of his convictions. For him, the Talmud and the Torah were revealed all at once. I told him that I would find it difficult to accept as divine each of the discrete little commandments and prohibitions, whereas I affirm the divinity of the whole with all my heart. It was a strange spirit that overtook me on the foredeck at night under the stars, talking about last things.

Alexandria. Mitzrayim: It is as if, after so many years, we were still here making bricks, for which we needed no visa—and then we were gone. And then there were great synagogues and a library here, and everything is as if yesterday and today. Great expanses of time are bridged in my thoughts. An ancient people that cannot be destroyed. We will always make our way; we must have this passionate devotion.

March 26, 1937   Off of Haifa

Passport control went smoothly on board. The commission worked quickly; disembarkation, then a long wait in the customs hall until each individual piece of luggage came out. Commission agent, porter, landing, everything together cost almost a pound. Finally came out, then frisked by a policeman down to the most intimate parts of the body. Then finally outside, Ernst, who has grown into a giant, almost unrecognizable, brown the way one imagines a chalutz to be. Very calm, anchored securely in himself. First evening Pesach with a lovely service, very conservative. Community singing. What emotions assailed me; I was close to tears. Pesach in Erez Israel. Only Jews. When I look down from the balcony, I see real people walking through the streets to the synagogue with their tallis and prayer books. There is an *eruv* around Haifa, and so people can carry things! Sun is shining. We are in Erez Israel!

Went to the Ahavath Torah Synagogue! We arrived, that is, Herr Schindler and I, after the scrolls had been taken out. The room is not very large! Many stand outside, including most of the women. A panorama out onto the sea. Strange emotions for me as I said the Shabbat prayer. I stayed outside for the priestly blessing. – Hardly any of the worshipers spoke Hebrew among themselves. German dialects were very common. I look over the sea. Cows are approaching. Automobiles are parked all around. A Jewish milieu.

Sunday, March 28, 1937   Haifa

Went up Mount Carmel with the Schindlers, Trudi, and Ernst; unbelievable contrasts. Modern houses built into the desert, then again a bit of forest, and asphalt roads, and from everywhere views overlooking the sea. It is very difficult to find anyone on Carmel because none of the streets are identified. Discussed my future with Wiener; he thinks that if my pension were transferred here, I would be able to live a modest life. His viewpoint is completely different from that of Hitachdut Olei Germania.[4] He also gave me some very valuable recommendations for taking care of the details. – I now feel much less agitated. Later, as we were walking down the main street, we ran into Dr. Rabin, the former rabbi at the Breslau Seminary. We walked some and stood some and talked mainly about cultural matters. He appears to have involved himself in the most various areas here and seems to live a somewhat splintered existence.

In the afternoon went with Trudi to see Dr. Rabin, who lives in a pretty little villa at 6 Achad Ha'am St. To get there, we went through the lovely gardens of the Technion, which with its Oriental forms meshes beautifully into the landscape. Discussed cultural questions; he gave me the program of the Jewish Scientific Association that he founded here. I discussed with him the possibility of my involvement. In his opinion, it all depends on my mastery of Hebrew. Frau Rabin thinks that a German Jew would not be capable of that.

Monday, March 29, 1937

Walked with Ernst through the lovely park created by the founder of Hadar HaCarmel, which is near here.[5] The sun did me good. The park was teeming with children, who just matter-of-factly speak Hebrew. Discussed some of Ernst's problems with living here. For him, the kibbutz is everything, and that is how I would see it, too. Seeing all the children, I am reassured about the future of our people; they will create what we elders are no longer able to.

What the union organization has accomplished here is impressive; you buy a ticket at the register for five grush; whatever you eat from a

4. An organization founded in Tel Aviv in 1933 for the purpose of advising Germans wishing to emigrate to Palestine.

5. Hadar HaCarmel is the part of Haifa situated between the lower town and the upper town.

remarkable selection of dishes is punched out on your ticket.[6] The remainder is returned to you at the register. Everything is spic-and-span, and tasty. The menu is in Hebrew. Everything is very reasonably priced so that workers can afford it. Across from the workers' kitchen, the spaces of the Poale of Agudat Israel; next to the worker's kitchen, the administrative building of the Histadrut, and a WIZO home for infants.[7]

Tuesday, March 30, 1937   Haifa
Guttmann was good enough to make time for me yesterday; we spoke about the possibility of doing scholarly work, and he pointed to the inadequacy of the libraries. I told him that I would like to get a sense of life at the university, which he enabled me to do. I told him that once I was here, I would be prepared to work in an honorary capacity, to which he replied that this would be possible, just so long as I understood that this implied nothing further about any future arrangements. I don't think that I would be able to earn additional income in Jerusalem, but I would like to live there all the same.

Tuesday, March 30, 1937   Givat Brenner
I am now ensconced in a tent, and I am infinitely happy that I have arrived at the goal of my desires. The trip up here was lovely, and everything has about it the fragrance of Paradise. We found many letters from friends that were addressed to us. Most of the people we wrote to get information actually tried to write us.

Wednesday, March 31, 1937   Givat Brenner
We slept very soundly in the tent last night; there was something almost romantic about it. I haven't spent a night like this since the war. While I am writing this, I hear no sounds other than those produced on the land. In the early morning I heard people take out the milk cans. The chaverim work from five thirty to eight o'clock, and then have

---

6. A grush (girsh in Arabic), also called a piaster, was a Palestinian coin.

7. What Cohn meant was Poale Zion ("Workers of Zion"), a Jewish workers party within the Zionist movement. The Histadrut (full name: HaHistadrut HaKlalit shel HaOvdim B'Eretz Yisrael, or General Federation of Laborers in the Land of Israel), founded in 1920, was a socialist Zionist organization of Jewish workers in Palestine. It served simultaneously as a trade union (under the legal name Hevrat ha-Ovedim, or Society of Workers). It also owned various public and private assets and enterprises.

breakfast. We ate somewhat earlier; matzoh, butter, sardines. Went to inspect the pumphouse, where a well almost 90 meters deep is operated electronically [*sic*]. The Arabs are still working with draw wells. Spoke Hebrew with a number of chaverim; walked by the school, where the teacher is already a third-generation Palestinian. Had a conversation with the Hebrew teacher of the kwuzah, and got permission to participate in his class from time to time.

I am now writing by the light of two petroleum lamps, while Trudi is already asleep. Ernst is at an *assefa* of the Youth Aliyah. In our tent there are always flowers, which nature richly provides. Nighttime is peaceful; only the sound of animals outside. Jackals!

Thursday, April 1, 1937   Givat Brenner
I walked on ahead by myself and watched the plowing and harrowing, all of which is done with the most modern machinery. Breathed in the hay of our land. I am intoxicated by what Jews are creating here; walking alone through the fields. I am able to immerse myself in my thoughts, and to enjoy what is going on, constructive labor all around. The Arab village of Yibna, the ancient Yavne, where Yochanan ben Zakkai founded the first house of teaching, it is not far from where I am walking.[8] The history that has so often been presented to us springs to life here.

Discussed the problems of our future with Trudi; laid out for her all the reasons why I would want to stay here. There is something life-fulfilling about it! If I could act according to my feelings, I know what decision I would make.

Friday, April 2, 1937   Givat Brenner
Ernst conducted us through the garden and the tree nurseries yesterday afternoon. Everything is optimally arranged. He explained all of it beautifully and full of love of nature. Everything grows unbelievably quickly here. Later—it is the last day of Pesach—I attended the small synagogue, which also serves as a dining room for parents. Here one can observe the most varied kinds of Jews. Chassidim and Galicians, Lithuanians, even a physician from Allenstein, a Dr. Romm. A *chazzan* led the prayers beau-

---

8. Yochanan ben Zakkai founded the so-called vineyard at Yavne, which after the destruction of the Temple in Jerusalem by the Romans became a major center of Rabbinical Judaism.

tifully, though I missed the congregational singing that is customary in orthodox Jewish communities. I prayed with all my heart.

Trudi doesn't understand my somewhat romantic notions and sees things much more soberly. I often find her attitude hurtful, but I see no possibility of changing things! Our discussion was not a pleasant one, and unfortunately there was no resolution. I sometimes get very tired of all these things, and I regret that they play such a large role on this trip.

Saturday, April 3, 1937   Givat Brenner
Went for a walk with Ernst in the afternoon and discussed all of our problems with him. The boy is infused with such extraordinary idealism. We had a funny experience. We ran into a grandmother and her grandchild. She has been in the country for two years and still can't speak a word of Hebrew; her grandchild speaks only Hebrew, so Ernst had to interpret for them.

The cemetery, where many Jews now rest in peace in the soil of Erez Israel, is situated at the outskirts of Givat Brenner. The place is marked by simple cairns bearing nameplates. No ornamentation, as our most ancient traditions would have it. A moving and deeply touching sight.

Sunday, April 4, 1937   Tel Aviv
Allenby Street, Café Atara. Rode here on the Drom Yehuda bus line.[9] The route went via Ness Ziona and Rishon le-Zion.[10] The bus accelerated whenever we passed through Arab villages. A lovely trip. We went by the Jewish Museum, looked at the main synagogue from the outside, across from the large Barclays Bank building. The impressions are powerful in that this is a purely Hebrew city, but in some ways also a certain mixture of the most modern and the East. On the beach, real beach life, full of Jews and English soldiers, all together.

Monday, April 5, 1937   Givat Brenner
I have much to catch up on because of the bus trip yesterday. The buses all have gratings on the windows, which is the best protection against

9. Drom Yehuda was a bus company that mostly ran routes in the south of the country. It merged with Egged in 1951.

10. Founded in 1882 by Russian Jewish immigrants, Rishon le-Zion (literally First to Zion) was actually the second Jewish farm colony in Palestine after Petah Tikva.

stones. Whenever stones are thrown, you have to pull the window down to protect against shattered glass. In the Arab villages, people sit on the ground hawking their wares. We observed the sale of a bed, around which a large crowd had gathered. Camel drivers sit on the ground right in the dirt of the street.

Trudi came back at about five o'clock from Ben Shemen, where she spent time with Hannelore Alexander. Had a discussion with her, and it is clear that she does not want to move to Givat Brenner. That puts an end to one of the dreams of my life. I can no longer indulge in battles! I had already grown accustomed to the thought, even though I sensed clear resistance. Nonetheless, I must try to maintain my equilibrium.

Tuesday, April 6, 1937   Tel Aviv
This morning at seven-thirty I took the bus down to Tel Aviv to settle some matters about the boat ticket. And I went to the Jewish Museum, which is very beautifully set up as an art museum.[11] Very cordially received by Dr. Schwarz, the director, whom I knew from a meeting of the Jewish Museum Association. Sought counsel from him, and he told me that I would be able to live here on 15 pounds. It was a very stimulating hour in an intellectual setting.

Wednesday, April 7, 1937   Givat Brenner
To the extent I am able, I would like to describe how a day is spent on the kibbutz. Somewhere between 700 and 800 people live here, among them 120 children. The *mazkirut* leads; especially important things are brought before the *assefa ha-clalit*. The *siddur avoda*, a committee responsible for the organization of work, plays a very important role in the internal life of the kibbutz. Each department has a chaver in a leadership position, with experienced workers who assist as needed. The level of Hebraization differs widely.

Work begins in the kitchen at four in the morning, and they work for nine hours. General wake-up is at five thirty, and work begins at six o'clock. A gong is sounded at eight for breakfast. Those working in the

11. Cohn visited the house of the former mayor of Tel Aviv, Meir Dizengoff, located on Rothschild Boulevard. It was turned into an art museum in 1931, and Karl Schwarz was its director in 1937. The State of Israel was proclaimed from this building, in 1948.

pardessim, in the fields and gardens, are brought breakfast and eat out-doors at tables and benches set up in *srifim*. They continue to work until eleven thirty. The entire chevrah gathers in the *chadar ochel* after the gong is rung, with the exception of those who are working externally such as in the port, in Tel Aviv. Naturally, whatever they earn also goes to the kibbutz. Then there is an afternoon break until twelve thirty, after which they work until four, when they have a snack. Dinner is at seven.

The children live in various children's homes; they are often seen in the late afternoon taking walks with their parents. I find the children to be in an excellent state. Many of the women are pregnant. They have a real family life. Books are lent out in the evening, and many chaverim make use of the library's rich holdings. Whatever foodstuffs the kibbutz needs to buy are available from Tnuva, the large sales branch of the kib-butz movement. The flowers come from a special cooperative.

The bread, which is produced by a cooperative bakery, is especially good. Givat Brenner has its own post office, which is managed by a chaver. His earnings also go to the kibbutz. The mail is brought to Rehovot at ten o'clock each morning; the arriving mail is distributed in the afternoon. Many of the chaverim now write only reluctantly because they feel unable to describe effectively how they actually live. One particular problem experienced by the kibbutz is how to integrate traumatized parents. They came here because their lives outside were no longer tenable, and they find fault with everything. They also eat separately and observe a strictly ritual kitchen. Most of them help with the work. And so you see old people with skullcaps and beards whose entire lives were once lived under very different circumstances.

Friday, April 9, 1937   Givat Brenner

Yesterday evening, the entire chevrah sang along with Kronenberg. This white-haired old gentleman used to live in Berlin, where he led such song societies. He uses the same method as Karl Adler, in Stuttgart, and it was a joy to see what he was able to coax out of the chaverim and chaverot.[12] The entire *chadar ochel* was full, and in the end everyone was singing along. They sang mostly uncomplicated Hebrew songs,

12. The music teacher Karl Adler (1890–1973) was director of the Stuttgart Con-servatory and founder and director of the Jewish arts community.

among others, "Who Sows with Tears Harvests with Joy." People's eyes beamed with pleasure, and you could see them begin to relax. It was very instructive observing people's faces.

Trudi told me yesterday that she doesn't feel very comfortable among these people, and has been unable to find any sort of inner connection with them. I regret this, of course, but it doesn't change anything. Trudi and I walked to the garden in the afternoon; on the way, she told me that she does not wish to live the rest of her life here in misery. I can no longer fight these battles, and so this dream is destined to go nowhere. My farewell will be very difficult!

Sunday, April 11, 1937   Jerusalem
At seven-thirty we took the bus along the now-familiar road to Tel Aviv, then switched to the Egged route and the indescribably beautiful trip to Jerusalem. Upon entering the city, the first thing I saw was the large German consulate general building near the hospital, which had hoisted the swastika flag on Sunday.

Jerusalem seems rather cold and raw after one has grown accustomed to the warmth. As I approached the city, I said the Shehecheyanu in gratitude. We are well lodged in B'nai B'rith's Bet Olim, on Abyssinian Street. Everything spic-and-span. I share a room with Trudi; Ernst sleeps in another room.

Monday, April 12, 1937   Jerusalem
I spent the morning partly writing, partly walking back and forth in front of the house, to the extent the sun permitted. It is very interesting studying the various types of people who pass by, especially the Abyssinians, with their pretty, black children. One can see the ancientness of their culture! I met a servant boy of Yemeni origin who attended the Bukharian school here.[13] I asked him, "Atah zaddik?" Whereupon he intelligently replied, "Hashem yodea."[14] He also knew which day of Sephira it was. What beautiful, black, and intelligent eyes the boy had!

13. Bukhara, one of the quarters of the city of Jerusalem, was named after an ancient city in Uzbekistan, the long-established home of approximately thirty thousand Jews who spoke a Jewish-Persian dialect.

14. Cohn asked, "Are you a Righteous One?" to which the boy replied, "G'd knows it."

How diverse our people are! Everything infinitely run-down. Jewish craftsmen mostly do their work outside! Butcheries! I am pleased to say that I can at least read most of the signs! Over time one gets used to the language! In the old Yishuv one sees more than a few dignified figures with their white beards. The boys with their *peyess* seem alien.

The inscriptions on the German Protestant Hospital are in German and Arabic; we also saw the large Jewish Bikur Cholim Hospital. Many charitable institutions sponsored by the Ashkenazi and Sephardic communities, also the court building of the Ashkenazi communities. Then walked a piece on Jaffa Road; an old Jew addressed me as "Herr Doktor" and wanted to sell me something. Much begging on the streets. Chaotic traffic rules: *shotrim* with white gloves stand on raised wooden platforms. It still amazes me that I am now in Jerusalem! Naturally, we carry a Jerusalem in our hearts, but not the modern parts of the city. But of course it cannot be strictly the old anymore after two thousand years, and we cannot begrudge the fact that like every other era, our own builds according to its particular architectural style.

Tuesday, April 13, 1937   Jerusalem
Accompanied Ernst to the German consulate general regarding his declaration of majority. First we waited in a small ground-level room and filled out a form stating what we were there for. After a short wait, which I spent reading the *Literarisches Centralblatt*, we were brought before an official, who gave us information in a very amiable manner. He then talked with Ernst and recorded his personal information. The result is that when Ernst turns 18, I will apply for his declaration of majority to the municipal court in Breslau.[15] They must consent, and then application will again be made to the consulate general.

Afternoon. Rode up to Mount Scopus, an indescribable trip. A fairly steep road passing by the English military cemetery, very moving. From Scopus, a view overlooking Jerusalem, just as I had so yearned to see it. Even though I didn't know all of the individual buildings, an image was nonetheless impressed in my soul, the Dome of the Rock on the Temple Mount, the ancient grandeur of our people!

15. Ernst was born on August 6, 1919, so he would have turned 18 in four months. With his parents' consent, he would be able to attain majority at 18; otherwise he would have had to wait until the age of 21.

To the amphitheater, from there a panoramic view overlooking the Judean desert, the Jordan, the Dead Sea, and the Transjordan Mountains. One could almost reach out and touch them, they seemed so close. And yet so far. That was when I understood what it meant to cast someone like Azazel out into the desert.[16] A tour through the library, which suffers greatly from a lack of space; found some of my own works in the card catalog. I had myself announced to the director, Weyl. After a short wait, he came out and I asked him the questions that I always ask. He thinks that I would have a difficult time running a household on the amount of pension that I would receive. I asked him whether I might be able to earn anything through the library if I first worked on an honorary basis. His response to that question was in the negative as well. He also told me that he has little influence over the filling of positions. I left after a very interesting and stimulating half hour that at least gave me a clear picture.

Then went to see Professor Julius Guttmann, who lives on Alfasi Street, where I was greeted by him and his wife, my old schoolmate Grete Henschel. He also gave me advice. He, too, sees few material prospects for me in Jerusalem, but he well understands the reasons why I would want to make aliyah. Then his wife showed us a glorious view of the surroundings and took us as far as the border between the Jewish and the Arab areas. We saw Bayit Vegan, a Jewish colony, and a Christian-Arab monastery whose old trees extend to the Jewish area.

A very full day, perhaps one of the most exciting of my entire life, and what I have been able to write down here after the exhaustion of the day is only a small attempt. One simply can't process everything that quickly. *But today I can say that I have found something of the Jerusalem of my heart.*[17]

Wednesday, April 14, 1937   Jerusalem

If Trudi, Ernst, and I have seen much here, we owe it to our outstanding guide, Dr. Golinski, without whom we would never even have dared to go into the Old City. First, he took us to see the Russian quarter, which is outside the Old City.

Then, we again found ourselves on the Jaffa Road, which we walked along past the new construction being done on the main post office

---

16. The scapegoat mentioned in Leviticus 16.
17. This sentence is underlined in the original.

(characteristically, only Arabs are employed to do that work), and then to the Jaffa Gate. From there, a final glance over Jerusalem's surroundings, and then plunged into the hubbub of the Arab souk, a foreign world, shop upon shop, coins, textiles, foods. It is important not to get lost in the side alleys because as a Jew today you risk disappearing without a trace. The main street is secured by the police. The English police are armed, the Jewish and Arab are not. It is a complete chaos that seems harmless enough on the surface, but any minor act of carelessness can trigger an incident. One had best pass through as if indifferent, as if uninvolved. Spanish riders (barbed wire barriers) are thrown up where the various quarters abut. They can be used in an instant to cut off access. I was overcome with a sense of home when I entered the Jewish quarter. Here we heard Hebrew again instead of Arabic sounds. We visited a number of synagogues.

The synagogues of Yerushalayim filled me with a wonderful spirit. Not all of them are beautiful in an artistic sense, but they are sites of Jewish prayer, sites of our faith. First we visited the Hurva Rabbi Judah Hechassid, known as the Hurva Synagogue, then the synagogue of the Cabbalists, the Eliyahu Hanavi Synagogue. The *shammes* told us that Eliyahu Hanavi always appears in one of the synagogues whenever there aren't enough to form a minyan for prayer. The Yochanan ben Zakkai Synagogue, the middle Sephardic Synagogue, the Stamboul Synagogue, and finally the Hasidic Synagogue, Tiferet Yerushalayim, which is generally known as the Nissan Bak Synagogue after its builder. From its roof (an agonizing climb for me; I lost my breath) there opened out a deeply heart-stirring panorama over Yerushalayim, the Holy City, especially of the Temple Plaza and the Wailing Wall. It is true that very little remains of the earthly magnificence of our holy sites, but the world of the Jewish spirit is infinitely great. It is Mount Moriah, where Abraham intended to sacrifice his son to G'd. It is the site on which the three temples stood.[18] Below us, the narrow houses where people live in mutual enmity, and yet so close together on the same soil.

---

18. In Jewish times, there were only two temples, King Solomon's and then King Herod's temple. After destruction of the latter in the year 70, the Romans erected a temple to Jupiter on the same site. Apparently, Cohn included this temple as well.

Yerushalayim, Holy City, when will you again arise in your ancient magnificence? And then we went to the Wailing Wall through narrow angular alleys heavily policed, again on Arab soil passing by police posts, and what a momentous occasion, standing before these ashlars, by which so infinitely many tears have been shed. True, the externals with all the beggars are not a pretty sight, but the stones bespeak our history. We said Tehillim. The psalm "By the rivers of Babylon."

Thursday, April 15, 1937   Jerusalem
Took a short walk along the Jaffa Road with Ernst yesterday evening. I was hoping that he would tell me a little about himself, but it was hard for him to express himself. The work makes one taciturn.

Friday, April 16, 1937   Jerusalem
In Beit Hakerem looked at the enormous grounds of the Jewish teachers college. A completely modern institution; one ascends a large flight of outdoor steps and finds oneself in a quadrangle, around which are the classrooms so that no further staircase is necessary. A wonderful classroom, a room with newspapers where students may congregate, a library available to the students, where hard work is in evidence. The institution consists of three parts, an elementary school, a gymnasium, and a teachers college. All in all it was gratifying to see so many young people growing in unencumbered freedom. The institution has been in existence only a few years.

Then spent some time at the home of Joseph Marcus, an old acquaintance, the former Oberregierungsrat in Breslau. Unfortunately he was not there. His wife, Käte Ephraim-Marcus, received us.[19] She had been a well-known painter for many years, after all, and is beginning to have some success here as well.

Visited Ernst Simon, in Rechavya. Trudi didn't want to come along, so Ernst and I went alone. Simon received us most cordially; we spoke about scholarly matters. He has a magnificent library; we talked about pedagogy and educating the next generation, for whom the Hebrew language is a given. We found that we are in complete agreement. If

19. Käte Ephraim-Marcus (1892–1970) was a portrait and landscape painter born in Breslau. In Berlin she studied under Max Beckmann and Lovis Corinth; she emigrated to Palestine in 1934.

education is not conducted on this basis, only complete Levantization can be the result. These are the sorts of conversations that need to be had more often at home.

Sunday, April 18, 1937   Jerusalem
Yesterday afternoon went to the Lebanon Restaurant and drank tea. Shabbat figures: people in fur-lined caftans. *Shtreimel!*[20] Later walked as far as Beit Hakerem in the lovely cool air. In general, one walks through Jewish territory; through Arab only when leaving Jerusalem. There the roads part.

Tuesday, April 20, 1937   Givat Brenner
Wrote a great deal in the early morning. There are so many sights that one would like to remember, for example, a girl standing on a wagon, driving the team of horses in all her youthful beauty. There is no more vivid an image of the renewal of our people. Wednesday is the day for German mail, and then one sees chaverim carrying thick letters. They continue to have many relationships in their countries of origin, but they are full of worries about their parents and family members, and about their futures.

Wednesday, April 21, 1937   Givat Brenner
Yesterday evening, Ernst and I took another walk out into the country-side and discussed what the future holds for him. It was a clear, starry night, the kind of night when people find peace and clear their minds. When I see the young people working early in the morning, I am over-come with a feeling of happiness that our people will renew itself. I feel almost sorry for the Jews who do not wish to understand that such renewal is possible only in this way.

Thursday, April 22, 1937   Haifa
The last night in the *srif*. Ernst is a person who does not readily show his feelings; when, standing by the bus, he said "Come again soon," that was a great deal for him! I saw how emotional he was, and then he left quickly. May G'd grant that I will see him again soon, and in good

---

20. The fur hat, often of sable, generally worn on Shabbat and on holidays by eastern ultra-orthodox Jews.

health. – He did everything he could during these weeks to make our lives easier in every way. It is not easy to bid farewell to a child!

Saturday, April 24, 1937   Haifa

Went to synagogue with Trudi. All traffic ceases shortly before Shabbat; only a few vehicles on the road! We happened to attend an eastern synagogue. Trudi was the only woman. Polish Jews prayed in Ashkenazi accents. Very dignified figures. I got the feeling that in these synagogues people are really praying, even though the hustle and bustle is distressing to our senses.

How diverse is our people. Children who grow up with Hebrew as a given; workers, who dominate the streetscape; and the old people, who in general try to live on just as they had at home. The older German Jews are undoubtedly no welcome addition; they live completely in the past and mourn their dashed hopes.

No real relationships have formed between the eastern and western Jews; they exist in completely separate worlds. One can only hope that the next generation will effect a reconciliation. After all, this is the only way we can become one people! The German Jews here quickly lose the veneer of European civilization, but without accepting Jewish values! And their social cohesion leaves something to be desired. They have learned nothing and forgotten nothing. For the eastern Jews it is, of course, difficult to adapt to a certain civilized state, but in turn they stick together and are extraordinarily modest, having very few needs or wants. I have a certain love for the eastern Jews because they are closer to Judaism. If they reject German Jewry here, it is in part because German Jews never treated them with particular humanity.

Sunday, April 25, 1937   Haifa

We sat for a time in Jakob Morenu's small inn by the hot springs in Tiberias. Arabs frequent the place as well. It seems to me that the relationship between Jews and Arabs is relatively good there. I looked at the bathing facilities. There are rough wooden tubs, one of them occupied by two Jewish men, one of whom is cheerfully singing. We then went into the Ora Restaurant, which is owned by a Jew from Germany. He recognized me by my similarity to Wölfl, whom he, in turn, knew from his days at the Sorbonne. Theo Harburger, whom I had met some years ago at a meeting of Jewish museum associations, in Breslau, joined us in the restaurant. He used to be curator of the art collection of the Jewish community in Munich, and he now owns the Pension Kinereth, in Tiberias, though at the moment, English soldiers are garrisoned there.[21] He leads a completely carefree existence because after half a year of waiting he is being well paid. He has gotten used to the climate on the Sea of Galilee. He took us to see Rambam's grave.[22] "From Moses to Moses, there was none like Moses." I recited a psalm and sat with Trudi for a time. This moment moved me deeply. A few steps away, the grave of Yochanan ben Zakkai. Spoke Hebrew with the Sephardic grave attendants.

Wednesday, April 28, 1937 Haifa
My last day in Erez Israel is approaching! It is a melancholy feeling for a person who would gladly stay here. But that is of no help. May G'd grant me another visit. I am grateful for the weeks that I was able to stay here. In spite of the immense difficulties that had to be overcome, they have been among the most eventful of my entire life. May G'd grant that I may soon return and participate in the reconstruction.

Onboard the *Champollion*. The passport formalities went very quickly, but then we had to wait a long time until, with all manner of pomp and circumstance, the emir of Transjordan had boarded. The national anthem, naturally, and then they ascended the stairs. The French ship officers wanted to force us third-class passengers to use the rear stairs; it was only through the energetic intervention of an English officer of the Palestine police force that we were able to get on board and to our cabins quickly. – This time we're traveling separately because we couldn't get a two-bed cabin. The ship is similar to the *Mariette Pasha*. There is a smoking room where I can work comfortably.

Thursday, April 29, 1937 On board the *Champollion*
My heart was heavy yesterday evening as the steamer slowly pulled out of the port of Haifa. I am leaving a country with which I feel deeply,

21. Kinereth is the Hebrew name for the Sea of Galilee.
22. Rambam, acronym of Rabbi Moshe ben Maimon, or Maimonides (1135–1204). The great philosopher and physician of the Golden Age of Jewish culture in Spain died in Cairo. According to legend, he was reinterred in Tiberias.

deeply connected! – It was a magical sight, all the lights as far up as the summit of Hadar, then the lighthouse of Bat Galim, and finally Bat Galim itself.

Sunday, May 2, 1937
We have been sailing along the coast of Calabria. The way Aetna projects through the clouds is fantastic. Now we can see the coast of Sicily, and we can make out individual towns. This reunion with my beloved Sicily, even if only from the sea, moved me greatly.[23]

Monday, May 3, 1937
I am feeling very alone. In many respects I have grown apart from Trudi; naturally, I cannot hold it against her that I have become in many respects another person with whom it is surely difficult to get along. Like the ship, life is slowly rocking toward its goal. We are borne forward. The wave holds, the wave bears us onward, and then we sink! My dialogue with this book gives me strength and peace.[24]

Wednesday, May 5, 1937   Paris, 30 Rue St. André des Arts.
We arrived at the Gare de Lyon yesterday just before eleven, and Wölfl was waiting for us at the station. I thanked G'd that this, too, had worked out so well! With the Gottgetreus by car to the hotel, where we stayed in the same room, and where Wölfl had prepared things beautifully! Told him a few things about Palestine and about Ernst, and then fell into bed, exhausted.

Friday, May 7, 1937   Paris
Today is Wölfl's birthday; it is the first time in five years that we have spent this day together, and this makes me very happy. My only worry is that he finds so little satisfaction in himself. I had a long conversation with him yesterday in which I tried to make clear to him how wrong that is, and how he has every reason to be content with himself.

23. Cohn had gotten to know Sicily on a scholarly visit in the spring of 1927. See Willy Cohn, *Verwehte Spuren. Erinnerungen an das Breslauer Judentum vor seinem Untergang*, ed. Norbert Conrads (Cologne: Böhlau, 1995), pp. 438–461. Six weeks later, Cohn was already planning a book about Sicily.
24. Cohn refers to his thick diaries as "books" throughout.

Monday, May 10, 1937   Breslau

I arrived safely in Breslau yesterday, thank G'd, and rode home quickly by car. There I found everything in good condition. All my worries were for naught, but better this way. Ruth looks very good and has gotten nice and plump.

Friday, May 14, 1937   Breslau

Have begun to work through my travel diary; it allows me to relive the entire experience. Went to Koebner's bookstore, where I had a long conversation with Herr Riesenfeld. He told me that my publisher, Marcus, has sold his publishing house and is moving part of it to Prague.[25] Münz is taking over publication of Judaica; Martin, the printer from Trebnitz, will take over the general education series. With that, all of my scholarly works will now be in the hands of others. And so, one business after another is being liquidated!

Whit Monday, May 17, 1937   Breslau

I have now been in Breslau again for a week, though it seems like an eternity if only because I have heard so much since my arrival. Yesterday afternoon, continued to work through my Palestine book, which pleases me greatly and allows me to enjoy my memories all over again.

Felix Perle invited us for after dinner. It has been a long time since we have visited the Perles; he has since been very ill and still looks terrible. He also spent a few days in jail at police headquarters in connection with the lodge affair, without, however, being deposed. Then he discussed with me my work at the seminary. I have the impression that it won't be of long duration; they seem not to be pleased with my remarks, and I am the least likely, at my age, to prove flexible. Basically, I have little desire to deal with all the *machlokes*, and if I could I would gladly shake the dust of Breslau from my feet!

In the morning went to synagogue. Rabbi Lewin spoke beautifully; I always like to hear him. I am in complete agreement with what he says. He spoke today about all those who in the past epoch turned away from Judaism and its knowledge and now stand before the ruins.

25. Max and Hermann Marcus founded the Verlagsbuchhandlung M. & H. Marcus in Breslau in 1862. Cohn's historical works were published by this house. It also had a Judaica section.

Sunday, May 23, 1937   Breslau

Today I visited the cemetery in the Lohestrasse, where I hadn't been for quite a while. Once a person has stood in a Jewish cemetery in Erez Israel, the difference is enormous. There stones, and here flowers; both grow out of the landscape. It has been a long time since I've been out here, and in that time more than a few of our circle have been called home to their Father. I sat for a good long time by our graves and prayed; then I made the grand tour, also stopping at Lassalle's grave! So many historical epochs of our Jewish existence rise up walking through this cemetery. I also stood at the graves of other departed intellectual giants of Breslau: Graetz, Brann, Guttmann, Rosenthal, Ferdinand Cohn. Left with Rabbi Brilling; visited Mother.

Tuesday, May 25, 1937   Breslau

I had to do a few things at the seminary at four o'clock; I began my lecture about literary history yesterday. It was very well attended, and I then lectured for an hour about the final days of Lothar III of Supplinburg. After that, there was a meeting of the Provincial League, which dealt with resumption of the teacher course. Obermagistratsrat Guttmann chaired the meeting; Rabbi Hoffmann talked a lot of nonsense. My suggestion was accepted, namely that we send a plan for the intended courses to the schools, and then wait to see how many respond.

Thursday, May 27, 1937   Breslau

Yesterday afternoon had a discussion with the faculty of the Jewish Theological Seminary about the organization of my lectures. Heinemann, Lewkowitz, Wahrmann, and Urbach were present. Everything went without a hitch; I elaborated on the program that I had established for my lectures in history and literature, which were met with general approval. So-called German-Jewish circles had complained about purported ironic remarks that I made, and stayed away from my lectures.

Sunday, June 6, 1937   Breslau

I read the Torah portion about the spies yesterday; here, too, a repetition of our history. The Jews even complained about Erez Israel, just like today. It is certainly true that we haven't made things easy for our Jewish leaders, but often enough we have also been punished severely for it.[26] Polished my writing. The results often depress me; I wish that Jews had not merely always been moneylenders and the like, but then when we look around now and see them making the same mistakes over and over again in their wanderings, it looks very bad. I read an item in the *Rundschau* about the enormous number of eastern Jews who have gathered in Paris without spreading themselves over the country as a whole.

Thursday, June 10, 1937   Breslau
Very unpleasant conversation with Trudi. She does not understand why spiritual common ground between us is so important to me. The discussion began around preserving and pickling. I believe that this conversation will have to be the last of this sort; I'm simply not making any headway, and it is just too exhausting! Problems with the nanny Else Eisenberg, who just dropped her work and left. She had become quite insolent, and now running the household will be even more complicated!

Saturday, June 12, 1937   Breslau
I wrote most of my letters by hand; Trudi typed two of them for me. She has a great deal to do now because she has to do it all! We don't talk to each other much.

Went to synagogue in the evening. All the things that happen these days. Here we have the son of Rabbi Lewin, who has emigrated and convinced his old father to give him the majority of his books, probably so that he can sell them off on the market! It has been very difficult for the old man to bid farewell to a library built up over a long lifetime. Fear that the books might be confiscated some time, completely incomprehensible.

Tuesday, June 15, 1937   Breslau
Meeting of the *Gemeindeblatt* committee at the Jewish Community. Now that the *Breslauer Zeitung* and the *Jüdische Zeitung* have gone

---

26. Cohn is referring to Numbers 13:1–14:9. In this story, after the Israelites receive the covenant from God, they begin their journey to the Promised Land. However, they complain of hardships all along the way and send spies into Canaan to ascertain whether it is worth continuing. They find it a "land of milk and honey," but the spies also believe that the people who already live there are more powerful than they, and so the Israelites rebel and refuse to go on. For this disobedience, God forces them to wander in the wilderness for forty years.

under, they are going to seek approval for a weekly edition of the *Gemeindeblatt*.[27] This is an urgent necessity because of all the personal announcements. This afternoon I have to go to Militsch, where I will speak about Palestine. Lecture paid for by the Provincial League of Jewish Communities!

Saturday, June 19, 1937   Breslau
I now buy the *Schlesische Sonntagspost* every Saturday because of a series of articles about the history of the Jews in Silesia, which makes use of my work. Of course, it is all very anti-Semitic, and I wish that I could refute the things they say. But I no longer think that is possible. In researching Jewish history, I am frequently struck by how unscrupulous we so often were in making money, and how little we have hewn to the tenets of our religion. In Jewish research it has frequently been overlooked that the precepts of the Torah and the Talmud were often less important than how things worked out in practical terms. In good times, it would have been difficult to preach moderation to the Jews.

Monday, June 21, 1937   Breslau
Went for a walk in the rain with Trudi yesterday. It was lovely, and we reconciled a little with each other. Trudi and I had a bit to eat by ourselves, and then we discussed various matters. Trudi read my two Palestinian sketches, the ones I wrote recently. She liked them!

Tuesday, June 22, 1937   Breslau
Much music and noise on the street at eleven in the evening as the Hitler Youth returned from their midsummer night bonfire. Yesterday, the newspapers carried stories about the fall of the Blum government. Even though it might be a good thing that a Jew is no longer leading the French state, we do not know to what extent this retreat might represent a station on the way to fascism. Naturally, I'm also thinking about it personally, and about Wölfl's future.

27. The *Jüdische Zeitung* ceased publication at the end of April 1937; the *Breslauer Zeitung* at the end of May 1937. The *Breslauer Jüdisches Gemeindeblatt* was published from 1924 to November 1938. See Bernhard Brilling, *Die jüdischen Gemeinden Mittelschlesiens* (Stuttgart: Kohlhammer, 1972), p. 43.

Saturday, July 3, 1937   Breslau
Received a very nice letter from Ernst yesterday; he was in Tel Aviv and is making inquiries for us. Who knows whether it will ever come to pass, or whether my health would even be up to it.

In the afternoon, I gave a lecture at the Jewish Theological Seminary, where I began to explicate Laocoön. Synagogue; in the evening walked a bit with Trudi to the Sauerbrunn, before that met Feilchenfeld and accompanied him home. He recently had his third child! I plan to travel to Glogau in the morning, where I received a very nice invitation to talk about my trip to Palestine.

Monday, July 5, 1937   Breslau
Had a conversation with Frau Witt, the teacher at the Jewish elementary school. I told her about Palestine. She was fairly astonished that I haven't talked about my trip here, but apparently there is opposition, probably from Frau Preuss and Herr Lux.

This morning worked a bit on my book; I am currently working on one section, about Jewish records relating to the Silesian Piasts.[28] Rode to Köbner's, where I acquired a volume of Herder, a classic that I don't yet have. I paid for it with two *Grüne Heinrichs* by Gottfried Keller. It's always like that: the books you are trying to sell are never in demand; the books you need are on everyone else's list too!

Sunday, July 11, 1937   Breslau
Took a long walk with Trudi. Immediately behind the train station toward Kundschütz, an entire barrack city has sprung up for the new air force installation. One can see sheds and large buildings. If only mankind spent only a fraction on building up of what it spends on destroying. But as long as human beings exist, the byword will remain: *Si vis pacem, para bellum.*[29]

Friday, July 16, 1937   Breslau
Good news and bad. Wölfl got a nice private tutoring position near Bordeaux, on the sea. This makes me very happy. Wrote an unpleasant letter to the Proskauers. There was still unfinished business to take

28. A branch of the Polish Piast dynasty had ruled parts of Silesia since the Middle Ages. The last Silesian Piast died in 1675.

29. Latin: "If you want peace, prepare for war."

care of. Met Trudi; in the evening, a lecture at the Jewish Craftsmen's Association at rooms provided at Glogowski's. I talked about my trip to Palestine, paying special attention to things that might interest craftsmen. It was well attended, and the evening was a success; walked home with Feilchenfeld and Sklarz.

Ruth returned home from her trip to Mittelsteine at four o'clock, in a good mood and sunburnt. Thank G'd everything went smoothly, and the trip was just right for her recovery. She started to tell us about it, how they fed everyone. In general things must have been quite harmonious; even their relations with the inhabitants of that Catholic region were good. Growing up in a youth league is so important, and I almost feel sorry for children who are not exposed to this on their path through life!

Sunday, July 18, 1937   Breslau

Actually already the tenth, but because the date of the destruction of the Temple occurred on Shabbat this year, it had to be "slid" over a day. The Eichahs are so beautiful and moving! Walked home with Rabbi Lewin. Discussed the case of Kommerzienrat Schwerin, who has now gotten out.[30] Each in turn is repaid by fate for his sins against others, and particularly against Judaism. Back when I was still serving at the Elisabethgymnasium, his second son was taking Protestant religious instruction, but what a fuss he put up about my honorarium when I taught his half-blind eldest son, who, it should be said, turned out to be a fine person. What is so unfortunate about such cases is that all Jews are held up for blame, and others, who are completely innocent, are made to pay!

Wednesday, July 21, 1937   Breslau

On the train to Kudowa. In the evening went for a walk with Trudi. It was cool and pleasant. Unfortunately, when we got home we had another discussion, the aftereffects of which were that I couldn't get to sleep until midnight. But in other respects I should be glad and grateful to have such a good companion in life as Trudi.

---

30. Kommerzienrat Ernst Schwerin (1869–1946) fled after his considerable fortune had gradually been "Aryanized." In 1938, the Nazi government revoked his and his family's German citizenship.

How is it that I am so alone in my thinking! I see so much more than most others how something new is arising from all of the crises of these times, something healthier. Certainly, this may sometimes hurt us Jews, but we have to maintain our objectivity; perhaps I should more often keep to myself what is in the fullness of my heart.

Friday, July 23, 1937
Yesterday during the night they came and plastered the entire neighborhood with posters saying, "Jews out!"; well, that touches me but little. Met a former student of mine, Kosterlitz, at the fountain. He took a photograph of me.

Now we have to be worried about the fate of the Palestine Germans; at least nothing will happen to them under Jewish leadership. What the *Schlesische Tageszeitung* says is undoubtedly false, namely that only Palestine Germans are planting Palestinian oranges. I am especially interested in the Palestine debate in the English lower house. The partition plan is to be presented before the League of Nations, and with that it will be done!

Friday, July 30, 1937   Kudowa
A major war has broken out in the Far East; in Breslau, a major song festival![31] What contradictions, and how little the individual knows about the sufferings of others!

Sunday, August 1, 1937   Kudowa
Trudi arrived unexpectedly just as I was sitting down to dinner; I was so happy to see her.

Monday, August 2, 1937   Kudowa
Went to the park, and Trudi admired the uniquely beautiful grounds. We had a nice, quiet conversation; everything is easier when your heart beats at least somewhat serenely. Lotte examined Trudi. The gallbladder thing that she suffered from in Breslau has not been resolved yet; she didn't look good to me and her face seems to have shrunk so. Much depends on the state of her health now; may G'd grant that she will soon be up to it again. We walked a little further past the Glatzer Rose,

31. Cohn was probably referring to the Second Sino-Japanese War, which began on July 7, 1937, and ended only with the end of the war in the Pacific.

a bit toward Gross Georgsdorf, and talked about our future. We talked about all the difficulties that aliyah entails, especially if you are not taking along good health, a pile of money, or an appropriate profession. I brought Trudi to the bus. When one is so close to a person, one feels terrible about each unkind word that one has ever uttered, and nonetheless it happens time and again. Trudi is such a selfless woman; perhaps I really don't deserve her.

Monday, August 3, 1937   Kudowa
I wrote Trudi a very loving letter; I felt guilty the entire day that I hadn't been nice enough. I increasingly suffer from the realization that I so frequently differ in my opinions from those of other Jews. They just don't seem to understand that it is out of my deepest love for the Jewish people that I must see matters this way. It is not always a pleasure to swim against the tide!

Thursday, August 5, 1937   Kudowa
Watched the harvest for a while; it is always wonderful when the farmers bring in the grain. I still see the wagons full of hay in Givat Brenner. Up here, the harvest has not yet concluded; in the low lands it is probably long finished. How much work goes into such a field.

Saturday, August 7, 1937   Kudowa
It is remarkable that even the press at large is running stories about the Zionist Congress, which is of particular importance these days because of the question, "Jewish state, yes or no?" The *Völkischer Beobachter* ran a lengthy, very factual essay about Zionism. I am in complete agreement with what they said about the emancipation of the Jews. I often feel lonely, very lonely; I so much wish that my relationship with Trudi were even closer, but about many things I feel resigned. That may also have to do with the circumstances in which we are living.

Tuesday, August 10, 1937   Kudowa
Monstrous, how the entire world arms itself; the arms magnates must be making a fortune, and one of these days the masses will be forced to pay in blood. My heart is somewhat quieter. Trudi wrote me a very nice letter; she tries so hard to be encouraging. Walked past a little farmhouse, and it struck me how lovely it would be to sit in peace

before one's hut. But life is now a struggle, and this struggle must be waged to the end.

Friday, August 20, 1937   Breslau
I arrived safely back in Breslau yesterday and took a taxi home. Thank G'd, Trudi didn't have a throat inflammation, but she does tend to spike a fever at night. Ruth was still lying on the sofa as well. Susannchen is doing well. Things are looking a bit better today! Had all sorts of discussions with Trudi that led nowhere, and which are perhaps best avoided in our mutual interest.

Tuesday, August 24, 1937   Breslau
In the afternoon to the Jewish Community reading room; I haven't been reading the Jewish newspapers for quite a while. They are currently in the process of shrinking because of paper shortages, and there is precious little room anymore for cultural essays. They are all full of news. Rabbi Lewin accompanied me a piece on my way home; spoke to Fräulein Guttmann of the Provincial League. She told me about how the synagogue congregation is shrinking. Outlying towns that in past years were able to muster three minyans now have to import people from Breslau just in order to pray. Jewish communities in the provinces are dying a very rapid death.

Thursday, August 26, 1937   Breslau
Big changes have occurred at M. & H. Marcus, the publisher and bookseller. Theodor Marcus sold the jurisprudence list to Herr Gerhard Martin, from Trebnitz, which means that my *Das Zeitalter der Hohenstaufen in Sizilien* and *Hermann von Salza* are now owned by that gentleman. What remains unclear is who will now negotiate with Catania about an Italian edition of the Hohenstaufen book. The historical studies series has not yet been sold, and so the fate of my *Geschichte der normannisch-sizilischen Flotte unter der Regierung Rogers I. und Rogers II.* is still unsettled. My *Geschichte der Flotte Friedrichs II.* has been taken over on commission by Stefan Münz, who recently founded a new Jewish publishing house. Naturally, Marcus did not sell voluntarily. He always belonged to the camp that believed that they in particular would survive. But the people who toppled him, according to Münz, have themselves now been toppled. Marcus is currently living in Prague,

where he is the director of another publishing house.[32] Münz is interested in a history of the Jews in Breslau and asked me whether I would be willing to write one. I didn't respond one way or the other but suggested that he negotiate with the Jewish Community. I then tried to interest him in a small volume of my historical essays and another of my sketches. He asked me to prepare the manuscripts and show them to him, which I will do as soon as possible.

Monday, August 30, 1937   Breslau

In the afternoon, Trudi and I prepared the essays that I had written over the past four years. I plan to present this selection to Stefan Münz for his new publishing house; perhaps he will even publish them as a volume, which would please me greatly. To date, I have not had any luck with other publishers. These days, if you want to find a home for a book with a Jewish publisher you have to have extremely good connections, and I'm rather incompetent when it comes that. As I was looking through my things with Trudi, which, as I said before were written over the past few years, it dawned on me how much I actually wrote during a time when I felt I was doing nothing at all. How I wish I could see my entire life's work within the covers of a nice little volume, but I don't think it that ever happen!

Sunday, September 5, 1937   Breslau

The year 5697 comes to an end today, and now we begin 5698, whose Hebrew acronym תרצ"ח means "murder," a terrible omen.[33] Best to

32. Theodor Marcus wrote about these times himself. He was deprived of his citizenship and fled to Prague, where he headed the Academia Verlag, until 1939. His relative Stefan Münz served as a "front man" for his publishing house in Breslau. See Theodor Marcus, "Als Jüdischer Verleger vor und nach 1933 in Deutschland," in *Bulletin of the Leo Baeck Institute* 7 (1964), pp. 138–153.

33. Numbers, including Jewish years, are indicated by Hebrew letters. To indicate that a succession of letters is to be understood as a number and not as a word, a sign called a *gershayim*, which looks like a double quotation mark ("), is placed above it before the last letter. Nonetheless, some sequences of numbers may appear to form words. In this case, the last three letters of תרצ"ח indeed form the root for the concept "murder." The first letter means "thou shalt." For some reason, however, Cohn did not in fact switch letters as he claimed. If he had, he would have written תרח"צ, the root for the more neutral concept "bathe" or "wash." The practice of transposing two letters is standard in such cases.

switch the last two letters as I did above in order to ward off that evil. Matters look malignant throughout the world, and war is breaking out in all sorts of places.

Personally, as always, when I review the year 5697 in its closing hours, I have cause to be grateful to Him, except for my deteriorating health. After all, the year brought me reunion with my sons. Separation from them is often very hard on me. But now I have the memory of those lovely hours. And, thank G'd, the two girls have also developed nicely; Trudi has always proved herself, and in the end I have proved able to feed my family decently. We have gotten through by dint of our own efforts! G'd even guided my old Mother through this year. And so, on the threshold of the new it behooves us to trust in the future.

Tuesday, September 7, 1937 Breslau
Rudolf spent New Year's evening with us; we had a comfortable time, without pitfalls. He spent his vacation in Schwarzort, in the Memel region, where he met a lot of eastern Jews! How this former Naumannite has changed! All the difficulties he used to cause for every sort of honorable Jew! Now he even wants to take a look at Palestine.

Wednesday, September 8, 1937 Breslau
Took the streetcar to the postal check office; switched at Fränckelplatz, which is now called Fontaneplatz; observed the walls of the old Jewish cemetery being blasted out. A small piece has now been seized and is being desecrated in the cause of redeveloping Fontaneplatz. This really pained me; these old walls have stood for almost 200 years, protecting the "eternal peace" of our ancestors. All the debris gathered together during the clearance process had been dumped in the old cemetery in the Feldstrasse. It is a sad sight in the middle of the city.

Thursday, September 9, 1937 Breslau
Rode into the city where, at Uwe Mayer's, I traded the books that Daniel and Czollak gave me for Rosh Hashanah. Among other things, I took the *Philo-Lexikon*, the lack of which I have always felt![34] Incidentally, my works are listed in it among the Jewish historians. The lexicon

---

34. The *Philo-Lexikon* was a Jewish reference work published by Emanuel bin Gordion, among others, in Frankfurt am Main, 3rd ed., 1936.

appears to be quite serviceable, better than I had expected given the "Philo" in the title.

Sunday, September 12, 1937   Breslau
Another powerful speech against the Jews was given at the Nuremberg rally! It makes me very unhappy that the Jews are frequently so politically prominent in Russia; they should finally learn to leave politics to the native peoples!

Monday, September 13, 1937   Breslau
Yesterday went with Ruth to the Industrial Arts Museum, which I haven't seen in more than four years. It is set up in an extraordinarily clear manner so that even the layman can profit from it! Early history is very much overemphasized and figures prominently, particularly that of Silesia, in order to underscore the German character of the landscape. I was very pleased that Ruth took such an interest in everything; she is now entering a period of development in which her intellect is being awakened. Given that she will go to Erez Israel when she is young, it is perhaps important that she take all of these experiences with her!

The morning mail brought me a letter that did not particularly please me. Frau Borger wrote from Givat Brenner that the *mazkirut* had denied our application. True, after all these many months I no longer expected anything, but nonetheless now that it is in black and white it is a terrible blow. I have had to give up one of my dreams; perhaps I might again have found something of a home there. In any case, I got very upset. They didn't give any reasons. Perhaps it has to do with the fact that Trudi wasn't able to adapt to the spirit of the community when we were there. People are very sensitive to things like that. Well, I will just have to try to get over this blow, but a heavy blow it remains, and I don't think I can take too many more. I often suffer from ghastly symptoms. I'll have to be very courageous to deal with them. How hard it is to generate new projects over and over again! I think I will let go of it soon. My soul was so counting on this plan, and Givat Brenner in particular seemed like a haven. Now, that is all done with, all done with.

Daily Life

Tuesday, September 14, 1937   Breslau
Bathed in the evening; the usual ablutions before Yom Kippur. Was in a terrible emotional state and had to take Eupako, a medication I am reluctant to use. On such days, I really feel sorry for Trudi; sometimes I have the feeling that my emotional reserves are at an end. I prayed that I might not wake up again. Perhaps that is a cardinal sin. Trudi countered my prayer with hers.

Wednesday, September 15, 1937   Breslau
Yom Kippur is over, and I feel very badly that I didn't fast, but with this heart of mine I simply didn't want to risk it. Trudi prepared everything beautifully as always yesterday evening; then all of us attended synagogue in the Rehdigerplatz. The children returned home earlier; it pleased me greatly that Trudi held on until the end. This day is one of infinite fulfillment for me, and I was able once again to find something in it for myself. Of course, we can't overcome all of our problems. I thought about my sons far away; may things always go well for them. Will we ever experience another Yom Kippur together?

Friday, September 24, 1937   Breslau
City library; spoke there with a Protestant cleric who used to work at the Johannesgymnasium. I think his name is Provost Oertel. He is always warmly interested in what I have to say; I told him about Palestine, and he told me that whenever he thinks about the Holy Land, it is always associated in his mind with battles and discord. And in fact, anyone reading the German newspapers would be hard-pressed to conjure up an image of Jewish reconstruction work.

Tuesday, September 28, 1937   Breslau

Yesterday, I went with the children to the Abraham Mugdan Synagogue for Simchat Torah. It was very cozy as usual, like in a large family. Whenever I see groups of children walking behind the Torah, I know that our people will continue to have a future as long as our children are raised in the spirit of the Torah. I also had the honor of bearing the Torah; old Grünmandel called me up because I am a frequent attendee, which elicited protests from some. Unfortunately, in my present state I am unable to go as often as I would like; I find it very difficult in the mornings in particular.

Thursday, September 30, 1937   Breslau

Didn't have a good night. I dreamed that I was dying a slow death by heart failure, that I was suffocating, and that only Aunt Amalie was being good to me! How long has it been since I have thought about her; she passed into the other world almost a decade and a half ago! It was almost as if she were trying to call me.

Friday, October 1, 1937   Breslau

There is a lot of little work to do on my book about pawnbroking. I don't think I will take much pleasure in this work. I've already spoken to a number of Jews about these things, and most of them respond apologetically, an attitude that I hate! And if I were to publish my book somewhere else, I might well be accused of anti-Semitism. But it had to be written nonetheless.

I entered the army 25 years ago today; I am passing through many anniversaries that I now celebrate in silence! I enjoyed being a soldier, and I would have wished that my experience might have been of use to Erez Israel. This morning I told Trudi a few stories from my time in the army!

Monday, October 4, 1937   Breslau

Today is our anniversary; we married 14 years ago. This year has brought us good things and bad, but I am thankful in my heart that I found Trudi, who has always stood by me. I am certain that it has not always been easy to be with me, and now I have unfortunately become a man whose strength is broken, and who simply drags along! Sometimes I think she should perhaps treat me differently because things tend to reverberate in me. But Trudi is also an impulsive person with a tendency to lash out when upset. Above all, in these 14 years I have not been able to separate her from her family, to which I feel no connection!

Sunday, October 10, 1937   Breslau
Yesterday morning I received a letter from the Ministry of Propaganda with all of the documents I must fill out to be approved as a contributor to Jewish newspapers. Because the questionnaire also asks about my political past, I doubt whether this approval will be granted. I have my heart set on this journalistic activity, and so I want to do everything I can to gain approval. It is less a material matter than an intellectual one. My daughters are a great comfort on days like this. Ruth is very good to me. Trudi's parents stand between us, however! There is nothing I can do about that.

The morning mail brought a letter from Ernst, thank G'd, with his signature certified in the presence of the consul in Jaffa. Unfortunately it cost him 85 piasters! I hope it will help him in the future.

Monday, October 11, 1937   Breslau
Dictated to Fräulein Cohn all of the documents to be submitted to the Ministry of Propaganda. Because Trudi didn't want to leave in the evening, and because I, on the other hand, still had letters to be mailed but didn't want to risk going alone, I asked Rudolf to pick me up, and we walked to post office 18 and back. It was good because it gave us the opportunity to talk again.

In the morning went to Ruth's school. Consulted with Fräulein Lange, her German teacher; they always tell me that the children themselves are wonderful, although their performance leaves something to be desired. The school is in the process of renovation; the top floor is being expanded into an assembly hall, and so the entire second story has to be buttressed.

Tuesday, October 12, 1937   Breslau
What is especially noteworthy at the moment is the increasing shortages of raw materials in Germany. Naturally, the newspapers report nothing about this but, for example, the reinforced concrete fencing along the Kaiser Wilhelm Strasse cannot be completed because there is no iron! Distribution of beef to the butchers is spotty; bacon is scarce as well. The sole difference between wartime and inflationary times

is that we can neither talk nor write about it. It simply doesn't exist. However, I am not one of those people who from these signs prophesizes the collapse of the regime! The German capacity for organization will deal with this, too! But in any case, the heavens are full of the most threatening clouds!

Wednesday, October 13, 1937   Breslau
A letter from Ernst. He is now on his way to his final settlement site, where it is undoubtedly more dangerous right now. May G'd protect him! I am proud of the fact that he has chosen a life as a builder of Erez Israel. I wish I could be at his side!

Saturday, October 16, 1937   Breslau
Susannchen helped me organize my library; I rearranged part of the literature section! There is a great lack of space in my library, but of course there is no money for an expansion!

Sunday, October 17, 1937   Breslau
Had a strange dream today. I dreamed that I visited Rabbi Friedmann, the wonder rabbi of Sadigura, and I gave him a slip of paper with my name on it.[1] My name was then called out. First, the wonder rabbi told me to shake off my hands so that he might take my hand. Then he looked me in the eye and said, "I do not like how you look," "Sick heart." I replied that it was the *tzores* of having one son in Paris and another in Palestine. This interested him greatly, and at that moment I woke up. The dream has given me much to think about.

A number of changes have been made in the Kürassierstrasse. The large building built by the Freemasons Lodge was sold and is currently empty.[2]

Wednesday, October 20, 1937   Breslau
What continually catches the eye in our area is the amount of construction going on! For example, an entirely new street was created recently: Anzengruberstrasse. Went for a brief walk with Trudi in the evening!

1. The widely revered Rabbi Israel Friedmann lived in Sadagora, near Czernowitz, until his death in 1906.
2. Oddfellow Hall was located at Kürassierstrasse 15.

Received a card yesterday from Ernst; he is in Maos, post office Ein Harod, which he likes very much. He is a courageous boy; things will undoubtedly be much more difficult for him there.

Saturday, October 23, 1937   Breslau
I wish to say a few things about the Jewish questions of our time. It is difficult to come to any common understanding with people who do not wish to see that the fate of the Jewish people is wholly bound up with Erez Israel; it is especially difficult to enter into community with those who see everything solely from the perspective of their own private benefit. This is why we constantly make the same mistakes! Those who, like our Ernst, exhibit true devotion and sacrifice their youthful energies and their enthusiasm for the people. My entire life has been just such a struggle for the Jewish people, and it often saddens me that I am unable to win over others. It is, however, my conviction that our people lives and will continue to live on.

Tuesday, October 26, 1937   Breslau
The war of economic destruction against the Jews in Germany is being conducted with all sharpness! Officially, Jews are not obstructed in the conduct of their business, but the pressure on Aryans not to frequent Jewish businesses is becoming ever stronger. Members of the NSDAP and officials in general are already forbidden, and because the party is now experiencing such an influx of new members, the number of people who ex officio may not buy in Jewish stores is becoming ever larger. This policy affects organizations of war victims, among others. And so the pressure to sell businesses grows from day to day. No need to worry about the big fish; the proceeds from sales will ensure them a secure life. But things are more difficult for small and medium-sized business owners who are unable to live from the proceeds, are unable to earn their livelihoods in other ways, and cannot send their money outside the country. Because these things are all done legally, this monetary aspect of the destruction goes relatively unnoticed. Each day, we see more and more stores displaying the word "Aryan" in their windows. If I ask myself why this war of destruction is being carried out with such intensity now in particular, I would have to say it has to do with Germany's position in the world at large.

Thursday, October 28, 1937   Breslau
Spent an hour and a half giving Latin exercises at the seminary. Kurt Schwerin from the Am Anger School is also participating now, although he was one of Professor Santifaller's students. Then rode into town again; I spoke to the Jewish Teachers Association at Glogowski's on the subject of "Problems relating to the teaching of Jewish medieval economic history." Rosenstein, a very amiable teacher at the elementary school in the Rehdigerplatz, led the proceedings. Although my presentation was well attended and the teachers paid attention, the discussion was fairly disappointing, as is so often the case. – I had expected more from a body of teachers!

I tried to be very clear in my conclusion, even though Feilchenfeld completely deflected the point of the discussion! The new head of the Am Anger School, the former Studienrat Pollack, from Hindenburg, behaved extremely foolishly. He, by the way, was also discharged under Paragraph 4, although he was able to convert this to a Paragraph 6. A man who replaces the detestable Schäffer, who was hounded from office, shouldn't even be treated like a colleague!

Friday, October 29, 1937   Breslau
In the afternoon, spent two hours at the seminary. Then Lewkowitz came into the teachers room and told me that he would again present my position before the board of trustees. The gentlemen said that they could not arrange compensation in any other way because the Reich Representation has been forbidden to hire anyone permanently. So, I will have to make do with that; in any case, it pleased me greatly that Lewkowitz was so good as to take on this matter. Community reading room. Book lending has increased now that my fee recommendations for instructive books have been announced and an article has appeared in the *Gemeindeblatt*.

Saturday, October 30, 1937   Breslau
I'm having something of an internal crisis about my big book; I am struck by how little understanding there is for what I am saying, even among intellectual Jews, as I recently saw in the discussion at the teachers association.[3] People are simply not willing to hear anything unfavorable, and

3. He is talking about his planned book about pawnbroking.

because the Jewish people is unwilling to learn from its own mistakes, it will be very difficult to ward off a repetition of its fate. Nonetheless, I will try to continue on this book and bring it to something of a conclusion, even though it may never be published in my lifetime.

Sunday, October 31, 1937   Breslau
Daniel came by yesterday, and we went for a brief walk together. He wanted to get my advice about his pedagogical examination. After we had fully discussed the matter, I told him that, when I am no longer among the living, I would like him to assume responsibility for my literary estate because what I am writing now is unlikely ever to see printer's ink! He promised that he would do so.[4]

Ruth took part in a big Jewish swim meet today and just called to say that she had done well and wouldn't be home until 10 o'clock. The Wolffs are hosting a party for the swimmers! She is now going out by herself! Met Rudolf, then went for a short walk. Trudi stayed at home! I am often grateful for my inner life, which helps me contend with many things that come along.

Tuesday, November 2, 1937   Breslau
Matters are increasingly coming to a head! One of these days a terrible world war will break out. I'm reading a book from my library by Egon Erwin Kisch, titled *Schreib das auf, Kisch*.[5] Such a moving book about the war. That is how the war really was, and it will ever be so!

Friday, November 5, 1937   Breslau
Seminary; read for two hours, then Trudi came for a visit with Susann-chen. Trudi was returning from her gynecologist; it is quite possible that something little is on the way. I would like to have many children. Worked for a while at the seminary; called Trudi again to inquire whether she had settled down.

4. Cohn had studied Hebrew under Rabbi Rudolf Daniel (1909–1995) for about two and a half years and had a particularly trusting relationship with him. Unfortunately for Cohn, Daniel emigrated to Palestine, in February 1939.

5. Egon Erwin Kisch (1885–1948) was a Czech writer and journalist from a Sephardic family who wrote about his experiences in World War I in the book that Cohn references ("Write it down, Kisch"), which was published in Berlin in 1930. Kisch was radicalized by the war and became a life-long communist.

Read the *Danziger Gemeindeblatt* in the Community reading room. The Jews of Danzig must have suffered terrible losses on account of the smashed windows and plundering. Fräulein Silberstein told me about a general meeting at Perlhefter's wholesale food company, where she works. Perlhefter stood before his mostly Aryan employees and described himself as the "better sort of Jew." That such people are still running around in the open. He even had his children baptized Catholic, and now they're Jewish again. The Aryans had a good laugh over this one!

Tuesday, November 9, 1937   Breslau

The Revolution broke out in Berlin 19 years ago today. A nice bit of history we have lived through since then. Today, this day is viewed by the NSDAP as a day of mourning because this date is when the putsch in Munich took place. Swastika banners have been unfurled. There is no longer peace in the world, and it will not soon return.

Wednesday, November 10, 1937   Breslau

Trudi went to see Dr. Schäffer because she has had a fever for several days. He told her to rest and spend time lying down. The best thing, of course, would be to operate soon, but the doctor hasn't said anything about that yet. Naturally, I'm against her going to Berlin on Sunday, but I won't get anywhere with that. I hate these Berlin trips. At the moment, Jew-baiting is again on the agenda. An exhibition titled "The Eternal Jew" is running in Munich right now; Streicher spoke at the opening.[6] I wish that our Jewish people were much tougher and didn't feel so sorry for ourselves.

Thursday, November 11, 1937   Breslau

Today is Ruth's thirteenth birthday. If she had been a boy, there would have been a big celebration.[7] As far as her character is concerned, Ruth has developed magnificently in every way. She is a great support to us and a very reliable person with a real sense of responsibility who proves

6. The exhibition, "Der ewige Jude" [The eternal Jew], opened at the German Museum, in Munich, on November 8, 1937, with speeches by Gauleiter Julius Streicher and Propaganda Minister Joseph Goebbels.

7. Reform Jews had already begun the practice of bat mitzvah for 12-year-old girls, a practice that a traditionalist like Cohn would undoubtedly have frowned upon.

herself in every situation! And I told her so myself yesterday evening! When you look her in the eye you know who you are dealing with.

Sunday, November 14, 1937   Breslau
Spent some time organizing my book on economic history. I will never live to see this book in print! No Jewish publisher will print findings that bring undesirable things to light; nonetheless, I will make sure that I bring the work to some sort of conclusion! I have already completed a book about the Jewish economic mentality in my head, which won't ever be published either.

Wednesday, November 17, 1937   Breslau
Meeting of the Provincial League in the meeting hall of the Community Representation; afterward, lunch at Glogowski's. Rabbi Ochs gave a good talk about the role of the priesthood in ancient Judaism. Also, two lectures by Dr. Weissenberg about the advisory board and one by Friedländer about labor welfare were of fairly high quality.[8] Otherwise, not a word about Erez Israel and the victims who are now dying there. Table conversation was at the same level as before the war. These people have learned nothing and forgotten nothing. Overall, I find this tendency abhorrent! At the table I talked mainly with Dr. Freyhan. Kammergerichtsrat Wolff was sent from Berlin by the Prussian State League, and Frau Professor Berliner by the Reich Representation. I simply can't understand these double expenditures. Herr Wolff didn't even have a kippah for the prayer. Anniversary speeches were given as if nothing were happening.

Friday, November 19, 1937   Breslau
My audience at the Jewish House of Teaching wants me to give a follow-up to my course; however, the leadership is refusing its consent because it doesn't wish to make an exception, even though there are enough people. I probably won't be able to travel to Switzerland because I won't get the necessary foreign currency. The people who applied in August are being taken first. And under no circumstances do I want to go to the foreign currency office about getting an emergency certificate!

---

8. Raphael Friedländer (born 1881) was an official of the Jewish Welfare Office and the Jewish Labor Welfare Office in Breslau. He emigrated to Palestine in 1939.

Monday, November 22, 1937   Breslau
The general situation for Jews in Upper Silesia is becoming increasingly dire; liquidations are continuing at a rapid pace. In Breslau, Jewish restaurants have been closed for purported "uncleanliness," and individual Jews have been punished. In Gross Strehlitz, an elderly Jew who was arrested on supposed morals violations took his own life. He was the owner of a large business! I think that the Jewish authorities will have to accelerate the liquidations.

Friday, November 26, 1937   Breslau
It is somewhat strange walking through the darkened Breslau, although one quickly gets used to it. Walked along the Gräbschnerstrasse, then Hohenzollernstrasse and Schwerinstrasse.[9] Some things look very different in the dark, and all of one's instincts from wartime, when we spent a good deal of time operating in the dark, are awakened.

Monday, November 29, 1937   Breslau
Yesterday, finished writing the section about the history of the Swiss Jews and waited for the mail. There was a card from Trudi, among other things. I am always a bit sad when she writes so impersonally. My creative life depends so much on the response that I find in her. In the morning, I went walking for an hour, but it was raw and miserable outside, and I couldn't make any headway against the wind. Went to the Kürassierstrasse and looked at the progress being made on streetcar construction. The city is expanding quickly. My interest in this used to be quite different; now I am an alien in my own home city.

Tuesday, November 30, 1937   Breslau
Yesterday, the morning mail brought a warmer card from Trudi, which pleased me greatly. Also two lovely cards from Ernst, who writes so well about his region. Lit Hanukkah candles with Ruth. In the evening, Ruth played the game of dreidel at the Schüftans; they invited me too, and I went downstairs for a short time so as not to offend them.[10] We talked for a time. It seems that another Jewish butchery, Moskowitz,

9. Poorly legible passage, but this would have been the way to Opitzstrasse.
10. A dreidel is a square top on which are written Hebrew letters. The game of dreidel is played on Hanukkah evenings.

has been shuttered in Breslau. More than 70 Jewish schnapps taverns have been closed down in Upper Silesia.

Friday, December 2, 1937   Breslau
Walked to the Hanukkah celebration at the seminary; first there was a celebratory service in the seminary synagogue. Nathan, whom I have known for many years from the Elisabethgymnasium, lit the celebratory candles. Another student led the prayer. Afterwards, there was a nice party in the rooms of the seminary library. The students put on humorous skits; the board of trustees, which apparently treats the students less than well, came off very badly indeed.

I was only able to stay until five forty-five because of a meeting about the teacher course at the Am Anger School. Only a fraction attended because of the Hanukkah celebration. Then I rode home, where I found Trudi and Susannchen, who, thank G'd, had come back safely from Berlin. However, Trudi was so filled with the Berlin spirit, which goes completely against my grain, that the evening was something of a torture for me. Perhaps I'm seeing ghosts where there are none, but I think I will increasingly have to get used to going my intellectual way alone. Trudi was also full of the rumors fed her in Berlin, all of which goes against everything I stand for.

Friday, December 3, 1937   Breslau
Trudi went to see Dr. Schäffer, who confirmed her pregnancy. May G'd grant that the child is born healthy and is a joy to us. I have always loved children.

Saturday, December 4, 1937   Breslau
I wasn't able to attend synagogue; I stayed at home the entire day, mostly in my armchair by the stove. To my great pleasure, Trudi has taken the time over the past few days to help me with my work. I hope that her interest will continue. She has come to terms with the idea of having another child and, with G'd's help, she will perhaps even come to feel happy about it!

Sunday, December 12, 1937   Breslau
Today I am in my 49th year going into my 50th. I can look back on many decades, and some birthdays from the past are particularly memorable. How many people who have offered me birthday congratulations

on this day are now in the other world. Wölfl and Ernst haven't celebrated my birthday here for quite a few years, but I am grateful to G'd
that they are doing well so far. I had hoped to celebrate this birthday in
Erez Israel; perhaps next birthday.

Monday, December 13, 1937   Breslau
Took a nice walk yesterday morning with Ruth and Susannchen. Walking was very pleasant in the cool air, and I was able to do it without
symptoms. Ruth loves to talk; Susannchen was exhausted by the end!
We rode from Südpark to Goethestrasse; went to see Mother, who is in
great pain. All my siblings eventually arrived; having all of us together
is a real rarity because emotionally we don't really have much in common anymore.

Rudolf now assumes that his boss, Herr Braunthal, is going to sell
Trautner; it is possible that two old employees, Kutscher and Briesenick, will buy it. Naturally, Rudolf is quite upset and sometimes loses
his composure. Mother as yet knows very little about these matters. I
accompanied Rudolf as far as Zwingerplatz.

Wednesday, December 15, 1937   Breslau
In the evening talked about Palestine with Trudi, but we haven't come
to any final decision about our aliyah.

Friday, December 17, 1937   Breslau
Yesterday morning rode into town soon after the mail came. Gave
Hans Thiem his Christmas present; he really deserves it because he
takes his duties as building caretaker so seriously. Rudolf then asked me
into his private office to talk about his emigration plans; I strongly advised him against emigrating to Chile, telling him that Jewish businessmen from Germany are not exactly a desirable commodity. Naturally,
he will do as he sees fit.

Sunday, December 19, 1937   Breslau
This morning I went to a continuing education course for Jewish teachers at the new assembly hall at the gymnasium. Guttmann, from the
Provincial League, opened in his usual rather cool manner. Then, Dr.
Heinemann Stern lectured about German instruction in Jewish schools,
very assimilationist. Lewkowitz was the first to speak during the discussion portion, then I spoke from a very *völkisch* perspective, saying that

we Jews in the Occident are Orientals too. I also took a position against the trivialization of what it means to be Jewish. I spoke rather sharply, but these assimilationists must be opposed sharply if we are to have even a ray of hope. I told Herr Stern that a Jewish school should concentrate only on that which is Jewish! This was met with much applause.

Monday, December 20, 1937 Breslau
Yesterday, I arranged my will with Trudi. For me, it is rather upsetting to put things in order for a time when I will no longer exist. But that is how the world turns. Later, went for a brief walk with Trudi after dinner. It was fairly cold out, but it was lovely nonetheless to be together again. Then Trudi accompanied me to the Jewish Gymnasium, where a study group under Dr. Bamberger was discussing the teaching of culture in a Jewish school. Bamberger comes to us from a Reform teacher seminary in Berlin.

Wednesday, December 22, 1937 Breslau
Evening before last, when I got home, I heard that Ludendorff had died. With his death, a major figure from the world war has passed, one who had been much celebrated since the taking of Liège. For us Jews, he was also the author of the proclamation, "An meine lieben Juden in Poilen," but he subsequently led the sharpest attacks against the Jews.[11]

Yesterday morning, I spent most of my time arranging my manuscripts; gives me some indication of just how much I have written over the decades. How much I would have loved to see a bound volume of my shorter writings! But I doubt that will ever happen! Trudi went to visit Mother in the morning with Susannchen, where she heard that Rudolf von Braunthal had been fired. That was to be expected.

Thursday, December 23, 1937 Breslau
Ruth came home with a rather bad report card; promotion doubtful. I did not, however, reproach her. I then rode to the train station with

---

11. Cohn is talking about the letter of General Erich Ludendorff (1865–1937), "Zu die Jiden in Paulen" [To the Jews in Poland], distributed in the fall of 1914, to foment a Jewish uprising in territories controlled by Russia. Text in full in *Der Querschnitt*, founded by Alfred Flechtheim, vol. 4, no. 4 (autumn 1924), pp. 191–192. Ludendorff became a right-wing nationalist and took part in Hitler's Beer Hall Putsch, in 1923. He later split with Hitler.

her; it was the first day that the holiday return tickets were valid, and there was an enormous crowd. I admonished her about Berlin. Naturally, her grandparents have the right to see her there once a year, but I don't like her to go because it is such a completely different milieu.

Four Jewish food stores have been closed for uncleanliness. This is surely a pretext in some cases! Among them were two stores, Somma and Kretschmer, which weren't doing well anyway!

Saturday, December 25, 1937   Breslau
It must be beautiful in the mountains in their white magnificence. In the past, I often had the opportunity to get out in the winter, and I especially yearn to see Landeck again. But I would be happy and grateful if I can make the trip to Switzerland in March.

Monday, December 27, 1937   Breslau
We are now sleeping together with Susannchen in the children's room in order to spare ourselves having to tidy and heat the bedroom. The mailman returned two small packages I'd sent to Ernst; he probably can't pay the duty on them! It makes me sad that he can't have this to help strengthen him. I will send him five marks each month, as I already did in November and December.

A detailed letter from Ernst arrived via Ella, in which he describes his life in Maos. There are a total of 60 people. How much I would like to give him something to improve his living conditions! But I can't even send small packages. Susannchen went to the circus with Hanne Schüftan. Susannchen was so looking forward to it, and we showed our gratitude to Hanne, who is always so good her. A happy childhood is the most lovely thing one can have.

Friday, December 31, 1937   Breslau
The year 1937 has come to a close; a review of what it has brought us could be rather drawn out. For many it has brought hardships; for many Jews in Germany the loss of their positions, separation from their loved ones; for many people in China and Spain, the end. We here in our small circle can be happy that our four children have, thank G'd, developed well, and that we were able to see our two grown sons again. The very best thing would be if we could reunite our entire family in Erez Israel.

Monday, January 3, 1938   Breslau
Went to the bank in the Gartenstrasse. I gave them the children's full savings cards, and had the interest added for 1937. The children have saved quite a lot and probably have enough for a ship ticket to Palestine! And so, all of us have a nice little nest egg. And Trudi's book already has 100 marks set aside for the birth.

Friday, January 7, 1938   Breslau
From a correspondence that I was given to examine yesterday, I gather that the seminary is imperiled, and there are forces at work in Berlin looking to close the Breslau seminary in favor of the Higher Institute in Berlin. Although three training facilities for rabbis in Germany may be too many, let us not, of all things, close down the old institution in Breslau. But I fear that this is what will happen. Overall, the offices in Berlin tend to push through whatever they want, especially since such decisions are not taken by people who understand anything, that rather by administrative lawyers who "understand" everything. I personally would feel very badly about the closure of the seminary, not so much for material reasons, but because I have come to love this work. Nonetheless, I think that these days we are not in a position to plan for the long term. There is, however, another possibility, namely that Professor Elbogen would come to Breslau; but then, of course, there would be even less room for me.[12]

Tuesday, January 11, 1938   Breslau
My nephew Gerhart Cohn came for a visit, something that I have long awaited, and he accompanied us together with his friend Tischler, a former student of mine. The English school seems not to agree with Gerhart; this type of training is a way of avoiding the big decision. But it is no wonder that Gerhart is not enthusiastic about being a chalutz. In general, he is a very amiable young man; it is of course sad that he is visiting his parents just after his father was fired.

Thursday, January 13, 1938   Breslau
At the Am Anger School, the continuing education course for teachers, spoke about Jews in the French Revolution. Then spoke with Fräulein

12. Ismar Elbogen (1874–1941) was a professor at the Hochschule für die Wissenschaft des Judentums, the Reform rabbinical seminary in Berlin. He emigrated to the United States in 1939.

Daniel about her brother, whom the Reich Representation is unwilling to register for the second examination because at the time he had not taken part in my seminar. This is fairly outrageous behavior on the part of the Reich Representation; for Daniel, who has completed the work, it means the end of his plans for the future!

Went into town with Susannchen. The child is always so delightful whenever I pay attention to her, and it is already worthwhile explaining things to her. I also brought along some oranges; the storekeeper told me that Jaffa oranges would start arriving soon.

Saturday, January 15, 1938   Breslau
I did not feel well enough to attend synagogue in the afternoon; I read the Torah portion at home, the "Song by the Red Sea" and the *haftarah* portion with the "Song of Deborah." Then I prayed the evening prayer alone.

I am apparently going to be placed under heavy pressure to sell the Ring building in order not to make things difficult for the reorganized Trautner company, a step I will never feel fully prepared to take. What so upsets me is the thought that now I am being asked to demonstrate a solidarity that was never shown to me, even during times that were particularly difficult for me.

Sunday, January 16, 1938   Breslau
I asked Herr Briesenick and Herr Kutscher to come and see me after dinner; they are the two old Trautner employees who would like to buy the store. They wanted to negotiate with me about rent. Presumably, they will enter into a contract. But first, they want to talk with Herr Grzesik to see whether he would want the front cellar! The negotiations proceeded calmly, much differently than I had been accustomed to from earlier times. Nonetheless, it upset me. A piece of family history will come to an end with the sale of this building. The gentlemen told me that business has increasingly been falling off. Increasing pressure has been exerted on customers not to buy from Jews. As I heard yesterday, Rudolf wants to move to Berlin, where he intends to make contact with foreign business representatives. I doubt that he will ever emigrate.

Thursday, January 20, 1938   Breslau

My nephew Gerhart came to visit me during the morning to say good-bye. He is returning to England. I doubt that I will ever see him again because his parents will probably emigrate, and it is unlikely that he will ever return to Breslau. Rudolf, who in his entire life never had any interest in Judaism, now has an exquisite understanding of how to harness the Jewish authorities to his wagon. He is completely *sans gêne*, as they used to say. So now he wants to go to England.

Sunday, January 23, 1938   Breslau

Trudi went to see the exhibition at the Jewish Gymnasium, which she says is lovely. I didn't want to risk going because of the three and a half staircases! Went with Trudi and Susannchen to Zimpel; we walked along a lovely footpath, along the recently opened Treidelweg as far as the bridges over the big shipping waterway and the outfall. Much has been built there, and you can see how Breslau has been growing on all sides. – Only we Jews are no longer involved in this blossoming, and perhaps it is good that way, even though our generation will not get over our sense of connectedness with this landscape.

Ruth was involved collecting nonperishables for Jewish Winter Relief. She is learning early to meet her social obligations! And in the process she has had the most curious experiences!

Tuesday, January 25, 1938   Breslau

To the bank; unfortunately, we had to withdraw some of what we had for the coming event. In spite of all frugality, one always needs more than one intends. On the way there, I noticed that the first *pardess* oranges this winter were on sale at the market hall![13] This is always a big event because the children so often think about Ernst.

Thursday, January 27, 1938   Breslau

Professor Andreae has been fired from the university because he has a Jewish wife; as far as I know, he is now completely without means.

---

13. Oranges were among the fruits imported to Germany before World War II. They came, in part, from the British Mandate for Palestine, and were called Jaffa oranges. There would have been no specifically Jewish overtones in this trade for the German consumer, but for Cohn, of course, they represented a greeting from the Promised Land.

Friday, January 28, 1938   Breslau

I had a rather peculiar anniversary yesterday. Twenty-five years ago, I marched in the Schlossplatz in honor of Wilhelm II's birthday. Paraded as a one-year volunteer in Field Artillery Regiment 6! Yesterday, the words of the last Kaiser came to mind more than once, "I am leading you into magnificent times."

At the moment, the Community is in something of a depressed state. The confectioner Michaelis took his life in jail, probably there for violating the foreign currency laws. A physician, Dr. Kupferberg, is said to have bolted (with wife and child) because he had been summoned to the Gestapo. All of them, people who never think in terms of collective responsibility! Such a man must have been up to something, otherwise he would have responded to the summons in good conscience!

Sunday, January 30, 1938   Breslau

The Third Reich was founded five years ago today. For us Jews, these five years have doubtlessly brought many hardships, but I am objective enough to recognize what they have meant for Germany and its resurgence.

This morning, I attended the annual celebration at the seminary; the weather was beautiful.[14] I was very satisfied with the seminary celebration today, if I ignore the fact that, as a "teacher 2nd-class," I was seated in the parterre. I got to hear the voice of Cantor Rossbach of the New Synagogue for the first time, who recited the El Male Rachamim for Kommerzienrat Fraenckel as well as a Hebrew psalm and a German *lied*. The lecture by Rabbi Ochs, from the seminary, titled "Masters and disciples in Talmudic writings," was quite an experience. Not only the fact that he had completely mastered this enormous corpus, he presented it in a manner that demonstrated a magnificent fervor for Judaism. It was so beautiful when he said that we must learn to replace the word לִי (me) with the word לָנוּ (us). If German Jews try to lighten their load by getting rid of the spiritual (throwing off the *tzitzis*), it will do nothing to lighten their load.

14. The annual memorial at the seminary in honor of its founder, Jonas Fraenckel.

Thursday, February 3, 1938   Breslau

In the show window at Trautner, floral arrangements to celebrate its takeover by Aryan owners. And so a piece of our family history has come to an end. This, too, a hurtful moment!

Walked a piece with Urbach. He is having difficulties with his trip to Palestine; because he is a Polish citizen, they don't want to allow him back into Germany.[15] Trudi is having symptoms associated with her blessed condition!

Sunday, February 6, 1938   Breslau

All the newspapers featured the news that the entire military leadership of the Reich has been entrusted to a single person; doubtless a very strong concentration of power.[16] Terrifying clouds are arrayed in the heavens for 1938. The sinking of so many English ships in the Mediterranean should give us pause. Travel to Palestine will surely be significant this time. Reservations are almost sold out. How lovely if we could finally get over there.

Tuesday, February 8, 1938   Breslau

Read a rather unpleasant story in the *Schlesische Tageszeitung* to the effect that "Jewish children" will no longer be granted tax abatements, and that this policy will go into effect with the tax assessment for 1937.[17] This means that we will have to pay a considerable amount in arrears. Apparently, emigration isn't going fast enough for the officials in charge, and they want to exert even greater pressure. For us it means a significant decrease in income; we will have to try to make do with this as with so much else. It was quite a shock.

On the other hand, the morning mail brought a very encouraging and magnificent letter from Ernst; it is wonderful to see how these young people, entirely on their own, and now in the rainy season com-

15. The *Mitteilungen des Verbandes ehemaliger Breslauer in Israel*, no. 56 (1992), p. 7, contains an obituary for Ephraim Elimelech Urbach (1912–1991).

16. As a consequence of the so-called Blomberg-Fritsch Affair, Hitler had on February 4 become the Supreme Commander of the Wehrmacht. This meant that all political, military, and economic powers were now in his hands.

17. The Gesetz zur Neufassung des Einkommensteuergesetzes [Revision of the income tax law] was published February 1, 1938, in the *Reich Law Gazette*, Part 1 (1938), no. 9, pp. 9ff. and went into effect on February 6, 1938.

pletely cut off from their surroundings, are going about body and soul building up the land. How lovely it would be if I could help. But I doubt that this will be granted me.

Saturday, February 12, 1938   Breslau
Synagogue, walked home with Rabbi Lewin and asked him to look after me if I am prematurely called away so that everything is done according to proper Jewish custom.

Sunday, February 13, 1938   Breslau
Yesterday was another one of those days, and it brought real turmoil into the house from a side that I had not expected. In the morning, I stayed at home and talked for a time with my father-in-law. After all, there were a few things that needed to be discussed because we so rarely see each other. I suggested that he visit Palestine instead of Italy as he intended.

At my suggestion, he and Trudi then went to talk to her mother. This resulted in a major upheaval. She accused us of never asking about Rudolf, who is currently in England.[18] On this occasion, Trudi, who is otherwise quite controlled, unburdened herself, and even though I felt a bit sorry that it upset Erna, it seemed to me necessary to get out into the open all of the sins that had been committed against us over the years. Trudi spent a lot of time at home crying, which in her present state is almost certainly harmful, and she will not be going to Berlin in the near future.

Friday, February 18, 1938   Breslau
Rode into town. Talked with Briesenick and Kutscher. They told me that if business gets going again, they will give Uncle Moritz something, a very decent attitude. The new rental agreements have been signed. A photograph of the Führer is now hanging in the private office; they sent me the family pictures some time ago.

Thursday, February 24, 1938   Breslau
Mother will have to decide whether to go into a private home or old-age home; she cannot get by with a housekeeper. I would feel very badly

---

18. Rudolf Cohn had gone to England to explore the possibilities there; a month later he was back in Breslau.

if she were forced to give up her household, but I don't see any other way. I will look into this matter next week when I am less busy.

Fifty years ago was the Year of the Three Kaisers, one hundred and twenty-five years ago the Wars of Liberation.[19] If I had had the opportunity, how many more essays would I have been able to write given what I know. But time has passed me by! Fate!

Sunday, February 27, 1938   Breslau
Erna called at four o'clock to tell us that Uncle Perls had taken his life; he reached the age of 77 and was ruined by these times, which robbed him of everything. He had felt very much alone. As long as I can remember, he has been our loyal physician and advisor. Now that he has passed over, it makes me wonder whether perhaps we should not have done more for him! Suicide must always be condemned! But unfortunately he lacked religion! May he find peace where he now rests!

Tuesday, March 1, 1938   Breslau
Very happy that Ernst sent a nice letter for Susanne's birthday containing a lovely picture of himself. The boy has developed magnificently during this year; unfortunately, he is beginning to lose his hair already. But thank G'd, he is the prototype of a new Jewish generation. Rode to a meeting of the *Gemeindeblatt* committee; as always, got upset by Rosenfeld's idiocies. A real *galut* Jew. Walked home!

In the morning I went to the police to confirm that I am still among the living; I have to do that each year. These people know me and are very nice. Then at the school department stuck the letter with said confirmation in the box.

Friday, March 4, 1938   Breslau
Czollak told me that many students will be leaving the Jewish Gymnasium at Easter and will not be replaced. At the moment, the pressure on Jews to emigrate is especially intense. With us, things frequently take the form of mass psychosis. It is certainly good that young people are leaving! I told Czollak that he ought to consider his future, too, before it is too late. There aren't all that many Mizrahi teachers!

---

19. Two Kaisers died in 1888. Wilhelm II (r. 1888–1918) was the third Kaiser that year. The anti-Napoleonic Wars of Liberation began in 1813. These wars have long played an important role in galvanizing German nationalist feeling.

Saturday, March 5, 1938   Breslau
A man from the local Sauerbrunn group of the NSDAP was here in the evening. At issue was a form to be filled out about our origins; it is apparently aimed at eastern Jews!

Later, I had various errands to take care of, among them the bank, where I learned that the money I applied for will be transferred to Rosette Ruf within the next 14 days. The bank official advised me to go soon before something happens to my passport.[20]

Wednesday, March 9, 1938   Breslau
Bank. I have finally received the Swiss money. I hope that nothing is done to my passport by the time I am able to go, but I should probably anticipate problems. Met my former colleague Freund, whose eldest son recently emigrated from Switzerland to China! Separation everywhere.

20. Cohn had planned a trip to Switzerland for the end of March, beginning of April 1938. Unfortunately, the diaries for this trip have been lost.

The Annexation of Austria

Thursday, March 10, 1938   Breslau

The Iron Cross was instituted 125 years ago. They will perform the Grand Tattoo tonight at the Schlossplatz. All those who have the Iron Cross are to line up; under other circumstances I would have gone!

Friday, March 11, 1938   Breslau

Rudolf called in the evening seeking recommendations for Prague. He's looking for business representatives for Australia. People always call when they want something.

Big things are happening in Austria. It looks as if Schuschnigg plans to go his own way; perhaps the consultations with the Führer concluded very differently from what we are told here. We are tapping around in the dark in our own times!

Saturday, March 12, 1938   Breslau

Austrian Chancellor Schuschnigg has supposedly stepped down. The National Socialist Minister of the Interior supposedly requested that the German government send troops! Italy has apparently rejected a request by France to consult together on the Austrian question. Public opinion appears to be divided in Vienna. For me, it is beyond question that National Socialism will succeed; no one will be able to keep Berlin from annexing Austria! Great national movements do succeed. What is still in question is whether the Western powers will approve this form of annexation of Austria to the German Reich at this particular moment! If not, it might mean a European conflict.

The Jews in Vienna have surely made a serious error over the past few years; they have probably still not understood that they would be best served if they withdrew from public life! Just today, I read in *Das*

Jüdische Volk about how young Viennese Jews lack a sense nationalism.[1]
How Herzl wore himself out over this. The Jewish people continues
making the same mistakes and will continue having to pay the price!

So, German troops have marched into Austria. The newspapers
write about the Liberation of Austria. Exactly how other countries will
respond is not yet clear; a report has been published in France to the effect that there is no reason to intervene. The nationalist movement will
be unstoppable.

Sunday, March 13, 1938   Breslau

I am very curious to read how the political situation has developed
overnight. We will have to pay attention to people like Seyss-Inquart,
the new power in Vienna.[2] I also read today's *Schlesische Zeitung*. Enormous enthusiasm in Austria; the Führer has crossed the Austrian border. It cannot be denied that this is a momentous event. If only we Jews
were firmly led by such a hand and built our future accordingly. But we
are internally split!

Monday, March 14, 1938   Breslau

Bought the newspaper on the way home. The annexation of Austria
by Germany will not upset the peace! One has to be impressed by the
energy with which everything was carried out! There will be hard times
for the Jews of Vienna, who so often, and here too, bet the wrong
cards and believed that their salvation lay in an alliance with the clerics.
The Viennese Jews were never particularly moved by the notion of
chalutziut; perhaps now they will be gripped by the Zionist impulse.
Perhaps we Jews in Germany should not be sympathetic to this national
uprising, but we are nonetheless, and any nationalistic person will feel a
certain kinship! We Jews should be united in just this way!

Tuesday, March 15, 1938   Breslau

Walked home; Fräulein Daniel, the teacher, accompanied me part of
the way. She told me that her mother is now in Erez Israel, but that she

---

1. *Das Jüdische Volk* was a weekly newspaper published in Berlin.

2. Arthur Seyss-Inquart (1892–1946) was an Austrian National Socialist politician. After the "annexation," he became Reichsstatthalter [Reich Governor] in Austria in 1938–1939, and in 1940–1945 Reichsstatthalter in occupied Holland. He was
sentenced to death and executed at Nuremberg.

had been so frightened by rumors that she would not be permitted to cross the border. But of course everything went smoothly; the way our people are rumor-mongering is a sin.

Wednesday, March 16, 1938   Breslau
Went to the bank and post office 5 with Susannchen. On the way back, I bought her a *Schmackoster*, one of those rods decorated with paper.[3] She is always very affectionate and charming when we are alone together. It is only after dinner that the girls don't get along. Heard part of the Führer's speech from Vienna at the bank.

Discussed economic matters with Trudi for when I am gone; after all, I have to put my affairs in order, especially since I have to put everything in order for the various administrative offices. As far as I can tell today, my lecture trip is secure; I will, G'd willing, leave on Saturday evening. Purim is this evening.[4]

3. Children in Silesia used to go from house to house on Mid-Lent (Laetare) Sunday with these colorfully decorated sticks asking for candy. The Jews of Breslau adapted this custom to Purim.

4. The diary breaks off here; the entries from March 18 to October 27, 1938, have been lost. This would have amounted to approximately four or five diary notebooks. This gap is all the more regrettable because this was when Jewish assets had to be registered and identification cards were made mandatory for Jews. For Willy Cohn they included a meeting with his son Wölfl, in early April 1938, in St. Gallen, and the birth of his daughter Tamara, on July 19, 1938.

The "Big *Geserah*" of November 9, 1938[1]

Saturday, October 29, 1938   Breslau

It seems that there won't be any lectures at the Jewish House of Teaching. Hinkel, the special commissioner responsible for monitoring Jewish cultural affairs, demands that all manuscripts be turned over. However, that either cannot be done at all or in any case not so quickly.[2] And so there are always changes, but they are just details in comparison to what is going on in the Jewish world at large.

Polish Jews were hunted down in Breslau evening before last. Poland will supposedly enact a law, on November 1, whereby all Poles who have lived outside the country for twelve years are to lose their Polish citizenship. As a result, Germany fears that she will not be able to get rid of her Polish Jews because they will have become stateless. On Thursday evening, they arrested these people wherever they found them and deported them. The story is told that Poland has refused to take in these poor people, and that they are now stranded in Beuthen.[3] They weren't allowed to take anything with them! Families were torn apart, and efforts are being made in Jewish circles to find homes for the children left behind. Manhunts in the 20th century. Naturally, people

1. *Geserah*, a threatening decree or persecution of the Jews. Cohn would not have known the term "Reichskristallnacht" (Crystal Night).

2. Reichskulturwalter [Guardian of Reich Culture] Hans Hinkel (1901–1960) was made special commissioner in the Ministry of Propaganda, in 1935, and department head, in 1938. He was also director of the Reich Chamber of Culture.

3. After a plebiscite in 1922, Beuthen had become a border town between Germany and the Second Polish Republic, but on the German side. The Jewish community of Beuthen was the first to be transported to Auschwitz for destruction, in February 1942. Now called Bytom, it is part of Poland.

were very upset yesterday, and quite a few who are regularly in attendance failed to show up at the Abraham Mugdan Synagogue. It's a bad business.

Today I got a letter from the Association for Jewish History and Literature to the effect that Jewish gatherings have once again been banned. I was supposed to have spoken there, something that I have always wanted to do. A ban on gatherings decreed for all of Germany would have hit me very hard at this time of year, but I will just have to find a way to muddle through. Under no circumstances will I let myself be broken by it.

Sunday, October 30, 1938   Breslau
The arrests and deportation of many thousands of Polish Jews have had tragic results! The Helfgotts told me about it. In one family, the only remaining member is a half-paralyzed man in a Jewish hospital. During the night from Thursday to Friday, 4,000 people were deported to Poland. Ruth just told me that Poland is only accepting those who have assets over there; the others were either deported back or will be sent to a camp. Ruth told me that people from her sporting club gave them food at the train station.

Tuesday, November 1, 1938   Breslau
Went to the seminary; there I heard that three attendees of Polish citizenship had been deported. However, news has already come from Rabbi Chameides, in Kattowitz, to the effect that everything has been done for them that could be done.[4] Nonetheless, they were forced to move on to Cracow because Poland has special laws governing who can live in border regions.

I heard more about the entire affair at an editorial committee meeting in the evening. Polish Jews were rousted out all over Germany. Thus, for example, a train from Saarbrücken was routed here through Chemnitz; as we were informed by the Jewish Community in that city so that the people could be fed here, which was in fact done. Vogelstein is said

4. Kalman Chameides (1902–1942 or 1943) was the last rabbi of the Jewish community in Kattowitz (now Katowice), on the Polish side of the border, just south of Beuthen. In 1937, he was appointed adviser on Jewish matters to the municipal courts of law.

to have made an all-out effort. A number of the transports then returned from the Polish border because Poland was unwilling to accept the people, who, it is said, looked in very bad condition. Officials here behaved very properly, helping with the food; the aid societies at the train station as well! Poland then immediately began deporting Germans. Negotiations are currently underway between the two states. – Fates.

Had a conversation with Rabbi Wahrmann at the seminary. Wahrmann is staying in Breslau at the moment; he is also a Pole and has to keep out of sight in Oels. Then I spoke with Hans Prinz about our aliyah, and how I might start the process for getting Susanne and Tamara over there because the pension benefits certificate isn't enough.[5] He recommended that I get in touch with Ahava, and possibly talk to them in person in Berlin.[6] He considers the matter very difficult.

Wednesday, November 2, 1938   Breslau
Terrible things appear to have happened while the poor people were being shoved over the green line! The entire action is said to have stopped as a result of Roosevelt's intervention! He apparently threatened to deport Germans. I have no idea whether this is true. Rosenbaum, a German citizen from Breslau, was apparently deported along with them. Rau, who is responsible for monitoring foreigners here, is said to have been especially vicious.[7] I've heard his name mentioned

---

5. In order to emigrate to Palestine, people needed a certificate from the Jewish Agency. These documents were granted only under certain conditions and were subject to a quota. Wealthy Jews received a capitalist certificate; Jews who were merely receiving a pension would be lucky to receive a pension benefits certificate. Willy Cohn's hopes for certificates for his two younger daughters were in vain.

6. The Ahava children's home was founded in Berlin, in 1924. The work of this home was continued, in 1934, at Kibbutz Kiryat Bialik, near Haifa. It included an Ahava school, where Rabbi Siegfried Ucko, who was originally from Breslau, taught. One of Cohn's hopes was that he might find a home for himself and his family there. See Regina Scheer, *Ahawah. Das vergessene Haus. Spurensuche in der Berliner Auguststrasse* (1st ed., Berlin: Aufbau Taschenbuch, 1993; 4th ed., Berlin: Aufbau Taschenbuch, 2004).

7. Here, Rau is merely mentioned briefly; later he is actually named. Walter Tausk also mentioned this particular police official as a "well-known and loathsome person." Walter Tausk, *Breslauer Tagebuch 1933–1940*, ed. Ryszard Kincel (Berlin, 1975; new edition, Berlin: Siedler, 1988), p. 170.

more than a few times. The older, upper-echelon police officials don't want this!

Saturday, November 5, 1938   Breslau

During the recent hunt for Polish Jews, a number of members of the Community representation and of the board, who were unable to show identification, were arrested. The Jewish House of Teaching has canceled lectures for this semester! Everything will become more difficult! How many synagogues in which I used to speak have now been sold. Rastenburg, Osterode in East Prussia, Kaiserslautern, all torn down!

Monday, November 7, 1938   Breslau

Herr Helfgott and Herr Bratmann were here yesterday. I helped them fill out the forms for their emigration. Helfgott went to the Palestine Office in Berlin today; everything is getting more complicated by the day, and many people find themselves in a real mouse trap. When the seminary closes its doors at Easter, it will have strong repercussions on our lives as well.[8] We will have to see how we can make do!

Tuesday, November 8, 1938   Breslau

The newspapers today are reporting terrible news for us. Vom Rath, the secretary of the German legation in Paris, was shot by a Polish Jew and severely wounded, a very cowardly act that will almost certainly have the worst possible consequences for us in Germany. I assume that there will be confiscations, imprisonments, perhaps even termination of Jewish pensions, and so forth. It was an unforeseeable and cowardly act resulting from a false desire for vengeance, which will have dire repercussions for all of us.

Wednesday, November 9, 1938   Breslau

Yesterday was a terrible day, and I am glad it is over. This morning, as I am writing this, I have no way of knowing what sorts of vengeful measures the government will decree against the Jews in Germany. I

---

8. As already mentioned in these diaries on January 7, 1938, the merging or closing of the Jewish Theological Seminary had already been planned before Kristallnacht, apparently for Easter 1939. The events of the coming days accelerated this process. The institution ceased operation on November 9, 1938. Willy Cohn returned his key on July 6, 1939. The building itself was torn down after 1945.

read in the *Schlesische Zeitung* yesterday evening that the assassin, Gryn-
span, is a 17-year-old man who acted in response to a postcard from his
parents.[9] They were among the people affected by the measures taken
by the German government against Poles in Germany. That may help
him get a milder sentence from a French jury, but it won't help us. One
cannot even imagine what they might do to us!

We had invited Rudolf for the evening, and so I had the entire day
to think fearfully about what was to come! Nonetheless, it went more
smoothly than I had thought; I very much wanted to host him before
his departure for Australia.

Today is November 9, a fateful day in history. It has now been 20
years since the Revolution in Berlin, which I experienced; 15 years since
those days in Munich (1923), which marked the beginning of National
Socialism! How much has happened since then! Back then, I, too,
made a November speech, which was duly noted, to my detriment!
And what does the world look like today! It feels like November again,
misty weather. We wish only to maintain an even keel emotionally, for
ourselves and our children.

Thursday, November 10, 1938   Breslau

Today I do not even know where to begin. There was severe rioting
overnight! The milk man told my wife this morning that the New
Synagogue had been set ablaze, and that businesses were demolished.[10]
In the meantime, Ruth has come home from school; school was let
out. Rosenbaum's pharmacy has also been demolished. Poor people!
Vom Rath has died, and these riots are most probably the consequence
of anger over this. Yesterday evening, I heard that all Jewish events and
the Jewish press have been banned for a quarter of a year.

Yesterday, I was still thinking about how hard all this would hit us
since we are so dependent on this income, but now all that recedes into
the background given such terrible Jewish suffering. Will this be the

---

9. Herschel Feibel Grynszpan (1921–after 1945, fate unknown; declared dead in
1960) was born in Hannover, the son of immigrant Polish Jews. His act of violence
was in response to the forced deportation of his parents and other Polish Jews from
the German Reich.

10. The New Synagogue had been designed by architect Edwin Oppler (1831–
1880). For many years, its 60-meter-high dome dominated the skyline of the city.

end of it? Who knows? When this terrible deed was done in Paris, it was clear to me that it would have repercussions of this sort! The notion that all Israel answers one for another holds equally in bad times as in good! The small number of remaining German Jews will not have an easy time of it. Perhaps the Polish Jews who were deported are actually better off. In these difficult times, may G'd protect all of my children, both here and abroad!

At ten thirty. Things seem to have been very nasty in the city. The New Synagogue is apparently still burning! Wolff's chocolate shop has been demolished. Our cleaning woman tells us that Jews have been taken into protective custody. Who knows what will come; we will simply have to endure. But who knows how our families will survive these next days? We must simply endure it! And be strong! In case I am arrested as well, I stressed to Trudi the importance of taking care of the children and of my work. I would hope that they would at least get through these times. I have already lived my life! I am having a hard time concentrating on work today.

The day has unfolded particularly badly. Curt Proskauer and Rudolf were arrested, and many others as well. I assume that I will be picked up at any moment. All Jewish stores have been destroyed, according to the *Neueste Nachrichten*. And the New Synagogue is still burning. All synagogues have apparently been destroyed.[11] Erna came here with Paul this afternoon; Erna is a model of composure. I tried to console her as well as I could, and I told her that I am sure that Curt will be released today. I don't believe it myself! I'm sure that this is not the end of the matter, and that even worse will follow when these things become known abroad. I feel very sorry for Ruth; she is conscious of everything that is going on. She says that she envies Tamara, who doesn't know what is happening.

---

11. Most of them were demolished, but the New Synagogue alone was set ablaze. One eyewitness reported as follows about the Zum weissen Storch Synagogue: "Its inside rooms were demolished, the Torah scrolls and all other furnishings and equipment were burned. The rabbi and the cantor, who were forced to witness the burning, sat on the floor afterwards and tore their clothes in an expression of sorrow." Karol Jonca, *"Noc kryształowa" i casus Herschela Grynszpana*, Acta Universitatis Wratislaviensis, 1312 (Wrocław: Wydawn. Uniw. Wrocławskiego, 1992), p. 180.

Friday, November 11, 1938   Breslau

Yesterday evening occasioned no further sensations in our inner circle, but we have no idea what is going on outside. Erna would have called us if Curt or Rudolf had been released. I am sure that these prisoners will be held hostage for the next few days. Much worse things are still possible; I am quite pessimistic. Matters for us will be made even worse because foreign governments will undoubtedly express their indignation. But there is no sense in worrying about it.

Ruth is 14 years old today; we wanted her to have a much nicer birthday, but that's not possible. In these 14 years she has always been a joy and a support to us. In these times children are called upon to absorb much that is distressing, and these things will affect them for the rest of their lives. Fate is stronger than a parent's love! What else will this day bring?

The dome of the New Synagogue has collapsed; the insides are completely burned out. New anti-Jewish legal measures are to be expected. What we hope for is a loosening of emigration policies. I no longer believe in a rebirth of Jewish life here in Germany, nor do I consider it desirable! This morning brought more excitement. Fräulein Cohn, whom I had asked to work with me, came at nine; I told her that our work together would now also be coming to an end because all further activity has ceased for me.[12] Today I would not have been able to dictate to her even if there had been something to work on.

Today I am organizing my stamp collection, the only thing that more or less distracts me during these critical days. Then Trudi came in to tell me that some people in the Opitzstrasse were being hauled away. She asked me to go take a walk. I did so for her sake, if reluctantly, because I believe that no one can escape their fate. And so, I walked as far as the Gräbschener cemeteries; it was tiring for me because there is no place to sit and no place where a person might duck in. My mood contrasted sharply with the lovely fall weather. I saw a number of elegant private automobiles with SS people, who I am sure are involved in the action.

---

12. As of December 8, 1938, Jews were forbidden to do any scholarly work at the universities and in libraries, something that Cohn probably knew was coming. See Joseph Walk, *Das Sonderrecht für die Juden im NS-Staat* (Heidelberg and Karlsruhe: C.F. Müller Verlag, 1996), p. 264.

I bought some wine at a fruit truck in order to get a ten pfennig coin to use the telephone. But then when I called home no one was there, and as I heard later it hadn't even rung. In other words, our telephone has been disconnected, and this has happened to others as well.

Then I went to the barber because a person is especially conspicuous with such dark stubble, and then when I saw that nothing was going on in our house, I went upstairs. As far as the children and my wife could tell, observing from the window, our house had been spared, but of course they can always make up for that later, even though I think that the action has been halted for today. Of course, it will be continued to-morrow. It looks as if all more or less healthy male Jews have been jailed or, in the official wording, taken into protective custody.[13] I do not know whether they will be transferred to a camp, although I suspect as much! Trudi is putting on a brave face, but I know it is probably much worse to be frightened for another person. Ruth looks very worn out. A terrible birthday; nonetheless, she is very happy that I came home at noon. She is very attached to me. I am going to stay home in the afternoon with my family for as long as they permit it. I would feel even unhappier elsewhere. My heart and blood vessels make things unimag-inably difficult for me; nor did I find any peace after dinner.

The mood on the street is thoroughly anti-Semitic, and people are happy that this has happened to the Jews. Just horrible, the description of the collapse of the New Synagogue in which my father prayed, and which is so connected with my earliest memories.

Saturday, November 12, 1938   Breslau
We heard from the Schüftans' daughter that the action against the Jews may have been halted. I hear the message, but I don't believe it! Lotte Helfgott came by in the evening completely upset because her father had

---

13. Figures differ as to the number of Breslau Jews deported to Buchenwald. The first report submitted by SS-Oberführer Fritz Katzmann (1906–1957), on No-vember 10, at 3 in the afternoon, stated that 600 men had been detained, although arrests continued. Walter Tausk estimated that 4,000 had been arrested, which is probably too high. According to Jonca's research, approximately 2,200 Jewish men were taken from Breslau to Buchenwald. Karol Jonca, *"Noc kryształowa" i casus Herschela Grynszpana*, p. 183 fn. 154. Here also p. 64, fig. 8, a photograph of the Katzmann report.

been arrested right off the street at three forty-five. I told her that she should not do anything further, but wait. This is especially difficult for our people, but this is the only possible course because nothing we do can make any difference! In the evening, we went to bed early; I even managed to get some sleep. What today brings is in G'd's hands. Because of incitement from the radio station in Strasbourg, we can expect any number of things. These gentlemen on foreign soil incite from a safe port![14]

The day has not brought anything out of the ordinary, but let us not praise the day before night falls. I did not go out; Trudi went for a walk with Tamara and Susanne; Ruth went after dinner! The two big girls are now at the Schüftans'. The Lewins just visited us. I like the old Rabbi very much; they wanted to arrest him as well, but they decided not to because he is 70. David Foerder is said to have been beaten up. Falkenstein, the cantor in Landeshut, was supposedly roughed up as well.

Sunday, November 13, 1938   Breslau
In spite of the house arrest I have imposed on myself, I still hear a few things about the outside world from people who come to visit. Duscha, the barber, and an old party comrade of mine, came at twelve thirty. He is very unhappy about these events, and he told me that even Aryans have to be extremely careful about what they say lest they risk trouble. People have already been arrested on that account. He thinks that prisoners over the age of 50 will stay in jail until the so-called foreign incitement has stopped; I think they will be sitting in jail for a good long time. Among other things, he also said that trains carrying prisoners had departed the evening before last, on November 11. I always assumed that they would be deported to a camp, because there is surely not enough space for them here at police headquarters. Those who have been released say that they were treated and fed decently. It is not in the nature of the old public officials to torment individuals. Longer imprisonment would be very bad for my brother Rudolf because his emigration is coming up soon! Those who can prove they are emigrating will probably be freed the earliest!

14. Between 1930 and 1940, Radio Strasbourg, in France, broadcast German-language programming that could be picked up in much of Germany, and it became an important source of information. The Third Reich demanded that it be shut down, but without success.

Luckily, the Torah scrolls at the Abraham Mugdan Synagogue were saved.[15] But there won't be many of them left in Breslau. In my opinion, these days are among the blackest not only in Jewish, but also in German history, and I believe that many Germans are ashamed of what is happening. I hope that at least a portion of the Jews remaining in Germany can be saved from this mouse trap.

The mail brought news that Friedrich Bloch, with whom I had such a harmonious relationship, took his own life on November 11, this *dies ater*.[16] I suspect that he made all necessary preparations for suicide. Trudi and I were very upset! He did not have what it took for these times, and I am sure that his emotional suffering was unbearable during these five and a half years!

The newspapers have published a portion of the new Jewish laws. One billion in collective penalties. A ban on attendance of entertainments, which sounds grotesque since who would do that now! Although, you can never tell with some of our people. A ban on all independent business activities, in other words, practically all means of earning a living. – The end of Jewry. Now there is only one way out, emigration, and we can only hope that more doors will open. The world's indignation appears to be enormous! Increasingly, we have the feeling that this entire action must have been prepared in advance; how else would it have been possible for synagogues everywhere to be set on fire at the same hour![17]

Sunday evening at five thirty. Herr Schüftan was just here! He told me that the prisoners are at the Neuhammer target range.[18] Things seem to have been terrible in Beuthen; even old Rabbi Golinski was arrested.[19] And homes were destroyed there as well. In Upper Silesia,

15. In 1938, the Abraham Mugdan Synagogue at Rehdigerplatz 3 was one of the few Breslau synagogues that escaped destruction.

16. *Dies ater* (Latin), black day, day of calamity

17. For an account based largely on Nazi documentation of how the riots were organized, see Raul Hilberg, *The Destruction of the European Jews* (New York: Holmes & Meier, 1985), vol. 1, pp. 38ff.

18. A large exercise grounds in Lower Silesia.

19. Ludwig Golinski (1879–1942); after his studies at the Jewish Theological Seminary in Breslau (1899–1908), he became a rabbi in Beuthen, Upper Silesia (1923–1939). He emigrated to Palestine in 1939.

events seem to have been especially grim! In Landeshut, Herr Schüftan's brother managed to bring two Torah scrolls out of the burning synagogue, but they were thrown back in, and he himself was arrested. One hardly knows what to believe! In Beuthen, they forced a Jew they had tied up to pray in front of the synagogue.

Public officials seem to have been decent everywhere; the people doing this are other elements. The entire people cannot possibly be this bad! But those who have been loosed upon us. Some seventy people, among them Spitz, the attorney, have been released.

Monday afternoon, November 14, 1938   Breslau

I am continuing with my voluntary house arrest, but Trudi, who went out, tells me that there are very few Jewish men to be seen on the street even though about ten of them were released yesterday. Trudi went to the bank with our two younger daughters; she was able to withdraw money freely. Naturally, we have to watch every pfennig now because I assume that I won't be earning money in the foreseeable future; in Germany, probably never again.

For me, a person who has always managed to pick himself up in every situation, it is almost as if I have been hit over the head. I still haven't processed what is happening. All Ruth talks about is emigrating; first, she wants to spend a year in France. But these are all utopian fantasies, and I myself see no possibilities for earning a living anywhere in the world given the poor state of my health. The children will make it with G'd's help. Even with all the languages I know, I doubt that I would be able to earn anything from them. I think that my life has reached a final turning point, perhaps an end point. Friedrich Bloch drew certain consequences from this, consequences of which I cannot approve. At the moment, this diary is the only literary work I am able to accomplish. I am emotionally cut off from all the rest, and I lack the concentration for scholarly work. So I read in the Bible. Today I worked my way through the Book of Joshua in Hebrew and German. I continually find things that relate to our times!

I will never forget how, on Friday morning, I made myself scarce for an hour at Trudi's request, and Ruth and Susannchen stood with worried looks by a window in their room, following me as I left the house. On days like this I see how attached Trudi and the children, my family, are to me. It is bitter thing that they should be forced to experience this as children. I do not believe that the matter is at an end. They will certainly view us as hostages in the face of everything that is going on in the world at large. I am sure that much more will happen. Nor do I believe that most of those in protective custody will be freed anytime soon.

How are we impoverished Jews supposed to come up with one billion. But that, too, is secondary, if only they let the people out without harassing them too much, because this sort of emigration brings endless trouble! I am also very anxious to get news from Wölfl! What a shock this must have been for the boys!

Duscha, the barber, came in the afternoon. He has children in Trebnitz, who told him what havoc was wreaked there. Durra is said to have been paraded through the city in chains, an old man in his nightshirt. Even the Aryans were upset about it. Duscha believes that the people do not want this. In the afternoon, Ruth went with Susanne to see their friend Ilse Häufler. She returned with news that the Jewish press and cultural activities are again permitted, but the question is whether we Jews will still be able to get them going again given that so much of substance has been destroyed. The main thing is that they should let the people leave.

Susannchen had a slight fever in the evening, and Ruth has gotten scrawny. Wherever the children go they hear the same conversations. In the evening they spent a little time with Mother, who is doing poorly. No news from Rudolf and Curt!

Tuesday, November 15, 1938   Breslau
Eleven o'clock. The *Schlesische Zeitung* carried an interview with Goebbels conducted by a Reuters reporter. I will mention just a few points. Jewish cultural organizations are supposedly operating again, there is no intent to force Jews to live in a particular quarter; only those who have 20 to 30 rooms (sic!) in a villa must give them up! Apparently, there has been quite a bit of pressure from abroad. In England, intercession services have apparently been held for the Jews, and Chamberlain does not dare say anything good about Germany. The latter from the radio. Furthermore, Goebbels said that the special tax of one billion will be paid by assessments on wealthy Jews! From this, one

may assume that pensions will continue to be paid. It is perhaps not right to think about such things, but of course I feel responsible for my family and my three small children. No one has heard anything about Curt and Rudolf. A transport train apparently went to the camp near Weimar.[20] A Herr Bär died on the transport.

Mother appears to have no money whatsoever. The Proskauers have no savings at all! If Curt has to stop working, they stand before the abyss. I was always clear about this, but I can't do anything for them. They never listened to me anyway. I hear that Erna looks very bad. Paul Proskauer went to Berlin about an American visa. But these things do not move that quickly. Rudolf's wife, Kaete, who is in Breslau right now, hasn't even gone to visit Mother.

Tuesday afternoon. People say not to be on the streets on Thursday, the day of vom Rath's burial. There is no way to know whether popular passions will again bubble up "spontaneously." Eventually, a person simply gets numb.

Wednesday, November 16, 1938   Breslau

Today, the newspaper reported the most significant fact, that in England, Eden, Germany's enemy and successor to Chamberlain, is advancing! For those of us remaining in Germany, this will do nothing to improve our situation. The newspapers are currently focusing a great deal of attention on how the English are proceeding against the Arabs in Palestine. They compare this with the way they are dealing with the Jews in Germany, thereby seeking to exonerate themselves! But that is something completely different! This was almost certainly an action planned in advance! The world is not fooled. I keep asking myself, though, why this happens to us over and over again because, as a historian, I cannot simply look to the latest instance. I must think about the deeper causes, and conclude that we are also at fault! But I do not think we can get any distance on the matter while we are still in the throes of the events themselves.

20. Since July 1937, the concentration camp at Buchenwald had, along with the one at Dachau, come to define the terror regime of the Nazis. A total of 9,845 Jews were deported to Buchenwald after November 9, 1938; more than 26,000 Jews were arrested throughout the Reich as a whole. By the end of the war, approximately 250,000 prisoners had been interned in Buchenwald, 56,000 of whom died there.

Thursday, November 17, 1938   Breslau

Another night over; outside, daylight is reluctant. It is raining; November weather that fits our mood. I'm very hungry for air, and I will be happy when I can end my house arrest. One hopes that perhaps some of the prisoners will be released from protective custody, once vom Rath is buried today in Düsseldorf. I don't actually believe that this will happen; rather, I think they will be kept hostage to the attitude of foreign governments.

I hear from Ruth, via the Schüftans, how poorly so many Jewish women are behaving; shaken, they send telegrams all over the world instead of simply allowing matters to take their course. Raphael Friedlaender, in particular, is overrun! He operates the Jewish office that is responsible for passport matters; he himself was only recently freed.

In the morning, I spent a great deal of time reading the Book of Samuel; then I did some work in my library. Given my sedentary life, I am trying to do at least some physical work. However, I can't do much because I run out of breath so quickly.

Took a nap after lunch, and now I am speaking French with Ruth about how to behave on a trip! Ruth wants to go to France to be with her brother, and to see something of the world! Outside, we see large numbers of swastika flags with mourning banners; I hope that the proceedings throughout the Reich go off without further endangering the Jews.

Saturday, November 19, 1938   Breslau

We hear more and more details about what happened in the province during that horrible night. A traveling trader from Klein Ellguth, who has a car, reports the following.[21] During the night he was forced to drive in the direction of Neustadt. Word was that things would get started at four o'clock. If I remember the report correctly, the order was announced at 12 o'clock. The man reported—I got this only indirectly because I have not been going out—that he was driving the worst of the men. Armed with rubber truncheons and iron bars, they attacked

---

21. Under special provisions governing Upper Silesia, where the Reich's anti-Jewish laws did not apply until League of Nations protections lapsed in July 1937, the Synagogue League of Upper Silesia had been able to lease the Ellguth-Steinau estate (not Klein Ellguth as Cohn believes), where they founded an agricultural school. It served to prepare young people for emigration to Palestine.

chaverim in Klein Ellguth. They also beat the girls after they threw themselves on the boys to protect them. This in the 20th century.

In addition, I myself had the following experience yesterday afternoon after it was already dark. I wish to record it in detail. All of a sudden, the doorbell rang once, which to us is a sign that it must be a stranger because people who know us always ring twice. Trudi opens the door, just as she always does these days, and an Aryan man is standing there and says he wants to talk to me. She doesn't know what to say. However, he tells her that she can let him in without fear. My first thought was that he was a Gestapo agent coming to pick me up. But matters played out much differently. He was a former student of mine named Sch.; he did his Abitur Easter 1924.[22] He is now a pastor near Oels, out in the countryside. A country pastor, member of the Protestant Confessing Church. He said that he had simply come to tell me that there are also decent people, and in fact he stayed for more than an hour, an emotionally satisfying hour, knowing that such people still exist. Sch. is now 30 years old, married, and very religious. He told me that he just walked past the ruins of the New Synagogue, and that only a few people he had seen walking by were not deeply affected. Sch. said that the German people does not think this way. I am so happy that a former student of mine still remembers me fondly after so many years. An arduous calling he has chosen.

Sunday, November 20, 1938   Breslau

I worked during the day; my productivity has not returned, if it ever will? My heart and nerves are in a fairly desolate condition! Nonetheless, I did some more work on my memoirs; I wish that the manuscript were in a place where it would survive these times. It is an attempt to describe the development of one Jew who came of age in a now disappearing German cultural milieu. But who knows what the fate of the manuscript will be. Everything is in flux.

22. Cohn abbreviates his visitor's name. In all probability, it was Heinrich Schulz, the pastor in Postelwitz and Mühlatschütz, in the district of Oels. Born in 1907, in Sophienau, district of Adelnau, Schulz belonged to the Confessing Church, and after the war he became superintendent of the church district of Salzwedel, in Saxony Anhalt. The editor is grateful to Dr. Christian-Erdmann Schott, pastor in Mainz, for this information about Schulz.

After dinner, I took a walk with Trudi for the first time since Friday a week ago and breathed fresh air for the first time! It did me good! A person feels like a criminal walking along empty and ill-lit alleys, hoping to avoid people (even from our own circle) who might ask, how come you aren't in a camp? Even among our Jews, there are those who do not wish me well because of my honesty and outspokenness. I keep wondering why it had to come to this. If we view world history from the perspective of space, the shortage of space in Germany is certainly an important factor. Space shortages have always caused such convulsions; I am not seeking to excuse, but perhaps it is an explanation.

Sunday, November 20, 1938   Breslau
In the afternoon dictated a letter to the Coch bookstore; I wish to sell several journal series from my library that do not matter much to me, and which I could not take with me in any case. They wouldn't mean anything to Wölfl either. I have a hard time separating from things like this, but it is better to sell them off slowly over time than to be forced to get rid of them abruptly. These journal series are also very heavy, and therefore costly to transport. I am a sentimental person; each book is associated with a memory. But none of this is of any help; in the end, we even have to separate from our children. And if I must now send my two girls away, I will consider myself fortunate to have found a place for them, regardless of how my fatherly heart aches.

Monday, November 21, 1938   Breslau
A rumor has been circulating that teachers, doctors, and all men above the age of 45 and young men below the age of 20 are to be set free today. May G'd grant that it is true; but so many rumors have been circulating over the past few days that I have become suspicious and unwilling to believe anything that has not yet come to pass. Last night, the synagogue of the eastern Jews, in the Friedrichstrasse, which they had seemingly overlooked, was set on fire.

The morning mail brought a circular letter sent by the Reich League of Jewish Cultural Associations asking whether I would be available to take part in events. The ban has been lifted, with the exception of lectures. The government wants to maintain the cultural associations. But I don't believe that Jews in Germany will ever again be capable of such a thing.

Trudi has just come back from her errands; she was able to save all of my books. The lecturers' room was spared; the auditorium and the lecture halls, on the other hand, were completely destroyed. Trudi spoke to Frau Heinemann; her husband couldn't talk as the board of trustees was meeting. Kober was not imprisoned, but Lewkowitz's son was, as were almost all of the audience members with the exception of a few foreigners! Frau Heinemann doubts that the seminary will ever reopen; another chapter in my life comes to an end. I am going to try to get a certificate, and to claim my honoraria!

I was intellectually occupied for much of the day; however, except for this diary only passively as my productive powers are still completely paralyzed! This old body simply does not want to anymore, and personally, I don't think I am fit for emigration. My main desire is to know that my older children are safe. I do not believe that I have much of a future, and to that I will have to reconcile myself.

Tuesday, November 22, 1938   Breslau
In a dream I spoke only French. Today, both children are in school again; Ruth as usual, and Susannchen for two hours. Up until yesterday evening, no one knew whether the teachers would be released.

Perhaps some Jews will consider me foolish for what I am about to write: I cannot imagine myself outside the German cultural milieu. True, externally we have long been excluded, and Jewish involvement in the German language will also die out. And yet, how could I live in a country with a language foreign to me where I have no potential for creativity. True, I might perhaps find a calling in Erez Israel, but in all seriousness I doubt that this will ever come to pass. I have never understood the point of nurturing relationships merely for the sake of it. It always seemed unclean to me; nonetheless, it is the unclean who seem to go farther. I feel very tired most of the time and no longer up to a new challenge. Luckily, Trudi is of a completely different constitution, and with G'd's help she will manage with the children. I spent myself too quickly.

Wednesday, November 23, 1938   Breslau
A letter to Ernst Simon. I asked him again to see about our aliyah. I don't think that he will achieve much, and fundamentally, I am really not capable of it anymore. I often wish that I could bed my tired body

here in the Lohestrasse.[23] My hope is that my children will carry on in my spirit.

The Max Nordau Hall in the Neudorfstrasse has also been demolished.[24] It had been erected with such love. For Ruth, this means the end of table tennis. Ruth is filled with immense rage, something one can well understand in young people. For me, my great love for Germany remains.

Yesterday, Fräulein Heinisch, the midwife, visited my wife, and she had some stories to tell! With the exception of uniformed groups in the movement, there seems to be a change in mood under way in the Aryan population. The synagogue burnings seem to have opened many people's eyes; however, that won't change the power structure. We have heard about a large number of Jewish suicides during those critical days.

23. That is, in the family plot in the Jewish cemetery.

24. The Max Nordau athletic facility was where the Jewish Bar Kochba sporting club practiced and played. It was named after Max Nordau (1849–1923), an important Austrian proponent of Zionism. It was designed by the architect Heinrich Tischler, and had only recently been dedicated, in 1936. The architect wrote about the dedication in the *Jüdische Zeitung*, vol. 43, no. 7 (February 14, 1936).

Efforts to Get the Children Out

Friday, November 24, 1938   Breslau

The second mail brought a card from Rosette Ruf, who is making efforts to find a place for Ruth and Susanne in Switzerland. In addition, Ruth may be able to go directly to Erez Israel; aliyah for children nine and older has been approved, and yesterday Marianne Lasker came by to ask whether we would agree to putting the child on the list. Naturally, we agreed immediately, and we hope that Ruth may perhaps be sent to Gan Megged, where she would be with her friend Esther Jacobsohn. The absorption of children seems to be very well organized. What our hearts will endure if we must send our children away is something best not talked about. But that is not the point; the main thing is that the children be safe in case these things repeat, which could quickly happen again! The children look forward to the prospect. The desire to get out transcends everything, particularly for Ruth. Rosette Ruf really is a true friend to make such efforts. It will take a few weeks, but the time will pass quickly. I still have not received any news from the Fraenckel board of trustees about whether I will be paid for the lectures I gave in November. I have no idea whether more might be in the offing, but I cannot even think about it. It doesn't help; one just has to take things as they come.

The newspaper reported today, among other things, that the first installment of the levy on Jewish assets, in the amount of one billion, is due on December 15. Only those who have assets greater than 5,000 marks are affected, and it is an open question whether I will be among them. In any case, my assets will have to be reassessed by December 12. I am especially sickened by the thought of all the extra work involved! But this, too, must be done! On such days, of course, there can be no thought of productive work. But who can even contemplate that now; we consider ourselves fortunate just to muddle through.

Friday, November 25, 1938   Breslau
Lay awake at night and thought about the pain of separation from Ruth and Susanne. But that is of no help; everything must be done in the interest of the children. Nonetheless, it is very painful for parents to send their children away at such a young age. This morning I wrote very detailed letters to Wölfl and Ernstl; the children will want to be informed of everything.

I also doubt that the majority of those interned near Weimar will come home anytime soon. They probably won't release them until they can prove that they are emigrating.

Saturday, November 26, 1938   Breslau
Rudolf has returned from the camp and will be emigrating in two days. I assume that he will say goodbye to me before he leaves; I just sent Ruth to visit him with a letter. Old Rabbi Hoffmann broke a leg in Buchenwald, near Weimar, and he is still interned there.[1] But my student, Paul Hirsch, has been released; on the other hand, Schüftan, from Erfurt, and Absberg, from Elberfeld-Wuppertal, are still in the camp. Those two hadn't even been sought; they were picked up while they were out walking. The seminary library is closed; the police took the key and said they would send an expert!

Went into town for the first time since the Jewish stores were destroyed. Boarded up windows everywhere; a scene of considerable desolation. We keep hearing reports that the police are confiscating plundered goods and placing them in safekeeping.

Sunday, November 27, 1938   Breslau
Frau Helfgott came to see us, completely despondent; she wants to take her life. She hasn't heard any news from her husband in 14 days. Today we are advertising our dining room furniture; it is difficult for me, but we will probably take in Mother on January 1, 1939.

---

1. Rabbi Moses Hoffmann (1873–1958) refused to be released until the last Jew had been let go. Walter Tausk, *Breslauer Tagebuch 1933–1940*, ed. Ryszard Kincel (Berlin, 1975; new edition, Berlin: Siedler, 1988), p. 202.

Monday, November 28, 1938   Breslau
Handwrote some letters; among other things I wrote to Verlinden about whether he sees any possibilities for me in Belgium. I hesitate to write such requests, in part out of principle: I am not used to harnessing other people to my wagon. For 50 years I haven't been able to do it, and then Palestine looked like an option. But now the situation is such that I have to consider all possibilities in the interest of my wife and children. I don't really believe that the letter will or can have a positive outcome, but Verlinden has always shown himself to be so decent and reliable in our scholarly correspondence that I believed I could write such a letter without compromising myself.

Read the Book of Job, which has much to tell us in moments like this. On the way to the post office, I met Alice Friedlaender, the daughter of Raphael Friedlaender, who is responsible for the Community's most important task. He has been able to get 10 to 12 people out of Buchenwald each day. About 300 people come to his office daily. The police have forbidden visits at his private residence. Spoke with Gidi Mandowsky, whose father is currently interned in Buchenwald. They have received a certificate, and so he will probably be released soon, and then emigrate. I think we can assume that this internment action will cause a majority of Jews to leave the country. What will happen to them outside is another matter.

Tuesday, November 29, 1938   Breslau
Herr Grzesik is coming this afternoon to discuss pre-negotiations for sale of the property. All this is very painful, but it has to be done. Called Bendix's office twice.

Rudolf did not even call to say goodbye. His dear wife probably prevented him. This is the thanks I get for decades of sacrifice on his behalf! But I'll get over it!

Wednesday, November 30, 1938   Breslau
We have been thrown out of the health plan. This was to be expected, but it is particularly inopportune right now as I may have to go to the hospital. Reports in the newspaper today underscore how hostile everyone is in the world. It has been decreed that Jews may not leave their homes on Saturday, the day of national solidarity, from 12 to 8 o'clock in the evening. All this has happened before on our painful path through history.

Ruth has just brought news that the father of one of the teachers died in Buchenwald, near Weimar. It is said that 70 Jews have died there already, among them a number of Breslauers; after all, they arrested quite a few over the age of 70. I still have not heard anything from Switzerland about the children; they are waiting expectantly! It is bitter that one must hope that positive news will arrive soon. I wonder whether Ernst Simon has been able to do something for me in Palestine.

All Jews are now talking about emigration and building a new life; I am very tired, and nonetheless I feel an allegiance to Germany, where I have lived for 50 years. I don't want to be a beggar and have to show gratitude somewhere out there in the world. Trudi is very competent and positive; she will always be able to make something of a life for the children. But for an intellectual like me it is very difficult; I doubt that I will be able to do it. It hurts me so much that Ruth and Susannchen have to hear about all of these things that are now simply in the air. But it can't always be avoided. Of course, it is a burden on their young souls, but that is how it is in most Jewish families now.

I have been writing a great deal in this book lately. If it survives these days, it may perhaps tell later generations what one Jew experienced and suffered in these times. Everything is in turmoil!

Thursday, December 1, 1938   Breslau
Herr Briesenick, one of the owners of Trautner, was here this morning. He is very interested in the building; perhaps he will take it for the first and second mortgage. That would certainly spare me the annoyance and upheaval of selling it.

Dr. Landsberger, the pulmonary doctor, is said to have died in Buchenwald; Feilchenfeld, the school head, as well. May G'd grant that it is not true.[2] Rudolf Daniel was at school again today. All the people there had been shorn bald. But that wasn't the worst of it; we heard about other things as well.

I have to do everything I can to ensure that Frau Freund, our housekeeper, does not unthinkingly tell the children horror stories at meal-

2. His fear was unfounded. Rector Heimann Feilchenfeld took up the reins again at his school in January 1939. He emigrated to Riga, Latvia in late April 1939, where he died in the occupation.

times. She is the sort of person who wallows in such stories and doesn't absorb better. Other than that, she is a good sort.

The head of the league, Marianne Lasker, called to say that one of us should come to the Hechalutz Office to give our consent for Ruth to go to Holland for a year. Separation from this child is now becoming a serious matter. But we must do all we can to save the children; we are not yet at the end of what faces us in the future. Three children in three countries!

Friday, December 2, 1938   Breslau

Yesterday afternoon, Trudi went there and gave our consent for Ruth's placement in Holland. The child has already gone to be photographed, and then she will be examined by Dr. Sgaller. – We will have to obtain a considerable sum of money. I have already turned to Bendix to find out whether some funds might not be obtainable from the inheritance for the purpose. Had a telephone conversation with Friedrich Schoeps, the subject of which was how to get Curt Proskauer out of the camp.

Discussed with Trudi all the problems associated with Ruth's aliyah. The prospect of separation is very painful for us. Nonetheless, it is best for Ruth's future; all else is of secondary importance. I also wrote to the boys; soon we will be writing to both of the girls as well. The seminary paid me for the lectures I gave in November, naturally not for the entire month, but I don't think I will get more. This may be the last money that I will have earned from intellectual work in Germany.

Saturday, December 3, 1938   Breslau

Yesterday evening for the first time since the *geserah*, I went to the Abraham Mugdan Synagogue, which I love so much. Services are again permitted there. With full hearts, we thanked G'd that we may again pray here, with our health somewhat intact. Badrian, the school caretaker, is attending the sick at Buchenwald, and our colleague Czollak is a cook. Helfgott wrote as well. Walked home with Rabbi Lewin, who already has a certificate awaiting him in Berlin. I told him that I was perhaps too tired to be able to accomplish anything outside, but he wouldn't hear of it!

Because all of us are under house arrest on account of the day of national solidarity, our neighbor Herr Schüftan visited me and engaged me in one of those conversations about emigration that are basically de-moralizing and lead to nothing. I always feel badly that I no longer feel the vitality within me to make a fresh start abroad, in areas that are not my specialty. I am just very tired. Of course, I would be happy if I could save my entire family, but could I save myself? Could I be replanted anywhere other than in Erez Israel?

Today, Jews are banned from going outside from 12 noon to 8 in the evening.[3] Such measures were once decreed by the Lateran Council; the history of the world is cyclical, the question is who gets hit!

Sunday, December 4, 1938   Breslau
Rudolf Daniel, who just returned from his "trip," came by in the evening. Except for a bad cold, he seems to have come through all right. We talked until almost 11 o'clock. He will presumably leave in January; his sister is doing what she can to push through his aliyah. We talked about the general situation, and that the Jews in Germany are approaching *neila*.[4] Jews may not own automobiles, and so most will have to make their way on foot. And there are certain streets in Berlin where Jews may not walk!

Monday, December 5, 1938   Breslau
Telephoned Inspector Utical from the tax office about the levies on Jews. He advised me to go to the tax office before January 15 to find out whether I have been assessed. This could easily turn into a big surprise for my 50th birthday; at least we are prepared! It hardly makes a differ-ence as is; at that point, we would have to use our life insurance policies to make up the shortfall. But the children will get out; the question is whether my wife will get any benefit from it? Do not set your heart by life's material goods!!

Went to the market. I had to look around for quite a while to get some oranges for Tamara. They are now a rarity! Bought some sausage at the store that used to belong to Glücksmann. They still produce sau-sage by the same new kosher method.

---

3. See Joseph Walk, *Das Sonderrecht für die Juden im NS-Staat* (Heidelberg and Karlsruhe: C.F. Müller Verlag, 1996), p. 261, no. 43.

4. Cohn uses this Hebrew word to describe the sense of resignation and doom in the country.

Went to see my current publisher Stefan Münz, the successor to Theodor Marcus in Jewish publishing. He just pulped 45 hundredweights of Jewish books; what all has been destroyed in the process. Nonetheless, the Gestapo made him agree to leave Germany in the very near future! He will be going to Montevideo! So, this is the last time I will visit these rooms. The first time I was here was during winter semester of 1909–1910, when I shyly offered them my book about the Norman fleet. Almost 30 years of scholarly association.

Tuesday, December 6, 1938   Breslau
It is hard to know where to begin in all of this turmoil. I met with the Hebrew teacher, Reznikow, yesterday and we talked about what is on everyone's mind: the sufferings and tribulations of the Jews.

The morning mail brought news that was partly happy, and partly other things. Wölfl wrote a card in which he told me that he has been able to place Susanne with Baron Rothschild's secretary, and asking for our consent. This morning I sent a telegram in the affirmative. It is hard to say what one feels at such a separation, and yet it would be such a good stroke of fortune for the child to find a home there. It may be that it will ultimately prove too bourgeois for her, but nonetheless we must be grateful to Wölfl for having made such efforts on his sister's behalf. The two of them got along so beautifully at Easter.[5]

Today, the newspaper reported about the Aryanization of Jewish-owned property, the sale of stocks, and so forth.[6] It amounts to an almost one hundred percent expropriation; but none of this seems to me as important as the fate of the children. Perhaps this will unburden me of all the depressing administrative work and responsibilities that have tormented me for years and for which I have received so little thanks! And if the children are taken care of, what do I care about the money?

5. Cohn took Susanne with him when he visited Wölfl at Easter, in St. Gallen, in 1938. A photograph of the two children together in Switzerland has survived, although the diaries from that time have disappeared.

6. For more on the expropriations and policy of Aryanization in Germany as a whole, see Raul Hilberg, *The Destruction of the European Jews* (New York: Holmes & Meier, 1985), vol. 1, pp. 94–138.

Wednesday, December 7, 1938   Breslau

Ruth had to race around town to get herself photographed again. Perhaps she will go to Holland on hachshara instead of to England.

Thursday, December 8, 1938   Breslau

Received a lovely letter from Rosette Ruf. She is making efforts on our behalf in Switzerland, at least for a temporary residency permit. But this would only be granted if we have been assured of a certificate for Palestine. I sent an urgent letter about this to Arthur Wiener, in Haifa. Lay awake for a long time at night; not particularly happy thoughts. But as I have my whole life, I am determined to meet my obligations to the fullest.

Friday, December 9, 1938   Breslau

After dinner, I had to dictate an urgent letter to Trudi about Ruth's emigration. The battle continues for the 750 marks that the executor of the will set aside for Ruth. We received 50 marks! We hope that the sale of one of our stocks will be approved. Trudi had to go to attorney Bendix's office this afternoon on this account.

Sunday, December 11, 1938   Breslau

Herr Nürnberger, who had also been at Buchenwald, visited me yesterday afternoon to pick up a letter from my brother-in-law Ernst Rothmann. They had met each other once in Gross Gaglow. Then my old war comrade, Hanke, came regarding postage stamps, and later Ruth Wolfsohn to pay her tuition, and to report on her family. Her father and her brother were in Buchenwald; the latter was very sick when he got out. Now they have to emigrate as quickly as possible, and it is very difficult to settle accounts on such short notice. Everywhere, fate! I urged her to attend a higher Jewish institution of learning so that she might yet get her Abitur! After all, until November 11 she had been attending the Südlyceum.[7]

Went out for a while with Ruth; this may be the last Sunday that she spends in Breslau. I went with her to the cemetery in the Lohestrasse, where she had never been before, so that she will at least have visited once the place where her ancestors are buried. Her great-great-

---

7. The Südlyceum was a private Catholic secondary school in Breslau.

grandmother, Philippine Hainauer, née Cohn, is buried there. I also explained to her the old gravestones from the thirteenth century, which are embedded in the wall. I told her about how Jewish history repeats itself. As we were walking, I told her that she should always remain true to the spirit of our home, and work on herself. This is now the third time I have talked in this manner to a child on the verge of leaving our inner circle. Very difficult.

Today I heard from Herr Bratmann that certificates may potentially be available for old Zionist fighters. Trudi then called Dr. Hans Prinz, who promised to see what he could do. Naturally this might apply to me; in any case, a glimmer of hope.

Monday, December 12, 1938   Breslau
Today is my 50th birthday; I never expected to see this day.[8] Yesterday, I tried to pour out everything that I feel in a poem. This, after all, represents a large part of a man's life, and in these times. But nonetheless we must remain positive. I received many lovely letters, among them a dear letter from Wölfl, and one from Rosette Ruf. Even a former student, Pepi Holländer, wrote.

The prospects look good for Susanne; we are now trying to get her an immigration permit. She would be going to the country, an hour from Paris, and so she would be able to see Wölfl each week. Rosette Ruf is sad that she won't be coming to St. Gallen, but that would have been difficult in any case. To my great joy, the evening mail also brought a birthday letter from Ernst, which he wrote on November 28 and was stamped on November 30. That the boys write so faithfully, and that my family here at home put so much effort into making this day a beautiful one, that was the best birthday present of all.

Thursday, December 15, 1938   Breslau
I spent some time yesterday afternoon freshening up my English, which can't hurt! It looks like winter is coming in earnest; we will have to cut our expenses, but it will be hard to adjust so quickly at home, particularly since our immediate future is so unclear, and we don't want to do

---

8. On February 17, 1939, the *Jüdisches Nachrichtenblatt*, no. 14, carried a belated appreciation of Willy Cohn on the occasion of his 50th birthday under the heading "From the communities."

things that are unnecessarily unproductive. The most important thing right now is the word we get about our assessment.

Walked home. It is always a shock to see the New Synagogue. Ruth just told me that Mono Czollak has been released from the concentration camp at Buchenwald, and has returned home. I am happy to hear it.

Saturday, December 17, 1938   Breslau

The first evening of Hanukkah. This morning I worked on my box of manuscripts and threw a few things out. This is the time of year when it makes sense to burn things. Delved into decades well before my birth, when my father built his beautiful store with iron determination! Life smiled on us German Jews back then.

Went to synagogue, Shabbat afternoon service; first day of Hanukkah. The men's section was very full, and we all proudly sang the old song of the Maccabees, which has been heard for more than two thousand years and will hopefully be heard for another two thousand. I firmly believe in the future of our people, and in its healthy inner life force. The Jews who pray in our synagogue, and who returned from the Buchenwald camp, all said the Birkat Hagomel, the prayer of deliverance.

Spoke with Tischler, the classifieds representative, and he told me that the *Familienblatt* has been liquidated, that Schatzky sold it. How many Jewish livelihoods are now finished as a result; there will be no renewal of Jewish intellectual life in Germany now that all of the major sources of income have been blocked.

Celebrated Hanukkah in the evening with all three daughters. Trudi held Tamara in her arms. It is my most fervent hope that my family will celebrate this day next year in Erez Israel, in freedom. Whether I can still accomplish that, with all the efforts needed to get ready! Tamara will be five months old day after tomorrow! Susannchen knows all of the verses of "Ma'oz Tzur."

This morning I sent both of my big girls to see Mother. Ruth was able to get half a chicken, and we sent a bar of soap along as well. Unfortunately, I can't do much; I'm short on money right now myself, and I don't know how we are going to get through this. I don't want to ask anyone, either. It is very difficult for a father when he is unable to do what he would like to do, but of course that is also happening to innumerable Jews right now. I think that few of us Jews will escape this mouse trap. Sometimes, a person must push his thoughts aside and bear in mind all of the good things that he has!

Sunday, December 18, 1938   Breslau

I don't think I have yet noted that Curt Proskauer returned home from Buchenwald. His health seems to have been badly affected by it. I called him yesterday.

I went to see Czollak to greet him after his return from Buchenwald. He was in bed because of a nail-bed infection; other than that, thank G'd, he did not look too bad. He is very impractical about his emigration plans. I will help him to the extent I can. Urbach, in Jerusalem, is treating him and Daniel very decently. We have to help each other through these times!

Monday, December 19, 1938   Breslau

Unfortunately, Trudi has to make the rounds of the police this morning about Ruth's passport. First the district station, and then headquarters. She doesn't want me to do it. The matter of Ruth's identity card seems to be going smoothly; she will pick up her passport tomorrow. I don't expect any other problems either. I am always quite anxious whenever one of my children's emigration approaches. But it is not helpful, and I just have to get through it. We must fight against every sort of failure.

Tuesday, December 20, 1938   Breslau

Two ladies looked at the dining room set in the morning; they liked it, but we haven't heard anything further. Separating from every little thing is hard for me, but it has to be done because we must make reductions, and because we can use the income to help us get through the winter. And what, after all, is furniture when we have to send our children away!

Betty Keschner called this afternoon to say that both students, Absberg and Schüftan, had been released from Buchenwald. We are happy about each one who gets out of there with his health. Tischler, the architect, died there, as did many others.[9] We hear about these

9. According to Tausk, the architect and painter Heinrich Tischler (1892–1938) died of a pulmonary infection that he had developed at Buchenwald, in the Jewish hospital in Breslau, only a few days after his release from the concentration camp, on December 16, 1938. Walter Tausk, *Breslauer Tagebuch*, p. 210, along with an appreciation of Tischler.

things only occasionally because there are no more Jewish personal announcements!

Thursday, December 22, 1938   Breslau
Walked into town! On the way there I went to the market and was able to get an orange. You really have to beg to get one, and then buy something else as well. We need an orange for Tamara each day. The world has these things in overabundance; our young people are growing them in Erez Israel, but here there is a shortage. The world is out of kilter. One feels like an alien downtown. The stores are full of people making their final Christmas purchases. We exist outside all that!

Saturday, December 24, 1938   Breslau
Went to synagogue in the afternoon, which is always very full. Later, studied the Torah portion with Daniel, the one in which Joseph dreamed about the fat and the lean years. We then talked about his situation. The University of Jerusalem has given its consent for him to enroll as a student; now the question is how the Mandate government will respond.

Today is the last day of Hanukkah, and Christmas. I want to go to synagogue again. The Christian faithful wish for "Peace on Earth" today; but how far removed is humanity from that ideal! Day after day, the newspaper reports on death sentences carried out in Germany. Peace on Earth! How many Jews died in Buchenwald, or from its consequences. Peace on Earth!

Sunday, December 25, 1938   Breslau
I went to synagogue again yesterday afternoon. It was the last day of Hanukkah, and there and at home we sang the "Ma'oz Tzur" with all our hearts, and if G'd wills it, we will be singing it still in 2,000 years. I, too, made an aliyah.[10] At home, I gathered the family once more around the Hanukkah table and wished them all a celebration in freedom, next year in Erez Israel. Will I still be with them?

The Zwingergymnasium, which absorbed our old Johannesgymnasium, will be moved to the building of the König Wilhelm Gymnasium, which is being dismantled. Also the Bethany and the Luther School, apparently all of them religiously conservative Protestant institutions.

---

10. Cohn means that he was called to the Torah during the service.

Monday, December 26, 1938   Breslau

In the evening, I filled out the various forms that are required to bear the additional names Sara and Israel, which are compulsory for Jews as of January 1, 1939.[11] There is always something to relieve the monotony. If only that were the worst of it!

Wednesday, December 28, 1938   Breslau

In the evening, I had a very upsetting conversation with Trudi in which I divulged my deepest feelings. I told her that it might perhaps be best if she built a future with the children in Palestine, and I would conclude the evening of my life here. The morning mail brought news from Julius Guttmann to the effect that there is nothing at the university. Scholars with an international reputation are given preference. Nor do they have the money. I hadn't expected much else, but this letter, too, confirms me in what I so painfully presented to Trudi yesterday evening. But it is all of no help; we have to call things by their right name!

Thursday, December 29, 1938   Breslau

The morning mail brought a letter from Youth Assistance, that they have not yet been able to commit to Ruth's emigration! I look at this with one tearful and one joyful eye!

It is extremely difficult to decide which payments are the most urgent at the beginning of the month. It is always a miracle how we get by and continue to feed ourselves decently, but it is very difficult. Because I received a reminder, I must turn to the Community for a postponement of taxes, something I do very reluctantly because I am sure that the Community needs every pfennig. It has always been my desire to meet my obligations punctually. – But all sources of income have dried up, and as I said, it is very hard.

Trudi wrote a very skillful letter to Rose Hoffmann, in New York, and asked whether she might be able to do something to enable us to go to Jerusalem. I myself am unwilling to write such letters anymore; I don't want to advertise my services. Machunze, the landlord. Up to now we have had a rental agreement renewable for a year. I wanted to change it to an agreement that could be terminated each quarter.

---

11. This decree was published in the *Reich Law Gazette*, 1938, Part 1 (August 17, 1938), p. 1044.

Machunze was very decent about it; just one word, and he did as I requested.

Saturday, December 31, 1938   Breslau
Yesterday's *Schlesische Zeitung* carried an interesting story about the coordination of Czechoslovakia in terms of Jewish matters. They are doing it precisely according to the German model. All teachers of Jewish extraction have been let go at the German university in Prague; the Nuremberg laws are used as a guideline for this policy. It was quite clear that once Czechoslovakia had been abandoned by the Western powers she would be completely dependent on Germany.

The former attorney Siegbert Kober, who once lived opposite us on the Wölflstrasse, just took his life. He was always a bit unstable emotionally, but unfortunately, more than a few have, sadly, lost their nerve.

Today is again the end of another secular year, and because we live our lives by this calendar, we inevitably look back in our thoughts. This has undoubtedly been the worst year in the history of the Jews in Germany since the Middle Ages. Undeserved? That is the big question! Externally, the world is still at peace because of the Munich agreement. However, 1939 will bring a clash of two worlds, if fascism has not by then already conquered the world, something I believe is not out of the question! It may also bring a sudden reversal; it is hard to predict!

I am going to go to the Hechalutz Office today about Ruth. These days, so many children who were never actively Zionist are being sent abroad on hachshara. If we don't make sure they keep her in mind, she may have a long wait. The children were harassed yesterday while skiing, Ruth was beaten. The children want out.

1. School-leaving exam (Abitur) at the Johannesgymnasium. A photo from normal times when the school was still a paradise of interconfessional tolerance. The school had approximately equal numbers of Protestant, Catholic, and Jewish teachers and students. This photograph was taken at the time of the Abitur, on February 14, 1931, as the date chalked on the door attests. Studienrat Willy Cohn is leaning up against the door. He was forced to retire two years later for political and racial reasons. Photo in private hands.

2. Immediately after they seized power, in 1933, the Nazis set up a concentration camp in the Breslau suburb of Dürrgoy. As an active Social Democrat, Cohn was shocked at how SPD politicians were treated. When Paul Löbe, president of the German parliament, was interred at Dürrgoy, on August 5, 1933, the other inmates were forced to form a gauntlet, and the newcomer was taunted with burning nettles and loud music. From Paul Löbe, *Der Weg war lang. Lebenserinnerungen* (2nd ed., Berlin, 1954).

3. The old tradition of the song festival was co-opted by the Nazis as a pageant to the new German national-racial community. When Breslau held its song fest, in 1937, most of the Nazi bigwigs attended, including Hitler, who basked in the adulation of the masses. Naturally, Jews were excluded from the festivities. On July 30, 1937, Cohn wrote, "A major war has broken out in the Far East; in Breslau, a major song festival! What contradictions, and how little the individual knows about the sufferings of others!" From Friedrich Heiss, *Das Schlesienbuch* (Berlin, 1938).

4. A snapshot from the 1934 Zionist conference at St. Annaberg, Upper Silesia. The speakers are just leaving the conference building. Front row, from left to right: Willy Cohn (Breslau), David Schlossberg (Berlin), and Hans Prinz (Breslau). Cf. diary entry of July 25, 1934. Photo in private hands.

5. The building owned by the Cohn family, at Ring 49, in about 1935. Geschwister
Trautner was on the first floor. The "Aryan" businessman Paul Grzesik rented the
upper floors on January 15, 1934. He bought the entire building on July 12, 1939.
The diaries note both events. Photo: Muzeum Historyczne we Wrocławiu.

6. Willy Cohn's children gave him this photograph on his 46th birthday, on December 12, 1934. It shows Ernst along with Ruth (left) and Susanne (right). Ernst left for Palestine on a Youth Aliyah in March 1935. Ruth followed him in 1940. Susanne shared the fate of her parents. Photo in private hands.

7. Willy Cohn on his way to Palestine, end of March 1937, on board the *Mariette Pasha*. At the time, many Jews were actively exploring emigration to Palestine. Cohn and his wife spent a month with Ernst, who had lived at Givat Brenner for two years. Unable to decide, the couple returned to Breslau, in May. Photo in private hands.

8. Willy Cohn at Kibbutz Givat Brenner, 1937. Photo in private hands.

9. Gertrud Cohn at Kibbutz Givat Brenner, 1937. To visitors, a kibbutz like Givat Brenner might well have seemed like a resort. However, life was regimented and difficult for kibbutz members. Cohn very much wanted to stay; his more practical wife Gertrud, however, doubted that they could adapt to the farming life. She would much rather have emigrated to America. Photo in private hands.

10. After Kristallnacht, on November 9, 1938, about 2,200 Breslau Jews were rounded up and taken to the concentration camp at Buchenwald. Some died; others returned broken men. Cohn expected to be picked up at any moment. His postcard of November 13, 1938, to his son Wölfl, in Paris, was a sign of life, letting him know that everyone was "well." The number 312 means that this was the 312th message that Cohn had sent to his son. In private hands.

11. This photograph was taken when Ruth returned to Breslau briefly, on September 15, 1939, before making aliyah. It was her farewell photo. Not yet fifteen, Ruth is flanked by her sisters Susanne (left) and Tamara (right). Ruth began her Youth Aliyah in Denmark, in 1940. From there she made her way via Sweden and the Soviet Union to Palestine. Photo in private hands.

12. The Jewish school at Rehdigerplatz 3, in Breslau, was built by the Jewish architects Richard and Paul Ehrlich. It contained a private synagogue that was named after the Breslau religious judge (*dayan*) Abraham Mugdan (1840–1927). Cohn loved this synagogue because of its intimacy and orthodoxy. The Abraham Mugdan Synagogue seems to have been overlooked during the *geserah* of November 9, 1938. It was the only synagogue that remained completely intact. Historisches Institut, Universität Stuttgart.

worden.

Über mein persönliches Schicksal: Ich sagte ihr, daß ich immer schlecht für mich habe etwas ausrichten können; er meinte, daß das ans meisten in der andern Welt angerechnet würde. Man solle euch nichts beweisen, was man getan hat. (dies im Bezug darauf, daß ich nicht in Palästina geblieben bin.) Ich begleitete ihn dann noch bis zur Kaiser Wilhelmstraße; nah in der Nähe, dort sagte er mir, daß ich mich stets an ihn wenden könnte, wenn ich etwas Persönliches von ihm wollte. Ich sagte, daß das nicht der Fall sein würde, mir wissenschaftlich. Er dankte mir noch sehr bei meinem Fortgang

13. The diary entry for September 14, 1940, is typical of the thousands of pages that Cohn wrote. In this entry, Cohn reflects on his meeting with Chief Rabbi Leo Baeck. Central Archives for the History of the Jewish People, Jerusalem.

14. No sooner had the architect Paul Ehrlich built the building at Ring 49, in 1902, than the family was forced to commission him to design the family gravesite in the Lohestrasse cemetery upon the death of Louis Cohn (1843–1903). Willy Cohn hoped that this would be his final resting place as well, especially after it became clear to him in 1935 that, "In Germany, cemeteries may soon be the only places where we are wanted!" Photo: Stefan Arczyński.

15. The courtyard of the Schiesswerder beer garden. Along with a thousand
other Breslau Jews, Cohn and his family were held captive in the beer hall itself between November 21 and 25, 1941. They then boarded a train destined for
Kaunas (Kovno), Lithuania. There, on November 29, 1941, all of the Breslau Jews
were shot. This photograph was taken, on April 9, 1942, during the next large
"Jewish action." Again about a thousand Breslau Jews were herded together at
the Schiesswerder beer garden, where they awaited "resettlement." The apparent
peacefulness of the scene is deceptive. The people shown here were deported to
Izbica, near Lublin, on April 13, 1942. Izbica was simply a station on the way to
the extermination camp. From Helmut Eschwege, *Kennzeichen J* (Frankfurt, 1979).

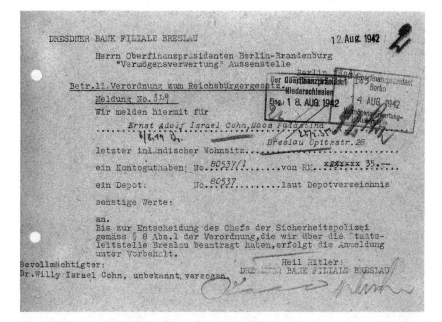

DRESDNER BANK FILIALE BRESLAU   1 2. Aug. 1942

Herrn Oberfinanzpräsidenten Berlin-Brandenburg
"Vermögensverwertung" Aussenstelle
Berlin

Betr.11.Verordnung zum Reichsbürgergesetz.

Meldung No. 319

Wir melden hiermit für

Ernst Adolf Israel Cohn, Haos Palästina

letzter inländischer Wohnsitz... Breslau Opitzstr. 28

ein Kontoguthaben; No. 80537/1 ......von RM. xxxxxxxx 35.--..

ein Depot: No. 80537 ....laut Depotverzeichnis

sonstige Werte:

an.

Bis zur Entscheidung des Chefs der Sicherheitspolizei
gemäss § 8 Abs.1 der Verordnung,die wir über die Staats-
leitstelle Breslau beantragt haben,erfolgt die Anmeldung
unter Vorbehalt.

Bevollmächtigter: Heil Hitler:
Dr.Willy Israel Cohn, unbekannt, verzogen.   DRESDNER BANK FILIALE BRESLAU

16. The assets of emigrated Jews were seized by the German Reich. This also happened to the blocked accounts and stock certificates belonging to Ernst and Ruth Cohn. In 1942, the Dresdner Bank reported to the Gestapo and the German treasury the assets that the bank still held. A copy was sent to Willy Cohn, "moved, address unknown." Cohn, his wife, and two youngest daughters had already been murdered. Archiwum Państwowe we Wrocławiu.

17. After his release from the French Foreign Legion, Cohn's eldest son, Wolfgang
(Louis), joined the British army, in which his brother Ernst, in Palestine, was
also serving. Both were granted leave in January 1945 so they could see each other
again. The photograph shows the brothers (left Wolfgang and right Ernst) in
Rome on the occasion of their first reunion in twelve years. Photo in private hands.

Willy Cohn

(1888-1941)

Historyk i nauczyciel, który jak nikt inny opisał żydowskie życie we Wrocławiu
i niesprawiedliwości doznane w czasie reżimu narodowego socjalizmu. Tym samym
stał się jednym z najwybitniejszych świadków swoich czasów. W roku 1941 Willy Cohn i jego
rodzina zostali deportowani z Wrocławia przez władze niemieckie i zamordowani w Kownie (Litwa).
Ta kamienica, Rynek 49, została zbudowana przez jego ojca,
żydowskiego kupca Louisa Cohna w 1902 roku.

A historian and teacher, who like nobody else described Jewish life in Wroclaw and the injustice
suffered during the National Socialist regime. Thus he became one of the most eminent witnesses
of his time. In 1941 Willy Cohn and his family were deported from Wroclaw by the German
authorities and murdered in Kowno (Lithuania). This building, Rynek 49, was built in 1902
by his father Louis Cohn, the Jewish merchant.

18. In May 2010, when the Zum weissen Storch Synagogue was reconsecrated
and a Polish translation of Willy Cohn's diaries was published, the city of Wrocław
(formerly Breslau) honored the author of these diaries with a memorial plaque. It
was installed at Ring 49, the building that Cohn's father had built for his business.
Photo: Stanisław Klimek.

Hopes for Palestine

Saturday, December 31, 1938   Breslau

The mailman brought sensational news this morning in the form of a letter from Arthur Wiener to the effect that Ernst had visited him, and that Kibbutz Maos had requested an application from us.[1] Ernst went to Haifa specifically to discuss all this with him. Naturally, this occasioned great joy in our home, and there are now many things to write about. I cannot possibly imagine all the details, but it would be wonderful if we could reunite the entire family. Ernst has behaved very well and faithfully, which is only to be expected. Our children remain our best calling card. By the time everything is in place, at least a quarter of the year will have gone by, and who knows what will be happening then. Things look very volatile again today; in particular, the increasingly bad relationship between Germany and the United States will have dire consequences for us, and it is an open question who of the Jewish men remaining in Germany will still be alive and in good health next month. But best not to think about that.

I spent many hours writing to Arthur Wiener, and to Ernst as well, whom I thanked from the bottom of my heart. Later, I went to the Hechalutz Office to inquire about Ruth's emigration. I spoke with Kurt Eisinger. They got together a group of especially dependable children who are supposed to go to England and then to Palestine. When they first arrive in England, they will be housed in a camp under medical

---

1. The British Mandate for Palestine set strict conditions for Jewish immigration. Immigration certificates were issued for the following categories: workers, young people (15–17 years), skilled craftsmen, relatives, capitalists, rabbis, and professionals. Cohn hoped to receive a certificate as a relative, i.e., a parent.

supervision, and then be assigned to individual families who are looking for children. I would have preferred a camp like the one in Wieringen, but we don't have any choice in the matter.[2] On my way back, I stopped in at the North German Lloyd office and inquired about the Messageries Maritimes ships, but the man didn't know much. It probably makes more sense to reserve spaces directly with the French travel agency in Berlin, if it comes to that.

Snow is falling without letup today, and the Aryans are driving off with their skis. Many memories for me. Long, long ago. In spite of it all, I remain attached to Germany.

Sunday, January 1, 1939   Breslau

I had a conversation with Trudi last night, and we glided lightly over more than a few things that happened this year. We also talked about our future in Palestine. The gentleman from the Schenker shipping company will be coming on Tuesday. We were awakened by cannon fire during the night, the usual New Year's Eve commotion; bells rang too.

This morning I asked Professor Wermke, the director of the city library, whether I could continue to use this library. Naturally, this is very important to me.

Tuesday, January 3, 1939   Breslau

A representative from the Schenker hauling company came today for initial discussions about transporting our things to Palestine. He was a very nice gentleman, who also loaded Vogelstein's library for transport to America and Heinemann's to Palestine. Heinemann left last Sunday. And so, what once was the intellectual core of Jewish Breslau is now dispersing. People no longer even come to say goodbye! We hear about departures by chance! It is extremely difficult for me to negotiate these matters.

Friday, January 6, 1939   Breslau

Went to synagogue. It was absolutely full. A large number have returned from Buchenwald, including Sklarz. Ruth and her chaver Günther Holz bought fruit and brought it over to him before Shabbat.

---

2. Between 1934 and 1941, there was an agricultural school (hachshara camp) in Wieringen, Holland, set up to prepare young German Jews between the ages of 18 and 24 for emigration to Palestine.

Daniel came, and we studied the Torah portion in which Jacob blesses his children, and the *haftarah* that goes with it about David's departure.

Saturday, January 7, 1939   Breslau
The morning mail brought a very lovely letter from Frau Borger at Givat Brenner, who is following our fortunes closely! The Hitachdut Olei Germania has 20,000 applications, and it seems highly unlikely that the country will be able to absorb all of them since that comes to at least 40,000 head. We keep hearing about Jewish emigrants who in their wanderings are exploited in other countries. The Schüftans, who live in the house and change their plans from day to day about traveling to one country or another, have now booked passage to Brazil for 2,000 marks each with a ship company that North German Lloyd has told them is dishonest, and they have sent their passports to Paris already. Their passports may be gone by now, and their money as well. This is the sort of exploitation that we have been subjected to since 1492. Everything is working up to a new world catastrophe, for which the Jews will be made responsible.

Monday, January 9, 1939   Breslau
The morning mail brought a card from Libertini, in Catania, with a lovely picture of Aetna. Because we no longer have a telephone, the mail is now our main connection with the outside world. Naturally, since the Jewish newspapers, and so forth, have stopped publishing, our mail has decreased as well.

Nowadays when I go out walking alone and there are so few people I know, I have more than enough time to think. Jews switch their Fatherland so easily; I can't do that. Erez Israel would be a new heimat, but anywhere else would merely be a new *galut*. If only I could earn my keep in Erez Israel to keep myself fed; but I despair of finding that again. I have always been a proud and independent man who doesn't like saying thank you. I would never want to be dependent on some aid committee. Other people make things easier for themselves. Trudi is of a different life force. I am sure I'm a ball and chain to her. I would need greater vitality than what is currently available to me. It is a relief to confide in this book because I often feel very alone. The great *geserah* was two months ago today, on November 9!

Tuesday, January 10, 1939   Breslau

I had a lengthy discussion with Trudi in the evening which went until ten thirty. My sense of fatigue is growing, as is my recognition that I don't fit into these times that no longer need people of my type. There are now red placards on the advertising pillars, announcing fat rations for less well-off people. In bold letters at the top: Jews excluded. And so, life is made ever more difficult for the poorest of our people.

The morning mail brought news from the Palestine Office telling us the number of our parents application. We then filled out the questionnaire, etc.; it is a good thing for us to do something actively, to know that we are making efforts on behalf of our emigration just in case there is a new wave of arrests. Trudi went to the Italian consulate, where they are "well aware" of my work. She also inquired about why she had been asked to appear in the spring of 1938, and they told her that at the time I was being considered for the board of the society, and that the consulate had made exhaustive inquiries about me. But since then, the consulate has heard nothing more on the matter. I wrote at length to Libertini today!

Thursday, January 12, 1939   Breslau

I started to translate my book about Charles I's fleet into Italian yesterday afternoon! It went well, and I enjoyed it greatly. The evening mail brought a letter with an affidavit of service from the hard currency office to the effect that I must now submit another inventory of assets. I am sure that withholding taxes and guarantees are at issue. These things cost us a great deal of work, but there is nothing to do but get through it. And just before, I was engaged in such a very different world.

Saturday, January 14, 1939   Breslau

I went to synagogue yesterday afternoon; it was completely full again. Afterward I walked home with Rabbi Lewin, who now has immigration possibilities in England and is wavering between England and Palestine.

This morning, Trudi and I finished the capital-flight tax declaration, and I took it to the hard currency office. Earlier, I took care of some letters by hand in order to relieve Trudi of the burden.

Sunday, January 15, 1939   Breslau
Today, the newspaper announced that Jews are forbidden to use the city library; I have been going there since 1904 and have always worked there faithfully in the name of scholarship. It will be very hard to get by without a library. Still, I have a substantial collection of my own that will stand me in good stead.

Monday, January 16, 1939   Breslau
The newspapers are raising a hue and cry about the lack of new intellectual blood. That's how it is! Well, that's not our worry anymore! I have an article about "the intellectual baggage carried forth by Jewish emigrants" all composed in my head. Perhaps I can dictate it soon. Met Rosenstein, the teacher; he will soon be emigrating to Holland. Another one who was held in Buchenwald.

Tuesday, January 17, 1939   Breslau
Went to the mailbox. Talked to the Helfgott boy; the family is going to go to Shanghai as England isn't taking Jewish boys anymore, only girls. The boys are said to have behaved badly. Sad!

Wednesday, January 18, 1939   Breslau
Spent several hours yesterday morning in the fresh air with Trudi and Tamara. We met my former colleague, Frau Lebek, Jewish by race. At the former Johannesgymnasium she always acted as if she were Protestant; now she shares the fate of the Jews—and her children as well: "He punishes the children for the sins of the parents to the third generation"!

Czollak was good enough to visit; he wanted to tell me about a potential opportunity. Apparently, a camp is being set up in England to house 300 old Zionists. Needless to say, I don't feel much enthusiasm!

Today is the anniversary of the founding of the German Reich and the coronation day of the Prussian kings! We have certainly lived through much history. What has there ever been that was not once magnificent and exalted that did not decay and pass away! Now we are living aside from the history in which we once played a leading role! Fate passes over us all; we must find the understanding to bear it. Today there is a melancholy rain; inside, I am feeling lonely, withdrawing ever more into myself.

Thursday, January 19, 1939   Breslau
Went to the Palestine Office, where I spoke with Herr Waldstein, who
was very nice. He will try to find out whether anything can be rescued
of my pension. If possible, they want to support my claim from here. It
would be wonderful if we could arrive not completely without means.
Everything is in turmoil. It was a good thing I went there because they
gave me some advice that will make it easier to negotiate the legalities
surrounding my assets.

Friday, January 20, 1939   Breslau
I met my former colleague Freund in the morning; he seems a broken
man. After November 9, they carried broken glass by the hundredweight out of Mugdan, the store that belonged to his wife and son. He
hasn't heard anything since December from his eldest son, who is in
China. Originally, he went to Hankow, which was then occupied by the
Japanese. – Fates. Emotionally, these Jewish Christians have it especially
bad, but that is Nemesis or the punishing hand of G'd. Dentists have to
stop working on January 31; I assume that a similar regulation will affect
doctors soon! Economically, things won't look good for the Proskauers
when that happens! But there is nothing I can do to change it!

The newspaper brought news that Professor Andreae has died! There
was a lengthy appreciation in the *Schlesische Zeitung*. He was treated
badly enough during his lifetime and never accorded a real livelihood.
That is often the fate of scholars. He was always very nice to me! Back
then, he asked me to write a biography of Brann for the *Schlesische
Lebensbilder*.[3]

Saturday, January 21, 1939   Breslau
Rabbi Lewin will soon set off on his aliyah; if G'd so grants, he will be
leaving with his spry 70 years. – Studied with Daniel the portion from
the Prophet Isaiah that is being read on Rosh Chodesh today. The

3. Rabbi Marcus Brann (1849–1920) had since 1891 taught history at the Jewish Theological Seminary in Breslau. In addition to his research on the history of
Silesian Jewry, he published *Germania Judaica* and the journal *Monatsschrift für
Geschichte und Wissenschaft des Judentums* [Monthly Journal of the History and Science of Judaism]. See Willy Cohn, "Marcus Brann," in *Schlesische Lebensbilder*, vol. 4:
Schlesier des 16. bis 19. Jahrhunderts, Namens der Historischen Kommission für Schlesien,
ed. Friedrich Andreae et al. (Breslau: Priebatsch, 1931), pp. 410–416.

text of the passage was fairly difficult. In the evening, I discussed our financial situation with Trudi, who urges us to scrimp. Perhaps we will again rent out a room.

Sunday, January 22, 1939   Breslau
Ruth went to the Hechalutz Office again. As she just told us, there was a young man from Berlin there who asked whether her parents would be opposed if a closed group set off on hachshara to Sweden or Holland. We certainly wouldn't be against that!

Tuesday, January 24, 1939   Breslau
There is no wood at the moment; Mother doesn't have a single stick in the house. Eggs are a rarity; a great delicacy now. Coffee is also extremely scarce. But on the other hand, we have oranges and tangerines again. Apparently, no hard currency is available; the only business that gets conducted occasionally involves barter transactions. Germany has been pretty much blockaded economically.

Wednesday, January 25, 1939   Breslau
Trudi went through the dining room yesterday afternoon and sorted out the old things that we certainly won't want to take along if we make aliyah. Breakable things can be put to better use here. I try not to live as if departing so that I can accomplish the intellectual work that is my life.

Thursday, January 26, 1939   Breslau
I must see how I will deal with life, and as a G'd-fearing man I must, like Job, continually take up the battle anew. But I am often so indescribably tired, and I would be happy if I were at the end. I often beseech G'd to let me go in peace to my eternal sleep. Nonetheless, I will have to carry on. I no longer feel the power within me to build anew. The hopes of my family now reside in my children, who will continue when I am no longer able. It is a bitter thing, but I intend to be honest in this book.

Among other things, the evening mail brought an inquiry from the Palestine Office. They are beginning to make efforts on behalf of the veteran fighters, the *vatikim*, opening a pathway to get out. I think, though, that for me all this will come too late because of the reasons I have stated. My tired body belongs with my ancestors in the Lohestrasse.

I read a deeply disturbing report about ships with emigrating Jews passing through Port Said on their way to Shanghai. They called it a voyage unto death. I myself thought something similar, and I did whatever I could to prevent people from traveling to Shanghai. But it happens to be the only country on earth with no visa requirement![4] If Jews had done more for Palestine earlier, it could now take in more of them.

Friday, January 27, 1939   Breslau

At Herr Perlhöfter's I met the former director of the Museum of Fine Arts, Dr. Wiese, who was also a very good friend of Friedrich Bloch, of blessed memory. Until recently, the couple had lived together. Talked to a lot of people. Feilchenfeld, Fräulein Dr. Weil, Frau Cohn, née Marcus, the secretary. She told me that again today someone had been arrested by the Gestapo who had booked passage to Shanghai and then changed his mind. Of course, it is stupid to do that because many people were released from Buchenwald on the explicit understanding that they would leave for Shanghai. Except in cases like that, I am against emigrating there.

Today the advertising pillars are full of *Stürmer* posters inciting against the Jews: "The Jewish problem not yet solved." Supposedly, they intercepted a letter from a Jew in Jerusalem to a Jew in Cosel, in Upper Silesia, threatening vengeance against the German people. It looks as if a new action is in the offing!

Saturday, January 28, 1939   Breslau

Went to synagogue in the afternoon, then walked home for the last time with Rabbi Louis Lewin; he will set out on his aliyah tomorrow. I will without a doubt miss him very much! We had much in common. He can be very pleased that he was still able to do it at the age of 70. He will see what he can do for me when he arrives.

I was awakened by loud music after I had already fallen asleep. The SA on the march. Apparently a victory march celebrating the fall of

---

4. While Shanghai did not require immigration visas, Germany did require visas to leave the country (see entries for February 12 and March 11, 1939). Nonetheless, approximately 17,000 Jews had emigrated to Shanghai by the summer of 1939.

Barcelona. Say what you will, it seems that fascism, or better said, the nationalist idea, is on the march everywhere.

Today I received a very nice letter from Rose Hoffmann in New York, who is working on behalf of our aliyah. She has done everything that she could to get me a certificate as a "research fellow." I answered her accordingly, but it is always problematic pouring such a letter into the right mold. I don't want to overwhelm her with requests, but everything has to be borne in mind. I then sent an application to the Palestine Trusteeship Office about transferring my pension.

Sunday, January 29, 1939   Breslau
We keep hearing about new material difficulties raised for people seeking to emigrate. Now people are only allowed to take one place setting of silverware per person. By the time it is our turn, we won't be able to take along much, but this is the bridge one must cross over to get out. That is the least of my worries, though; other Jews get so upset about these things!

Monday, January 30, 1939   Breslau
I applied to Jewish Youth Assistance in Berlin as a teacher. Hedwig Bermann conveyed farewell greetings from Bruno Schwarz, who is going to Capetown. He's considered a remigrant there. Spoke with the wife of Stadtrat Frey on the street. She looked especially unwell, as do many of our people. She and her husband will be following their children to Brazil.[5] I also met Ellguther, from Glatz; even these old people want to get out! Everyone is trying to get out, but how many of them will ever reach a safe harbor?

The newspaper carries stories about the misery of the Spanish refugees trying to get over the border to France. These people are barely able to save their lives, the arm of vengeance at their backs! Eventually, people simply become indifferent to the misery on this earth; the heart simply cannot comprehend it all.

---

5. Apparently, the Freys were unable to flee to Brazil as Stadtrat Hugo Frey died in the Gross-Rosen concentration camp, in 1944. See Isabell Sprenger, *Gross-Rosen. Ein Konzentrationslager in Schlesien* (Cologne: Böhlau, 1996), p. 186.

Tuesday, January 31, 1939   Breslau

Trudi took apart a tailcoat of Franz's to make a winter dress for herself! I felt each rip. But perhaps he would have understood the need to make something useful out of it.

The *Morgenzeitung* carried a big speech by the Führer yesterday, much of which dealt with us again and was, of course, extremely sharp.[6] There was—unfortunately—much in what he said that I must agree with. We are harvesting more than a few things that we sowed, and the incitement abroad is making matters even more difficult for us. I can understand that the German people needs living space, and if that living space had been granted, this enmity toward the Jews in Germany would never have developed.

Wednesday, February 1, 1939   Breslau

Trudi went to the Palestine Office about a letter from Rothschild, in Basel, which I received yesterday. I must avail myself of every possibility that offers itself to get to Erez Israel, at least for the family. I continually try to shore up the will to live in others; in me it is completely extinguished. I want to get my family safely to Erez Israel, and then join my ancestors in the Lohestrasse. All I want is that my children and my books and my students bear witness to me. I myself am probably done for.

Saturday, February 4, 1939   Breslau

I wrote a letter to Trudi in the afternoon in which I presented my position; however, we are still so far apart, and it is questionable whether we will ever reconcile, or at least not in the foreseeable future.[7] This, too, I must bear. I wasn't able to do any translation today, but I was able to help others!

6. Cohn was referring to Hitler's notorious Reichstag speech, on January 30, 1939, in which he threatened the "destruction of the Jewish race in Europe."

7. The Cohns' marital relationship was stretched so thin by worsening conditions, their differing religious and political views, and their attitudes toward emigration that Willy Cohn was now communicating with his wife in writing. In several passages, Cohn referred to Trudi as "my wife," an indication of emotional distancing.

Sunday, February 5, 1939   Breslau

No mail from Ernst today either. I am very anxious to hear from him because I am very worried about his welfare. There must be a reason why he doesn't write, but I am completely powerless, sitting in my armchair, waiting. I have aged terribly over the past few weeks. Fräulein Silberstein told me, among other things, that Herr Bielschowsky didn't want me for the orphanage because I am intellectually superior to him.[8] One reason after another.

Monday, February 6, 1939   Breslau

I was rewarded this morning. I received a completely normal card from Ernst, dated January 26. He went to see Arthur Wiener again, who wrote me at the same time. The application has been sent, but at the moment there are no certificates. I am most deeply grateful to G'd for this mail! I wrote a long letter to Arthur Wiener thanking him for everything. He is a faithful friend. That must serve to compensate for much else!

Tuesday, February 7, 1939   Breslau

Last night I dreamed that I was reading the *Historische Zeitschrift* again, and I was sitting on a horse. Wishful dreaming about a now nonexistent world! Trudi went to see Waldstein about the Basel certificate, but that won't be easy to get anymore either. The parents application is still the safest route.

Wednesday, February 8, 1939   Breslau

The newspaper today published, among other things, a speech by Rosenberg, in which he stated that the Jewish problem will only be solved in Germany when the last Jew has left the country.

Thursday, February 9, 1939   Breslau

With Susannchen, I accompanied her friend Eli Feilchenfeld home; the boy was quite naughty. The things that children talk about these days! The boy said that they have made some progress with their emigration. Yesterday, Ruth was punched in the stomach by a Hitler Youth boy; foolishly, she didn't immediately report the incident to a Schupo.

---

8. Cohn was apparently hoping to be hired by the Jewish Orphanage, a position that went to Martin Bielski.

Friday, February 10, 1939   Breslau
Of all the German despots, Rosenberg is currently the sharpest in his incitements; apparently, he said, among other things, that even Alaska is too good for us.

Sunday, February 12, 1939   Breslau
This morning, the mail brought a relatively favorable letter from the Paltreu, to the effect that it will be possible to salvage my pension through the Haavara if we have the certificate in hand.[9] Naturally, this would give our aliyah a completely different financial footing. That would be a stroke of good fortune.

People are having terrible difficulties. Every time they think that they are about to leave, there are new obstacles. Helfgott wants to go to Shanghai; he has two tickets, but now he doesn't have a visa for China. The *Jüdisches Nachrichtenblatt* reported that Woburn House has received 25,000 applications for temporary residence in England.[10]

Friday, February 17, 1939   Breslau
Tormented by nightmares again. Among other things, I dreamed that I had been sent as the cardinal's representative to a conclave in Rome, and I didn't know whether or not I had voting rights. A strange dream!

Now to go visit Daniel to say farewell before his aliyah. He is leaving on Monday from Trieste, on the *Galilee*, the same ship that Ernst took four years ago. This time, Rabbi Moses Hoffmann will be going along with many from the Breslau Youth Aliyah. I am more and more alone. Daniel told me that Jerusalem University approved five scholarly certifi-

9. Paltreu was the abbreviation for Palästina-Treuhand-Stelle zur Beratung deutscher Juden [Palestine Trust Office for Advice to German Jews]. The Haavara Agreement, signed on August 25, 1933, between the Zionist Federation of Germany, several other agencies, and the German regime, was a transfer agreement designed to help German Jews emigrate to Palestine. Part of the agreement was that Jews gave most of their assets to Germany, which could then be repurchased as German exports.

10. All Jewish newspapers were banned after Kristallnacht. The *Jüdisches Nachrichtenblatt*, however, was permitted to continue as the semiofficial organ of the Reich Association of the Jews in Germany until July 1943. However, it was largely limited to announcing new Nazi laws and decrees for the Jewish people.

cates, one of which Lewkowitz will be getting. However, the Mandate government has not yet consented. My farewell from Daniel became fairly difficult; intellectually, he gave me a great deal. He was always a good friend. Who knows whether I will ever see him again.

Sunday, February 19, 1939   Breslau
The *Jüdisches Nachrichtenblatt* had a very nice item on the occasion of my 50th birthday written by Fritz Günther Nathan.[11] I was very pleased!

Saturday, February 25, 1939   Breslau
Now, all objects of value owned by Jews must be turned over, sold to pawn offices within fourteen days.[12] It is one thing after another, but even that wouldn't be so important if I were able to build a new life with my family in peace and in health in Erez Israel. Worldly goods don't mean much to me; the things that are truly valuable are in oneself.

Tuesday, February 28, 1939   Breslau
Trudi went to the Glogowskis to the farewell party for the Mandowskys, where all their best acquaintances met. Most of them are getting ready to leave. Frau Viktor, from Hindenburg, who is not yet 35 years old, received a chalutz certificate, and she can take her children with her. The Foerders are still waiting for a parents application! Trudi just told me about all of their experiences packing, etc. It's important after all.

---

11. The brief item in the *Jüdisches Nachrichtenblatt*, no. 14 of February 17, 1939, p. 7, reads as follows: "Recently, retired Studienrat Dr. Willy Israel Cohn celebrated his 50th birthday. Born in Breslau, he studied in Breslau, Heidelberg, and Munich, obtaining his doctorate in 1910. Dr. Cohn, who enjoys a reputation as a meritorious teacher, dedicated himself to fostering awareness of the Jewish cause even as a young teacher. In addition to his work in Jewish journalism and scholarly journals, he also published a number of studies of Jewish medieval history and of the history of the Jews in Silesia. As a lecturer at the Jewish House of Teaching and the Jewish Theological Seminary, his audience had ample opportunity to appreciate his love for the Jewish people and for Erez Israel, which remains a guiding principle of his Jewish ideals."

12. On February 21, 1939, all Jews were ordered to surrender within two weeks any object in their possession made of gold, platinum, or silver as well as those containing jewels and pearls. This decree was of a piece with others that forced Jews to give up their automobiles, telephones, radios, among other things.

Wednesday, March 1, 1939   Breslau

Alice Friedlaender had some interesting things to tell. The Gestapo made all sorts of concessions to her father, Raphael Friedlaender, if only he would stay. They even wanted to give him a pension; but he rejected all of it. His departure will be a heavy loss for us Jews in Breslau because I doubt we will be able to find anyone able to continue his work. Nor did he get much thanks from the Jews, only insults and attacks.

Friday, March 3, 1939   Breslau

As I was getting ready to leave, Dr. Mende from the Reimitz broker-age house came to see me about the sale of the building at Ring 49. A knowledgeable man, Dr. phil., student of German and English litera-ture. I discussed the building situation with him; perhaps he will be able to find a buyer. I told him that given our prospective emigration, we were hoping for a certain haste.

Saturday, March 4, 1939   Breslau

Susannchen is seven years old today. The child is my heart's consola-tion and my sunshine. I cannot imagine ever separating from her. In any case, Susannchen had a very nice day; she is now at the "Storch," to hear the *megillah*.[13]

This evening a hachshara transport will be leaving to go abroad, taking, among others, my student Schatzky. It is really happening, via Vienna to the Promised Land. They are now trying to bring as many young people into the country as possible! Everyone considers himself lucky, even if he arrives without assets other than courage and health!

Tuesday, March 7, 1939   Breslau

Met Frau Muhr; she is waiting for a capitalist certificate from Palestine. Everyone is waiting. Went to the police station to certify that I am still among the living. I had to wait a long time, but I was well treated. To the bank; then met Hugo Mamlok, who told me that Hanne Brienitzer left after all, the previous Monday. They fit her in at the last moment.

---

13. Evidence that services had been resumed at the Zum weissen Storch Syna-gogue after its devastation on Kristallnacht.

Thursday, March 9, 1939   Breslau
Bought two small things for Trudi at food stores. Buyers and sellers alike are complaining! The scarcity of lard, butter, and margarine are hard on consumers. The scarcity of coffee is also being felt; coffee is sold only in the smallest quantities once per week. Recently, cut half and half with grain coffee. Germany is supposedly no longer getting coffee from Brazil because it was reselling the coffee it got to Yugoslavia. Naturally, I have no idea what is true. The sellers have to listen to all sorts of complaints from their customers. Reminiscent of 1917. There are plenty of eggs at the moment. I am noting these things only because they may be of interest in the future.

Friday, March 10, 1939   Breslau
This morning, I started to read the Torah portion about the Golden Calf, which seems to fit nicely with having to surrender my valuables.

Saturday, March 11, 1939   Breslau
Spoke with all sorts of people at the synagogue; the Helfgott family will not be going to Shanghai; as stateless people they can't get a visa for China, and since they have no visa they cannot get a French transit visa. Jewish fates. Walked home with Rabbi Erno Hoffmann; I will try to study Gemara with him, something I want to familiarize myself with.

Sunday, March 12, 1939   Breslau
Went to see retired Amtsgerichtsrat Laskowitz, whose advice I wanted about whether to apply to the authorities yet about transferring my residence abroad. After due consideration, we came to the conclusion that I shouldn't, but wait until the certificate arrives. It may not be a good idea to draw their attention too soon. Laskowitz, who has to report to the Gestapo each month, wants to get out. Emotionally, he finds reporting to them very difficult. One face after another is disappearing from our circle!

Monday, March 13, 1939   Breslau
Herr Schimbach visited at quarter to, quite despairing because he isn't making any headway with his aliyah. His residence permit expires on March 31, and he missed the deadline for applying for an extension. Now he is full of the darkest thoughts, and it was all I could do to comfort him somewhat.

In the afternoon, Ruth brought home bad news: the *Galilee*, carrying 800 persons, went aground off of Crete. Apparently, no one was hurt; everyone was taken on board another ship. Hanne Brienitzer was on that ship as well. May G'd grant that nothing happened to her. It is really tragic; people have finally made aliyah, and now this happens.

Wednesday, March 15, 1939   Breslau
I'm awaiting the mail today with particular urgency because I am somewhat anxious about Wölfl. Of all the things that fate burdens us with, this waiting for mail is among the most difficult. There is a rumor going around that private Jewish libraries are being inspected for undesirable books. It would be terrible if my book collection were to be torn apart in this manner. But, like much else, we just have to wait and see.

Thursday, March 16, 1939   Breslau
Today's newspapers report that the invasion of Bohemia went peacefully as planned, and that the Führer has already entered Prague.[14] Thankfully, there have as yet been no complications of an international sort. However, I see black for the Jews in Bohemia. Their enmity toward Germany will be repaid! Politically, a situation has been created in Bohemia as it existed for millennia, and an unnatural state has disappeared.[15]

Trudi wants very much to leave, but I see so little future for myself! Perhaps I should really make the trip to the Palestine Office, in Berlin, to try to do something in person, but then again, my bad relationship with Trudi's family holds me back. I don't want any upheaval, but per-

---

14. In violation of the provisions of the 1938 Munich Agreement, Hitler had occupied "rump Czechoslovakia" on March 15, 1939, and on March 16, he proclaimed Bohemia and Moravia a German protectorate.

15. Cohn exaggerated somewhat. The Kingdom of Bohemia was part of the old Germany for only a few centuries. Most German emperors had, from the fourteenth century to the dissolution of the Holy Roman Empire of the German Nation in 1806, simultaneously been kings of Bohemia. Like many Germans and Austrians, Cohn, too, viewed Czechoslovakia as a construct of the Versailles Treaty, an "unnatural state." Bohemia contained a very large ethic-German population.

haps I am not acting as I should and not thinking enough about the future of my family. In fact, many are much more active than I; I fit very poorly in these times.

Saturday, March 18, 1939   Breslau
Raphael Friedlaender and his family, who are setting out on their aliyah tomorrow, came for dinner. It was a cozy Friday dinner in our dining room, which we heated for the purpose. We sang "Shir HaMaalot," and Herr Friedlaender led the prayer. Lovely, when a family is able to say that they are leaving together, and that this is their last Shabbat in the *galut*. After dinner, Herr Friedlaender and I spent some time by ourselves in my study. He told me about his last trip to Holland and England, which brought him together with important Jewish personages. His entire life revolves around working for Jewish emigration and for the well-being of the Jews, and he intends to continue in this endeavor there as well. In spite of his 58 years, he is much more fit than I. The evening ended with a big argument after the Friedlaenders had left. Once again, Trudi and I were of different opinions. Trudi constantly tells me that I need to go to Berlin about our aliyah, but I cannot and do not wish to be with her family.

Sunday, March 19, 1939   Breslau
Trudi is separating out the silver that we are permitted to keep, all Jewish things from these times. But that isn't the worst. I just heard on the radio that the synagogue in Brünn is burning, and that people have been arrested. It was to be expected that the same things would happen there, and that many of our people would suffer.

Now for some more pleasant news: the 500 chaverim and chaverot who went on hachshara abroad have arrived safely in Palestine and will certainly be useful in building the country. Many of our acquaintances are among them. Young, happy people!

Tuesday, March 21, 1939   Breslau
Trudi demands that I go to Berlin regarding our aliyah; I will simply have to do it tomorrow, even though I dread it because I would have preferred to avoid seeing Trudi's family. But that is of no help; I must not be accused of having neglected a duty involving the future of my family.

Wednesday, March 22, 1939   Berlin, Meinekestrasse 10[16]
I arrived here yesterday afternoon, and after telephoning, my father-in-law was waiting for me at the Charlottenburg train station. I am staying with him at Xantenerstrasse 20 V.

Had a long conversation with Dr. Pick, and I was treated very well in every respect. We will be given preferential treatment and, with G'd's help, will receive a certificate during the summer, a C certificate.[17] All of the work that I have done has actually been recognized here. Now I am waiting to hear about Ruth. Negotiated with Youth Assistance about Ruth; she will be placed in a preparatory camp, and certified from Germany.

Dr. Pick also strongly advised me against applying to transfer my residence abroad for the time being. I was very satisfied with our discussion. Against expectations, everything went well.

Saturday, March 25, 1939   Breslau
I reported everything in detail to Trudi yesterday; I was unable to go to synagogue. Went into town with Trudi, Susanne, and Tamara to have photographs taken for our identity cards. The photographs have to be taken such that the left ear is visible because that is where criminal characteristics reside. Neither Tamara nor Susanne need to be photographed yet. On the way, met Rosenfeld, the director, who said goodbye to me. He will be emigrating to Shanghai within the next few days. Met Ilse Häufler, who will be leaving with her mother for Palestine by packet steamer on Monday, from Hamburg.

Monday, March 27, 1939   Breslau
Trudi went with my old war comrade Hanke to the pawn office to surrender our valuables. A large number of Jews were there, and they had to stand in rows. The young official issued commands in the new German tone. They didn't give us money right away; we will be noti-

16. At this time, the Palestine Office and other Zionist associations were housed at Meinekestrasse 10.

17. The category C certificate was for workers and employable laborers. However, it also included Zionists who had performed meritorious service. Cohn always expected that his services to the cause would be recognized in this manner, and so he was understandably pleased with this recognition.

fied in three weeks, and then we can come in and exchange our receipts for cash. Some of us will have a very hard time separating from these things, particularly from objects used for religious purposes. I couldn't bear looking at the individual pieces; some of them had been in our family for a very long time, and we prayed so often before these Friday evening candlesticks.

Dresdner Bank. The children have now received papers from the bequest, and I gave an order to sell for 1,000 marks so that Trudi could purchase a few things. Over the past few years we have been able to buy very little.

Thursday, March 30, 1939   Breslau

While visiting Mother, I heard that Father's only living brother, Moritz Cohn, who is over 80, just emigrated to Argentina with his wife Emma, née Dorndorf! His children are living there.

At the bank, I sold the children's papers in the amount of 1,000 marks so that Trudi can now make some purchases which we had continually postponed. I also permitted myself a pair of slippers.

Friday, March 31, 1939   Breslau

While looking through my coin collection, I found an old silver goblet that Father had received for his 50th birthday, and which Mother later gave me. Now it, too, has found its way to the pawn office; today is the last day to surrender these items legally. I have done everything correctly. Parting with this goblet, which my father was given on his big day, was very hard for me. But all that is of no help; I have had to part even from some of my children.

Saturday, April 1, 1939   Breslau

At night, pleasant Friday evening with tin candlesticks that we borrowed from Frau Freund. Whether silver or tin, it makes no difference.

Met Herr Nathan, the father of Fritz Günther, who is now in Jerusalem and is doing well. He is attending a Seder at the Heinemanns'. Met old Professor Gutwein on the way home. He has always been very devoted and has shown great interest in how we are doing. In addition, met Lux, the attorney, who will be making aliyah in mid-April. A former student, whose name I don't recall, said goodbye to me. He will be setting out on Hachshara B next week.[18] Of Ruth's friends, Mira Cohn will be making Youth Aliyah.

Tuesday, April 11, 1939   Breslau
The mail brought confirmation of a certificate from the special section of the Palestine Office. Now we will slowly have to turn our remaining possessions into liquid assets. I was given a special honor today at the synagogue as I was permitted to carry the Torah. Maskir, stirring; we also prayed for the victims in Erez Israel, and for the victims since November.[19] Director Abt spoke; but even though his words went straight to the heart, we know so much that is unfavorable about this man that even the most beautiful words fail in their intent.

To our great joy, the evening mail brought a letter from Ernst, which we had long awaited. He writes full of satisfaction about the growth of the settlement! They already have 150 people. They are beginning to harvest now.

Wednesday, April 12, 1939   Breslau
Spoke with Lewkowitz, whom I hadn't seen in five months. He, too, complained about Dr. Kober of the board of trustees. Apparently, all he thinks about is how to get out. I have always hated such egocentric thinking.

On the way home met a former student, Egon Goldschmidt, who is getting ready to go to Cuba. Recently, during the summoning action, which was conducted street by street, he was summoned to the Gestapo, where he was treated quite roughly. But as he tells me, he responded forcefully. The interesting part was that the official said that his intentions toward him were good, and that he should get out of Germany as quickly as possible before the next action. It is possible that he was just saying it.

18. Hachshara B was another name for Alyah bet, also referred to as "special hachshara." After Kristallnacht, the Reich Association of Jews in Germany tried to get young people to Palestine on old ships that they had rented. These attempts at immigration, which bypassed British Mandate quotas, often failed.
19. Maskir is a prayer recited in memory of the dead in the German-Jewish tradition. The term commonly used outside that tradition is Yiskor. Cohn actually uses both words interchangeably in his diaries.

Thursday, April 13, 1939   Breslau
Picked up the photo identity cards this morning. Met Director Gabriel, who was very solicitous, asking about each of us. Went to the Hamburg-America Line office to get information about our trip to Palestine. The route via St. Gallen, Paris, and Marseille will probably remain just a fantasy. Messageries Maritimes isn't accepting payment in Reichsmarks anymore. The nice official told me it was quite improbable that we would ever be permitted passage through Switzerland to France. We might conceivably travel with the German Levant Line and perhaps talk with Wölfl at a French port. But that is far in the future.

Saturday, April 15, 1939   Breslau
Yesterday evening we ate the first *eshkoliot* in remembrance and in our hopes for Palestine. Susannchen extinguishes the candles every Friday. It is so adorable to watch how she covers her eyes with her cute little paws. An interesting item in the *Jüdisches Nachrichtenblatt*. Because of the shortage of manpower, Jews are to be put to work again—but separated from the rest of the workforce—probably on the roadways. It will do some of them good to do physical work, thereby preparing them for emigration!

Monday, April 17, 1939   Breslau
Yesterday, Trudi and I took our first trip. It was also the first time since our trip to Palestine that we have set foot in a train together. We were received warmly in Schweidnitz. I was shocked when I saw the place where the synagogue once stood. In addition, the Community had to pay 3,000 marks to have it torn down. Schweidnitz is also one of the few communities where even the cemetery was destroyed; the mortuary had to be dynamited and the stones knocked down. Even women were arrested. We then took a tour of Schweidnitz and its magnificent parks. Passed the Friedenskirche, which commemorates the peace treaty that ended the Thirty Year War.

Tuesday, April 18, 1939   Breslau
Went into a number of stores asking for apples because Tamara needs them, but except for bananas there is no fruit to be had in the entire city. In one store I was told that these are hard times.

Wednesday, April 19, 1939   Breslau
Hedwig Bermann told me about an article in *Das Schwarze Korps* to the effect that the Jewish problem could be solved in sixty minutes if only Roosevelt minded his own business.[20] Supposedly, the Americans responded that they already have enough Germans.[21] Had an argument with Trudi about purchases for our emigration! I think that we should stop buying. Who knows when we will get out, and we must continue living here for the time being.

Thursday, April 20, 1939   Breslau
The *Jüdisches Nachrichtenblatt* reported on a change in the policy on certificates. In contrast to practice up to now, the High Commissioner for Palestine has set monthly quotas, and about 1,000 persons will be permitted to immigrate in April. At the moment, Hachshara B is creating problems, and the ships are apparently unable to dock. Then, there was another pleasure in the form of a circular letter from Rudolf, in Melbourne, who also addressed a few lines to me.[22] It was infinitely painful that he never even said goodbye to me when he left. In any case, I can now write to him.

Saturday, April 22, 1939   Breslau
In the morning, I took care of correspondence as usual, then I put my Hebrew library in order again, something that was well past due. Recently, I was given a number of machzorim and siddurim with family entries.

20. *Das Schwarze Korps* was the weekly battle organ of the SS. The newspaper was published between 1935 and 1943 and served to glorify Hitler's elite organization.

21. Presumably to go up against the Nazis.

22. In fact, Cohn wrote immediately to his brother, in Melbourne, and Rudolf responded warmly to him in his next circular letter, dated June 30, 1939. This is the only circular letter to the family in Breslau that has survived.

Commission from *Germania Judaica*

Sunday, April 23, 1939   Breslau

Wrote a letter to the Institute for the Science of Judaism; they have asked me to write for *Germania Judaica*.[1] Had a bad night; I experienced my own death and said the prayers offered for the dead.

Curt was just here; he asked my advice about his emigration problems. He has lost his nerve a bit; in the near future they want to go to England. In some Jewish circles there is also apprehension about the Reichstag session on April 28. This no longer scares me. Everything is happening as it must, and there is no sense in making decisions in panic.

Monday, April 24, 1939   Breslau

Took the streetcar to police headquarters, where I was ordered to appear at 7:15 about the identity cards. Things went fairly quickly and painlessly. One of the officials was somewhat abrupt and brusque. They also fingerprinted me like a criminal, and because I had to sign for Susanne and Tamara, I had to sign 15 times. They did not want to fingerprint my children. I'm feeling a bit numb, otherwise I would have gotten upset at this humiliating procedure.

---

1. This marked the beginning of a scholarly engagement that Cohn pursued until the end. By the fall of 1941, he had written approximately eighty articles for this planned encyclopedic reference work, of which all have disappeared with the exception of an article titled "Breslau." See also, Norbert Conrads, "Die verlorene *Germania Judaica*. Ein Handbuch- und Autorenschicksal im Dritten Reich," in *Berichte und Forschungen. Jahrbuch des Bundesinstituts für Kultur und Geschichte der Deutschen im östlichen Europa* (Munich: Oldenbourg Wissenschaftsverlag, vol. 15, 2007), pp. 215–254.

Tuesday, April 25, 1939   Breslau

Met Fräulein Hoffmann, the daughter of the rabbi who emigrated, whom Rose Hoffmann asked us to look after. Of her family, she alone remained behind. Her father is in Petah Tikvah. Warnings are going out from Erez Israel at the moment about the so-called Hachshara B. Transports are being turned back, or the people are arrested. Our return to the land of the Jews is not being made easy.

Wednesday, April 26, 1939   Breslau

I have received a firm commitment for several articles for *Germania Judaica*, and another for a Lag BaOmer day. I enjoy such varied activity; intellectual work helps me to forget!

Coffee is now extremely scarce, to be had only in the smallest quantities much like during the continental blockade.

Thursday, April 27, 1939   Breslau

Frau Häufler and her daughter Ilse, Ruth's friend, tried to get to Palestine by Hapag steamer, without a certificate! The girl was given a certificate en route, but her mother was not permitted to step ashore. She is now adrift in the Mediterranean. She certainly can't come back here.

Saturday, April 29, 1939   Breslau

We received notification from the pawn office that we may pick up our compensation for the valuables that we delivered up. Because it had to be done today, on Shabbat, I walked to the pawn office, where I was given 102 marks, surely only a fraction of what it was worth, but still better than nothing. At my family's urging, I immediately used the money to buy things that I need: a pair of shoes, two pairs of socks, a suit with two pairs of pants. In fact, all of my things are fairly shabby as it has been years since I have bought anything for myself. I don't place much value on my external appearance even though I probably should. And then, I don't like frequenting these stores, which no longer employ Jews. But this is of no help. The best thing to do really is to spend the money on some clothing so that I won't have to buy so much later on.

On the way home, I ran into Machunze, our landlord, who always likes speaking with me. He has several enemies in the house, and so he cannot risk renting empty apartments to Jews. Everyone has his own fears.

Sunday, April 30, 1939   Breslau
The Feilchenfelds bid us farewell yesterday; in the evening they went to Riga, in Latvia. Even with all of the goodbyes that one has to deal with these days, this one was especially difficult. He is a guileless soul, the sort of person I like being with. And Susannchen is losing a good friend, their son Eli. Later, the Feilchenfelds will probably emigrate to Erez Israel via Riga. And so our circle is getting smaller by the day.

Friday, May 5, 1939   Breslau
Telephoned Waldstein at the Palestine Office. He thinks that there is now no purpose in going to Berlin as there are no certificates available from the April allotment. He is hoping for May—those certificates have not yet been issued. I am to call him in ten days at the latest.

Saturday, May 6, 1939   Breslau
The mail brought a particularly lovely letter from Wölfl, which included a letter especially addressed to Ruth. Regarding our aliyah, he thinks that because of Tamara we should take the most convenient route, as much as he would like to see us. The letter was in every respect a great joy.

   This afternoon, Hedwig Bermann was here regarding her affairs. Among other things, she told me that the wife of the late consul Smoschewer had taken her life. She did not want to join her children empty-handed—as if everything always revolves around money! It is sad when people lose their nerve like that!

Tuesday, May 9, 1939   Breslau
Hedwig Bermann came to see me this morning extremely distraught. Early in the morning, she had been summoned to the Gestapo to report on the state of her assets. However, she couldn't because her accountant and tax advisor always take care of these matters. She now has to furnish that information by three o'clock.

Wednesday, May 10, 1939   Breslau
The implementing provisions to the new rental laws for Jews have now been announced. Landlords will have to register their Jewish renters in order to afford an overview of the community. This law won't have any immediate consequences for us.

Saturday, May 13, 1939   Breslau

Czollak will soon be going to a camp in England, and his wife is tearing her hair out about whether or not to take furniture along to Palestine. Went to synagogue in the evening; it is now no longer so full. Many are now going to the Storch Synagogue, and in addition so many have left.

Tuesday, May 16, 1939   Breslau

Walked into town with Trudi and then rode back. She wanted to look at the stores and see what sorts of goods are still to be had. The question is whether we should buy now. If our aliyah falls through and we have to stay here for any extended period of time, then we will need the money. These things cannot then be sold! Perhaps we will find out this week!

The remains of the New Synagogue are now being torn down. The enormous plaza is boarded up on all sides so that no one can watch. Supposedly, they are working day and night. I don't know whether this is something that the Jewish community will have to pay for. A place for me so rich in memory!

Wednesday, May 17, 1939   Breslau

A letter arrived from Rudolf in Melbourne, which I will be receiving by way of Erna. Everything in this world is so scattered. Economically, Rudolf is having a very difficult time in Australia; we have been reading about this in the *Jüdische Zeitung*, too.

Monday, May 22, 1939   Breslau

Anita Lasker, one of Ruth's last friends, was here for dinner. A very pretty and graceful girl; she wants to be a cellist.[2]

Trudi returned from the Palestine Office with rather unfavorable news. It is now very doubtful that we will get a certificate. Waldstein told her that no certificates for *vatikim* have been released.[3] None of the April certificates went to Germany. May certificates have not yet been distributed. Waldstein views the entire situation as rather precarious

---

2. Lasker's cello saved her life by making her useful to the concentration camp administration. See Anita Lasker-Wallfisch, *Inherit the Truth, 1939–1945: The Documented Experiences of a Survivor of Auschwitz and Belsen* (New York: St. Martin's, 1996).

3. Cohn hoped to get one of the immigration certificates for meritorious Zionist fighters (*vatikim*). Cf. diary entry of December 11, 1938.

and thinks I should try to go to England. Trudi agrees, whereas I am unwilling to go to some other country and live the life of a beggar.

Because I had not yet sent a letter to Wölfl, I added a note asking him to look into possibilities for Susanne, even though I cannot imagine separating from her! I really don't know what is the right thing to do.

Tuesday, May 23, 1939   Breslau

Went to synagogue in the evening to say Kaddish: Franz's yahrzeit. With his death, I not only lost a brother but a very good friend. First we studied Tehillim; between Mincha and Maariv Abt lectured about the prayers. Intellectually, he did a very nice job! Nonetheless, I don't like him, but I learned a few things.

Wednesday, May 24, 1939   Breslau

Went to synagogue in the evening, the first day of the Feast of Weeks. The synagogue was beautifully decorated in green. In our apartment, Susannchen decorated the *mezuzot* beautifully. She is an observant child; on the other hand, I cannot get Ruth to go to synagogue at all. She has now received her call to go to Winkel, and she will leave at the beginning of June.[4] This farewell, too, will be very hard on me.

Dr. Mende from Reimitz's office called in the afternoon. Grzesik has received approval for the buying price from the Regierungspräsident, and he is anxious to conclude the agreement. Too stupid that this dumb real estate transaction had to come today of all days. I hope that Dr. Reimitz will settle the matter. All of the things that keep circulating in my head!

Thursday, May 25, 1939   Breslau

Ruth spent the afternoon packing with Frau Rinka Cohn! The customs officials were very friendly, but they looked closely at each item! Frau Cohn does not yet have a stamp to reenter Poland. I often get things mixed up in this book, but sometimes the flurry of details is too much.

---

4. The Winkel estate near Spreenhagen, in Brandenburg, was originally the country home of the Jewish Schocken family. After 1931, it was used to train chalutzim. Starting in 1933, under the leadership of Martin Gerson (1902–1944), Winkel became an agricultural preparatory camp for young emigrants. It was dissolved by the Nazis in 1941. See Ilana Michaeli and Irmgard Klönne (eds.), *Gut Winkel—die schützende Insel, Hachschara 1933–1941*, Deutsch-israelische Bibliothek 3 (Munster: LIT, 2007).

Whit Sunday, May 28, 1939   Breslau
Yesterday spent a good deal of time writing for *Germania Judaica*; organized everything that needs to be said about Silesian towns in general. I spoke with Police Inspector Heinrich at Sauerbrunn in the morning; he is always anxious to hear my opinion about the situation. The "District Air Command" is now housed in the old Schottlaender Castle, in Hartlieb. What a transformation!

Easter Monday, May 29, 1939   Breslau
I turned my attention to the Silesian Piasts yesterday afternoon. For *Germania Judaica*, I have to take the general historical circumstances into account. Ruth's friend Anita Lasker came over in the evening. She brought her stamp album with her, and I pasted a large number of my duplicates in it for her, and in return she gave me one that I didn't have yet. The two girls then went for a walk, and I was worried because they were gone so long.

Thursday, June 1, 1939   Breslau
Rode to the Cathedral Archive, where I now have permission to work on *Germania Judaica*.[5] Very nicely received by Professor Nowack, the director of the Diocese Archive.[6] How happy I was to work once more in a scholarly setting. How resplendent the cathedral island is in its summer magnificence.

Friday, June 2, 1939   Breslau
I heard from Fräulein Silberstein that Jacobi, the former probationary teacher who made things so difficult for positive Judaism at the Am Anger School, is now an editor in Jerusalem. This upset me greatly because it is so unjust. I simply don't understand how to maneuver myself into the foreground, and I will probably never make aliyah. I'll just have to live with it. But such things are really painful. At the mo-

---

5. Ever since being barred from using the city and other libraries, on January 15, 1939, the Catholic diocese library was the only one open to Cohn. He had received permission to use it on May 21, 1939, and he began working there for the first time on June 1. Until his deportation, the diocese library in Breslau and the adjacent archive served as both his scholarly and social refuge.

6. Professor Dr. Alfons Nowack (1868–1940), spiritual counselor, 1918–1939, director of the Diocese Archive.

ment, the matter of certificates is very unfavorable overall, and I should not expect to be called anytime soon!

Friday, June 2, 1939   Breslau
I worked for several hours in the Diocese Archive this morning, where I feel very comfortable and found much material for *Germania Judaica*. I haven't been to this part of the city for a long time, and much has changed in town. The big government building on the Lessingplatz is approaching completion. Large transports with "illegal" immigrants have been stopped before reaching Palestine. What is especially bitter is that these are all subtracted from the number of certificates so that hardly any certificates will be made available in Germany for the foreseeable future!

Sunday, June 4, 1939   Breslau
Ruth is out today with her friend Peiser. Tomorrow, the leader of the Werkleute, Marianne Lasker, is going to England, and one of her friends, Illa Guttmann, is also going to England as a so-called guarantee child.[7] Ruth's circle of friends is getting ever smaller!

Monday, June 5, 1939   Breslau
This morning I was able to work undisturbed for several hours in the Diocese Archive, for which I am grateful every day. Doing this work, I forget all my cares. Left with Dr. Jedin at twelve thirty, when the archive closes, and accompanied him as far as the indoor swimming pool.[8] Talked about general problems.

---

7. After Kristallnacht, British Prime Minister Chamberlain and leading Jewish figures in England agreed on a campaign to save Jewish children from Germany. The Jewish community in England pledged 50 British pounds as a guarantee for each child. Hence the term "guarantee child."

8. Hubert Jedin (1900–1980) qualified as a lecturer at Breslau University in 1930, but lost his permission to teach (the so-called *Venia legendi*), in 1933 because his mother was Jewish. From 1936 to 1939 he worked as an archivist in the Diocese Archive in Breslau. Under the protection of the Vatican, Jedin was able to go to Rome, where he began the work that made him one of the leading Catholic Church historians. His autobiography was published posthumously: Hubert Jedin, *Lebensbericht: mit einem Dokumentenanhang*, ed. Konrad Repgen (Mainz: Matthias Grünewald, 1984).

Tuesday, June 6, 1939   Breslau

Ruth rode to the train station this morning; Marianne Lasker is emigrating to England, for now![9] The girl is not yet 19, but firmly committed to becoming a chalutz and marrying Kurt Eisinger. Sometimes, young people know exactly what they want.

Wednesday, June 7, 1939   Breslau

Rode with Ruth to the cathedral island. She has not yet taken in consciously as an adult the beauties of our city. I also took her for a moment into the consistory of the Kreuzkirche. Completely awed, she asked whether we were even permitted! Worked for several hours in the archive and gathered much lovely material. But when you have been writing for three quarters of an hour without letup, you get a little soft. They are so very nice to me there. Professor Nowack and I spent a good deal of time today discussing Hermann von Salza. The Archive of the German Order, in Vienna, is now also in the hands of the state.[10] I really am extremely grateful for permission to work here.

9. Marianne Lasker (1920–1952) was the eldest of the three Lasker sisters. Some of Anita's letters to Marianne, in England, are reprinted in Anita Lasker-Wallfisch, *Inherit the Truth*, pp. 21ff.

10. Prof. Nowack told Cohn that the Nazis had even begun to confiscate Catholic archives such as the Archive of the German Order. This news greatly affected him because he had done a good deal of scholarly work on the German Order, also known as the Teutonic Knights.

Ruth's Departure

Thursday, June 8, 1939   Breslau
Ruth says that Curt Proskauer and his son Paul are in Berlin today; one of them races here, the other there to get tickets to Shanghai! What insanity! I have no influence. Curt and his not so fine son are responding to fear alone! Erna sacrifices herself for that boy, and he is so horribly self-centered. I must push these matters from my mind! I have nothing but bad luck with my surviving siblings!

The second mail brought Ruth's call to go to Winkel; she has to be there on June 14. Of course, she is very happy at this turn of events. I'm making the separation very difficult, after all she is the third child to leave home. But none of this is of any help: the future of the children is more important than a father's heart!

Sunday, June 11, 1939   Breslau
Ruth made the rounds to say goodbye; the Proskauers and Brienitzers gave her all sorts of things! People were very nice to her everywhere! Ruth also told Paul Proskauer exactly what she thought of his passivity; but that is no longer our problem! They have given up on their crazy Shanghai plans; now they are waiting to hear from America. Then Frau Cohn, who is returning to Poland on Tuesday, came by. Because the consul refused to give her a Polish reentry visa, these poor people will be forced to cross the heavily guarded green line, an extremely hazardous undertaking. The German border police have agreed to this; no one knows how the Poles will respond. Manhunts in the twentieth century.

Monday, June 12, 1939   Breslau
Worked in the archive. Dr. Jedin, who has been so helpful to me in my work, is a non-Aryan by family history, and so he was stripped of his

Venia legendi, in Cologne.[1] His maternal grandmother is buried in the cemetery in Münsterberg! His mother was baptized in the crib; these are also fates. In Germany he is considered a Jew, but in England he was denied a position because he is considered German. He hopes to obtain a position in Rome, at the Vatican.

After the archive closed, he took me up to his apartment on the Domplatz; he has a magnificent library, with a particular focus on the history of the Council of Trent. – Trudi prepared a special lunch for Ruth's last day. Last meal, Ruth called it sardonically.

Tuesday, June 13, 1939   Breslau

Ruth just left the house, and with her a piece of my heart. She has really proved herself, particularly during the past few months when Trudi no longer had household help. Just like her brothers, she will do honor to us in the world. And so, our home becomes ever lonelier; but the happiness of our children must be our only goal. It is hard nonetheless. Trudi prepared everything calmly and with discretion, and yesterday afternoon brought her baggage by car to the train station. Ruth is spending the night in Berlin, and if G'd wills it, will continue on to Winkel tomorrow.

Sunday, June 18, 1939   Breslau

A Jewish couple from England has been in Breslau to ascertain the situation of the Jews for the Jewish aid committees in England! I am told they were particularly taken by the children's Hebrew singing in our Jewish school. They then promised the children that they would be brought to Palestine as soon as possible!

Sunday, June 25, 1939   Breslau

Spent the afternoon outside with Susannchen. Sometimes, a person is granted insight into the soul of a child. She tells me, "Most of the children play with me, but two children won't. They know that I'm a Jew!"

Monday, June 26, 1939   Breslau

Rode to the cathedral island in an open streetcar; the morning was especially beautiful. Worked hard in the archive for several hours; looked

---

1. Hubert Jedin actually obtained his *Venia legendi*—and had it revoked—in Breslau.

through much important literature. Because Dr. Jedin keeps giving me the latest journals, my work is in no danger of being outdated. While I am excerpting, it is interesting to see the various people who come and go. The cathedral night watchman came in to get a few books today. He praised his former Jewish doctor, Feige, who is supposedly better than more than a few of the Catholic ones. Talked with Jedin on the way home. He has been helpful to me in every way. After all, he bears a similar fate.

Wednesday, June 28, 1939   Breslau
An important letter from the pension certificate department of the Palestine Office arrived with the afternoon mail. They want our personal information by telegram or telephone, but because Herr Schüftan happened to be going to Berlin, I gave him the letter, and Trudi will surely have received it yesterday evening. Up to now, the pension department had turned down a certificate for us; just how I finally get a certificate is of no concern to me. It is a good thing that Trudi is in Berlin right now and can take care of the matter.

Friday, June 30, 1939   Breslau
Phoned Trudi yesterday. She is very diligent and takes care of these details much better than I would. We will presumably get a pension certificate. She plans to visit the Palestine Trust Office about the pension transfer. I wouldn't have been able to do all that.

Saturday, July 1, 1939   Breslau
Yesterday I received a lovely letter from Ruth; she has done so well in Winkel that they are sending her to Palestine in September. She is very happy about that. This time, I'm not making matters so difficult for myself because we may be arriving there at about the same time. Waited for the "money mailman," who paid me my pension for July. Worked at the archive; because of Dr. Jedin's kindness, I discovered a number of Silesian towns in a document of Charles IV that had Jewish populations of which I had not been aware. Stefan Brienitzer also came by to say goodbye; he is leaving for Scotland early next week.

Trudi just sent news that the pension certificate has been approved for me personally; however, it is not yet clear how Trudi and the children will be dealt with! In any case, a monumental step forward, and for this I am very grateful to Trudi. An enormous turning point lies before me, and even though I am happy at the thought of reuniting with my children, the greatest happiness in the world, I would be dishonest if I did not acknowledge in this book that leaving Germany, which I have always loved, will be very hard for me.

Sunday, July 2, 1939   Breslau
Yesterday, I began drafting my first two articles for *Germania Judaica*; gathering all of the material is the hard part. But I enjoyed it, and then the writing was easy!

Wednesday, July 5, 1939   Breslau
Received a long letter from Trudi. She took care of everything at the Palestine Office, in Berlin; it is always stressful and somewhat upsetting to do these things! Sent an application to the school administration for permission to transfer my residence to Palestine. A decisive step. The mail brought confirmation from Paltreu that they will transfer my pension. This is enormous progress.

Thursday, July 6, 1939   Breslau
Went to the board of the Fraenckelsche seminary in the morning, where I received some very important articles by Brann. Handed in my key; another chapter come to an end.

Saturday, July 8, 1939   Breslau
Yesterday morning was very pleasant and productive; I was able to finish two articles for *Germania Judaica* and made considerable headway on my lengthier article about Neisse, in Upper Silesia. A letter from Trudi, which was certainly well intended, gave me much to worry about. The pension certificate only covers two persons, and Trudi thinks that I should leave with Susannchen. I'm sure that her offer is intended to be very generous, but I rejected this course of action in a detailed letter. I don't feel up to it. Nor do I want another tear in our family! Perhaps a way out will present itself.

Sunday, July 9, 1939   Breslau
Curt Proskauer, Erna, and their son flew to Milan via Berlin. Ate lunch with Susannchen; when I arrived home I found very unpleasant news. The English consulate will not give me the pension certificate if the

issue of Susanne and Tamara is not cleared up. I immediately sent Trudi a letter by special delivery and asked her, if she thinks it useful, to stay in Berlin one more day and do whatever she can to facilitate our aliyah! Such things never go smoothly! In any case, the news really affected me. Even our child is now talking about certificates of nonobjection. I told her that they are playing games, and to leave these matters to the grown-ups!

Wednesday, July 12, 1939   Breslau
The building was sold yesterday evening in the presence of notary Kenhardt, Tauentzienstraße 2; Alice Halle had arrived from Berlin and was brought directly from the train station to the office by car.[2] I didn't much like the notary, whom I don't know, nor actually Dr. Reimitz, less even than I did from his voice on the telephone. The most decent person in the room was the buyer, Grzesik.[3] It took a fairly long time because everything had to be discussed, and then a clean copy drawn up. I find it hard to bear the behavior of these people of the other race, their cheerfulness, which stands in such stark contrast to our suffering. Saying goodbye to this building, each stone of which I saw being set, was very difficult for me. But that is now of no help.

Friday, July 14, 1939   Breslau
The second mail brought a very loving letter from Wölfl. He needs a health certificate for Susanne, and immediately. I took care of it and sent it to him by air mail in the evening.

2. In the expectation that he and his family would soon be emigrating to Palestine, Cohn accelerated the sale of his parents' building at Ring 49, which housed Trautner.

3. This judgment was probably colored by his relief at having the matter over with. In fact, Paul Grzesik was one of the profiteers who benefited from the policy of Aryanization in Breslau. Earlier, he also managed to get his hands on a company owned by the manufacturer Ernst Schwerin, who had left in 1938.

Coercion and Seduction by the Gestapo

Sunday, July 16, 1939 Breslau
At the request of the Gestapo, I am to take part in a discussion with
Dr. Arlt about matters concerning Jewish history. This can easily cost
me my aliyah because if the police use me to research the history of the
Jews, I will have a hard time getting a passport. But I will just have to
wait, and I will write to the Community about it. It is most inopportune that this is occurring just as our aliyah might be granted.[1]

Monday, July 17, 1939 Breslau
Worked in the archive again, primarily excerpted for *Germania Judaica* from the German town book. Discussed a number of scholarly
and other matters with Dr. Jedin. He is of great help to me, and I
am able to gain access through him to a number of things that might
otherwise escape me. I even hope to find primary sources for my book
on lien law.

---

1. This marked the beginning of Cohn's brief involuntary stint helping the State
Office for Race and Clan Research. This office was directed by Dr. Fritz Arlt, a
member of the SS and a Gauamtsleiter, who played a very shady role in Poland and
in Breslau. It is unclear whether Cohn fully understood Arlt's deceitfulness. In the
later diary entries, when he referred to Arlt, it was because he thought Arlt might
protect him from the Gestapo. At the time, the State Office for Race and Clan
Research was consulting on how to manage the certificates of Aryan descent. But
at the same time, it was compiling an "alien race" file with "important documentation for racial measures to be undertaken in Silesia." See Heinrich Tewes, "Die neue
Gausippenstelle Schlesien," in *Schlesien—Volk und Raum*, Vierteljahresschrift (July
1938), p. 130.

Wednesday, July 19, 1939   Breslau
Many letters; among other things, I had to send an application in triplicate to the Reich Ministry of Education for residency approval. Yesterday, our neighbors the Schüftans packed their property for emigration to Chile in accordance with customs regulations. Things went very well; one of the older customs officials was there, and he didn't make things hard for them. The *Jüdisches Nachrichtenblatt* announced yesterday that there won't be any certificates this winter because of the many illegal immigrants. In the situation that the Jewish people finds itself, a very bad decision indeed.

Thursday, July 20, 1939   Breslau
Fräulein Silberstein was here for dinner, as was Anita Lasker, who brought a very lovely poem that Ruth had written on her hachshara! This gave me at least a little insight into their lives at Winkel since Ruth writes little, which I can understand given all the many things she must absorb. Once we have raised our children, they just slip away.

Saturday, July 22, 1939   Breslau
Yesterday was a horrible day. Terrible upsets, with Trudi as well. Arrangements for additional payments to the Palestine Trust Office so that we can at least take Tamara with us. To the bank, where I spent an hour negotiating; then came Dr. Latte, whom we had selected as our foreign currency advisor. We found a possible way out, namely if we can use the boys' money that was placed in blocked accounts, we may be able to take Susanne with us. I cannot even imagine separating from the child.

Regarding yesterday, I must add that I was summoned to the Gestapo in the morning in the context of a so-called "street action." They wanted my family's personal information to the extent that they are registered in Breslau, and then he asked, "When are you emigrating?" I told him that my son had applied for me. "How long could that take?" I replied, "A few months." "You can go home now," he said. The whole matter took a few minutes.

Sunday, July 23, 1939   Breslau
I went for a short walk; we are no longer permitted to sit down in the Hindenburgplatz. All the benches have signs reading, "Forbidden to Jews."

Wednesday, July 26, 1939   Breslau
Yesterday was an extremely strenuous day for me. I had a three and a half hour discussion with Herr Dr. Arlt of the State Office for Race and Clan Research, at Teichstrasse 24, the former Catholic workingmen's hostel, which had been closed for reasons of "uncleanliness." I dictated a lengthy typewritten note about it, so I won't go into it here. I was treated very properly, although one can never really know where the fly in the ointment might be. I then assembled all of the materials that I had promised Herr Dr. Arlt, and he gave me his word of honor that he would return all of it.

Friday, July 28, 1939   Breslau
Worked in the Cathedral Library; told Dr. Jedin about my discussion with Dr. Arlt. Went to the wedding of Moritz Kalischer and Meta Kohn at the Wochentagssynagoge.[2] This was the first time that I've been in the little Storch Synagogue.[3] Pakulla sang beautifully. Reinhold Lewin, whom I hadn't heard in more than 21 years, spoke very correctly, but somewhat distantly.

The evening mail brought a very loving and devoted letter from Wölfl, about which I was very happy. He is very confident about Susanne, but if things work out with Palestine, we will of course take her with us.

Monday, July 31, 1939   Breslau
This morning was a fairly strenuous but also interesting morning. At seven thirty met with Dr. Arlt and his secretary, Frau Kuhl, on the Holteihöhe, where I gave them an introductory lecture. Later, we drove through Breslau by car, about which I will dictate a report. Then to his office in the Teichstrasse, where I worked with him and his graphic artist. A morning like that is difficult because each word must be carefully weighed.

2. Literally "Weekday Synagogue." It was a prayer room in the administration building adjacent to the Am Anger Synagogue, which was destroyed 1938. After Kristallnacht, it was used by the Gestapo.

3. The so-called Kleiner Storch was a prayer room located in the first floor of the community center in the Wallstrasse, immediately adjacent to the Zum weissen Storch Synagogue. It continues to be used by the tiny Jewish community in what is now Wrocław, Poland.

Thursday, August 3, 1939   Breslau

Dr. Arlt and Herr Schubert picked me up at seven thirty. We first drove by the Jewish Gymnasium, which I talked about, then to the piece of land in the Menzelstrasse, where a synagogue might perhaps once have stood, then the hospital and the Jewish buildings there, the Lohestrasse cemetery, where I made a special point of discussing the older portion! Lassalle's grave, near which a final resting place was being dug for another exhausted Jewish wanderer. It was a somewhat melancholy tour. I also showed him the memorials for the Jews who fell victim to the enemies of Germany! Both gentlemen were very appreciative! Then back in the office, I worked through the list of city councilors and discussed a number of other things as well, about which I will dictate a report tomorrow!

Monday, August 7, 1939   Breslau

Yesterday morning I began dictating an article: "The significance of the Jews for the book trade in Breslau." The topic was chosen by Dr. Arlt. The material is fascinating; it will be published in book form.

Tuesday, August 8, 1939   Breslau

Dr. Arlt asked me to come in and see him; in his office I ran into my former student, Kienitz, who is working there. He has since earned his doctorate at the technical university and wants to qualify as a university lecturer. It is always strange to meet a student under such completely different circumstances, but in some ways he seemed completely unchanged. I went through the Jewish associations with him, and then with his secretary, Frau Kuhl, after he had left. He asked me whether it would be all right for him to put another person in the room with us. I told him that I considered it doubly desirable because I would not want to be left alone in a room with an Aryan woman.

Returned home exhausted. Fräulein Silberstein was there; she brought us the so-called municipal certificate of nonobjection, one of the most important documents needed for emigration. Then Herr Tiemann came from the Bohne company, to which we will consign our things to be transported. It will cost a minimum of 3,000 marks, but we want to do all we can to salvage my library. Trudi will have to take care of the details.

Received a letter from Dr. Latte, to the effect that it is still unclear whether Paltreu will issue the necessary certificate for the English consulate.

Friday, August 11, 1939   Breslau
Received an inquiry from the Oberpräsidium regarding my application to the Reich Minister of Education to have my residence transferred to Palestine. Taking care of this matter cost me a good deal of work; new difficulties keep arising, and I cannot imagine that we will be finished with it by October 1.

Anita Lasker and Edith Miedzwinski were here in the evening. Anita brought me stamps; she had also received a letter from Ruth. I then tried to listen to the radio through the wall; the Führer was speaking, and even though I couldn't understand everything, it was clear that the foreign policy situation is very dangerous.

Monday, August 14, 1939   Breslau
Took both children to Dr. Latte; this was the first time that Tamara had ever ridden in a streetcar. There I met Dr. Kloss, who used to work at the museum and now works in a state office charged with receiving works of art.[4] At least I was able to have an intellectual discussion for half an hour, a very rare pleasure. Then discussed immigration questions with Dr. Latte. Actually, things don't look that unfavorable given that Paltreu has certified that the 10,000 marks are guaranteed, so that we should be issued a certificate in the near future. This is a giant step forward. Now we have to make the various applications and fight for the finances. This will all take a lot of work, and even though we have the certificate, we won't be able to leave without permission from the Reich Ministry of Education. I can't risk leaving without it because then I would lose my pension.

Wednesday, August 16, 1939   Breslau
Yesterday was an especially difficult day, but also a nice one in some respects. Dr. Arlt picked me up in his car shortly after seven thirty. We

---

4. Although the art historian Ernst Kloss was not Jewish, he was a constant guest at the Latte home. He committed suicide when the Red Army entered Breslau. For more on Kloss, see Peter Schneider, *"Und wenn wir nur eine Stunde gewinnen . . ." Wie ein jüdischer Musiker die Nazi-Jahre überlebte* (Berlin: Rowohlt, 2001), pp. 21 and 66f.

drove to his office in the Teichstrasse, where we worked mainly on an index of Jewish associations in Breslau. Naturally, our conversation lit upon other things as well. Among other things, he had made inquiries about me with a number of university historians, who told him approximately the following: Cohn isn't like other Jews who copy everything from others. Rather, he has enriched scholarship by his own research. Of course, I'm flattered to hear such things. But these hours have been quite stressful; it is unavoidable that our conversation will stray into volatile border areas, and then one has to think about each word so as not to say something stupid. But mainly, it seems to me that complete frankness will achieve the most. Among other things, Dr. Arlt told me that it is important to him that my wife and I leave well provided for.

Saturday, August 19, 1939   Breslau
I had it out yesterday with one of the officials at the post office regarding my reply coupon. He claimed that I already had one; I told him that I haven't had one in almost two months, and that an old soldier doesn't lie. And so he gave me one. Those are the small battles.

Monday, August 21, 1939   Breslau
Things look very martial out in the Scheitnig section of Breslau. A column of automobiles just raced through the Scheitnig star; trucks with steaming field kitchens requisitioned from the province of Saxony, all on their way to the Polish border. The *Breslauer Neueste Nachrichten* writes that Danzig and the Polish corridor question must be resolved in favor of Germany. From what I saw in Scheitnig, it felt as if an attack were imminent, but apparently there was no attack during the night. Had a conversation with Dr. Kloss outside, later worked with Dr. Latte on my emigration; drafted a response to the school department that is under the Oberpräsident.

Tuesday, August 22, 1939   Breslau
Once again, the political situation looked very threatening in the *Abendblatt*. In Poland, "conditions are untenable," terror has become intolerable, and all the other phrases that we remember so well from when the Sudeten German area was occupied. I cannot say whether the decision will be made for war or for peace, but what is certain is that

this unresolved situation cannot long endure. As far as Ruth's Denmark matter is concerned, I have decided to let her go with her group. It cost me tremendous internal struggle, but it is probably best for the child's future, and my own desires recede in significance. Nor am I at all certain that our own aliyah will be settled quickly.

A massive realignment has occurred in our politics. What some had long presumed has now occurred. An agreement has been signed between Germany and the Soviet Union, initially in the area of trade policies, although a nonaggression pact will follow! And so, Poland will have to bend to German will, and perhaps there will now be progress in pacifying the world.

Wednesday, August 23, 1939   Breslau
Instead of his usual seven thirty, Dr. Arlt came at eight o'clock. I had to wait for quite a while. We then drove to the university in his car, and I had to climb the many stairs to the University Archive. There I met Dr. Kowalik, whom I recently saw incognito in the Cathedral Archive, where he is working on the Silesian book of documents.[5] I certainly get into the oddest situations. I didn't let him know that I had seen him before. I took an immediate dislike to the man, a very fussy gentleman!

I also got to know a very pretty young girl named Sawade, 19 years old, about to take her Abitur at the Victoria School. She had already examined the index file of lecturers for those of Jewish origin, and my task was to supplement her work. I discovered a host of other ones; however, we will need another session to finish up. Perhaps we will go through the student files as well. I had them look for my own card. I never thought that I would ever have access to this material! To our joy, the evening mail brought the binding preliminary notification about the 10,000 marks.

Friday, August 25, 1939   Breslau
The second mail brought an outrageous postcard from Rabbi Brilling, in Tel Aviv, in which he rebuked me for taking over the article about

---

5. Cohn incorrectly spelled his name Kowallek. After Friedrich Andreae's death, Dr. Alfred Kowalik was named head of the University Archive. He had received his doctorate with a dissertation about the history of Breslau. Alfred Kowalik, *Aus der Frühzeit der Breslauer Tuchmacher* (Breslau: Brehmer & Minuth, 1938).

Silesia for *Germania Judaica*. I set him straight on the matter.[6] Dr. Latte came by. It is always hard to get rid of him quickly. He brought one piece of good news, namely that the Paltreu has now approved the sale of stock. Nonetheless, in view of the current situation, we may not want to sell any time soon.

6. Apparently, Brilling had been given this work prior to his emigration from Breslau. See Robert Jütte, *Die Emigration der deutschsprachigen "Wissenschaft des Judentums." Die Auswanderung jüdischer Historiker nach Palästina 1933–1945* (Stuttgart: Franz Steiner, 1991), p. 20 fn. 20.

The Outbreak of the World War

Saturday, August 26, 1939   Breslau
Yesterday morning I worked in the University Archive with Fräulein Sawade, about which I have written my own notes so that I need not spend much time on it here. It was a very pleasant collaboration. The girl grasps things quickly. Hedwig Bermann came by. I feel very sorry for her; unfortunately, she isn't making much headway with her money matters or her emigration. The woman has gotten into the wrong hands.

The streets are now very much dominated by the military, and the sound of airplanes continues into the night. Up to now, I still believed in peace, but the way it looks today it seems rather likely that this slim thread of a possibility will break. Some things I do not even dare think about, such as the possibility of being completely cut off from the children, and what will become of the boys!

Sunday, August 27, 1939   Breslau
We prepared supplies for the cellar yesterday evening, only the bare necessities in case we have to go downstairs: spirits of ammonia, absorbent cotton, cookies for the children! – Such times.

Monday, August 28, 1939   Breslau
I spent yesterday afternoon thinking through the article about Silesia for *Germania Judaica*. The city continues to be at peace except for the schools, which have been turned into barracks. Nonetheless, everyone feels that something is in the offing. Yesterday, our neighbor, Frau Fulde, who is in charge of organizing air raid precautions, rang. From now on, rationing will be introduced for the most important necessities just like during the world war! We seem to be heading toward an eventual war economy.

No patriotic enthusiasm is evident on the streets as there was in August 1914. Rather, it seems as if people are silently despairing. No non-local or foreign mail was delivered today either; train traffic has apparently been reduced to a minimum.

Tuesday, August 29, 1939   Breslau
The morning mail brought a lovely letter from Ruth, which I had been expecting. I constantly wait for mail from one of my children. She is, thank G'd, doing well; naturally, they are sitting by the radio listening to reports. I went to the police station to have my signature certified so that she can get a passport. The political situation continues to be clouded; we hear that the question of war and peace will be decided within 24 hours.

Thursday, August 31, 1939   Breslau
Herr Grünmandel told me that the churches in Oppeln have been cleared out to make way for soldiers. I heard the radio here and there, but nothing certain. News of terrorist acts by Poles have become a daily staple! It appears that rail traffic between Danzig and Poland has been cut.

Then I had to go to the Jewish Community about Susanne's possible emigration to England. Naturally, we need to wait to see whether we will be able to emigrate to Palestine; matters do not look unfavorable at the moment because I have also received a certificate from the tax office that I need for the Oberpräsident! But all that takes a back seat to the general situation! Things still look very dangerous. Poland has mobilized fully and blocked all traffic in the corridor. Nonetheless, we must continue in our private lives as if nothing were happening. Spent some time talking with Dr. Rechnitz about my work with Dr. Arlt.

Friday, September 1, 1939   Breslau
This morning toward five o'clock, a succession of heavy squadrons flew at a great height in the direction of Upper Silesia, but other than that nothing seems to have happened during the night, except for the ban on air traffic announced several times on the radio. The hum of motors in the air is constant!

Toward eight o'clock. Unfortunately, it looks as if the attack has begun. The Poles have purportedly broken through at Gleiwitz.[1] The Führer has apparently formulated 14 points directed at Poland, to which they have not responded. The radio just announced that Danzig has been declared a part of the Reich. And so, the calamity has begun. The others will also intervene now, and that means world war. Inconceivable. Aside from my overall worries, my thoughts are with Wölfl and Ernst; the former, in particular, seems imperiled. May G'd keep his hand over him!

The streets have taken on a completely military appearance today; I even saw SS people from the Death's Head Regiment marching. On the street ran into legal consultant Dr. Tarnowski, who is just returning from the foreign-exchange office.[2] Apparently, it has now been decreed that Jewish assets are not to be disbursed. This will result in inconveniences for many. The Jewish Hospital was cleared for military purposes.[3] Air defenses have been mobilized, and from now on, Breslau is under a blackout. At police headquarters, I saw cellar hatches being sandbagged.

1. The so-called Gleiwitz incident occurred during the night of August 31. German agents dressed as Polish soldiers "attacked" the German radio station in Gleiwitz (now Gliwice, Poland). The Nazis used this manufactured provocation, among others, to justify the invasion of Poland.

2. Since 1938, non-Aryans were forbidden to work as attorneys, but under exceptional circumstances they could represent Jews as so-called "Konsulenten" (consultants).

3. Among the arbitrary measures carried out after 1938 and at the beginning of the war in 1939, were the confiscation by the military administration of the large Jewish Hospital located at Hohenzollernstrasse 92–96, and the forced clearing of the facility within two days. The hospital synagogue was desecrated even as they were leaving. The Jewish Community had no choice but to convert the adjacent Jewish old-age home into a hospital. When it, too, was confiscated, at the end of November 1939, the internal medicine department was transferred to the Community's administrative building, or more precisely, to rooms occupied by the Jewish school in the Wallstrasse. The surgical department was housed in a small empty private clinic at Viktoriastrasse 107. Dr. Siegmund Hadda, who was chief physician at the time, was an eyewitness to these events. See Siegmund Hadda, "Als Arzt am Jüdischen Krankenhaus zu Breslau 1906–1943," in *Jahrbuch der Schlesischen Friedrich Wilhelms Universität zu Breslau* 17 (1972), pp. 198–238, esp. pp. 224ff. Also, Andreas Reinke, *Judentum und Wohlfahrtspflege in Deutschland. Das jüdische Krankenhaus in Breslau 1726–1944* (Hannover: Hahnsche Buchhandlung, 1999), pp. 273ff.

Saturday, September 2, 1939   Breslau
Thank G'd, the first nightly blackout went without incident. Sat on the balcony. There was a nice breeze, and I could see the darkened city. Toward evening, Trudi returned from shopping with the news that the airport in Warsaw had been bombed, and that Pless, in Polish Upper Silesia, had apparently been leveled. In the morning we will hear what is true and what is not.

I didn't attend synagogue in the evening, nor did we light the Kiddush candles. Lay awake in bed thinking about Wölfl. We are completely cut off, and our thoughts alone connect us. It is sometimes difficult to turn them off. Emotionally, in fact, I have lost all hope that our emigration to Palestine might succeed. One has to consider the loss of money that would make possible such a transfer. But it makes no sense tearing my hair out about that now; all I can do is live from hour to hour. At this moment, I have no idea how the other powers will respond to the German–Polish war.

From a Jewish perspective, I can say the following about the situation. The Aryan population is surely not well disposed to us, and if Germany suffers failure in Poland, we can almost certainly expect pogrom-like assaults. Today on the street for the first time I heard two older men make an anti-Semitic remark: "The Jews must get out." It wasn't aimed at me, but that makes it all the more characteristic.

Monday at nine thirty, September 4, 1939   Breslau
I just returned from the barber, and I am completely aghast: France and England have intervened in the war, against Germany. The disaster begins anew. Who among us will live to see the end of this war? When I am not thinking of myself, I think first about the fate of those from whom we are completely cut off. What will happen to Wölfl? I won't be able to write to him or to Ernst. May G'd protect them. This dashes our plans, and my suspicion that my fate will be that of Moses seems to me headed for fulfillment. We simply weren't able to make aliyah in time.

Tuesday, September 5, 1939   Breslau
Yesterday evening I took a walk in the darkness. The streets appear quite different; they were very empty with few pedestrians, only people returning home from work. We darkened the bedroom differently. Instead of roll blinds made of black paper, we have glued black paper to

the insides of the windowpanes so that we can turn on the big light. I tried it out from downstairs, and couldn't see anything. Today we will do the same in the children's room. These are the small worries in a time of blackouts. Other than that, we are living at the edge of world history, disconnected from actual events.

Wednesday, September 6, 1939   Breslau
We had intended to prepare the certificate of nonobjection for the tax office, but there is now no point. The Palestine transfer is also done for, and so all our hopes have collapsed. But what is the point of all this.

Thursday, September 7, 1939   Breslau
I did some work on *Germania Judaica* yesterday afternoon. This article is largely completed. On the way home, I met Hadda, the architect, and I sat down with him here. We discussed the situation; we view many things the same way and believe that the democratic world is finished.

Friday, September 8, 1939   Breslau
The battle in Poland is progressing rapidly; German troops are already before Warsaw. The Polish campaign will soon come to an end, and perhaps a world war can be averted after all. Reimitz told me that the Breslau armored regiment apparently suffered heavy losses. He sees the future blacker than I do. I continue to hope that the conflict will remain local.

Sunday, September 10, 1939   Breslau
Went for a walk with Trudi yesterday afternoon. But it was no unalloyed pleasure; the mood has become extremely anti-Semitic, with one woman yelling "pack of Jews" after us. I assume that the anti-Semitic mood will continue to grow as the privations of war hit the people and casualties increase.

We will have to be prepared for all sorts of things. Yesterday, six Jewish women who were sitting on a bench in the Hohenzollernstrasse were arrested; someone claimed that they were laughing at the hospital where wounded soldiers are lying. The women have to report to the Gestapo. The newspaper reported today that bread rationing may be introduced. Cocoa, which is not rationed, is not to be had: hoarders have stockpiled it all.

Monday, September 11, 1939   Breslau

Discussed the situation with Trudi, but of course on fundamental questions she is of a completely different mind. She simply cannot understand my loyalty to Germany, or my respect for the people who are risking their lives for their Fatherland. Received a card from Ruth telling us to have courage even if we don't hear anything from the boys. Then she asked us about the certificate of nonobjection from the Jewish Community; in other words, her emigration to Denmark seems to be getting serious. I rode to the Community, where I applied for a certificate, which we will get this afternoon. Then I had to fill out a number of lists, which must be filled out by all Jews between the age of 16 and 55. I called the Gauleitung of the NSDAP from a payphone to talk to Dr. Arlt. The Race Policy Department told me that he is with the Wehrmacht, and I sent him greetings. So, this period of collaboration is also at an end for the time being. I hope he makes it safely through the war.

In addition, we Jews are under house arrest as of this evening at eight o'clock. Perhaps it is a good thing because then they can't claim that we committed acts under the cover of darkness. But it is an offense against our honor! One more worry, and yet I would make myself available if Germany needed me. In spite of everything, I consider its cause to be just.

Wednesday, September 13, 1939   Breslau

Today is erev Rosh Hashanah, and once again we are taking stock of the past year, 5699, coming to an end in blood and murder. Europe's eldest young people are slaughtering each other. Each war brings about a negative selection. The best sacrifice themselves for their Fatherland. If I survey my own life, the end of the year has brought a heavy fate, cut off as I am from my two beloved sons, and not knowing anything about them. For a loving father's heart this is the worst. My health has also deteriorated, as has my strength. Nonetheless, some good things have been granted me, as I gratefully recognize. All five children have, thank G'd, developed well, and Trudi has been a good companion in all these often difficult circumstances. And so, we hope to enter the new year trusting in G'd.

Rode to the Cathedral Library. Dr. Jedin told me that all communists have been released, which was to be expected after the pact with Russia.

Thursday, September 14, 1939   Breslau
First day of Rosh Hashanah. I attended synagogue yesterday evening; it was a downcast service, given the times, and I directed my most fervent prayers to G'd, that he protect my two sons from all evil. Grünmandel read the war instructions from the authorities to the Jewish community. We may pray in the Abraham Mugdan Synagogue, but women and children may not attend; in addition, we may leave home only in twos. No praying at all in the other synagogues!

Friday, September 15, 1939   Breslau
As I was returning home from visiting Mother, I saw Ruth striding toward me. She looks radiant, has gained eight pounds, and is very happy. She will be here for less than 24 hours. Very difficult because who knows whether we will ever see each other again. But we can't think about that! We must hope for the best and trust in G'd, and so my third child is now going out into the world. But it is in her best interest, and I am sure that she will be well treated in Denmark, even though she will have to work hard. But her heart and soul are in the work.

In the evening, the two older girls prepared our holiday dinner, and Ruth told us about her life. The newspaper reports that the Soviet border has been violated by Polish flyers, which will serve to pull the Russians into the war. It seems certain that the repartition of Poland is imminent. Visited Mother with Ruth; Mother is very weak. The farewell was upsetting, and Mother wept and said that she would be emigrating soon as well. Ruth was also very affected by this visit, but it was only right that they should say goodbye. As a memento, Mother gave her six napkins, which she counted out, her hands trembling. Susannchen waved from the kitchen!

Anita Lasker came for tea, and I have now discussed the most important matters with Ruth, things that I could not write in letters. This sort of final discussion with a child is a terribly difficult matter.

Saturday, September 16, 1939   Breslau
Ruth's train will be leaving in fifteen minutes. Trudi took Susannchen with her to the train station; I stayed at home so as not to leave Tamara

alone.[4] It is hard to say what a person feels at such moments; it is as if everything has frozen up. Nonetheless, I must reconcile myself because it is in my child's best interest. The tragedy of our times is that we must send her on her way completely alone much too early, but hopefully it is best for her. The generations that came before us were independent at this early age, too.

While I am writing this, she is probably already sitting in the train, which will leave Breslau in a minute. And then, her childhood and her heimat will be a thing of the past. But I think that she will take with her out into the world lovely memories of her childhood; we always lived for the children. And now the train will have pulled out of the station, and Trudi will be weeping.

Monday, September 18, 1939   Breslau
The newspaper reports that the Russians have invaded, and that the Polish government, with President Moscicki at the head, has fled. Polonia is done for. The *Schlesische Tageszeitung* excels in extremely abusive anti-Semitism against Polish Jews; I cannot bring myself to imagine what will happen to these people.

Went for a walk with Susannchen; the twilight hours are now the best time because one is unlikely to encounter hostile stares. The child told me that she would be happy to be out already because she doesn't like it here anymore. I can certainly understand that, even though I find such statements painful. The child is being robbed of her innocent childhood years. We try to be as good to her as we can.

Thursday, September 21, 1939   Breslau
The foreign currency office has now placed a restraint on disposal on my property, which makes everything more complicated. We are going to be held liable for the many Jews who did not properly take care of their affairs!

Went to the bank about the restraint on disposal, then back to the foreign-currency office. I was sent from the main building to Höfchen-

---

4. Ruth later wrote that her father stayed home because he would have found saying goodbye at the train station unbearable. Ruth Atzmon-Cohn, "This Is the Story of Those Times," in Marcin Wodziński and Janusz Spyra (eds.) *Jews in Silesia* (Cracow: Księgarnia Akademicka, 2001), pp. 421–422.

strasse 15a, where I was fortunate enough to be seen by a polite official. He told me that this had been done to get Germany through these difficult times somehow; I couldn't very well tell him that in that case it should have included the Aryans as well. But I did tell him that we are being made to pay for the Jews who skipped out.

Friday, September 22, 1939   Breslau
Yom Kippur—services not being held in the Abraham Mugdan Synagogue, probably for the first time in centuries that no prayers will be said on this day.[5] I will try to pray at home!

Saturday, September 23, 1939   Breslau
The authorities have chosen this day to confiscate all radios from Jews. Mother was visited by an official from the Gestapo this morning, who ordered her to turn over her radio between nine and twelve at Tauentzienstrasse 12. Frau Gebauer, the caretaker, went there three times; at six o'clock she finally managed to get rid of the radio. Five Schupos were needed to handle the traffic. They seem to be afraid that Jews will listen to foreign stations. We haven't had a Yom Kippur like this in centuries, but every now and then things are different. We are an ancient people!

Sunday, September 24, 1939   Breslau
Mother died at five forty-five! When I arrived at eight o'clock, I looked into her room through the open window, and I saw that it was over. Even now, in the afternoon, I cannot comprehend that Mother will never sit at her window again! While spending time alone with her recently, we drew closer, and now I will miss her very much. The morning brought me numerous obligations. Isidor Lichtenberg, who now leads the chevrah, came by with Hugo Mamlok, and we discussed everything. Her body will be transported at nine o'clock, and she will be buried on Tuesday at eleven. Frau Neumann sat watch, and Trudi helped to sew Mother's shroud, which is considered a great mitzvah.

---

5. For more on this ban on religious services, see Walter Tausk, *Breslauer Tagebuch 1933–1940*, ed. Ryszard Kincel (Berlin, 1975; new edition, Berlin: Siedler, 1988), p. 234.

Monday, September 25, 1939   Breslau

Fräulein Silberstein told me that the people who surrendered their radios were treated very badly. They had to stand for hours; one old woman said that she was feeling sick, whereupon the official replied, "You have no idea how sick I get just looking at you." They asked Ehrlich, the old master builder, who he was. When he said, "Regierungsrat Master Builder Ehrlich, retired," the official responded, "Another one who pushed his way into a civil service job," an accusation that surely doesn't apply to old Ehrlich! Petty people!

This morning was very difficult for me, and bitter! No one can relieve a son of the feelings he has on seeing his mother lying in a coffin and being carried out. We Jews must now carry our dead out almost in secret! We dare not draw any attention to ourselves. We wanted to hire a car so that we could at least ride behind the hearse to the Lohestrasse as is the custom, but cars no longer carry Jews. The driver asked Fräulein Liebe whether she was Jewish or was inquiring for Jews, and so we could not accompany Mother on this last journey, which pained me greatly. Fräulein Liebe was also very upset about this meanness. But none of this is of any help.

Most of the stores, to the extent that they have groceries for sale, have signs saying that they won't sell to Jews. We're supposed to get by with the officially rationed foodstuffs, and are to receive no eggs, no poultry, no fruit preserves, no unauthorized foods of any kind. The population doesn't approve of this, nor do many storekeepers. Trudi got her eggs at a creamery today, and the owner told her only that he would have to refuse her in front of other customers. Naturally, the population draws completely different conclusions.

Wednesday, September 27, 1939   Breslau

Arrived at the cemetery yesterday at ten thirty. Only a small number of people had gathered there; how many would have been there just a few years ago! But only a few people knew about it. Pakulla sang beautifully in Hebrew, and Rabbi Hamburger spoke very affectingly; he may have placed me too much in the foreground, which was a bit embarrassing, but overall he held to the matter as I had given him to understand it.

I cannot at this moment describe what I felt as Trudi and I, the sole members of the immediate family, walked behind the coffin on the long walk to our family grave. Outside, the rabbi told us that he hoped that this grave would never be desecrated.

Thursday, September 28, 1939   Breslau

Warsaw has capitulated, and 100,000 men have surrendered. This ends the Polish invasion; a military government will now rule over occupied Poland, with General von Rundstedt, the father of one of my scholarly colleagues, at the head. If the entire German air corps can be mobilized against the West, the war may end quickly. I do not believe that the Western democracies will be victorious; if Germany and Russia combine forces, these powers may easily give the world an entirely new look.

Friday, September 29, 1939   Breslau

I had hoped that we would hear something about Ruth's emigration today, but we did not. It is almost grotesque for a father not to know whether or not his child has emigrated. Went to the barber. He told me the following, among other things. He is very well informed, and if England continues the war, they intend to intern all Jews in concentration camps, and to place the children under state care. For this we have world Jewry to thank! When I talk to Duscha, who is a man of small intellect, I see clearly the effect of propaganda.

Germany and Russia have come to an understanding about Poland, and the agreement about the demarcation line has now been finalized! And so, Europe now has a different look, and I doubt very much that anyone will be able to challenge this astonishing unity between Russia and Germany. The world will have to get used to it!

Sunday, October 1, 1939   Breslau

At the Mincha service, I was actually called up, and I said Kaddish. The morning mail brought a card from Ruth, telling me that she had arrived in Copenhagen. She was very well received, and has even gone to the movies. She will be going to live with a teacher named Jensen, in Mors, in Jutland, where I am sure she will prove her worth. I now have three children in three different countries.

I walked along the embankment with Susannchen, and through the new park at Kinderzobten. Susannchen is now afraid that benches will bear signs saying that Jews are forbidden. I try to talk her out of this complex!

Tuesday, October 3, 1939   Breslau
Kaiser Wilhelm Strasse was full of troops returning from Poland; I am sure that more than a few who marched forth will not be returning home! The women on the streets were enraptured and tossed flowers into the cars. The soldiers are probably on their way toward the West.

Saturday, October 7, 1939   Breslau
Read the Führer's speech, which was measured and sensible and could be a bridge toward peace if the others are reasonable as well. It is doubtful, however, whether England will give in. Nor was the speech particularly anti-Semitic. We must recognize the greatness of this man, who has given the world a new look.

Monday, October 9, 1939   Breslau
In Sedlaczek's little shop on the Ring, bought a pin for my black coat to identify my order, then we warmed ourselves up in Jendritzko's bakery in the Antonienstrasse, which used to belong to Siedner. Only Jews go there; we are grateful that there is any place at all for us to sit.

October 10, 1939   Breslau
The mail brought me a larger commission from the Institute for the Advancement of the Science of Judaism, about which I am very pleased. Scholarship is always something marvelous. I spent the morning writing, later rode to the cemetery, where I negotiated with Geppert, the master stonemason, about the inscription, and with the grounds administrator about covering the graves. When I asked whether there would be room for a fifth plot for myself when it came to that, the answer was in the negative.

Thursday, October 12, 1939   Breslau
At the moment, Dr. Reimitz is in the process of traveling to Buchenwald; 50,000 Czech Jews are said to be interned there, and he will try to get a few of them released. Dr. Reimitz has also heard that England intends to continue waging war; it is said to be building 2,000 airplanes each month, and that production will be doubled next month. If all this is true and Germany is forced to continue the war, we Jews will be subjected to all manner of rage. The evening mail brought us great joy in the form of a letter from St. Gallen with an enclosed card from Wölfl dated September 30, the first news we have had from him in months. I

now content myself with very little; a few lines in his handwriting, and the knowledge that he is still breathing and alive is all I need. About Hanne and Steps Brienitzer, he reported that Steps is no longer in Edinburgh, which has been evacuated.

Saturday, October 14, 1939   Breslau
This afternoon on the Kaiser Wilhelm Strasse I saw many cars with soldiers returning from the East and on their way to the West. A chalk figure of a Jew in caricature was drawn on one of the vehicles along with the words, "The dream is over." Exactly which dream is over we don't yet know!

Wednesday, October 18, 1939   Breslau
We have now outfitted the dining room for blackouts. I'm going to be sleeping there for a time; I'm having differences with Trudi about turning out the light, and it is perhaps better this way until I have recovered somewhat, which I don't really believe will happen. Lay awake for a long time.

My big joy today was a very loving and detailed letter from Ruth from Nykøbing. I think she is in the right place there, and she is developing physically. She is growing out of all her things. Perhaps we can get some new ones for her from America; I always feel badly when I can't do things for my own children, but that is now up to a higher power.[6]

Thursday, October 19, 1939   Breslau
Cathedral Library. Received very warmly again. Professor Nowack inquired about what I'm working on. Dr. Jedin is very concerned for me, and he will go to the university library to pick up some books that I need for my current work. I was able to take two important books out of the Cathedral Library.

Saturday, October 21, 1939   Breslau
Trudi picked up the food rationing cards; the Aryans get them delivered at home, the Jews have to pick them up at the Society of Friends, but everything was well organized and took only a few minutes.

6. These clothes would have come from Rose Hoffmann, in New York, the daughter of a Breslau rabbi and a friend of Trudi's.

Tuesday, October 24, 1939   Breslau

The *Breslauer Neueste Nachrichten* announced a fifth levy on Jewish assets; they haven't reached a billion yet, and given our reduced assets this will hit many very hard. Who knows whether this will be the end of it. For this week, the newspapers announced an increase in the butter ration. In practice, this has resulted in a reduction. The reduced availability of fish makes clear the extent to which England still rules the seas.

Wednesday, October 25, 1939   Breslau

Very important mail arrived today: the Reich Ministry of Education has approved the transfer of our residence to Palestine. This is a document that I have long been waiting for, although it has probably come too late. Nonetheless, I will do everything that is my duty to make our aliyah possible, although personally I think it is hopeless.

Saturday, October 28, 1939   Breslau

This morning I was visited by a Gestapo official who inquired about how far along I am with my emigration. This probably had to do with the way I filled out the card file a while back, saying that I would be emigrating to Palestine in a few months. I told him that under prevailing conditions getting a certificate was out of the question, and furthermore I told him that at the behest of the Gestapo, Herr Dr. Arlt enlisted me to assist him in work about the Jews in Silesia, and that I was not to emigrate until this work was completed, but that as a result of the outbreak of war this work had now been interrupted. I dictated all of this for the report that he submitted! Over the course of our conversation, I told him, among other things, that I might request of the German people permission to die here, where five generations of my family lie buried, where the grandfather of my wife fought at Königgrätz, and each generation of us had been frontline soldiers. That made an impression. He was one of the old officials, not one of the new ones.

Sunday, October 29, 1939   Breslau

I have been sleeping in the bedroom again for some time now, and I told Trudi how hopeless I believe my personal situation is, and that it would be best if she and the two children emigrated alone because I simply no longer have the strength. But she wouldn't hear of it.

A postcard that was returned to me today reveals the fate of us Jews these days. I had written to Frau Rinka Kohn, Mira's mother, at her supposed address. The card was returned with the notation: Deported.[7] Perhaps this only referred to the people at the address to which she wanted mail delivered, but that is bad enough. These times bring such suffering.[8]

Friday, November 3, 1939   Breslau
I got another letter from Rosette Ruf today with a very encouraging letter from Wölfl. The decency of his character is evident. He is trying to keep up connections with his far-flung siblings. When I am no longer, which sooner or later will be the case, the boy will prove himself a very good male head of the family. He thinks of everything!

Friday, November 4, 1939   Breslau
We hear terrible things from the province of Posen. Letters sent to Jews, for example in Kempen, are returned with the notation: Unknown, moved. In official German, this translates as deported, probably to Lublin, and now in the middle of Polish winter, and I doubt they took anything with them.

Sunday, November 5, 1939   Breslau
Terrible stories are being told about the fate of the Jews in Poland. But perhaps these things that are happening in Poland and are *not* initiated by the military will achieve precisely the opposite effect: the unification of humanity. Did it have to be this way? Is it not a shame for the loftier parts of the German people, large swaths of which surely reject these things and are now being dragged down into the calamity? I believe that terrible times are ahead for the rest of us German Jews; but sometimes, things turn out differently than one expects, and only our trust in G'd can help us to overcome.

Tuesday, November 7, 1939   Breslau
Rode to the Cathedral Library, where I heard that Dr. Jedin will be

7. Willy Cohn later supported Rinka Kohn, sending her packages to the Weruschau ghetto, in Reichsgau Wartheland.
8. This notation may have been written by the mailman; the official terminology was "Moved." It is clear from this entry that Cohn had not yet grasped what was really happening.

leaving for Rome tomorrow! He has long talked about this, and one certainly cannot begrudge him. He will be freed of all other duties and can simply live for his work. He will be residing at the German College of Campo Santo! Of course, I am extremely happy for him, but for me it will be a heavy loss. He facilitated my scholarly work in every way, and was always kind and obliging! I doubt that I will ever find anyone who will help me as much.

For him as a person of mixed blood it is of course the best solution, and his great talents will benefit scholarship, particularly in the history of the Church! He recommended me warmly to Walter, his successor in the archive.

Wednesday, November 8, 1939   Breslau
Had a conversation with Trudi in which I argued that I am no longer able to emigrate. I suggested that she emigrate alone with the children because it is our duty to save them, and I am simply unable. Trudi decently rejected by suggestion, which I understand but do not think is right! I myself am simply finished.

Thursday, November 9, 1939   Breslau
Trudi has a hard day ahead of her as well because she has to go to the grocery store in the morning and then to the butcher in the afternoon! We are limited to buying on one day of the week. Susannchen returned home upset, less for herself than for her friend Rita Wechselmann. They were harassed by rude schoolchildren in the Rehdigerplatz. Such things are to be expected on this day. The child has now gone to bed for the afternoon. She says that she has a sore throat, but I think that it has more to do with the stress. She says that she got frightened this morning already, when she looked at the calendar and saw that it was November 9.

Saturday, November 11, 1939   Breslau
Günther Brienitzer was here and showed me a lovely letter from Rosette Ruf. It said, among other things, that Ruth had written to St. Gallen. It is gratifying to see such a young girl fulfilling her family obligations. Fifty Jews have been arrested in Breslau, 25 of whom were released yesterday. The rest are to be freed today. No one knows why they were arrested.

Tuesday, November 14, 1939   Breslau
Today, I had the great joy of receiving the first news from Ernst himself via St. Gallen, which he had written on October 27. Very quick, given the current postal situation. This is the first time since the war broke out that I have seen his handwriting, and I was very relieved to hear from him directly again. He is continuing in his work. His letter gave me energy for the entire day.

Wednesday, November 15, 1939   Breslau
A grotesque little story of the times. We Jews, as is known, must buy from certain butchers only, hard-core party comrades who are thereby given an extra source of income. The NSDAP is showing gratitude toward its old fighters by doing something for them. The Zionists, unfortunately, don't do the same. But this is not what I wanted to say here; this butcher is now making all-beef sausage specifically for his Jewish customers.

Saturday, November 18, 1939   Breslau
Most stores aren't selling sweets to Jews anymore, and so we try to buy these things for our children on the sly at vending machines. Hirschel, my neighbor in the temple, received news from his sister, in Kalisch. She has been forced to leave her home in Kempen. These unfortunate Jews from Posen province will probably be displaced further toward Lublin.

Monday, November 20, 1939   Breslau
Frau Freilich came by this morning, the Aryan wife of a stateless eastern Jew who was arrested six weeks ago. First he sat in jail here, then in Nuremberg. Later he was deported to Schubin, Posen province, from where he last wrote: hunger, nothing warm to wear; a man suffering. This is how our people are being destroyed. I am hearing of one such case; there must be innumerable others.

Dr. Reimitz visited in the evening. He shares my view, namely that I should not emigrate, and that if Trudi agrees, she should do so by herself with the children. He thinks that in my condition I should not leave without the financial means! I was very pleased to hear my view confirmed by another person. I then showed him some of the books that I have written over the course of my life, which made it clear to him that I cannot do otherwise.

Tuesday, November 21, 1939   Breslau
Downtown, we increasingly see signs, "Jews not served," and the like.
We rarely encounter Jews anymore.

Wednesday, November 22, 1939   Breslau
This morning, I left relatively early because the master stonemason
asked me to meet him at the cemetery so he could show me Mother's inscription. An old journeyman followed me to the grave. The inscription
was just as I wanted, and as long as the cemetery stands, it will proclaim
Mother's caring for her family. There is a little room left over at the top
of the plaque; perhaps my name will eventually be inscribed there.

Friday, November 24, 1939   Breslau
Except for the blackouts and the dearth of younger men, the war is
not particularly noticeable here in Breslau this November. The bits and
snatches of conversation that I hear on the street are mostly about buying groceries. Up to now the allotments have been adequate.

Monday, November 27, 1939   Breslau
Unfortunately, a number of Breslau Jews were killed on the steamer
Simon Bolivar when it hit a mine. The former Breslau attorney Hannach
(the elder); his wife was severely wounded. She's the mother of Wölfl's
schoolmate Günter Riesenfeld. The wife and child of Schäfer the der-
matologist are also said to be among the dead. Very, very sad. So much
is sinking into the ocean.

The old-age home, which was one of the few remaining parts of the
Jewish Hospital, must be turned over to the military administration by
January 1, 1940. They say that the Community will be compensated.[9]
The father of Dr. Freund, the chief physician, just told me that. This old
gentleman of 80 hopes to emigrate to Chile in a few weeks! Some have
courage; I am so tired that I no longer feel any energy.

Wednesday, November 29, 1939   Breslau
Dr. Hirsch-Kauffmann told me that 80 people were supposedly arrested on November 9, including some Aryans when the Jews they
were looking for weren't at home. Apparently they then just arrested

9. This was the second confiscation after requisition of the large Jewish Hospital.
The Jewish Community was left to replace the three-story old-age home on its own.

others. Attorney Lasker has been arrested because he behaved foolishly in front of the Gestapo. Usually, there is a reason for such arrests.

Thursday, November 30, 1939   Breslau

It is hard to believe all the things that have apparently happened in Poland. Helfgott's mother and sister appear to have died in Praschkau, in Congress Poland.[10] Was this the result of local pogroms or of military actions? The mail brought much that was encouraging: a package from Ruth containing butter, cheese, and chocolate. It is so touching to be cared for by our child.

Friday, December 1, 1939   Breslau

Trudi went to the Palestine Office this morning for a frank discussion with Fräulein Levy. The special hachshara will not accept such small children; however, she could get *us* out by this means. So, at the moment there is nothing to do. Fräulein Levy thinks that we should perhaps find the children a home elsewhere, but we don't want that.

Tuesday, December 5, 1939   Breslau

I did my own work this morning; I have now put together an index of all the articles that I consider ready for publication, but which cannot now be published. This sort of exercise makes you cry and makes you laugh at the same time. I so wish I could see them in black on white before me!

Dr. Latte, whom I haven't seen in many months, was here in the morning. I sent him with the files to Dr. Reimitz, who is now negotiating for me at the Palestine Office. Latte has also been to the Berlin office; we lull ourselves in the hope that a few pension certificates will be granted, and then I would be among the first considered! But in reality, I no longer harbor hopes; nor do I believe that I personally still have a future. I have done with life and feel fortunate just to be breathing.

Thursday, December 7, 1939   Breslau

The food rationing cards were distributed to Jews yesterday; all of the sections with extra allowances for things like rice, cocoa, and the like, have been crossed out and invalidated.

---

10. Originally, Congress Poland denoted the Kingdom of Poland created by the Congress of Vienna, in 1815. It lasted in that form until 1830. Cohn uses the term in a more general sense to denote central Poland.

Saturday, December 9, 1939   Breslau
We looked at the atlas, especially at Denmark, where Ruth is. This country appears for the time being to be outside the arena of conflict. We aren't living all that badly right now given that we have no telephone, radio, or car, and almost no streetcar.[11] It is a simpler life, and we walk a lot and are dependent on our own resources and on each other.

Sunday, December 10, 1939   Breslau
Duscha, the barber, was here. I showed him our ration cards full of "Jew" stamps that invalidated many of the sections.

Tuesday, December 12, 1939   Breslau
Susannchen recited a poem for me this morning; I also received a small present from her, and from Trudi and Tamara. Anita Lasker came by, but not for my birthday. She wanted to tell us about a letter from Ruth. She didn't show it to us; girls of that age don't do that. Her father has now been released and must report by the beginning of January where he will be going. Just technically, I doubt that this is possible.

Wednesday, December 13, 1939   Breslau
Rechnitz, the former administrative director, and Dr. Weissenberg emigrated to Chile some time ago. A boat built to accommodate 800 people took 1,600. The people arrived half starved; this is how Jews are treated! Like in 1492!

Thursday, December 14, 1939   Breslau
The restraint on disposal has brought us another difficulty: the life insurance premiums are no longer payable beyond the exemption limit.[12] We have to submit a special application. These are the small difficulties

11. In fact, Willy Cohn had always gotten along without a radio, which is why he barely made note of the radio confiscations during Yom Kippur. He had already given up his telephone in early 1939. A passionate train traveler, Cohn never had an automobile, so this ban didn't affect him either.

12. Cohn first mentioned the "restraint on disposal" (the so-called *Sicherungsanordnung*) in his entry on September 21, 1939. Originally this instrument served to ensure that Jews could not take much money with them when they left Germany. Later, Jews were forced to deposit their money in a "blocked account" (*Sperrkonto*), from which they could withdraw only up to a set limit to cover daily expenses. Certain additional expenses such as taxes, doctor bills, and life insurance premiums

we are faced with in life, but we have to deal with them. The afternoon mail brought a bar of chocolate from Rosette Ruf. This made me very happy, apart from the fact that Swiss chocolate is now a scarce treasure for the children. The bar is to be divided up on a special occasion! It becomes us well to be so modest in our needs.

Attended synagogue in the afternoon; it was the last evening of Hanukkah, and the menorah was fully lit. It is a large Palestinian menorah that was donated to the synagogue many years ago. My wish is that my wife and my children are safely in Erez Israel next year, and that I will by then have found my peace. I am not up to aliyah anymore.

Did a few shopping errands for Trudi. It makes me understand how difficult it is for women standing in line. At the dairy, a few women left after having waited a long time because they ran out of skim milk. I had a conversation with the young woman in the chocolate store. It was clear to me how badly it made her feel that she was not permitted to sell us anything other than Russian bread and malt candies![13]

Monday morning, December 18, 1939   Breslau
One hundred and twenty thousand Germans must return to the Greater German Reich from the territories conquered by the Russians; this cannot be pleasant in mid-winter. All Jews must leave Danzig. This wasn't reported in the newspaper; we heard it from Frau Rosenbaum.

Thursday, December 21, 1939   Breslau
In the afternoon. This morning worked on the index in which all my books and articles are filed. I can see just how much I have written over the years; I so wish that I could see all of them bound together in an edition of my collected works.

It seems to me that the political situation in Germany has deteriorated greatly over the past several days. – "Should I think of Germany at night, it puts all thought of sleep to flight."[14] Germany will sink to the conditions of 1648.

---

were exempted from this limit. However, as of December 14, 1939, life insurance premiums had to paid from daily expenses, making life all the more difficult.

13. Russian bread is a sweet crispy pastry, especially at Christmas. Children love them because they are cut in the shape of letters of the alphabet.

14. First verse of Heinrich Heine's poem "Nachtgedanken" [Night thoughts].

Sunday, December 24, 1939   Breslau

Today is Nittel, the Jewish contraction of "Dies natalis," that is, Christmas. I have many memories of this day, especially early childhood at home, where this holiday was often celebrated together with Hanukkah, and war Christmases in the field, where I often spoke and tried to encourage people in my own way.

Afterward, there was a horrible scene with Trudi. I was consumed by a terrible rage; I even smashed a few things. Such violence is rare for me, but so much has been stored up that an explosion was inevitable. I felt very sorry for her afterward, and sorry for the good things that were made to pay for my blow-up, a beautiful cup from Mother, among others.

Monday, December 25, 1939   Breslau

How beautiful it must be in the mountains, and how I wish I could walk without a care through these beloved mountains of my Silesian heimat. But that is all over now. For me there is no solution other than to be released by our beloved G'd as soon as possible from the torments of earthly existence, to escape all of these differences. Now isolated, I see no way out anymore. Trudi went to see the Brienitzers and Fräulein Silberstein. At the former, she heard that the archive of the synagogue community, which had been confiscated on November 9, 1938, has now been picked up by the State Office for Race and Clan Research. Perhaps I will see it if I ever work in the Teichstrasse again.[15] This archive was built by Jews with the greatest of love.

Thursday, December 28, 1939   Breslau

Yesterday morning, I went to the regional office for Jews in the Schloss-Ohle in order to get a soap coupon for Tamara. This office is manned by two officials, one of whom is a particularly repulsive type. One gets the feeling that he sees his task as one of offending Jews. It was unbelievable how he treated a pregnant woman. The other was all the friendlier, and he calmly did what needed to be done. I received my soap coupon.

---

15. The entire archive had not, in fact, been confiscated as Cohn found the majority of it in place, in August 1941. However, the State Office for Race and Clan Research did take all personal indexes and files needed to ascertain Jewish descent. For more, see Bernhard Brilling, "Das Archiv der Breslauer jüdischen Gemeinde," in *Jahrbuch der Schlesischen Friedrich-Wilhelms-Universität zu Breslau* 18 (1973), pp. 258–284, esp. pp. 271ff.

In one case, a father returned to the miscreant the coupons for his son, who had emigrated to Palestine, whereupon he replied, "Well, one bread coupon more." What does a fellow like this know about what it means to be separated from a child.

The morning mail brought me a detailed letter from the Rufs with a long letter from Ernst, the longest since the beginning of the war. He warmly congratulated me on my birthday. In a letter that was meant more for the Rufs than for me, he wrote that Kibbutz Maos is making difficulties for our application. This was basically our last hope for emigration to Palestine, and even though it was a very weak thread, we nonetheless clung to it. And so this news really hit my life energies, and I don't have much of this energy left.

Sunday, December 31, 1939   Breslau
The year 1939 ends with an especially hard winter. One automatically takes stock of one's life. Two calendars coincide in this year: the turn of the century according to the Jewish calendar, and the beginning of a new decade according to the Christian one. This decade begins under the poorest auspices! Half the world is in flames, and the prospect that the rest of the world will be set ablaze as well.

Thursday, January 4, 1940   Breslau
Rosette Ruf wrote yesterday that Rabbi Rothschild is taking an interest in our situation and has also written to us. Nothing has arrived yet, but perhaps he has had some success. Nonetheless, until I have an actual certificate in hand, I will believe nothing.

Went with Susannchen to the Cathedral Library, where there have been big changes. Old Professor Nowack retired on January 1, 1940; Konsistorialrat Engelbert has been named director. He introduced himself to me; he seems to be very open-minded.

Saturday, January 5, 1940   Breslau
Dr. Reimitz has not transferred the 2,000 marks that Susanne and Tamara are still owed from the bequest; I bought securities in the amount of 1,500 Reichsmarks, and bonds, which guarantee a consistent return, to the extent such a thing even exists under the current circumstances. Still, the care that my departed father exercised for so many decades

will help us through these critical times, and that, after all, is what he intended in his benevolence.

Late afternoon, January 6, 1940   Breslau
Mother's investments have now all been disbursed; it would have been much better if she could have eaten on them while she was still healthy. But the good thing is that we have no material worries for the time being, and for this I am extremely grateful.

Monday, January 8, 1940   Breslau
My wife, who is so extraordinarily competent in all these external matters, had to do a great deal of running about. For one thing, she was able to obtain three hundredweights of coal and briquettes, which Herr Hirschel picked up from the Kiese coal yard. They won't deliver anything anymore for lack of personnel. Many people have no heat at all in this cold weather; we gave our Eva a handbag of coal to take along. All those who were unable to buy potatoes during the fall don't have any potatoes now either. A very hard winter.

Sunday, January 14, 1940   Breslau
Had dreams all night that Wölfl and Ernst were back home; woke up very unhappy. There are rumors again about resettling the Jews in Lublin. But I don't really believe it. Apparently, things went very badly for the Jews in Warsaw; the Germans took revenge for what supposedly had been done to the ethnic Germans.

Thursday, January 18, 1940   Breslau
Duscha, the master barber, told me, "If only this awful mess were at an end." To which I asked, "What awful mess are you talking about?" To which Duscha responded, "The war." I said, "You call that an awful mess," to which he replied, "Yes, I call that an awful mess." The others supposedly weren't forced into it. I am writing this down to make clear that the popular mood is no longer particularly enthusiastic about the war.

The province of Posen has now been almost completely cleared of Jews. Among others, the Rohr family has been deported.[16] Their prop-

---

16. This was the second time that the Rohr family had been displaced. In 1933, they left Silesia after Hitler's seizure of power, renting their estate at Gross Breesen to the Reich Representation of German Jews.

erty is being divided up. Baltic Germans are being repatriated to take the places of the Jews who have been removed from all these territories. In addition, the Jewish deportees were forced to place their baggage in the baggage car, and underway the baggage car was disconnected. Their property was simply stolen. Apparently, they were permitted to take money along.

Saturday, January 20, 1940   Breslau
My entire life is now merely a struggle from hour to hour: worry about my children abroad, caring for my children here, and ever fewer hours in which to do some work. And no hope for the future; and often the sinful entreaty that I be released from these horrible torments, which will probably not happen so soon.

Thursday, January 25, 1940   Breslau
Went out for a while and had the good fortune of getting a hundred-weight of coal, which Eva then transported home on the sledge. We heard that all Jewish men in Kalisch have been jailed. One gets the impression that because the Germans are getting nowhere with the outside world, they are intensifying their harassment of defenseless Jews.

Friday, January 26, 1940   Breslau
Went to synagogue in the afternoon; heard terrible things about the behavior of the Germans in Posen, and in Poland. The cemetery in Lissa is said to have been completely desecrated, with not a single gravestone remaining. In Praschkau, the Jews have been herded together, and they are going to be deported.[17] It is said that they are dying like flies in Warsaw. People are being left with inadequate food and heat at this time of year. Why doesn't civilized humanity intervene? Treating people in occupied territories in this manner absolutely violates the provisions of the Hague Land Warfare Convention, but

---

17. These events are much better understood today. The arrests usually followed the same pattern: early-morning raids by an overwhelming force, at which time people were ordered in no uncertain terms to be prepared to evacuate, after which they were loaded into cattle cars and taken east. In Praschkau (Polish: Praszka) they were temporarily crammed into an improvised ghetto. See Michael Alberti, *Die Verfolgung und Vernichtung der Juden im Reichsgau Wartheland 1939–1945* (Wiesbaden: Harrassowitz, 2006), pp. 133 and 203.

why doesn't anyone care? The Gestapo is again summoning Jews, including Frau Alexander, probably to force her to emigrate. But for most this is no longer a possibility. In Cracow, Jewish stores have been closed down for "price gouging." And I doubt that the Jews will ever see their property again. Total war is being waged against us; we will suffer heavy casualties!

Sunday, January 28, 1940   Breslau
In the mail I received, among other things, a letter from Dr. Jedin with a piece of information of scholarly significance. Of Wölfl's money, 200 marks have finally been released for the support of Grandmother Proskauer.

Tuesday, January 30, 1940   Breslau
Today is the birthday of the Third Reich: seven years. It makes me think of Fontane's ballad "Archibald Douglas." I have borne it for seven years, and I can bear it no more.[18] And of Joseph. Were they the seven fat years or the seven lean years? Spoke with Frau Alexander, who told me about her summons to the Gestapo; the letter A was processed yesterday. Evidently, all Jews are now being watched and their emigration controlled. The letter A is to be summoned again in mid-March. She was told not to go out after eight o'clock in the evening, except when accompanying a child who is emigrating. Even then, one must seek permission. No travel without permission, all changes in personal status, employment, and so forth must be reported. Evidently, they are again trying to promote a state of disquiet among the Jews. Because my name comes early in the alphabet, I expect to be summoned within the next few days.

Wednesday, January 31, 1940   Breslau
The Führer spoke yesterday evening. In any case, he screamed loudly; that much I heard on the radio in the neighboring apartment. It is always the same thing, and then the unconditional promise of victory. Toward us Jews, only insults. Daladier gave a speech in which he talked about the enslavement of Poland. Unfortunately, we know all too well how right he is, at least with respect to the Jews.

---

18. Freely cited from Theodor Fontane's poem "Archibald Douglas."

Thursday, February 1, 1940   Breslau

This morning we got a hundredweight of coal, a major event. Eva picked up the coal with the sledge; she is always so accommodating. Most coal dealers now refuse to sell coal to Jews—with the temperature what it is. So much for humanity.

Thursday, February 8, 1940   Breslau

I'm going to describe my summons to the Gestapo yesterday! I was summoned for ten o'clock, but arrived a quarter of an hour early so that I could slowly negotiate the three long staircases. On each landing I read postings about attacks, executions, and manhunts. Upstairs, at the Gestapo office, there is a grating behind which is seated an SS-man with a particularly brutal face. We then had to wait in the corridor in two lines, mostly old people over the age of 70. We were not allowed to speak; the man next to me, who may have voiced his indignation, was bellowed at by the SS-man: "I'm going to punch each hair out of your head one by one." His entire tone was horribly coarse. Then someone came out and announced to the entire gathering that we were now forbidden to leave the house after eight o'clock and must seek approval for any intended travel two days in advance. Anyone who contravenes these provisions may count on the most severe punishment from the Gestapo. Emigration is now under the control of the Gestapo, and the next time we report, we must present evidence of everything that we have done on behalf of our emigration. Standing was the most stressful part; there were very few seats, and those were taken by disabled war veterans and the extremely infirm. I walked home, and then I had to change my clothes because such emotional upheaval makes me sweat profusely.

Friday, February 9, 1940   Breslau

Hedwig Bermann was here while I was out; she reported on a new scheme of the Reich Association together with Hapag to get people to Palestine. People are supposed to claim how much money they have available; the dollar conversion is calculated at 40 marks. I have little confidence in this scheme.

Saturday, February 10, 1940   Breslau

Religious services, which mean a great deal to me, will no longer be conducted because no fuel is available. We would have continued to pray in the unheated room, but the Community doesn't want that. Perhaps this would have upset the "national comrades," who might then claim that the Jews do have coal after all.

Tuesday, February 13, 1940   Breslau
At the moment, instead of briquettes, we are using pieces of wood from an old bed from the Ohlauufer that we sawed up, and which give off a lot of heat. Many Jews now have nothing at all to heat with. If I had known that this winter would be so cold, I wouldn't have sold Mother's old furniture for a few marks, but have had it sawed up for firewood. But one can't know these things.

Thursday, February 15, 1940   Breslau
Trudi had to race around town to get matzoh, meat, and fish. It is anything but easy for housewives now; I minded the house. It continues to snow uninterrupted; when I look out the window now, the Opitzplatz looks more like a landscape in Greenland. People are heating with old boxes and, in the end, pieces of furniture. I don't believe that Germany will make it through another such war winter. The *Breslauer Neueste Nachrichten* is now published in a single four-page edition. No newsprint is available.

Synagogue; accompanied old Grünmandel to his home. He is expecting his daughter to return from Bratislava today. It is terrible having to travel at this time of year. He told me about a Jew who, after having waited in line for three hours to buy a half a hundredweight of coal, was ordered by the Schupo to empty his sack again. Terrible times, but the others have probably had more than enough of it themselves.

Friday, February 16, 1940   Breslau
To our great joy, the mail brought a lovely letter from Ruth, in which she describes her Sunday with five meals. She has sent us butter, and is awaiting permission to send us a large package. Her host donated a chicken, but everything else is from her.

Sunday, February 18, 1940   Breslau
From the newspaper, I gather that milk and butter prices are going to be raised. For the first time, holes are being punched in the price-control system! Quotations on bonds—these are controlled prices anyway—have also been raised.

On all the streets one sees sledges onto which people have loaded the humblest quantities of coal which they have managed to garner after standing in line for hours and are now taking home. At Kiese, the coal dealer who now refuses to sell to Jews; there were long lines at noon, with the Schupos trying hard to maintain order. Some of the people are said to have been standing since two thirty in the morning. I myself try to pick up coal on the street; on such days I can find quite a bit! Susannchen looks out for coal too. "You may be certain of the Fatherland's gratitude." We aren't permitted to buy coal.

Synagogue, very cold! Today is the 10th of Adar, the date of Moshe Rabbenu's death.[19] The 18 men, who in Breslau are only 12 now, continue their rounds in the Lohestrasse and Cosel cemeteries in spite of the cold. Theirs is a heroic honorary office.[20] All the more admirable the accomplishments of these men and women who day in and day out continue to perform these services to the dead, knowing that the necessary cloth is no longer available for the dead, and that even the living cannot clothe themselves. The entire ceremony upset me. It reminded me of last things. שויתי יי [לנגדי] תמיד כי מימיני בל אמוט "I have set the Lord always before me; because he is at my right hand, I shall not be shaken."[21]

Monday, February 19, 1940   Breslau
Great excitement when we received notification of a customs package from Switzerland; clothing for Susanne from America. These things can be put to very good use because we aren't allowed to buy anything, even though I find it uncomfortable to accept gifts because I would rather do everything on my own. Frau Schmidt, unfortunately, has just returned from her unsuccessful expedition to procure coal. When Frau Schmidt told Kiese that there was a small child in the house, and that we needed coal, and what did he think would happen without it, the

19. Orthodox Jews refer to Moses as Moshe Rabbenu, "Our Leader Moses." The traditional date of his death is actually the 7th of Adar.

20. Cohn was praising the Chevrah Kadisha, a Jewish burial society that had been in existence in Breslau since 1726.

21. Psalm 16:8. The tetragrammaton of the biblical text יהוה is generally replaced by יי as Cohn does here. The word that is actually missing, לנגדי (before me), was added above.

scoundrel replied, "Probably freeze to death." People like that will be made to pay. Trudi got very upset and wept terribly.

At noon, an officer from the police station came by to inquire about my citizenship. After I had cleared that up, I used the opportunity to describe to him Kiese's behavior. He was beside himself; it is a good thing for decent officials to know what sort of riffraff there is out and about. He was a decent man.

The First Deportations

Tuesday, February 20, 1940   Breslau

What does the concept of justice even mean anymore? Violence is all there is. In the Community sitting room yesterday I heard that the Jews in Kolberg and Stettin were deported with only their rucksacks.[1] If this is true, it would mean that the Germans are planning a major action in Scandinavia; the Norwegian violation of neutrality would offer the needed pretext because there are no "ethnic Germans" whom the Norwegians might have oppressed.[2]

Today is Trudi's thirty-ninth birthday; this year, it is coming at a bad time, and all I can wish her is that things will be different next year. She surely doesn't have it easy, although she takes great pleasure in the children.

Wednesday, February 21, 1940   Breslau

In the afternoon, Trudi and Susanne were overjoyed to receive a large package of clothing from America, which the Rufs had forwarded from St. Gallen. Susannchen will be well provided with clothes for at least a year. Trudi also got two dresses. Naturally, the material is first class. I tend to feel more comfortable as a giver than a taker, but in these times one must adapt, and those outside know what is happening to us.

1. On February 12 and 13, 1940, approximately 1,500 Stettin Jews and other Pomeranian Jews were deported to the so-called "Jewish Reservation of Lublin" on orders of Pomeranian Gauleiter Franz Schwede (1888–1960).

2. This refers to the Altmark incident in which the German tanker *Altmark* passed through neutral Norwegian waters carrying about 300 captured British merchant sailors. After three perfunctory searches by the Norwegian Navy, the British Royal Navy boarded the vessel, on February 16.

Friday, February 23, 1940   Breslau

Slovakia is full of German troops, and it is to be assumed that something will happen in the southeast. There are 2,000 Jewish emigrants from Germany in Bratislava, most of them housed in a powder factory. Rose Hoffmann, the daughter of Rabbi Hoffmann, and a former teacher in the Jewish school here, is among them. An entire transport of special hachshara people intending to push on to Erez Israel is stuck there. But they are being taken care of.

Saturday, February 24, 1940   Breslau

A strange accident occurred at our cemetery in Cosel. An airplane flew too low, grazing the dome of the chapel, which caught fire and burned to the ground. The airplane crashed, and the entire crew died. And so, the war even encroaches upon the dead. I myself have seldom been in Cosel; the last time I was in the chapel was at Hugo's burial eight years ago. Twenty-eight years ago when I was in the Field Artillery Regiment von Peucker, the present airfield was our drill ground for horse-drawn exercises.[3] How often were we ordered when setting the cannons, "General direction: the Jew," by which was meant the top of the cemetery chapel.

This afternoon, Ruth's package arrived, a lovely chicken weighing eight pounds, a present from the Jensens, and from Ruth herself a cheese, butter, and a bar of chocolate for Susanne on her birthday. Our joy was enormous, of course; but such moments always pain me, that I must accept the fruits of a child's labor. She must have amply proved her worth, otherwise these people would not have sent us the chicken, and of that I am very proud. We are living under extraordinary conditions. By the way, this is the first chicken that we have eaten since the beginning of the war.

Tuesday, February 27, 1940   Breslau

One must be content with the small joys in life. Yesterday afternoon we had a part of the chicken that Ruth sent, and it was a great source of pleasure watching Susanne picking at the bones because we haven't

3. The Field Artillery Regiment von Peucker was the Silesian Veterans Regiment Number 6, named after Eduard von Peucker (1791–1876), a Prussian general from Silesia.

seen chicken bones in a long time. We are trying as best we can to provide the child with as happy a childhood as possible. Unfortunately, we
cannot shield her from all that is going on; she dreams about bombers
and the like.

Wednesday, February 28, 1940   Breslau
Animated discussion, with Trudi as well; naturally, she is worried given
the events in Stettin. It seems to have been confirmed that all of the
Jews there were deported, about 900. Among them, the father of Dr.
Barasch, who lives here. He wrote to his father, and the letter was returned with the notation, "Addressee unknown, moved"! When he tried
to call, the operator told him that service had been disconnected at the
request of the subscriber. What mendacity! We have no idea what has
happened to these people! It may well be that we will experience similar
things here since I have the feeling that events are simply out of control.

Thursday, February 29, 1940   Breslau
Anita Lasker and Konrad Latte came by yesterday, at seven forty-five,
an impossible hour; naturally, I wouldn't receive them.[4] Those are not
visiting hours. I heard from the Brienitzers that the Jews are being
cleared out of Hamburg and Bremen; Jews from Stettin were sent to
Lublin and Kielce, where one death has already occurred.

Sunday, March 3, 1940   Breslau
Bürckel, the Gauleiter of the Saarpfalz, gave a speech in Kassel in commemoration of the fifth anniversary of the vote—since the Saar region
has evidently been cleared of civilians—in which he stated that at the
end of the war no Richelieu will dictate the peace; the document will
simply bear the signature: A. H.[5] Regardless of the outcome, this for-
lorn heap of 200,000 Jews in the Old Reich will be the pawns. Trusting
in G'd, let us continue to peer into the future. In Lublin there will be a
minyan, and people will continue to pray!

4. Anita Lasker and Konrad Latte remained close friends throughout their lives,
bound especially by their common musical interests. Both of them survived as a
result of their music, Lasker as a cellist in Auschwitz, and Latte in the underground
in Berlin.

5. Josef Bürckel (1895–1944) was Gauleiter of the "Saarpfalz" [Saar Palatinate]
from 1926 to 1944. He is presumed to have committed suicide.

This afternoon I wrote a very lengthy letter to the Institute for the Advancement of the Science of Judaism. I asked whether they would entrust to me the co-editorship of the second volume of *Germania Judaica*! And I requested that my name also appear on the title page!

Tuesday, March 5, 1940   Breslau
Susannchen's birthday went very nicely, and what our dear child will remember from this day is that parental love did all it could to make it as happy as possible. Two hundred grams of cocoa arrived from Switzerland, an especially luxurious item in these times. Grandmother Proskauer will move out of the Lothringerstrasse and into the Beate Guttmann Home.

Friday, March 8, 1940   Breslau
At the moment I am wrestling with an idea: I want to come to a scholarly understanding of the cause of the fate of the Jews in the Diaspora. Previous Jewish historiography has never seriously considered this question because it has always become stuck in apologetics. I doubt that my weakened powers will suffice to come to a resolution, but at least I want to gather as much material as possible, even though I will be unable to work through it. It is a shame that intellectual maturity so often increases as physical stamina wanes.

Sunday, March 10, 1940   Breslau
At 12 o'clock, we heard the broadcast of the celebration in the Zeughaus in Berlin. I heard the Führer's speech from one of the loudspeaker columns.[6] There is always something electrifying about hearing him speak like this. His reasoning is difficult to refute. But it is bitter that there is

6. This is Cohn's first reference to the outdoor loudspeaker system that broadcast propaganda throughout the Reich. Shortly before it hosted the 1938 German Gymnastics and Sports Festival, Breslau became the first city in Germany to be outfitted with an operational "model Reich loudspeaker column network," with a total of 100 such "Reich loudspeaker columns." With this network, the regime had at its disposal "an effective means available at any time to conduct propaganda work about the movement and the state." The "total unity of the network and its immense area of coverage" were evident in the fact that in certain parts of the city it was impossible to escape exposure. See the article "Reichsminister Dr. Goebbels nahm Musteranlage des Reichslautsprechersäulennetzes in seine Obhut," in *Schlesien—Volk und Raum*, July 1938, p. 146.

so much poverty and misery behind all this world history that we are living through, and we have no idea when it will end. A person must remain sober and objective when, as it happens, his son or sons must fight within the ranks of the enemy. After all, they went out into the world to create a new life for themselves in peace, and now all of this has to occur. If only we didn't have to think so much.

Tuesday, March 12, 1940   Breslau
Yesterday at the synagogue, I read a shocking card from a Jew from Pomerania, who was deported to the area around Lublin. The poor people appear to have been robbed of their possessions; they repeatedly use the same trick, disconnecting the baggage car while underway!

Saturday, March 16, 1940   Breslau
The barber was very upset. His guild has decided that Jews, to the extent that they are served at all, must be served only before nine in the morning! And I arrived at noon! He is terribly afraid of being spied on by his customers.

Friday, March 22, 1940   Breslau
Today is Good Friday. During the Middle Ages, Jews were generally not allowed to go out on this day; the Good Friday liturgy still prays for the *perfidi Judaei*, a passage that as a rule is translated as "faithless." However, a comparison with other passages makes it clear that this can refer only to unbelieving Jews. I discussed this matter with Dr. Jedin, who at first disagreed, but was then won over to my interpretation.[7]

Saturday, March 23, 1940   Breslau
Received a very nice letter from Baeck for the Institute for the Advancement of the Science of Judaism that reinvigorated me, something that I need occasionally to do this work. This morning, after Dr. Jedin sent me

7. Interestingly, this conversation recapitulated a controversy within the Catholic Church. Between 1926 and 1928, a movement involving approximately three thousand priests (including cardinals and archbishops) known as the Amici Israel attempted to reform the Good Friday liturgy using similar arguments. Their purpose was primarily to facilitate Jewish conversion. However, the Amici Israel was dissolved by the Holy Office on doctrinal grounds and its leaders forced to recant. See Hubert Wolf, trans. Kenneth Kronenberg, *Pope and Devil: The Vatican's Archives and the Third Reich* (Cambridge, MA: Harvard University Press, 2010), pp. 81–125.

the material I needed, I managed to finish a fairly difficult article about Luxembourg for *Germania Judaica*. The next town I plan to work on is Enghien. No one knows what fate awaits him. Recently, Herr Helfgott related the following at the synagogue: 1,000 Jewish war prisoners from Poland had been transported to Lublin, released there, and their clothes taken from them. They were then forced to beg their way home. Such is the humaneness of these times! Never has brutalization been greater!

Wednesday, March 27, 1940   Breslau
Yesterday, Berlinger told me about the last Gestapo summonses. There was a tremendous bellowing and shouting, and in particular a search for hard currency. Certificates from Jews are no longer recognized; a district physician has to issue a new certificate, otherwise a person may not sit down. Naturally, fees must be paid accordingly.

Friday, March 29, 1940   Breslau
Today, we were summoned by the Gestapo to the Am Anger School, the subject of so much internecine Jewish feuding in the past.[8] That seems like such a long time ago! I felt so pained as I walked past the now completely leveled synagogue. In any case, I want to describe this visit in detail as it may perhaps serve as a historical document sometime in the future. The tone was more decent than the first time; perhaps the Jews will be terrorized next time. How often have I been in this building, where lectures were given at the Jewish House of Teaching, and where the Jewish Community Library was housed. On the site of the latter is now the doorkeeper's box, where the SS-man is seated. We then had to wait in the inner courtyard for more than half an hour. This was not pleasant because it began to snow heavily. They then formed two groups; one contained all the Cohns, and the other everyone else who had been summoned. And within the group of Cohns they proceeded alphabetically by first name so that in fact I had the good fortune of being the very last.

Inside, the interrogations proceeded very quickly: identity card, what have you done in connection with your emigration? I pointed to my pension certificate; he saw from the yellow paper that I also have

8. The building of the Reform Am Anger School had been confiscated on November 24, 1938. It was located next to the site of the now-destroyed New Synagogue and diagonally opposite Breslau police headquarters.

the Apala papers.[9] I said that I didn't think it would come to much; he thought that the Apala documents were the only thing that mattered. This proved to me that German officials are particularly interested in this material because they intend to pocket one hundred percent of the resultant hard currency. They won't earn any hard currency from the other things. He then asked me what I was living on: pension, savings, and when I tried to tell him that my assets and the children's are separate, he told me not to talk so much. I told him approximately 9,000 marks in total and 325 marks in pension. All in all, I spent one minute in the room.

Saturday, March 30, 1940   Breslau
Attended synagogue yesterday evening; old Grünmandel was very moving as he bid farewell to our little synagogue; he will be leaving for Pressburg/Bratislava on Tuesday, probably for good. I'm sure that his daughter more or less forced him; otherwise, he might have been able to survive on the rest of his assets, but as it is he has sold all of his things, and he can't take any of the money with him. There are some strange people; they get more upset when a Jewish child does not obey his parents as he should than when an official of the Gestapo yells at them.

Monday, April 1, 1940   Breslau
I rode to the tax office at about eight thirty. It is always a relief to be treated well at one of these offices. Outside in the corridor, I had a conversation with a Jewish woman who knew me. She said, "Who doesn't know you?" I'm always flattered to hear things like that.

Walked across the Lessing Bridge to the Diocese Archive; there I heard that Nowack, the previous director, had died at the end of March.[10] May the earth lie lightly upon him. He was very good to me, and it was through his kindness that I was able to do scholarly work for the past several years. Spoke with Konsistorialrat Engelbert, the new director. He told me that the cathedral had been offered the shelving

9. 9. Apala (actually Ha'apala) refers to the so-called Aliyah Bet, which Cohn calls Hachshara B. This was the illegal immigration to Palestine outside the British Mandate quota system; the Zionists called it "clandestine" immigration.

10. Alfons Nowack (1868–1940), the archive director, died on March 13, 1940.

from the Fränckelsche Foundation's library, but at a very high price. They knew nothing of the fate of the library itself.

Sunday, April 7, 1940   Breslau
Afternoon. The morning mail brought a card from Erna today. Her eldest son [Hans Proskauer] has now left Naples for America on the steamship *Rex*. They have also received a visa and will soon be setting sail. We three surviving siblings will then be living on three different continents.

Monday, April 8, 1940   Breslau
Yesterday, a lecture by Rabbi Hamburger about Pesach; it has been made particularly hard for us this year. The authorities in Breslau are the most radical, and have refused to release the flour certificate for the matzoh factory, even in exchange for bread coupons as was the practice in all other cities. The Reich Association has now approached the police authorities about extending the curfew in consideration of summer time, and for suspending the curfew on Seder evenings, but no one is expecting much success. They have no interest in making life easier for us.

Tuesday, April 9, 1940   Breslau
This morning, German troops advanced into Denmark and have occupied Tondern and Esbjerg; even Copenhagen has been occupied. Once again, another country is returning home to the Greater German Reich, and the King of Denmark will become a German Gauleiter. Is the world going to swallow this as well, or will the powerful neutral countries like the United States intervene on the side of France and England?

I wonder how our big daughter is faring? I'm sure she is very upset because she knows what a German occupation means for her personally. No sooner have we gotten our Jewish children safely to neutral Denmark than that country, too, is drawn into the war. In the end, all of Europe will go up in flames.

Monday, April 15, 1940   Breslau
In the morning, Stadtrat Less sent a messenger; he wants me to call him or come over soon. If I had known that the matter only concerned whether I would assume responsibility for the Community Archive, I wouldn't have hurried as much. We then had a lengthy discussion

about more general things; in terms of the matter at hand, I will discuss it with Dr. Halpersohn to see whether I might get involved. I would do it only if it were under my sole direction. I also told him that I would not accept compensation. I doubt that anything will come of it because Dr. Halpersohn would surely wish to maintain his supervisory role, but I won't do it under those conditions.

Friday, April 19, 1940   Breslau

Trudi returned very late from the butcher, where she stood for an hour and a half. I felt very badly for her. It is surely a particular form of harassment that Jewish housewives may make purchases only during very tightly controlled hours. I spoke with Dr. Freund at the synagogue; he just returned from the deathbed of his son-in-law, Spiegel, at the concentration camp at Sachsenhausen, close to Oranienburg, near Berlin. He had to wait there for three hours, which they apparently used to return the dead man to a state in which he could be shown. His face was uninjured, but one arm was apparently not. In addition, they had apparently permitted him to starve. They make people work in the concentration camps and then don't give them anything to eat. These things that are being done to poor, defenseless human beings will one day come back to haunt Germany. But the people who have died under such miserable circumstances can never be brought back to life.

Sunday, April 21, 1940   Breslau

A very fast letter from Ernst dated April 10, a speed record for this distance. He writes, among other things, that they are tilling their fields in peace while Europe has nothing better to do than to smash heads. But the most important news for us is that Kibbutz Maos is prepared to accept us; to our great joy Ernst has succeeded in his efforts. But whether we can take advantage of it remains more than doubtful.

Tuesday, April 23, 1940   Breslau

The Seder evening yesterday went very nicely. In spite of all the difficulties, which have to do with the times, Trudi was able to prepare everything, and the Seder plate looked very respectable. Susanne did a wonderful job asking the questions, and I tried as best I could to explain everything. We remembered the children who are outside Germany, and we were very happy to spend the Seder evening with such good news from all of them. Susannchen very much wants to be in Palestine next year, and she sang לשנה הבאה בא"י with great enthusiasm.[11] I hope with all my heart that her wish will be fulfilled, but no one knows where the apple will roll!

Thursday, April 25, 1940   Breslau
Anita Lasker visited yesterday afternoon; she had actually wanted to say goodbye to us because they planned to leave for Bozen on Friday, but at the last moment they didn't get an Italian visa. Inquiries must again be made to Italy because they are Jews. Dr. Lasker had a nervous breakdown. Personally, I don't think I can bear all of the upheaval associated with these things.

On the way back, I visited the "Freundehaus" to enquire about matzoh. You have to make a legally binding declaration that you won't eat meat for the entire year. Naturally, I refused to submit to such a stipulation.

Thursday, May 2, 1940   Breslau
Went to the cemetery this morning, then to the stonemason's office and consulted on renovations to the family grave. It was peaceful and quiet; Susannchen said a prayer for her grandmother. Flowers are beginning to poke up everywhere. I also found the grave of one of my sisters, who I knew had lived, but who died at the age of six months.

Friday, May 3, 1940   Breslau
Yesterday afternoon as I was going to shul, a group of little tykes threw stones at me as I came by and called out, "Here comes another fat old Jew," or the like. Repulsive children. I regret that I can't just give these little fellows a pasting, but that would endanger the synagogue.

Sunday, May 5, 1940   Breslau
Yesterday, toward evening, my neighbor Herr N., who is a court cashier, told me about the many Aryans being arrested by the Gestapo based on denunciations; all of the people convicted of listening to foreign radio stations had been denounced.[12]

---

11. Susanne sang "Next year in Erez Israel"; actually "Next year in Jerusalem" is sung at the end of the Seder.

12. Cohn was surely protecting his informant by abbreviating his name, but he occasionally talked to a neighbor in the apartment by the name of Nikolaus.

Took a walk with my child as far as our old neighborhood, the Kirschallee and Wölflstrasse. Jews are now forbidden to sit on any of the benches on the Hohenzollernstrasse at Hindenburgplatz. We sat for a while in the Kürassierstrasse; it was quite cold out.

Monday, May 6, 1940   Breslau
Trudi had to stand in line for a very long time today at the Lukas grocery store, and then for a reply coupon at the post office. Usually I do this, but I found the stairs especially hard to negotiate today. At the last moment, the city food supply office invalidated chocolate for Jewish children only. Such petty harassment would otherwise surely be unnecessary.

Tuesday, May 7, 1940   Breslau
Attended synagogue. Walked part of the way home with Heilborn the pharmacist; a six-year-old child was standing in front of the school yelling "Jew snot." This is how these small children are being incited.

Thursday, May 9, 1940   Breslau
The morning mail brought me the great joy of a Red Cross letter from Ernst in which he writes that he is pressing our application. It made me very happy to see his handwriting again. Later, accompanied Trudi to Dr. Freund, first in the Victoriastrasse, where we heard that he is seeing patients in the Wallstrasse, where a part of the Jewish Hospital is now located on the second floor.

Friday, May 10, 1940   Breslau
Heard some big news on the loudspeaker on the way to the bank. German troops are on the march against Belgium, the Netherlands, and Luxembourg. On the radio, Goebbels proved that the others had violated neutrality. I'm certain that in the Netherlands they will encounter the stiffest of resistance.

Saturday, May 11, 1940   Breslau
I spoke with my cobbler, Kulissa, from whom I picked up a pair of shoes. He is a most intelligent man. He thinks that Germany is just waiting for the other side to drop the first gas grenade, whereupon they will let loose a terrible barrage of gas such that nothing will be left alive.

Today, possibly for the first time, I personally experienced an anti-Semitic act. I sat down with my newspaper on a bench in the Hohenzollernstrasse with no sign on it. A rather unfriendly looking Aryan women was sitting on the other end. Later, a man came and sat down between us. Under her breath, but still loud enough for me to hear, she said to him, "There are still so many Jews running free." I immediately left without glancing at her; however, behind my back I heard her say, "Look at him beat it."

Tuesday, May 14, 1940   Breslau
The newspaper reports huge victories for the Germans. All of northern Holland is in German hands. German airborne troops are already in Rotterdam. This war is advancing at breathtaking speed, and unless there is a miracle I think that the continental war will soon be decided in favor of Germany.

Wednesday, May 15, 1940   Breslau
Received a number of encouraging letters yesterday. The Proskauers have finally gotten tickets on the next Italian ship, the *Conte di Savoia*, which will be departing Genoa day after tomorrow. May G'd grant that the future will not hold too many difficulties for them. After all, she is my sister, and she has been faithful in her correspondence and tried to make things up to me.[13]

Susannchen heard an ugly remark from an elderly man today in the dairy. Once the war is over, the Jews won't be allowed to run free here anymore. I always feel so badly when the child's impressionable soul is burdened by such remarks; as for myself, I no longer pay them much heed.

Thursday, May 16, 1940   Breslau
A request from Stadtrat Less for a discussion about the matter of the archive. I was first announced to Dr. Tallert regarding the archive matter, but because Less was unavailable at the moment I went to the office to inquire about work deployments.[14] Less was very formal, as always,

13. Between August 7, 1939, and May 15, 1940, Willy Cohn wrote about forty detailed letters and postcards to his sister in Italy. These letters are a valuable supplement to the diaries and are in the possession of Louis Cohn's descendants in France.

14. Jews were continually required to do work for the city. Even though Cohn was exempt for health reasons, he evidently wished to make inquiries.

but I got into a rather heated clash with Rabbi Dr. Halpersohn; in the end, I requested that I be withdrawn from further consideration.

Tuesday, May 28, 1940   Breslau
Went to the Palestine Office, which is now located on the second floor of Wallstrasse 5. I handed in the so-called Apala questionnaire; for us it is merely a formality since we don't qualify because of the small children! But, you have to be able to show the Gestapo what you have done.

Saturday, June 1, 1940   Breslau
Received a long letter from Herr Kohn, in Schweidnitz; the Jewish cemetery has again been vandalized there. The work of evil people. Trudi left early in the morning. Ration card controls are being introduced to ensure that Jewish households are buying from the right stores; however, the controls have been postponed to Tuesday.

Tuesday, June 4, 1940   Breslau
It is a good thing that one can't look into the future. My own personal situation is especially tragic. My inner sympathies happen to be with Germany, which I am convinced is fighting for living space, but my eldest son, whom I love so dearly and who I had always hoped would be my successor in the intellectual arena, must now fight for the other side.

Friday, June 7, 1940   Breslau
Jewish emigration will now be banned. Controls at the Gestapo are being limited purely to the reading of names! The pressure has been removed for some, but others who had completed all the preliminaries can now no longer leave! The fate of the Jews will be decided along with the fate of the world. From now on, the conversations of Breslau Jews will no longer revolve around the Gestapo as much. As it is, I live my life as reclusively as possible.

Saturday, June 8, 1940   Breslau
Spoke with Professor Weis, my old teacher and colleague. He is absolutely convinced that Germany will be victorious, and when you read the newspaper today, a person cannot but feel that the firestorm breaking over France, this old, civilized country, cannot be halted: Breakthrough at all points along the Weygand line; evacuations in Paris; more than 150,000 children to be transported away from there.

And I sit at home frightened for my eldest son and cannot do a thing to help him.

Wednesday, June 12, 1940   Breslau
Read in the newspaper, the terrible descriptions of the pulverization of France. Clouds of artillery smoke already envelop the Place de la Concorde. Paris, the unique and magnificent! The United States will in all likelihood start to send over whatever war matériel can be sent, but it will probably arrive too late.

Friday, June 14, 1940   Breslau
Flags were hung out everywhere toward noon: Paris has fallen. That has been expected for the past several days, but now that it is a fact, I find it hard to get it into my head that this *ville lumière* is now in German hands. They saved the city as such by declaring it an open city at the last moment so that it would not suffer the fate of Warsaw, and so at least its unique cultural treasures will not be destroyed even as German tanks roll through the streets of the city. It is almost unimaginable.

Thursday, June 20, 1940   Breslau
Here, all of the benches are now stamped with signs saying that they are forbidden to Jews. A sad action in the petty war against us; now even our little bit of summer will be made more difficult for us.

Friday, June 21, 1940   Breslau
This morning I had to report to the Gestapo; the next time will be on September 11. Except for the fact that I had to stand for two hours because I was at the very end of the alphabet, it was not particularly trying. I didn't have to present my emigration papers; only a few were asked about their emigration status. He asked me what avenues I was pursuing. I told him Palestine and "non-quota" immigration to America.

Sunday, June 23, 1940   Breslau
During the night of June 21–22, Berlin was for the first time attacked by airplanes; there were deaths among the civilian population. I fear that the war will become ever more merciless. The English will not so easily allow world hegemony to be torn from their hands.

Rode out to Scheitnig alone with Tamara in order to give Trudi a rest. We rode as far as the Japanese Garden, and then walked in the old park, which was beautiful. We sat on several benches. At the moment they are not stamped "Forbidden to Jews." I must feel contented with each day that I can do something for my body.

Wednesday, June 26, 1940   Breslau
Rode out to the Südpark, and walked back along the bypass railroad! At Hardenberghügel all the benches are now stamped "Forbidden to Jews." The petty war against us is continuing.

Thursday, June 27, 1940   Breslau
Rode out to Gräbschen with Trudi in the evening. We took a nice stroll through the fields, but I misjudged the time somewhat. We now have to be at home at nine o'clock, and we arrived at nine minutes past, and I had to run the final stretch, which was a considerable effort. It took an hour for my heart to calm down. If you aren't punctual, you always run the risk that some scoundrel will denounce you to the Gestapo. – My brother Rudolf and his wife have been stripped of their citizenship.[15]

Saturday, June 29, 1940   Breslau
The mail brought two encouraging letters yesterday, one of them from the Proskauers. Curt immediately found a paying position at the Academy, apparently the Academy for the History of Medicine. To our astonishment, Hans is working as a waiter. In any case, they will get by materially, and that is very reassuring. I'm very happy, especially for Erna.

Sunday, June 30, 1940   Breslau
Rode with Tamara to Scheitnig; there, too, they are beginning to stamp the benches "Forbidden to Jews." Harassment of defenseless people.

Thursday evening, July 4, 1940   Breslau
Once again the *Abendblatt* brought us a nasty surprise. The English have attacked the French war fleet in Oran, in Algeria; several warships were

---

15. On June 12, 1940, the *Deutscher Reichsanzeiger und Preussischer Staatsanzeiger* [German Reich Gazette and Prussian State Gazette] announced not only Rudolf Cohn's deprivation of citizenship, but also the revocation of his doctorate by the law faculty of the University of Breslau.

blown up.[16] The roadsteads had been laid with water mines; and so the war is continuing on its insatiable course. Who knows whether Wölfl isn't in this region right now![17] The Warsaw newspaper reports denials about the relationship between Germany and Soviet Russia, but exactly what is going on there is not at all clear to me. I anticipate that the Russians will continue their advance, and that the General Government will be occupied.[18] I think we are just at the beginning.

Sunday, July 7, 1940 Breslau
Heard bits and snatches on the radio of the Führer's triumphal entrance into Berlin. Isn't talk of triumph a bit premature?

We took a very nice walk, and it was so pleasant for the two of us to be alone together. We saw fields again, ripening grain, picked flowers, saw places where I had spent my childhood. I dearly love my Silesian heimat, even though my joy in heimat has become anything but. All is peaceful here; and none of the benches have signs saying they are forbidden to Jews.

Tuesday, July 9, 1940 Breslau
After dinner, went for a walk with Susannchen; we walked as far as Leedeborntrift and wanted to sit down there. But since the last time, "Forbidden to Jews" has been stamped on all the benches; we managed to find a waiting bench at a streetcar stop, but all of the simple pleasures of life are being made more difficult.

16. Although not at war with France, Britain feared that French naval assets would end up in German hands as a result of the French armistice with Germany. About 1,300 French servicemen were killed in the English action, known as the Attack on Mers-el-Kébir. Several warships were sunk as well.

17. After the German occupation of France, Cohn's son was conscripted into the French Foreign Legion and stationed in North Africa. Cohn knew about this, but he did not know that Wölfl was placed in a penal company, in 1941. However, service in the Foreign Legion was no protection from possible deportation as the German consul in North Africa had noted the names of all Jewish legionnaires. Only the Allied landing, in 1942, precluded his being sent to Auschwitz.

18. With the defeat of Poland and the loss of territory to both the Soviet Union and the German Reich, the rest of occupied Polish territory, the so-called General Government, was administered by Governor-General Hans Frank, with his headquarters in Cracow.

Saturday, July 20, 1940   Breslau
Walked with Trudi through the Südpark, where we haven't been for a while. All of the benches are stamped "Forbidden to Jews" although only the fewest benches are occupied. Pure harassment. Nonetheless, the park was lovely.

Thursday, July 25, 1940   Breslau
The morning mail brought very exciting if disquieting news that Ruth will be continuing on to Palestine with the special hachshara. As wonderful as it is that she will now be reaching her final destination, I cannot close my eyes to the dangers that such a trip entails under present circumstances. Fräulein Levy did much to reassure me. The children will not be leaving on the so-called special hachshara, but will be traveling separately, she assumes via Moscow, and she thinks that they will be well cared for. May G'd grant that she is right.

Saturday, July 27, 1940   Breslau
Walked with Eugen Perle after the service. He told me that Jewish tenants continue to be evicted, often with 14-day notice. The reason: they need the apartments for other purposes. Legal terms of notice are no longer observed. Arbitrary measures at every turn. Apartments are almost the last thing that can be taken away from the Jews. All it takes is for someone else to like the apartment, and then you are out.

Monday, July 29, 1940   Breslau
Heard on the radio a police decree that Jews may no longer buy fruit: "the petty war." Today begins the 13th rationing period. The war has lasted for 48 weeks. Bread rations have been reduced for all by 150 grams per week. Today there is air raid training for the Jewish homes, and the leaders of the Children's Home must participate. They seem to be expecting air raids!

Wednesday, July 30, 1940   Breslau
Yesterday we again saw evidence of the existence of personal loyalty on the part of Aryans. Frau Gallwitz, the building caretaker who operates a laundry, procured nine hundredweights of coal for us. At the present time, no coal may be delivered to Jews; what will happen later is also a question. In general, we often experience decency and loyalty, even though there is also a great deal of incitement. Some try to blame the

Jews for everything, but there are also people who think differently, and who blame the leadership for these offenses.

Thursday, August 1, 1940   Breslau
Unfortunately, the evening mail returned our farewell letter to Ruth. It contained a single Hebrew word, *chalutz*, and that was enough for the censor to take offense. We felt especially badly about this letter because we had poured our hearts into it.

Friday, August 2, 1940   Breslau
This morning, I went to the Cathedral Library again after a longer hiatus. Much has happened for the better since the last time, especially in terms of organization. One of the nuns is keeping a tight rein on the reading room. The reference library has been newly reorganized and the journals bound! New stacks have been put up, the shelving that used to stand in our Jewish Theological Seminary, in the Wallstrasse, and was sold to the cathedral. Herr Walter, the archivist, apologized to me for having to work in those stacks. Very tactful!

Sunday, August 4, 1940   Breslau
The evening mail brought an appreciative letter from Baeck, at least some compensation. A person needs such written recognition, especially when he works in the sort of isolation that I do where it is not possible to exchange ideas with like-minded colleagues!

Monday, August 5, 1940   Breslau
Worked in the Diocese Archive again this morning; I have it very good there. The new director, Konsistorialrat Engelbert, asked me to look at a number of manuscripts that were bound together using old Hebrew manuscript texts, and if possible determine their provenance. He also showed me the rooms of the archive where the shelving from our seminary has been set up. I heard a number of other interesting things there as well. The nuns were denied clothing cards. In addition, they are no longer permitted to minister to patients at the front.

A Polish pastor—a man in his mid-50s—was sent to a stone quarry in Linz, from where it is unlikely he will return alive.[19] The Catholic

---

19. A reference to the Mauthausen concentration camp, in Austria, which was located at the edge of a granite quarry.

Church has its own worries. I am happy that the Diocese Archive is providing me such favorable circumstances in which to work.

Friday, August 9, 1940   Breslau
My father-in-law is very afraid of being deported to Lublin, and because of this he wants to go to South America. Such thoughts are very foreign to me!

Monday, August 12, 1940   Breslau
Spent an interesting morning in the Diocese Archive. First, I had a very interesting conversation with the director, Konsistorialrat Engelbert, about scholarly problems. He told me that he had discovered a Hebrew gravestone in the Mauritius Church, which he wanted me to take a look at. Of course, it can only have come from the old Jewish cemetery. Engelbert thought that my theory, that the Jews had originally lived on these cemetery grounds, was very convincing.

I was able to establish that five old Schweidnitz manuscripts, which were from the sixteenth century and are bound in with wonderful Hebrew manuscripts, are parts of a prayer book that was in all probability once used by the cantor of Schweidnitz. Engelbert even suggested that I publish my findings in the *Zeitschrift für schlesische Kirchengeschichte*.[20] But it seems to me that publishing in that journal might endanger him. In any case, I was very pleased with the offer. Furthermore, Engelbert told me that he rejected an offer to collaborate on a history of the city of Breslau, which is to be published on the city's anniversary. He did not wish his name to appear on the title page along with that of the former mayor, Schönwälder, a former stonecutter; nor did he wish to write what they had or would have demanded of him. Someone with backbone and bearing. He also discussed frankly his displeasure with Aubin's *History of Silesia*, which had completely glossed over Church history.[21] It is a commonplace that the things one wishes to conceal are simply never pre-

20. The actual name was *Archiv für schlesische Kirchengeschichte*. It was edited by Kurt Engelbert and ceased publication in 1940 (vol. 5). The regime stopped distribution of the already printed and bound volume 6 (1941).

21. Nor was the ideologically motivated and unscholarly neglect of the history of the Catholic Church (and of Jewish history) corrected after the war. Rather, this neglect on the part of the Historical Commission for Silesia continued to be viewed as merely a "deficiency resulting from the times." Preface to *Geschichte Schlesiens*, ed.

sented. The same thing is being done to the Jews. The war has penetrated into the realm of scholarship. Such scholarly discussions are for me more necessary than food and drink; I have been without them for too long!

Tuesday, August 13, 1940   Breslau
Met with Herr Schatzky, who is supposed to leave with the special hachshara. About 4,000 people in all have been notified, but not told where they are going, although Palestine is surely the final destination. It is assumed that they will first go to Yugoslavia. To me, it feels like another sort of deportation, but nobody knows whether they might not have made the better decision in spite of everything.

I read an article today in the August 8 edition of *Das Schwarze Korps* that impressed me. I am not generally inclined to believe everything I read in the newspaper, but *Das Schwarze Korps* is the official organ of the SS, and it has in the past announced official measures in advance. For Germany, the Jewish problem will be solved only when the last Jew has been driven out. It seems to me symbolic that I should have read this article today, the 9th of Av, a day on which great persecutions have so often been initiated.

Tuesday, August 20, 1940   Breslau
Went to the administrative office of the Jewish Hospital, which is now located at Höfchenstrasse 101, to talk with Dr. Lydia Aschheim-Baruchsen, who translated a Polish article for me for *Germania Judaica*. I haven't talked to her for a long time; a very charming woman. Her husband tried to reach Palestine illegally and was interned at Atlit.[22] He is free now.

Saturday, August 24, 1940   Breslau
Went to synagogue to pray because I miss it terribly if I don't go at least on Friday evening. Talked with Eugen Perle about the sale of the cemetery in the Claassenstrasse. Less has suddenly had religious misgivings, which are almost certainly out of place since otherwise the cemetery will face a much worse fate!

---

by the Historische Kommission für Schlesien (St. Michael: J.G. Bläschke, 1983), vol. 1, p. 7.

22. Because the painter Isidor Aschheim tried to immigrate illegally, he was taken by British Mandate officials to the Atlit internment camp south of Haifa, and later settled in Jerusalem.

Tuesday, August 27, 1940   Breslau

We experienced the first English air raid last night; August 27 will be remembered in the history of the city of Breslau. The detonation didn't wake me since I had already lain awake since one o'clock. This was the first aircraft bombing that I had heard since 1918. For some time, I had the feeling that there were airplanes over Breslau at night. Apparently, the bomb came down not far from us, in the area of Alexis- and Kopischstrasse, and it caused quite a bit of damage.

Wednesday, August 28, 1940   Breslau

The night passed without air raids. Leaflets were apparently dropped in Görlitz bearing the message, "Of us there are eight, we will return each night." I went for a walk yesterday evening; it gets dark again between eight and nine, and when it is dark the "national comrades" talk more loudly. Yesterday, there was only one topic: the bombings. There was a real migration of people toward Kopischstrasse; I didn't quite go all the way because I didn't want to be noticed, but today I will. The Hardenberghügel has been closed off; searchlights have been emplaced there. The blackout was scrupulously observed!

Thursday, August 29, 1940   Breslau

I had the great joy yesterday morning of receiving news from Wölfl by way of the Rufs. We haven't heard anything from him in more than three months. He is well and is in a munitions depot, not in the desert. I can imagine a number of things from that description, but in any case he is alive and healthy, and that is the main thing. With G'd's help, the African climate will continue to suit him. Also received a card from Ruth, full of the spirit of the youth movement; she complains about not having found herself emotionally there. We wrote her a detailed letter and said, among other things, that she has great cause to be thankful. Of course, it is sad not to be able to talk to one's child, but that is of no help now.

Saturday, August 31, 1940   Breslau

The Jewish school building has been confiscated by the Air Office; the school will probably have to be cleared out.[23] More harassment.

---

23. Cohn is talking about the school building at Rehdigerplatz 3. The Abraham Mugdan Synagogue was also there. Cf. the entry of December 14, 1940.

Perle told me that the Aryans are running around saying that Jewish emigrants are responsible for the air raids, otherwise the bombs would not have been so accurate. The Jews are to blame for everything. If the bombs fall on civilian buildings, these are considered indiscriminate attacks; if they hit their target, the Jews betrayed their location. Childish; after all, maps of the city can be had anywhere. Be that as it may, if the bombings begin again we need to be ready for all sorts of consequences.

Sunday, September 2, 1940   Breslau
Went for a walk with Trudi and Tamara; we walked along the bypass railroad and then rode back on the streetcar. Now all of the benches there, which used to be available, are stamped, "Forbidden to Jews." The German people have serious worries. According to reports in the German newspapers, bombing raids on Berlin were very destructive.

Friday, September 6, 1940   Breslau
I often walk by the Hardenberghügel just as the soldiers are climbing up to the antiaircraft searchlights. It is lovely walking through the darkened city at night; I walked as far as the loudspeaker column in the Leedeborntrift, but it wasn't turned on. The reports are mostly the same these days. I cut old Gottheiner short when he asked me why I wasn't in Palestine. Why are people so tactless. I think he felt pained by the incident as well.

Sunday, September 8, 1940   Breslau
Took a long walk with Tamara; the child likes to walk, except that it is difficult because we aren't allowed to sit down on any of the benches. I sat her down on a stone wall, and a working woman told me I shouldn't do it because it isn't healthy. When I told her that we weren't allowed to sit down anywhere, she said, "Those idiots. I used to work for a Jewish employer, Kaliski (the cabinetmaker), and things were better then."

The cemetery in the Claassenstrasse. This is the first time I've been there, which really isn't right. A contemplative spot. Everything is overgrown, and if you want to read the individual plaques you need to climb over graves, which is actually against religious law. We looked for some of the more important graves such as those of Meyer Hilsbach, Jonas

Fraenckel, and the memorial to the cholera victims.[24] However, I didn't find the grave of my grandfather, Isaak Hainauer, which is still listed in the index. The grave must have been in the area that is now partly Bahnhofstrasse and partly air raid pool. I found two other Hainauers in the index as well. The prospective sale of the cemetery is still in its initial stages.

The orphanage has been confiscated for use by Germans from Bucovina and Bessarabia. Everything gets done at the expense of the Jews, although they say that other schools have been confiscated as well. But for the others it isn't such a loss.

Monday, September 9, 1940   Breslau
Buildings have also been taken from Catholic institutions to house returning ethnic Germans, but of course there's a difference, it isn't like with our orphanage, which is pretty much the last thing that we have. Mother Innocentia, with whom I often converse, was very upset. She told me about a prophecy, that Germany would get so big that it would fit under a tree.

Tuesday, September 10, 1940   Breslau
The orphanage had to be cleared out today.[25] Some of the children were taken to the Kirschallee, to the attic of the old-age home, some to the neurology department in the Wallstrasse. It is astonishing that people still find a way.

Wednesday, September 11, 1940   Breslau
Reported to the Gestapo, which went without incident today. The official asked me, "What efforts are you making," whereupon I replied, "To my son in Palestine, and if that doesn't work, to America with an employment contract." To which he said, "You can go." The worst part is standing for so long.

The *Abendblatt* carried a detailed report about the bombing of Berlin the previous night. An incendiary bomb even fell on the Branden-

---

24. Lieutenant Meyer Hilsbach (1793–1813) volunteered to fight Napoleon and was the first Jewish Prussian officer to die in battle at Grossgörschen.

25. For a personal account of the end of the Jewish Orphanage in Breslau, which was located at Gräbschener Str. 61–65, see Klaus Aufrichtig-Arkwright, "Unvergessene Junge Freunde," in *Mitteilungen des Verbandes ehemaliger Breslauer in Israel*, no. 62 (1997), pp. 8–9.

burg Gate, and the diplomatic quarter had to be cleared for a time. An incendiary bomb also hit the Reichstag, but it is used to being burned.[26]

Thursday, September 12, 1940   Breslau
I was told in the Cathedral Library that a Jewish old-age home in the north of Berlin was hit. I can't even imagine the details. In any case, it seems clear that the English will fight for their island to the last man. The Germans cannot at the moment bring their land superiority to bear; in the air, the English are up to the challenge, and on the seas, they have superiority.

Friday, September 13, 1940   Breslau
Went for a walk with Tamara. She wanted to sit down and rest in the Reichspräsidentenplatz, but of course we aren't allowed. It is hard to explain that to a small child. We then sat down at the corner of Kürassierstrasse and Gabitzstrasse on waiting benches that belong to the streetcar company and are not stamped "Forbidden to Jews."

Saturday, September 14, 1940   Breslau
In the evening, a relatively luxurious dinner considering the times: warm mushrooms, potatoes, and pudding, and a glass of very good Hungarian wine. At my age it does me good every now and again. Nonetheless, had a relatively bad night, lay awake for many hours even though I took sleeping pills. It was especially unpleasant this time because I had an appointment with Rabbi Dr. Leo Baeck from Berlin, a discussion that I had long been looking forward to. Nonetheless, I managed this morning and presented to him all of the things that are on my mind. Let me go down the list!

Early in the morning, I first telephoned his brother, the dentist [Dr. Richard] Baeck, who told me to pick up Rabbi Baeck at the Pension Brinnitzer, Charlottenstrasse 7.[27] To get to the point, I got to know a truly outstanding scholarly and Jewish personage, and realized once again how much I miss discussing scholarly matters with others. He

---

26. Here, Cohn is making sardonic reference to the Reichstag fire of February 27, 1933, after which most civil liberties were suspended in Germany.

27. At the time, both Dr. Martin Baeck, from Liegnitz, and Dr. Richard Baeck lived at Zimmerstrasse 5. However, only the latter had a telephone.

told me that he has had six different offers from abroad, but that he has rejected all of them because he doesn't want to desert his people, a point of view with which I completely concur. He also made clear how upset he is at the failure of the German rabbinate. It is an admirable stance to take, a stance with which I am in deep agreement. How many Jews think only about themselves! On the way to the Diocese Archive—we had to walk back and forth because of Shabbat, which was an extraordinary strain for me, much more so than for Baeck, who is 67 years old—we talked about various scholarly matters:

I. *Germania Judaica*. The main task of the teaching institution is to safeguard as much material as possible; everything is copied in triplicate and deposited for safekeeping abroad. Final editing can be done at a later date. I raised the question of whether the work might not be expanded to other epochs; however, he thought it would be better to limit ourselves, but was in agreement that I should also gather material about later epochs, just as long as the work on this volume is not hindered. And they will honor that. He apologized for the minor criticisms of my work, but after all we want to learn from each other. At the Diocese Archive, he looked at the Hebrew manuscript fragments and naturally found some things I had been unable to decipher. But the things that I had managed to translate were correct.

II. The Schweidnitz manuscripts. In Rashi script, a Hebrew commentary on portions of the machzor.[28] Hebrew in a later hand as well: suggestions for dotting. Very interesting variants to the texts that are customary today. Some *piyyut*, which might not otherwise exist.

III. Another manuscript: a fragment from Baba Mezia and a commentary on the Talmud. Another: a liturgical piece for the Shabbat para, the Shabbat for the red cow. He discussed with Konsistorialrat Engelbert photocopying everything in the state library. Baeck has specialized literature in Berlin that is not available to me; he was fascinated by everything and considers this trove to be of scholarly importance. Baeck is very formal in his manner.

On the way there and back I showed him my beloved city; he studied in Breslau years ago, but he was once again impressed by old Breslau and its incomparable cityscape. On the way back he told me

28. Rashi script is a general term for medieval Hebrew scripts.

that Professor Täubler is now also leaving Germany.[29] Just last year he helped work on a handbook of classical antiquity by Iwan von Müller.[30] One volume by Selma Stern, *The Prussian State and the Jews*, has been completed, and the entire edition has been deposited abroad for safekeeping.[31]

As for my own personal fate, I told him that I have always been bad at arranging things for myself; he replied that this would be counted to my credit in the next world. One should not regret anything that one has done. (This in reference to the fact that I did not remain in Palestine.) I accompanied him to the Kaiser Wilhelm Strasse, and at the door he told me that I should get in touch with him whenever I needed something from him of a personal nature. I told him that I would never do that, only for those of a scholarly nature. He thanked me, whereupon I replied that the thanks were completely mine.

He also expressed displeasure at the spirit that had prevailed at the seminary of late. About that we both concurred. He asked what happened to the seminary library, and I told him what Dr. Arlt had told me. I also told him about the work I had done there.

Regarding the general situation: difficult to foretell. The possibilities: Russia is victorious, possibly a later absorption into the Soviet Union: culturally dismal. England is victorious; the United States of Europe. Germany is victorious, the end of Jewish cultural life in Germany, and the obligation to rebuild in America.

I found Baeck very inspiring; he said that starting at the end, I should write my memoirs about my life in the Jewish community in Breslau.

Sunday, September 15, 1940   Breslau
Grandmother Proskauer told me that the Protestant Sisters of St. Trinitatis immediately offered to help when they heard that the orphanage

---

29. Eugen Täubler (1879–1953) taught at the Hochschule für die Wissenschaft des Judentums, in Berlin. He and his wife, Selma Stern-Täubler, emigrated to the United States in 1941. Täubler became a professor at Hebrew Union College, in Cincinnati.

30. Iwan von Müller (1830–1917) began publishing the *Handbuch der Altertumswissenschaft* [Handbook of the study of antiquity] in Munich, in 1885.

31. Selma Stern's completed seven-volume work was titled *Der preussische Staat und die Juden* (Tübingen: Mohr, 1962–1971).

had to be emptied in 24 hours, and they sent food as well.[32] I think that the government is badly served by this measure. Each injustice must eventually be expiated.

Thursday, September 19, 1940   Breslau
I went for a walk in the evening; it was a lovely clear night. However, I had to hurry at the end because an English bomber appeared at a great height. The searchlights had pinpointed the airplane in crossing searchlights. It was apparently looking for Breslau. However, it was flying so high that the antiaircraft guns stayed silent. I haven't seen such a display of searchlights since 1918.

The morning mail brought us the joy of a letter from Switzerland with news from Wölfl, dated August 29, in other words, very fast. Now I know where to direct my thoughts to him; he is in the province of Oran, in Algeria, and seems to be suffering from loneliness. But he is well, and that is the main thing. This letter made me very happy.

Saturday, September 21, 1940   Breslau
I attended the service at the Beate Guttmann Home in the evening; on the way I met Frau Wittenberg, who lost a son in the world war. She was exhausted, leaning against a light pole. She is not permitted to sit down on a bench. "You may be certain of the gratitude of the Fatherland."

Thursday, September 26, 1940   Breslau
A transport with children from England has gone down, probably torpedoed; only a few children were saved. There is no humanity anymore! I heard something yesterday that was already known to me, namely that three ghettos have been formed in the General Government: Lodz, Lublin, and Cracow; that is, Lodz, which today is called Litzmannstadt and belongs to the Warthegau, according to the new geographical realities. The Jews in Lodz will be given a quarter of a pound of horse meat per week; in addition, they are allowed to raise rabbits. When Duscha told me these things, I told him I doubted that

32. The Parish of St. Trinitatis in the Friedrichstrasse ran two homes for the sisters in the Gräbschener Strasse, the larger one in the garden house at Gräbschener Strasse 49.

rabbit feed grew in the middle of Lodz. They are undoubtedly pursuing a ghastly policy of destruction against the Jews and Poland. The war is taking ever more grisly forms.

Saturday, September 28, 1940   Breslau
Walked home with Herr Perle after service. We are told that an action is being planned against the Jews on October 6, but these announced plans tend not to occur. I went for a short walk with Tamara in the morning; one has to watch out for this little personage because she always wants to walk around on her own. Whenever someone asks her name, she says sweetly Tamara Sara.

Monday, September 30, 1940   Breslau
I pressed sauerkraut with Trudi in the afternoon. I learn things; this time I smashed my hand a bit. The morning mail brought a very nice letter from Herr Grünmandel and a very detailed letter from the Proskauers, which also contained news from Rudolf. His son, Werner, has already had his bar mitzvah. Erna writes very affectionately.[33] Today was a good mail day.

Tuesday, October 2, 1940   Breslau
We all bathed yesterday evening, a very rare pleasure. We often have to go without because of the coal shortage. With that, all of the dust of the year 5700 has been left in the tub. We stayed alive this year, and with the help of the Almighty we hope to continue into the next. For our close circle, it is my greatest wish that this year, 5701, we will see our children who have left. We also ask that we be permitted to stay in the apartment; it is the last thing that makes our life comfortable. Nonetheless, we would have to come to terms with its loss.

33. On September 9, Cohn had started a lengthy letter to his sister Erna, in New York. When he received the good news he concluded his letter with the following: "There is no need for you to worry about our fate. Rose Hoffmann knows what we need and what we do not need. In the final analysis, we are all just clay in the potter's hand, as is said in one of our prayers, and we do not wish to lose sight of life's goal." Erna and her family left Naples in May 1940, and their correspondence resumed after they reached New York. Cohn's last letter from Breslau to the Proskauers was dated November 5, 1941.

October 3, 1940 Breslau

Trudi prepared everything beautifully yesterday evening; she had saved some meat so that we could have meat yesterday and today. Susannchen recited a New Year's wish; she was very happy with her modest gifts. The main gift was a pair of slippers that Trudi and I had made ourselves. Children growing up in these times are very modest.

Writing His Memoirs

Friday, October 4, 1940   Breslau
I attended services again today at the Beate Guttmann Home; Trudi even accompanied me there so that we could at least talk a little on our wedding anniversary. I discussed with her my plan to dictate my memoirs to Fräulein Cohn. She agreed; it should be done before it is too late. I hope that G'd gives me the strength to complete this work since the first manuscript of my memoirs was lost.[1]

Monday, October 7, 1940   Breslau
Official propaganda is now focused on the redivision of the world; sounds fine enough, but in the end it means nothing other than the enslavement of the entire world. Countries like Romania, which are now ruled by Germany, must copy Germany's Jewish laws. The Jews are always the first to be targeted. Today is Himmler's 40th birthday. The blood of the Jews who died in the concentration camps sticks to his name, the Führer of the SS and the head of the German police.

Tuesday, October 8, 1940   Breslau
This morning, I first went to the ration coupon office to get an additional soap coupon for Tamara, which went quickly. On the other hand, I had to go again about gloves for the children because coupons aren't being given out for those at the moment.

---

1. Cohn had once before written memoirs, between 1935 and 1938, although their scope is not known. In April 1939, he gave his only handwritten manuscript to an acquaintance named Alfred Bruck, who was emigrating to England. Bruck, however, was arrested by the Gestapo and the manuscript seized.

Thursday, October 10, 1940   Breslau
Worked with Fräulein Cohn in the afternoon; I have started dictating my memoirs. It is joyful work for me, if only G'd will give me the strength to complete it. It will be a thick book that will bear witness to what German Jewry once was. A large Jewish old-age home in the Kirschallee had to be cleared out.[2] Now many old people will have to be accommodated elsewhere.

Saturday evening, after the end of Yom Kippur, October 12, 1940   Breslau
I attended services at the Beate Guttmann Home yesterday evening. They began late because the move from the homes that have been dissolved had not yet been completed. The Beate Guttmann Home had to take another 30 persons. It is a misery that old people should be forced out of their homes; a merciless war. The bedrooms are filled beyond capacity. Nonetheless, the Kol Nidre service is always very powerful.

Wednesday, October 16, 1940   Breslau
This morning, went with Susannchen first to the Diocese Archive, where the child was spoiled, both by Mother Huberta and by Mother Innocentia, and likewise by Director Engelbert and Walter the archivist. She was also given many things to read. She can be very adorable when she wants to! Afterward, went to the botanical garden, where I haven't been in decades. In the hothouse, Susannchen saw palm trees for the first time.

Saturday, October 19, 1940   Breslau
Yesterday I heard from Herr Perle that the Jewish cemetery in Dyhernfurth had been completely destroyed in November 1938. The property was sold to the domain![3] The end of another important chapter in Jewish history. Today, for the first time, I saw the ethnic German "evacuees" in our lovely former orphanage.

Thursday, October 24, 1940   Breslau
Grandmother Proskauer told me that I had been classified as unfit for work; from Perle I heard that a total of 68 Jews were recorded as fit

2. This was the Schottländersche Stift (foundation of the Jewish Schottländer family), diagonally opposite the Beate Guttmann Home.

3. The Jewish cemetery was located within Dyhernfurth, the domain of Thassilo Count Saurma-Hoym. Cf. diary entry of May 12, 1935.

for work. A decree has now come down from Berlin that Breslau must provide 4,000 Jews, Stettin 2,000 Jews, even though almost all of the Jews in Stettin have already been deported to Lublin. The Provincial Labor Office in Breslau has decreed that as of November 1, there may be no unemployed Jews under the age of 60. They are at cross purposes.

Saturday, October 26, 1940   Breslau

Yesterday morning, to our great joy, we received a very detailed letter from Ruth, which nonetheless betrayed great anxiety. She has no one with whom she can talk, and this is especially necessary at that age! She wrote about this less in our letter than in a letter she enclosed to Anita Lasker. Being torn away from one's children is the worst of it.

The *Geserah* of the Baden Jews

Wednesday, October 30, 1940   Breslau

When visited Herr Perle, he told me what happened in Baden and in the Palatinate. About 7,000 Jews were evacuated, and they were given only an hour and a half to ready their baggage. Each was permitted to take a hundred marks with them. A severe stroke of fate, but given today's circumstances, one never knows what will turn out to the good. They were taken to unoccupied France, probably to a barracks camp. In all probability, some Gauleiter wanted to make a name for himself and make his region "Jew-free."[1] How many human tragedies must have played themselves out there. No one knows whether we may not be facing a similar fate. Tomorrow has been declared a day of fasting because of the *geserah* in Baden.

Thursday, October 31, 1940   Breslau

I was affected all day yesterday by the implications of the news. My heart is full of sympathy for the victims; there is nothing we can do about what lies ahead of us except to keep our suitcases at the ready with the barest necessities so that at least the children are protected from the worst. In spite of these intrusive thoughts, I managed to get a good deal of work done yesterday.

1. This information was correct. Between October 22 and 23, 1940, about 6,500 German Jews were deported from Baden and the Saar Palatinate to the concentration camp at Gurs, in southwestern France. This deportation was initiated by Gauleiter Joseph Bürckel, and it occurred at the same time as the resettlement of larger population groups from the provinces of Alsace and Lorraine, which had been annexed by Germany. It remained the only deportation of Jews to the west.

I spent this morning in the Cathedral Library; told Konsistorialrat Engelbert about the events in Baden and the Palatinate. He was very upset. We also discussed the transfer of my personal library to the Cathedral Library should I ever be deported; however, he doubted that the Nazis would view such an arrangement as valid.

Friday, November 1, 1940   Breslau
Talked with Trudi in the evening; in any case, we will put together a few things in the event that we are suddenly forced to leave.

Saturday, November 2, 1940   Breslau
Yesterday afternoon before synagogue I made a long-intended visit to see the wife of Sanitätsrat Spitz at the old-age home in the Kirschallee. She gave me a number of very significant things having to do with her father, Dr. David Honigmann, who was a well-known personage here in Breslau. I also received a whole stack of letters from Abraham Geiger.[2] Then she related the entire odyssey of her children. Briefly: Barcelona (Spanish Civil War); flight from Barcelona via Perpignan, France, to Italy; then return to Barcelona, where they dug their things out of the rubble; now in Bilbao; in the process of going to the United States. Daughter in the Dominican Republic, two sons in England; the fate of the Jews in our times. At one time a sheltered family. The old lady, now over 80, is here all alone. The Rehdiger school has to be cleared by January 1, 1941, and given to the Air Office. And so, one institution after another is disappearing; total war is being waged against us. Yesterday evening we packed a few suitcases so as to be prepared in case the worst happens and we are driven out. Hopefully it won't come to that.

Sunday, November 3, 1940   Breslau
Conversations automatically keep returning to the sad events that took place in Baden, and in the Palatinate. This morning, I spent the larger part of my time working on my memoirs, and again made good progress. If only I am able to get this manuscript into safekeeping for later times.

2. Abraham Geiger (1810–1874) was a German rabbi and scholar who propounded a dispassionate, "scientific" Jewish historiography. A convinced assimilationist, Geiger was one of the founders of the Reform movement in Judaism.

Tuesday, November 5, 1940   Breslau
Yesterday, I had the great pleasure of a visit from Anita Lasker; she will not be going to Berlin, and I can understand why her parents would not allow it. The girl's appearance is completely captivating.

Thursday, November 7, 1940   Breslau
Our grocer, Münzner, was summoned to police headquarters because of us.[3] That hideous Frau Belit denounced him because he sold fruit to Trudi. It may well be that we will receive a summons as well on that account; there are too many subhumans.

Friday, November 8, 1940   Breslau
I reorganized my old scholarly correspondence yesterday morning. I was in contact with so many people, and if I have the time, I intend to add notes to the letters with the most important material about those men and relationships, a piece of scholarly history. Sometimes life now seems to be purely vegetative. It is a good thing that I have found a refuge in the Cathedral Library.

Sunday, November 10, 1940   Breslau
In the afternoon, I dictated a nice piece of my memoirs, describing my father's death. This brought up many things from the past. – Fräulein Silberstein set the record straight about the actions in Baden and the Palatinate. Only eight people took their lives, not 80; eleven attempted though. By notarial action, the remaining property of the deportees was transferred to the Reich Association. And six hours were granted for preparations.

Thursday, November 14, 1940   Breslau
I dictated a lengthy letter to the society in the afternoon; I am constantly dealing with Baeck's minor editorial criticisms. He wrote me a letter that was very nice in form, but there are always these details that he objects to. I took another pill to strengthen the heart, and it allowed me to work better. Visit by Molotov; they are preparing their propaganda campaign. Enemy of the State No. 1 is now the Führer's friend.

---

3. Franz Münzner had his store at Opitzstrasse 28, in the apartment building in which the Cohns lived. The family of Master Sergeant (for maintenance) Belit lived diagonally across at Opitzstrasse 27.

Saturday, November 16, 1940   Breslau
Terrible bomb attacks on Coventry.[4] Thousands dead. A horrific war.

Wednesday, November 20, 1940   Breslau
I received a card yesterday morning from Professor Goerlitz, inviting me to visit him.[5] He was a student at the Johannesgymnasium and did his Abitur in 1903. We got into a conversation about old teachers and about how well the students of the various confessions are doing. Goerlitz told me that he does not belong to any part of the party. Our conversation mainly revolved around the Jewish settlement in Breslau, and his calculation of the size of that community. My view on the matter seemed plausible to him. He took great interest in the fate of the Jews overall, consistently speaking of Jewish citizens not "racial comrades," as is so frequently the custom here these days. I came away with the feeling that he is a very distinguished and goodly person. I showed him my identity card; he was very upset by the "J."

Saturday, November 30, 1940   Breslau
Yesterday morning went to the barber and then the bank, where I conducted business for three quarters of an hour, settling the difficult matter of the accounts of the children who have now emigrated. In any case, we will get 300 marks from Ruth's money, which will make things easier. I will have an additional 300 marks transferred to my in-laws. Paid the rent, then my quarterly report to the Gestapo. This time, we didn't have to congregate outside but went into the former Wochentagssynagoge.

Tuesday, December 3, 1940   Breslau
I got ready at six o'clock this morning to go visit my former student, Dr. Hermann Kienitz, the deputy director of the State Office for Race

4. The bombing of Coventry occurred on November 14, 1940. The raid was considered such a triumph that the verb *coventrieren* (to "coventrate") entered the vocabulary of the Third Reich to describe the leveling of a city.

5. Thus began an animated scholarly exchange with legal historian Theodor Goerlitz (1885–1949). The Herder Institute, in Marburg, now has his papers. It contains five letters from Willy Cohn to Goerlitz from the period between December 8, 1940, and June 4, 1941.

and Clan Research.[6] Kienitz arrived punctually at seven o'clock; I received the majority of the material that I had lent to Dr. Arlt when he was still there; a small part of it was not there. Dr. Arlt is in Kattowitz, in the district of Bielitz, directing the resettlement of ethnic Germans from Galicia and Volhynia.

Wednesday, December 4, 1940   Breslau
Went to the barber first thing in the morning. He showed me the decree stating that Jews may no longer be shaved; however, he says I should continue to come anyway. Had a very interesting time with Professor Goerlitz. He told me that at least twelve scholars were dead at the Polish university in Posen, and that a Polish city archivist with years of service had been expelled from Thorn to the General Government, and other terrible things. Goerlitz even asked about his many Jewish schoolmates at the Johannesgymnasium! It was a very stimulating hour!

Thursday, December 5, 1940   Breslau
Worked in the Cathedral Library this morning after taking a few days off. Director Engelbert began to worry about me because I hadn't been seen in several days. His concern was very touching; they really spoiled me there today, both intellectually and bodily. Engelbert asked me to evaluate a parish history, which was submitted for Church imprimatur. I considered this great recognition of my scholarly work. However, a brief glance sufficed to show that the article did not meet basic scholarly requirements.

I was also spoiled bodily. Frau Jilek, the gatekeeper's wife, sold me some food that she had left over, including some goose fat. She told me that she once worked as a maid in a Jewish household and was apparently treated very well.[7]

Thursday, December 12, 1940   Breslau
Trudi set a birthday table for me, mainly very practical things for my office, which continues to expand. I could work more if I had the

6. See Hermann Kienitz, *Das sippenkundliche Schrifttum Schlesiens 1935* (Breslau: Schlesische Arbeitsgemeinschaft für Sippenforschung, 1937).

7. Like Engelbert, the widow Anna Jilek lived in the Cathedral Library building. She demonstrated such humanity toward Willy Cohn that she deserves special mention.

strength; there is no shortage of material. I am 52 years old, and sometimes I feel as if I were an old man; but occasionally I am young and enterprising again, although those days are very rare.

Friday, December 13, 1940   Breslau
The morning mail brought the news that Ruth has left Denmark; she wrote from Copenhagen. I hope that this will be for the best for our child. It was thrilling news. She is very excited about being with Ernst again, but we may not hear anything from her for months. It is not easy being Jewish parents these days! Also received very fresh news from Wölfl, dated November 21.

Saturday, December 14, 1940   Breslau
Discussed a number of things with Eugen Perle. The gentlemen from the Abraham Mugdan Synagogue, which is to be closed next week, have managed to throw a wrench in the works for the board.

Wednesday, December 18, 1940   Breslau
We were elated to receive a letter from Ruth, from Stockholm. She writes enthusiastically about all the beautiful things she has seen, and she thinks that she may reach her destination by December 22, in other words in four days. Apparently they will travel through Russia; she is completely consumed by the prospect of what lies ahead. For all the pain of separation, I am nonetheless happy that I have set her on the right path. Only such people can ensure the rebirth of the Jewish people!

Thursday, December 19, 1940   Breslau
Archive; Engelbert told me, among other things, about the sharp contrast between the military and the SS in occupied Poland. The SS doesn't want the military to give the population so much as a single morsel of bread. We were in agreement about the overall situation.

Sunday, December 22, 1940   Breslau
Day before yesterday, for once, I didn't go to synagogue; it was very cold out. In the afternoon, our neighbor in the house, Herr Teuber, brought us peas and apples; we gave him milk. This is how we help each other; we have some very decent neighbors in this house.

Monday, December 23, 1940   Breslau
Received a card from Ruth, from Helsinki, the capital of Finland. She writes that she was very well received there by the Jewish community. The trip has been a remarkable experience, but somewhat stressful. She hopes to be with Ernst on December 26.

Director Engelbert gave me a can of condensed milk, a bar of chocolate, and a can of sardines. When I asked him how much I owed him, he asked me for postage stamps I have in duplicate and envelopes with printed stamps. I also bought some wonderful things from Frau Jilek, some of which she wanted to give me: carp, a piece of meat, various fats, sardines, sausage. It is touching how this woman cares for me; I have experienced much love there. Regained much of my belief in humanity.

Wednesday, December 25, 1940   Breslau
We gave Hanukkah presents to Susanne and Tamara in the afternoon. The dining room table was divided into two halves, and Trudi set it up very nicely for the children, the way we do it for the older children, who are now far away, and for whom I was especially fearful yesterday. But that is of no help. The two youngest were very happy, which makes all the work that we have done the whole year through worth it, just to see the happiness in our children's eyes.

Monday, December 30, 1940   Breslau
Susanne had a Hanukkah celebration in school, which is now located in the Friends' House. I rode to the Cathedral Library, where I had a meeting with the director.[8] We also discussed the general situation; Roosevelt is said to have spoken in favor of giving the most energetic support to England in order to alleviate the German threat, even though they themselves had not been directly attacked. I again received some wonderful food items from Frau Jilek at very inexpensive prices. She is a very good woman.

8. Today we know the reason for their meeting. Willy Cohn brought Engelbert the first installment (pages 1–147) of a typewritten carbon copy of his memoirs for safekeeping. He did this a total of five times, the last installment being delivered on September 23, 1941. This complete copy, which was discovered only in 2007, is housed in the Archiwum Archidiecezjalne we Wrocławiu, Sign. VIII J a (papers of Alfons Nowack).

Tuesday, December 31, 1940   Breslau
New Year's Eve, and our thoughts drift back into the past and out toward the future! I wonder how my three children outside are faring, and where they are. If only I knew that Ruth had arrived safely! But there is nothing I can do. I recall many pleasurable New Year's Eves of the past, many a peaceful hour in my beloved Silesian mountains, to which I would so like to return. What will the world look like in a year! Much will have been blown away that today thinks itself so grand.

Sunday, January 5, 1941   Breslau
Yesterday morning went to the bank, the coal depot, Ilse Passia's lending library. To my great joy I received a certificate for five hundredweights of coal so that we are covered for January. But running around was very strenuous.

Monday, January 6, 1941   Breslau
Today I experienced an especially great joy: I received news from Youth Assistance that Ruth arrived safely in Palestine, on December 24. I am deeply, deeply grateful. Two of the goals that she had set herself in life have been accomplished. Her third goal is our aliyah.

Wednesday, January 8, 1941   Breslau
The 200 marks of support money from Ruth's account have been transferred to my father-in-law. The bank director told me that we Jews must now pay a special tax of 15 percent that had previously been charged only to Poles, because we enjoy the protection of the Reich without being ethnic Germans. This is a tremendous new encumbrance, but I no longer get upset about financial matters. We will just have to continue to cut down.

Saturday, January 11, 1941   Breslau
Yesterday morning's mail brought a great joy in the form of a lovely and detailed letter from Ruth, from Constantinople. The group sailed across the Black Sea, and Ruth got sea sick. She found people living in misery in Russia; she toured two cities, presumably Moscow and Odessa. The letter was an enormous joy for us. Herr Neustadt told us about the lamentable state of the files of the synagogue community archive, half moldy. Deplorable. I really had tried to make myself available back then.

Monday, January 13, 1941   Breslau
Dictated ten typewritten pages of my memoirs; at the moment that is
the work I find most fulfilling, but it is to some extent a luxury that I
can afford only when everything else is done. Trudi Silberstein came by
in the late afternoon. She was very depressed because her friend, Herr
Nellhaus, had taken his life, obviously mentally disturbed because there
would have been no other external reason. I felt very badly for her because she has too often experienced disappointments in life.

Tuesday, January 14, 1941   Breslau
Worked in the Cathedral Library again yesterday morning; it was quite
cold because the great hall isn't heated at all on Sunday. I was offered
a pound of lentils by Frau Jilek, which I bought. The woman is touchingly attentive.

   Newspaper: an item about the social insurance contributions of the
Jews, which cost us another considerable part of our income, but that
is the least of it these days. Still, we need money to live. Somehow we
will muddle through.

Friday, January 17, 1941   Breslau
Exchanged books yesterday morning. Fräulein Passia told me that the
Jewish circles with which she associates all expect to be deported. I
told her that Jews are making their own lives more difficult with such
thinking.

Monday, January 20, 1941   Breslau
The bank. In particular with regard to the accounts of our emigrated
children; perhaps I will be able to get the interest from Ruth's money
with the approval of the hard-currency office. Met my colleague Kliefoth
on the way to the library; we both enjoyed the great beauty of the cathedral island in its winter coat.

Saturday, January 25, 1941   Breslau
In the afternoon, went to pray in the Beate Guttmann Home, and
because I arrived too early I was able to take a short walk through
the alleys of Kleinburg. I rarely get to this area. Ethnic Germans, all
very simple people, are now living in the former old-age home in the
Kirschallee.

Tuesday, January 28, 1941   Breslau
Worked hard yesterday afternoon; rewrote a short article for *Germania Judaica*. I will do my duty in this regard until the last moment. Corrected my memoirs; I don't enjoy the things I've written myself, but there is no way around it. Here in Germany, mentally ill persons were gassed to death in an insane asylum; the Pope is supposedly looking into the matter.[9] It is difficult for a human being to comprehend such a thing, even though these poor people may have found release from their suffering.

Monday, February 3, 1941   Breslau
Suppelt, the dairyman, involved me in a discussion about the general situation this morning; Aryans like to do that because they hope to hear our opinion about how things really are. Suppelt remarked that during the world war they also kept saying that the war effort was going splendidly, but in the end we lost everything.

Tuesday, February 4, 1941   Breslau
Anita Lasker visited us; I told her a few things about Ruth. She is going to school again, seventh year in secondary school. In the early morning went to the Cathedral Library and organized registry volumes. Engelbert was very grateful; it is work that I enjoy doing, and it allows me to reciprocate for the hospitality that I have for so long enjoyed there. And in the process, I learn quite a bit in an area in which I have much to learn. That was all I worked on.

Friday, February 14, 1941   Breslau
Went to Haupt & Hoffmann to pick up a certificate for coal. We are permitted to use seven hundredweights more coal by March 31. I think

---

9. Starting in 1939, mentally and physically ill persons, who were considered "unworthy of life," were "euthanized" throughout the German Reich under the so-called T4 program, short for Tiergartenstrasse 4, the headquarters of the Gemeinnützige Stiftung für Heil- und Anstaltspflege [Charitable Foundation for Curative and Institutional Care]. On August 20, 1940, the German Conference of Bishops forbade Catholic institutions to collaborate in this murderous state program. T4 was an important precursor to the Final Solution. For more on the T4 euthanasia program, see Robert N. Proctor, *Racial Hygiene: Medicine under the Nazis* (Cambridge, MA: Harvard University Press, 1988), pp. 177–222. Also Götz Aly, Peter Chroust, and Christian Pross, *Cleansing the Fatherland: Nazi Medicine and Racial Hygiene* (Baltimore: Johns Hopkins University Press, 1994), pp. 22–93.

that may even be enough. I had an appointment at 12 o'clock with Professor Goerlitz, and we spent another stimulating hour together. I am always thankful for such conversations, and he is very well disposed toward me. He himself is studying the medieval Magdeburg Rights and the opinions of the court of lay assessors in that city. We talked about how, in the course of German colonization, Jews entered these eastern lands along with the Germans. Naturally, and how could it have been otherwise, our conversation also touched upon everyday matters, that is, the events of the day.

Wednesday, February 19, 1941   Breslau
Today already a fairly busy day. Barber, then the bank, where they had Wölff's certificate of nonobjection, and where I spent a good deal of time. Perhaps I will even manage to have some funds released. Everyone was astounded that I had been able to get a nonobjection for someone living in an enemy country. Then rode to the cemetery in the Lohestrasse; today would have been Father's 98th birthday. I brought him greetings from all those who could no longer come on this day. I am the last of six siblings still able to stand at the graveside. So many things go through my mind at such moments.

Took the 26 to the archive, past the house at Ohlauufer 15, which on this date had hosted so many happy people.[10] People at the cathedral are always concerned when I fail to come in for a few days; that is why I put in an appearance today and told them I would not be returning again until Tuesday. Engelbert's concern for me is touching.

Friday, February 21, 1941   Breslau
Yesterday, I went for a walk with Trudi for an hour in honor of her birthday. Various guests came by in the afternoon: Uncle Mamlok and daughter, Grandmother Proskauer, Hedwig Bermann, Eva Nürenberg; I slipped out after a decent interval.

Monday, February 24, 1941   Breslau
Yesterday was an especial *dies ater*. In the afternoon, a very regrettable incident with Trudi. I often curse my life, and then I think to myself

---

10. This was the house in which Willy Cohn was born. See Willy Cohn, *Verwehte Spuren. Erinnerungen an das Breslauer Judentum vor seinem Untergang*, ed. Norbert Conrads (Cologne: Böhlau, 1995), p. 18.

that it would be better not to wake up next morning. Trudi would then raise the youngest children herself; I'm just a dead weight on her anyway. Yesterday was a horror, and it took all my strength and willpower not to end my life. Everything seems to have become so meaningless, as if I am standing before a great heap of rubble.

Thursday, February 27, 1941   Breslau
Worked hard yesterday afternoon with Fräulein Cohn; again, I managed to complete a larger section of my memoirs. Luckily, my head is still functioning though other things sometimes break down, and intellectual work comforts me through the added suffering that has visited me since Sunday.

Gestapo, where they neither asked about my emigration nor bellowed at me. I am to report again on May 21; much can have happened by then. Hard-currency office, where I was summoned on account of Wölfl. I had requested that 200 marks be released as a present from Wölfl to Susanne. Initially, the official told me it was out of the question because Wölfl is living in an enemy country, but in the end he approved it for this one time only, but insisted I tell the bank not to view this as a precedent. I was very happy about this accommodation; it makes things much easier.

Sunday, March 2, 1941   Breslau
As usual, I was awakened by a nightmare. I dreamed that I was in the house at Ohlauufer 15 and got into a big argument with the owner. Herr Himmler will be speaking in Breslau today.[11] He is chief of the infernal hosts and probably the most dangerous enemy of the Jews. The Bukovina Germans are getting their citizenship.

11. Heinrich Himmler, the head of the SS spoke to the Bukovina Germans at the Jahrhunderthalle, ensuring them of their old living conditions and the restoration of their German citizenship rights.

Insecurity and Harassment

Monday, March 3, 1941   Breslau

I went to the police station to confirm that I am still among the living, as I must each year. It took only a second. Then to the bank and archive, where I had a lengthy conversation with Engelbert. I managed a good book trade; I received a copy of Caesarius of Heisterbach's *Dialogus Miraculorum*. Engelbert told me that the Catholic bishop of the Netherlands has been imprisoned because he forbade membership in the National Socialist Party.

Today, as we were eating, a lady came, supposedly at the behest of the price-control office, to look at our apartment.[1] She was actually a very nice lady, obviously relocated here from elsewhere, who also found the situation awkward. She didn't like the apartment anyway. I don't believe that the price-control board sent her to our apartment; she was probably sent to look at the Schüftans' apartment, and then neighbors pointed out ours as well.

Wednesday, March 5, 1941   Breslau

Bank, then the archive, where I stayed for a fairly long time discussing with Engelbert corrections to his history of St. Michael's Church. He is grateful for any assistance, and I was able to suggest a number of significant improvements. There was a session of the consistory yesterday; Engelbert told me that in the Warthegau the profession of clergyman no longer counts as a primary profession, but only as secondary. The

---

1. According to the Breslau address book of 1941, the chief of police also administered a price-control office whose main activity consisted in monitoring and establishing retail prices. Apparently, this office also had a department overseeing "Jewish rentals." Cf. diary entry of July 22, 1941.

clergy were given to understand that they should look for another primary profession. This is completely in keeping with the spirit of the times.

Saturday, March 7, 1941   Breslau
Dictated my memoirs for almost four hours today, which brought me to the end of the war. Once again, these reminiscences moved and engaged me greatly. The newspaper carried a noteworthy and lengthy article today about Jewish labor deployment to the effect that deportations will be held off for the moment because they need the labor. Naturally, the lowest work is just good enough for Jews.

Saturday, March 8, 1941   Breslau
Went to see Grotte in the afternoon and discussed some problems regarding my article about Prague, and I gained some insight into the Old New Synagogue. It is astonishing how elusive things are, even though much work is now being done on Prague these days. Grotte intends to join his son in Bolivia; he is an architect and apparently doing quite well. Attended services at the Beate Guttmann Home. Today is Shabbat Zachor.[2] "And remember what Amalek did to you; you shall not forget," an adage that has been with us Jews throughout our history.

Thursday, March 13, 1941   Breslau
A small package that we sent to the poor Jews in Litzmannstadt was returned; only letters up to twenty grams are delivered. The people are being allowed to starve. From others we have heard that the Jews there are being given only eighty grams of bread per day. Ghastly. But this, too, will be bitterly avenged.

Sunday, March 16, 1941   Breslau
Went for a walk in the afternoon with Susanne; when I walk alone with her she talks more openly. She told me that she often cries at night thinking about her brothers and sister, and that she makes plans for the future, all of them about Palestine. Today is Heroes Memorial Day, and the swastika flags are once again unfurled. Who still commemorates the Jews who died in the first world war?

2. "Sabbath of remembrance," immediately preceding Purim.

Wednesday, March 19, 1941   Breslau
Archive. I had doubts today about whether to go, but my instinct told me that it was the right thing. Worked for a time on the Hebrew manuscripts, excerpted a few things, and had a brief conversation with Engelbert. I was especially pleased to be there because Professor Goerlitz came to look through the registry volumes for his work on the opinions of the Magdeburg court of lay assessors. When I returned home, a Gestapo agent was there about the apartment. Apparently, all Jewish living quarters are being written down as a precaution in case there are further bombing raids in the west.[3] I gave him my little speech from Dr. Arlt and showed him a letter from the mayor, which Baurat Stein had signed. This apparently made an impression on him, as did my library. I believe that the apartment is in no danger at the moment.

Friday, March 21, 1941   Breslau
Worked in the archive again yesterday morning; I don't feel quite right when I don't go. Mother Innocentia, with whom I get along very well, told me that Mother Huberta had said that I endanger the archive by my presence, and that she didn't understand how the director could permit me to work there. I will consider by Monday whether to discuss this with Engelbert.

Friday, March 28, 1941   Breslau
Went yesterday morning to see Fräulein Levy at the Palestine Office. This office is now being drastically cut back, and it isn't even certain whether Fräulein Levy will keep her paid position. She has sacrificed her entire life for the movement without being able to make aliyah herself. Herr Foerder told me that they intend to pulp a large number of books, and I was able to save quite a few, which I will have sent here.

---

3. On September 27, 1940, Hitler decreed the evacuation of mothers and children from areas in Germany under air bombardment. These evacuations, which initially involved 3.1 million mothers with children up to the age of six, and then another 2.8 million between the age of ten and eighteen, increasingly came at the expense of Jews, who were ordered out of their homes. Eventually, an estimated 11.77 million people were evacuated to the east and to rural areas from the big cities. See Michael Krause, *Flucht vor dem Bombenkrieg. 'Umquartierungen' im Zweiten Weltkrieg und die Wiedereingliederung der Evakuierten in Deutschland 1943–1963* (Bonn: Droste Verlag, 1997).

As long as I have this apartment, I will continue to collect books, some of which I will undoubtedly be able to trade with the Cathedral Library.

Saturday, March 29, 1941   Breslau
Jewish secondary school is to be completely discontinued, and only the most talented will be sent to Berlin. This will cost a large number of teachers their livelihoods. However, there seems to be no way to avoid these reduced circumstances. We must adapt. Big anti-Jewish speech at the concluding session of the Institute for Study of the Jewish Question; a Jewish reservation is to be established under tight police supervision, which will eventually contain all of Europe's Jews.[4] But first, the war must be won.

Sunday, March 30, 1941   Breslau
Naturally, the teachers at the Jewish schools are quite upset about the terminations; it is to be hoped that the Jewish authorities will at least carry out the dismissals in a fair manner. I saw something very bad yesterday morning. As I was leaving the book room, a car from the medical examiner's office, the former anatomical institute, came up the Viktoriastrasse, corner of Höfchenstrasse, and a few moments later someone was carried down on a stretcher. I gathered that it was a Jewish suicide because I then saw a woman, supported by two others, being led into a neighbor's house.

Went to the cemetery. I felt the need to be there after Father's yahrzeit. The Menzel School is now a field hospital. The soldiers throw all sorts of garbage down into the cemetery, so I had to remove a piece of a comb and orange peels from the family grave. – Respect for the dead!

Tuesday, April 1, 1941   Breslau
A quarter of the new year is over, and next year promises to be even worse for the afflicted. But for Germany, the situation has deteriorated considerably. Waited for a long time to buy milk. Went to the bank, very pleased that the school had deposited 100 marks. Money is not all

---

4. A meeting of the Institute for Study of the Jewish Question took place in Frankfurt am Main, on March 26, 1941. This "institute" had been founded by Alfred Rosenberg (1893–1946), one of the chief ideologues of the National Socialist movement. Since 1940, the Nazi regime had been considering deporting the Jews to the French island of Madagascar.

that important to me, but one does need it to live. And I must consider myself lucky that I am still permitted to earn. I witnessed something very sad at the bank. I saw an older Jew paying a bill from the insane asylum in Chelm, near Lublin. This is the asylum where, we are told, all mentally ill Jews are being killed.[5] I asked him, full of sympathy, whether he was paying for someone who, hopefully, was still alive, whereupon he replied that his wife was no longer among the living. I asked him where she had been previously: "in Braniss."[6] And then whether she had been completely insane, whereupon he said that she had suffered from mania. It is simply grotesque how sick human beings are being treated.

Three people are rumored to die each night in the concentration camp; next morning, the blankets of the dead must be presented at roll call.

Sunday, April 6, 1941   Breslau

In order to survive mentally and spiritually, I must concentrate ever more on my work and embrace the children, and I must tell myself that I have something to work toward. With that, I hope that there will be no repeat of the eruption of a month and a half ago. In the morning, dictated a lengthy piece of my memoirs and some letters. Sometimes,

---

5. On January 12, 1940, all 440 patients at the Chelm (Polish: Chełm) asylum had been murdered and the facility closed for good. For more, see Alfred Konieczny, "Rozwiązanie i zbrodniami hitlerowskimi" 18 (1995), pp. 235–260 (*Acta Universitatis Wratislaviensis* No. 1715). Cohn could not have known that in April 1941 he was witnessing a massive fraud within the T4 (euthanasia) program. Chelm was in the General Government, that is, not in Germany proper. However, the actual killings were being done at T4 sites in Germany, and so the patients were transferred there. But because the T4 program was paid only up to the time of transfer, an elaborate scheme was concocted, including forged "Chelm" death certificates and couriers to take them back to Chelm for the requisite postmark. Hence the notion that people were being killed there. In any case, this elderly gentleman may well have paid for his wife's murder. See Henry Friedlander, *The Origins of Nazi Genocide: From Euthanasia to the Final Solution* (Chapel Hill: University of North Carolina Press, 1995), pp. 263–283, esp. pp. 276–277.

6. This undoubtedly refers to Branitz (District of Leobschütz) in the preceding footnote, where in 1940, 1,600 patients were housed in an asylum. See Georg Beier, *Die Dörfer des Kreises Leobschütz 1914–1946* (Dülmen: Oberschlesischer Heimatverlag, 1990), pp. 96–98.

remembering the past is the best thing to do now that the present is no longer what it was.

Tuesday, April 8, 1941   Breslau
Yesterday afternoon, I again took up my book about lien law, and I have decided to have another section copied so that there will be several copies of this book, which cost me many years of effort but will never see print. The attack on Yugoslavia is being justified with the same words as the attack on Poland. Bismarck's dictum, that the whole of the Balkans isn't worth the bones of a single Prussian grenadier, has been forgotten.

Good Friday, April 11, 1941   Breslau
Day of preparations for Pesach. Looked through old family papers. My dear departed father was such a generous man, full of love for humanity! During the night of the 10th, the English conducted a massive bomber raid on Berlin and appear to have wreaked havoc in the downtown. The State Library appears to have been damaged as well. If masses of American airplanes join the fight, we will have to be prepared for something much worse. Troop transport trains continue rolling toward the East.

Saturday, April 12, 1941   Breslau
Trudi made great efforts preparing the Seder; such things are a lot of work for a housewife. I went to pray at the Beate Guttmann Home in the morning. Afterward, I went for a walk with Herr Eugen Perle, even got as far as the Südpark. Less is supposed to emigrate sometime this month. Perhaps Emil Kaim will become first chairman of the Jewish Community, which I would applaud because he is a man full of energy who doesn't simply fall apart at every opportunity as was the case with Less.

Wednesday, April 16, 1941   Breslau
Did some work on *Germania Judaica* yesterday morning; the Easter break is now all but over. Later, did some errands with Tamara; I'm always happy holding her sweet little paw in my hand.

Thursday, April 17, 1941   Breslau
Today I went to see Oberbaurat Stein, who had written to me about the Hebrew gravestone that was removed from City Hall. I took a look

at it in his office in the old building of the Elisabethgymnasium; only a portion of it remains, and so it is almost illegible. Nonetheless, I was able to explain to him the general sense of the Hebrew writing and the disposition of the gravestone.

Friday, April 18, 1941   Breslau

My in-laws have now received their papers for Argentina and will emigrate as soon as they have dealt with the travel complications. Seventh evening of Pesach, Eugen Perle brought me two matzos so that I could recite Kiddush. Yesterday, received eggs and bacon from Frau Jilek at the Cathedral Library. She is always so attentive.

Sunday, April 20, 1941   Breslau

I attended services yesterday morning for the last time this week of Pesach; it was Yiskor, the memorial for the dead. It always affects me, and I conjure up the faces of many who have passed on. Went with Susanne to the cemetery in the Claassenstrasse, where I had an appointment to meet with Professor Goerlitz at 11 o'clock. However, we had enough time to visit Herr Wenglowitz, who lives there, and on this occasion I found the grave of my great-grandfather, Abraham Hainauer, who was born in 1801 and only lived a few years beyond 50. He occupies an important place in my family tree. Susannchen placed a stone on the grave of her great-great-grandfather.

Professor Goerlitz visited Bojanowo, which is now called Schmückert.[7] The Jewish cemetery there has been turned into a tennis court even though the last burials took place only a few years ago. The trees have been chopped down; the old-age home turned into a home for young women in the labor service. Goerlitz was very upset about the lack of reverence for the cemetery; we couldn't have imagined such a thing to be possible as little as ten years ago. I had the feeling that this visit to the cemetery affected him greatly.

Russia now denies all transit visas; this effectively puts an end to emigration to Shanghai. Perhaps this is all to the good! Many Jews from Poland will now have to perform forced labor in Silesia.

---

7. Bojanowo (district of Rawitsch, Posen) was renamed Schmückert in late 1939.

Saturday, April 26, 1941   Breslau
The Krietern Infants Home is being turned into a reserve field hospital; the Community was asked which they would rather give up, the Krietern Home or the Beate Guttmann Home for the Aged. They chose the former because the relatively small number of infants can be accommodated elsewhere.

Wednesday, April 30, 1941   Breslau
My in-laws plan to emigrate at the end of the month and have invited us to Berlin. As far as I am concerned, the invitation is out of the question because Berlin is so threatened by air raids, nor do I want the children to make the trip. Of course, I can't very well hold back Trudi. I feel so badly for her.

Less wanted to talk to me at the Jewish Community at 11 o'clock; he intends to leave for Montevideo shortly. I wished him the best of luck for the future, and I told him that if he would permit me to make a single criticism of his performance in office, it would be that he had been too soft. He heaped me with praises, which I declined.[8]

Thursday, May 1, 1941   Breslau
Today is May Day, and it has gotten somewhat warmer. Nine years ago today, I for the last time took part in a march for world peace. And where do we stand now? I believe that we may definitely anticipate that the United States will enter the war.

Wednesday, May 7, 1941   Breslau
Here, ever more people are conscripted. An enormous area is now occupied by German troops. I left the archive earlier than usual today because of the cardinal's visit. I considered this more tactful. I actually walked the entire way. At least today it is more like spring.

8. The emigration of Georg Less, the chairman of the Breslau Jewish Community, is not only the last emigration from Breslau mentioned in the diaries, it may well have been the very last. By August 17, 1941, Cohn knew that Less had arrived in Montevideo. Whereas in 1940, 544 Breslau Jews managed to emigrate, by the spring of 1941, only very few made it out. See Karol Jonca, "The Final Solution to the 'Jewish Problem' in the Silesian Province 1940–1945," in Marcin Wodziński and Janusz Spyra (eds.), *Jews in Silesia*, pp. 159–171, esp. p. 162.

Saturday, May 10, 1941   Breslau

There was great agitation at the Beate Guttmann Home when I went there to pray. The home is to be confiscated by the military authorities and must be cleared out by Thursday. Even if they are given 14 days more, it will still be terrible for the old people who thought that they would be able to spend the evening of their lives in peace. Naturally, people tried to reassure them as best they could, but it is nonetheless a hard stroke.[9]

Monday, May 12, 1941   Breslau

Trudi is taking the early train to Berlin today; I hope that she returns safely. A trip to the Reich capital is a dangerous undertaking these days. The morning mail brought great joy, a very long letter from Wölfl, dated April 20. It made me very happy. The young man writes so courageously, even though I am sure he doesn't have it easy. But he is full of worries about the family and tries to find a good word for each of us. And then, in the evening, another joy in the form of a sign of life from Ernst. March seems to have been a good month for him; now all I need is to hear something from Ruth.

I then went over to the Beate Guttmann Home to bring Grandmother Proskauer the happy news of Wölfl's letter; that's when I received the news from Ernst. It is really distressing to see how this lovely home is being dissolved, and how the old people are forced to sell their things. There is no news yet about which house will be made available.

Friday, May 16, 1941   Breslau

My old barber, Duscha, was all upset this morning. Yesterday evening he had received a summons from the local group of the NSDAP because he was caught shaving a Jew. I felt sorry for the old man. Now he understands what all this spying and informing leads to. He, too, felt badly that he would no longer be able to serve me; I have been his customer for more than seven years. He recommended a Jewish barber named Müller. I have his address, and I'll try to reach him tomorrow.

9. The Breslau address book for 1941 locates the Beate Guttmann Home at Kirschallee 36a and lists all "occupants" by name.

Saturday, May 17, 1941   Breslau

I changed and went to the Beate Guttmann Home for services, where everything continues to be up in the air. Grandmother Proskauer has already moved out, even though I had advised her against it.[10]

Sunday, May 18, 1941   Breslau

Grandmother Proskauer was here in the afternoon; she says she feels comfortable in the Hadda Home. Then, Herr Sander brought me the architectural plan of the burned synagogue in Trachenberg.

Monday, May 19, 1941   Breslau

Archive; just as I was about to go up to the reading room, a gentleman drew me aside and introduced himself as Professor Hoffmann. I knew who he was, the Silesian Church historian.[11] We got into a lengthy conversation, in part scholarly, but he also asked me about various Jewish scholars.[12] Hoffmann made a very good impression on me; he's an important scholar.

Wednesday, May 21, 1941   Breslau

Yesterday, I heard a conversation between two young girls who were talking about the fact that all girls over the age of 15 who are not needed at home must now work in munitions factories. What is Germany planning now? Rumor has it that the Führer will visit Breslau! Perhaps it has something to do with the Ukraine? Massive troop movements over the past few days!

Thursday, May 22, 1941   Breslau

Yesterday morning paid synagogue taxes. Reported to the Gestapo,

---

10. Selma Proskauer, apparently still a very active woman, had found permanent lodgings at Willy Hadda's private old-age home, located at Lothringer Strasse 8. As a result, she did not immediately share the same fate as the other inhabitants of the Beate Guttmann Home.

11. Hermann Hoffmann (1878–1972) taught at the Catholic St. Matthias Gymnasium, in Breslau, from 1902 to 1927. He describes his unconventional life in his memoirs. Hermann Hoffmann, *Im Dienste des Friedens. Lebenserinnerungen eines katholischen Europäers* (Stuttgart: K. Theiss, 1970).

12. In his memoirs, Hoffmann described the burning of the New Synagogue, in 1938, after which he sought out the chief rabbi of Breslau to express his sympathies and indignation. See Hermann Hoffmann, *Im Dienste des Friedens*, p. 292.

which luckily transpired without any major uproar. The morning mail brought a very lovely letter from Erna; she is making great efforts outside on behalf of all the children. She even sent Wölfl some money.

Because the library was closed today, I took a walk to the cemetery in the Lohestrasse to visit my parents, and to convey to them greetings from all those who have emigrated! I also found the graves of my great-grandparents Jaffé, and so I have been able to make some progress recently on my family tree. It is very beautiful and peaceful here, except that the soldiers who are staying at the field hospital in the Menzel School dispose of all sorts of garbage there, orange peels, entire sausages. These people are still too well-off.

Saturday, May 24, 1941   Breslau
Yesterday afternoon went to the Beate Guttmann Home for the last time to pray; the home is supposed to be cleared out by May 30, but as late as yesterday the people had no idea where the elderly would be taken. It is so distressing. I had a conversation with a 90-year-old woman, who knew my father when he was young. She talked about the old days, 70 years back, when old Fräulein Trautner was still alive. I felt just terrible that this is the last time I can go to pray there, and I do not yet know where to go the next time. But of course, wherever he may be, a person can find a path to his G'd.

Friday, May 30, 1941   Breslau
In the afternoon, I sent a package to Weruschau, traded a book, went to the barber. I am now reading Hitler's *Mein Kampf.* It is a book with which one simply must engage. In many respects, it seems to me that his characterization of Jews is not completely wrong.

Saturday, May 31, 1941   Breslau
Yesterday morning I spent almost four happy hours dictating my memoirs; I made good progress. I'm still describing my trip to Sicily; those were lovely weeks back then.[13] When I'm able to work, I forget everything that depresses me.

13. Cohn was reminiscing about his study trip to Sicily, in 1927. See Willy Cohn, *Verwehte Spuren. Erinnerungen an das Breslauer Judentum vor seinem Untergang*, ed. Norbert Conrads (Cologne: Böhlau, 1995), pp. 438ff.

Whit Sunday, in June 1, 1941   Breslau
First day of the Feast of Weeks. I went to the Storch Synagogue, where I haven't been in a very long time. It was beautifully decorated; I stood next to Eugen Perle, and was called to the Torah! Frau Dr. Aschheim, who will be receiving a salary for the last time on July 1, spoke. Advised her and her mother![14] Money is no longer to be spent on cultural efforts.[15]

In the afternoon. Today I attended services with the Reform Jews in the Storch Synagogue at 10 o'clock. It was quite full; Lewin's sermons are always a big draw. I didn't wait to listen to it; no one wore a tallit, and there was much talking! The service, which began with the Hallel, is basically very dignified. I sat next to Justizrat Peiser, who now leads the Fränckel Refuge in the Friedrich Wilhelm Strasse.[16] Outside, in the courtyard, he told me how sorry he was that the *History of the Jews in Breslau* had never been written. I told him that it was the fault of Reform Jewry that such tasks had been neglected.

Whit Monday, June 2, 1941   Breslau
Second day of the Feast of Weeks. Went to the Storch Synagogue with Susannchen; she, too, liked the decorations. I was already there this morning taking part in the Conservative services; they are very different from the Reform. Here you get the sense that a whole community is praying.

Afterward, spent some time with Perle at his apartment, which is nicely located in the former Palestine Office. He told me that the idea has been raised of relocating the Beate Guttmann Home to the former Leubus Abbey. I warned him against this course of action because of the danger that none of the occupants might ever return.[17] The state has

14. Lydia Aschheim's situation had been precarious ever since her husband, the painter Isidor Aschheim, emigrated to Palestine, in 1940, leaving her behind. Her mother, Flora Baruchsen, née Segall, who came from Latvia, was, if anything, in an even more uncertain position. Cf. diary entry of October 21, 1934.

15. Cohn is implying that his work on *Germania Judaica* will be unremunerated.

16. Among the benevolent activities of the Fraenckel Foundation was a refuge for Jewish families impoverished through no fault of their own.

17. Since 1930, there had been a provincial facility for caring for the mentally ill at the abbey in Leubus, and in the neighboring small town of Leubus. Cohn feared that relocation of Jews to Leubus meant that they might fall victim to the ongoing

a rather remarkable conception of "useless eaters." He will discuss my fears with Rabbi Lewin, but with no one else. Perle also introduced me to the new head of the Jewish Community, Landgerichtsrat Kohn, who it appears already knew me.

Wednesday, June 4, 1941   Breslau
My colleague Freund visited yesterday afternoon. He brought me the very sad news that he is being evicted from his apartment. But he is taking it like a man. I gave him some advice, and I also offered to let him stay with us while he is moving.

Monday, June 9, 1941   Breslau
Today's *Morgen Zeitung* brought very important news for us Jews. The English offensive in Syria has begun. I had always anticipated that, and surely Palestinian troops will be involved, and Jewish blood will also be shed. I wonder whether this will involve Ernst. On the other hand, according to the German newspaper, the English there are in such a superior position that serious French resistance is unlikely, even if Pétain makes an appeal. The Vichy government is not particularly powerful. This morning, I paid a considerable amount of income tax to the tax office. That's one place with no sign saying that Jews are not served.

Thursday, June 12, 1941   Breslau
Grandmother Proskauer visited yesterday afternoon. She told me that the question of relocating the Beate Guttmann Home has still not been decided; negotiations are taking place about relocating to Görlitz.[18] The people would have had to be housed privately here!

Saturday, June 14, 1941   Breslau
Happy event here this morning. We received two very lovely letters from Wölfl, the second one from the end of May, heartfelt as always, but this time with news from Ernst and Ruth. He describes their reunion; Ernst didn't even recognize Ruth! Ruth is happy and contented

---

policy of euthanasia. Leubus had already been rendered "Jew-free." Cf. diary entry of April 1, 1941.

18. What is notable here is that the relocation of the occupants of the home to Görlitz was still being viewed as a solution to the problem of accommodations. In fact, this relocation to Tormersdorf, near Görlitz, was to be the first step in the deportations to a concentration camp.

with her work and enjoys the land and nature. So, we raised our children right after all. Wölfl would also like to emigrate to Palestine, but that isn't possible at the moment.

Monday, June 16, 1941   Breslau
Rode to the archive and worked for several hours. I try not to get into conversation with Mother Huberta, if possible. Mother Innocentia told me that she had said that I endanger the archive. Luckily, the director is the one in charge, but it is nonetheless an unpleasant feeling to be working in the same room with a person who really doesn't wish me well. But, we've experienced all sorts of things these past eight years.

Tuesday, June 17, 1941   Breslau
In the Beate Guttmann Home, the fate of which is still undecided, 90-year-old Frau Leipziger, a childhood friend of my late father, mother-in-law of Herr Taterka, attempted suicide! How horrible! People's nerves are completely frayed!

Wednesday, June 18, 1941   Breslau
Visited Dr. Richard Baeck in the Zimmerstrasse this afternoon in order to speak with his brother. Unfortunately, he wasn't there, so I waited for him in front of the synagogue. The ceremony at the synagogue was a special event because of Leo Baeck's oration; his words were filled with the deepest wisdom. He said that when, in the future, an objective historian judges the Jews in Germany, he will praise them because they maintained school, religious services, and charity throughout these times. In earlier times, he said, we had much security and little conviction; today we have conviction and little security. What he said lifted my spirits. Of the musical offerings, the pieces played by Benjamin Freund, my old student, affected me most deeply. In addition to the liturgy, particularly the chorus from Mendelssohn's *Elijah*, "Thanks be to G'd." Anita Lasker played cello.

Good news today. The Berlin Palestine Office sent me a message via Fräulein Levy to the effect that I will receive a certificate for my family from a neutral foreign country.[19] Apart from practical matters,

19. Evidently, Cohn was hoping that it might come from Rabbi Lothar Rothschild, in Basel, Switzerland—a neutral country.

what pleased me the most was that it warmly recognized my services to Zionism.

Thursday, June 19, 1941   Breslau
Went to Pension Brinnitzer, Charlottenstrasse 7, this morning to greet Rabbi Dr. Baeck. He told me why the Reich Association has such limited means. It receives only a certain amount each month; there is also a tendency not to spend anything on cultural efforts. In addition, there is a desire to consolidate Jewish funds because after the final victory, the Jews will have to emigrate, which will cost a great deal. And of course, the authorities aren't interested in making our lives easy.

As far as my work is concerned, I told him that I will continue to do it without remuneration, and I also said that it makes no sense to expend too much effort on individual edits because I constantly do this myself. I asked him whether they were otherwise satisfied with my work, which he heartily affirmed. He was especially interested in my memoirs, which he is eager to read. Perhaps it will be possible to send a copy abroad for safekeeping; in any case, I will soon send him a copy. It is regrettable that one so seldom has the opportunity to converse with a man like him. The moments I spent with him were stimulating in any case. I asked him about the fate of the Beate Guttmann Home; it will be relocated to Rothenburg, in Oberlausitz.[20] I related my misgivings, but he said he thought that there was no need for concern for the elderly; other old-age homes had been relocated and, in contrast to the mentally ill, nothing unseemly had happened to them.

20. In other words, Baeck was informed of the relocation to Tormersdorf, not far from Rothenburg, and Cohn at this time was not. In Tormersdorf, there was a facility for the mentally ill run by the Protestant Zoar confraternity. In May 1941, at approximately the time that the Beate Guttmann Home was being confiscated, a Jewish commission was sent there to determine whether Tormersdorf would be suitable as a Jewish old-age home. The commission's positive evaluation was tantamount to a death sentence for the then occupants of the Tormersdorf facility. Between June 17 and 19, 1941, approximately 100 to 120 of them were taken to Sonnenstein, near Pirna, where they were killed. This made room for the old people from the Beate Guttmann Home, who arrived on July 8, 1941. Reinhard Leube, "Preisgegebene Menschen. Zwangslager und Judenghetto Zoar/Martinshof in Rothenburg 1941/42," in *Jahrbuch für Schlesische Kirchengeschichte* 83 (2004), pp. 135–152.

The Russian Campaign
and the War against the Jews

Sunday, June 22, 1941   Breslau
I am starting this book on a day of great historical consequence. What
was to be expected after the massive troop transports through Breslau
of the past weeks has now become a certainty. It has come to war with
Russia, and Germany now finds herself in a situation similar to that in
1914, but with the difference that her troops are now spread over a far
wider area. Germany is once again more or less encircled, and intervention by the United States is now only a question of days! Russia has
conserved its forces and is now preparing to advance, whereas Germany
has already squandered so many men. All of her previous successes are
now being eroded! The Führer's proclamation was published in a special edition. What is for certain is that the war will now begin in earnest!

Thursday, June 26, 1941   Breslau
Worked in the archive yesterday morning; spoke with Professor Hoffmann, who is always warmly interested. He told me that Simonsohn's
library is being sold by Poppe, the antiquarian. One of the trustees
probably sold it to them. I so wish I could acquire one or another of
those volumes.

At the moment, there is a great shortage of vegetables, and the "national comrades" are making sure that none of them get sold to us.
Except for potatoes, we aren't allowed to buy anything from our green-
grocer, and even at the truck, the woman made difficulties for our
Edith, denouncing her. There are some nasty customers about.

Sunday, July 6, 1941   Breslau
These days, I have been following world developments. By yesterday,
the Germans had already reached Smolensk. I don't think that their

advance will soon be brought to a halt. The fighting in the East must be horrific. Entire cities are going up in flames. Yet all that suffering will do nothing to alleviate our own.

Wednesday, July 9, 1941   Breslau
A comet passed across the skies. Comets have always portended catastrophe! We have no understanding of cosmic influences on the human soul.

Friday, July 11, 1941   Breslau
It looks as if the German advance in the East has been brought to a halt. The losses appear to be terrible! At the same time, the Americans are entering the war! The prognosis for Germany is not favorable!

Sunday, July 13, 1941   Breslau
Fräulein Silberstein came by toward evening with what are called atrocity reports. Rumor has it that the Gauleiter has completed plans for evacuating Breslau Jews to the General Government. Of course, there is no way to know whether this is true; there are rumors that entire towns are to be evacuated in western Germany, and that these people will be relocated in Jewish dwellings. Of course, it is impossible to know what is true. The source from whom Fräulein Silberstein received this information seems quite impeccable! There is nothing to do other than to peer into the future, trusting in G'd, and at most prepare a few small bags. We are living in catastrophic times! In my opinion, things do not look good in the East; there is talk that the German armies have been surrounded in the Rokitno swamps, but it is also possible that these are just rumors. Up until now, after all, the Germans have been lucky in spite of what have surely been enormous losses. On the other hand, the deployment of American troops in Europe is coming ever closer. And Germany no longer seems to have the upper hand! The French army in Syria must capitulate, and as a result, the situation in Palestine is considerably more favorable, and the land will probably expand northward to its historical boundaries. The power of the government in Vichy is getting ever weaker! But for now the Jews, who remain as pawns in the hands of the Germans, will be made to pay for all this. Of course, matters could come to a head more quickly. The newspapers outdo each other in inciting against the Jews; however, I don't believe this makes much of an impression on the population anymore!

Monday, July 14, 1941   Breslau
I sent a letter to Baeck, in his capacity as chairman of the Reich Association, about the threatened evacuation. For our immediate circle, what is important is whether the planned evacuation of Breslau Jews will or will not take place. Rabbi Lewin reacted with detachment to the news from Fräulein Silberstein. Hope for the best!

Tuesday, July 15, 1941   Breslau
Eugen Perle came by yesterday afternoon; naturally, we also talked about the feared evacuation, which the board has long been discussing. In Königsberg, this threat was averted by making available 500 rooms previously belonging to Jews. They are going to try something similar here, but we have no idea whether it will work.

Wednesday, July 16, 1941   Breslau
Susannchen played in the Cosel cemetery in the afternoon; the children are now playing in a part of the cemetery not yet in use. That is all we have left. In order to get to their playground, they have to walk through the entire cemetery; Susannchen was somewhat awed by the sight of it!

Thursday, July 17, 1941   Breslau
First spent a few hours yesterday morning working on *Germania Judaica*, then rode to the Community administration to discuss with Dr. Tallert the possibility of giving private lessons. He thinks that I would have to get a teaching permit, and the question is whether I should do that! Also spoke with Emil Kaim and Eugen Perle. As to the question of relocation, all we know is that room is to be made for 1,000 persons, who are to be employed in a shoe factory, in Rothenburg, near Görlitz. Also for 100 families!

I went to see Professor Goerlitz in the afternoon to discuss my situation with him. He is going to make a special trip to see Oberbaurat Stein. I told Goerlitz that I believe it is one's fundamental duty to share the fate of one's people. He agreed with me, but on the other hand, he said it was in the general interest for me to remain here. In any case, he was of an extraordinarily humane readiness to help others, and the realization that such a thing even exists these days made our conversation personally worthwhile. I will presumably meet with him again next Monday because he is traveling to Posen on Friday and Saturday.

Friday, July 18, 1941   Breslau

Worked in the archive again yesterday morning; spoke with Professor Hoffmann and told him about things that are in the air. He invited me for coffee next Thursday; he lives in the convent of the Sisters of St. Elisabeth, in the Antonienstrasse. Newspaper: daily incitement against the Jews. Kishinev, in Bessarabia, has been captured; another sadly famous place in Jewish history.[1] One hears that nine million men are currently facing each other in the greatest battle in world history.

Saturday, July 19, 1941   Breslau

Eugen Perle, who told me that barracks have already been built for the Jews in Munich. This seems to be part of an action aimed at evicting Jews from their dwellings throughout Germany. When and how is not yet known. I received a letter from Rabbi Baeck yesterday that was reassuring, if only for the moment, but in the final analysis we must be clear that none of us really knows anything.

Tuesday, July 22, 1941   Breslau

Professor Goerlitz went to see Oberbaurat Stein regarding my situation. Goerlitz told Stein more or less the following: if there are evacuations, he wants me to be the last to go. Stein agreed, and he then called an official he knows at the price-control office in charge of "Jewish rentals," who told him that they were merely the executing authority in all these matters, and that the actual decisions are made by the price-control office.[2] The Jews who now have the least desirable dwellings are in the best position; if someone likes an apartment, it will be given to them! What is clear is that Oberbaurat Stein had no idea about any planned large-scale evacuations, nor did the other office, which was somewhat encouraging, especially for the Jewish community of Breslau. I was touched by Goerlitz's initiative, and by Oberbaurat Stein, with whom I have rarely spoken but who apparently has a favorable impression of me! In the end, and this is very gratifying for a scholar, objective

1. A reference to the pogroms that took place in Kišinev (Romanian: Chişinău) in 1903 and 1905. Cf. Willy Cohn, *Verwehte Spuren. Erinnerungen an das Breslauer Judentum vor seinem Untergang*, ed. Norbert Conrads (Cologne: Böhlau, 1995), p. 60.

2. Regarding the price-control authorities and their responsibility for Jewish dwellings, compare diary entry of March 3, 1941.

research always makes its way and is recognized even in "Aryan" circles these days. I was especially pleased with their humane readiness to help! These are bright spots in these times. Goerlitz also told me how decently the new mayor of Breslau, Dr. Spielhagen, behaved when he was to be relocated into a Jewish apartment.[3] The story he told about the fate of the Romanian Jews was less pleasant. His nephew, who is a first lieutenant in the Luftwaffe, wrote that what was being done there was nothing short of butchery. Horrific!

Newspaper: victories piled upon victories in the East, whereas apparently everything in the West is being destroyed. It is said that only one church remains standing in Munster, in Westphalia! In Schweidnitz, the Ursuline cloister, home to 80 nuns, had to be evacuated again.

Wednesday, July 23, 1941   Breslau
In the afternoon, worked hard on *Germania Judaica*. After dinner, went and got the food cards from Fräulein Silberstein; I personally received none because I received packages from abroad. In reality, all I have received recently was 400 grams of cocoa. In any case, I will have to go to the district office tomorrow, which will waste more valuable time! They are trying to make life as difficult for us as possible!

Friday, July 25, 1941   Breslau
Went to the district office yesterday morning to get my food cards. They didn't subtract anything for the Chinese cocoa, but standing around was very strenuous for me, and I came close to fainting. Unfortunately, my own "racial comrades" behaved with such little discipline that in the evening Herr Foerder told me they called the Gestapo and asked that a policeman be sent to restore order. Sad.

I was invited for coffee in the afternoon by Professor Hermann Hoffmann. Professor Hoffmann lives in the convent of the Sisters of St. Elisabeth, in the Antonienstrasse. The peace and cleanness in such a convent is remarkable! It was a beautiful afternoon. The main thing was not that I was served zwieback and coffee made from real coffee

3. Wolfgang Spielhagen (1891–1945) was the deputy mayor of Breslau from 1940 and 1945. On January 27, 1945, Gauleiter Karl Hanke (1903–1945) had him arrested, court-martialed, and executed because Spielhagen had criticized plans for the military defense of Breslau.

beans, but that the spiritual atmosphere was so elevated, and we talked much about scholarly work. We also exchanged books. I gave him a complete machzor, which pleased him greatly, and he gave me his comprehensive book on the history of the Jesuits in Schweidnitz, and some other things, including Simonsohn's dissertation. Professor Hoffmann will visit us as well at some time. Professor Hoffmann also told me the ghastly, almost incomprehensible, news that 12,000 Jews were shot in Lemberg.[4] Apparently the work of the SS.

Saturday, July 26, 1941   Breslau
Storch Synagogue; rather somber mood. On Thursday, 51 Jews will have to relocate to Tormersdorf, near Rothenburg, not far from Görlitz; people have been evicted from ten apartments, and that is just the beginning of this action, as Community chairman Dr. Kohn was told at the Gestapo.[5] Apparently, they don't want this; the order is coming from elsewhere. The stated reason is always the need for apartments. Apparently people found Rabbi Lewin's announcement, which I didn't hear, very upsetting, and so I wouldn't be surprised if there were suicides during the night. I consider his behavior to be very wrong! But I don't have any influence on him. We are now permitted to buy food only between the hours of eleven and one.[6] Each day brings new restrictions. Increasing vengeance against the Jews!

---

4. Quite accurate information. These killings were perpetrated in Lemberg (Lvov) by Einsatz Commandos (mobile killing units) 5 and 6 belonging to Einsatz Group C, with the participation of Ukrainian nationalists. For more about the mobile killing units in the East, see Raul Hilberg, *The Destruction of the European Jews* (New York: Holmes & Meier, 1985), vol. 2, pp. 291–317.

5. At this time, Cohn often misstated the name, writing "Thomasdorf." Only later did he get more precise information about the place, of which he knew only that it was near Görlitz. Over the following weeks, the facility run by the Protestant Zoar confraternity, in Tormersdorf, was filled beyond capacity with Jewish transports from Breslau and other Silesian cities. This "Jewish residential community" quickly took on the character of a ghetto. It should be noted that the Jewish Community had been informed of these relocations. On July 25, 1941, the chief of police of Breslau issued a decree setting these measures in motion.

6. Ever since the regulations of June 10 and 17, 1941, Jews received their food ration cards separately from the rest of the population. On August 7, their rations were even further reduced.

Sunday, July 27, 1941   Breslau
Did a few things on *Germania Judaica* yesterday morning. Rich material is available for the section about Saxony and Thuringia. In the afternoon, I did some more on *Germania Judaica* and worked on deciphering the Hebrew photocopies!

In the East, Germany is trying to turn the Russians against their government. However, I don't think that Germany will succeed in ending the war before the onset of winter.

Wednesday, July 30, 1941   Breslau
Did some work of my own yesterday morning, then rode to Scheitnig with Trudi. It was lovely and restful; walked, particularly in the old part. Stood at the Schiller Memorial and admired his imposing face. There is still nobility in the German spirit. And how beautifully situated is the Eichendorff Memorial in the park. In the afternoon, worked hard on *Germania Judaica*. I then went to the barber, and from there to see Hedwig Bermann, who lives very nicely in the Museumsplatz at Frau Schmidt's, the pharmacist's wife. The rear of the building looks out onto the Friends' property; it is amazing to see how many trees there are in the old city. The widow of the artist Laboschin was also there.[7] It brought back old memories.

Thursday, July 31, 1941   Breslau
Yesterday morning went to the school department about the teaching permit. I was seen by a very nice official who told me what sorts of formalities I had to go through to get this permit. There are many, the most important being a certificate of good conduct from the police. That shouldn't be hard.

Friday, August 1, 1941   Breslau
I spoke briefly with Director Engelbert yesterday about the general situation and my own! We more or less agreed in our evaluation! There doesn't seem to be any real progress in the East, and a position war will probably develop there. Worked on *Germania Judaica* in the afternoon; wrote the article about Meiningen, and I am making good progress on the section about Thuringia.

---

7. Siegfried Laboschin (1868–1929) was a painter, graphic artist, and art critic well known for his paintings of the Jewish milieu and of old Breslau.

The first group of Breslau Jews left on the regularly scheduled train for Tormersdorf yesterday; Frau Heti Cohn, who once played a role on the board of the Social Group, and who likes me very much, was among them. It is impossible to know whether the Jews in Tormersdorf will have a better future than we; everything is up in the air. At the hospital in the Wallstrasse, a Frau Schreiber jumped out the window. Dead. Some just lose their nerve!

Saturday, August 2, 1941   Breslau
Spent a few happy hours yesterday morning and dictated a nice piece on my memoirs. These days, I seem to live on memories of times gone by. People continue to be evicted from their apartments on the shortest notice. A letter from the Jewish Community board is on its way asking me to administer the archive. Halpersohn has retired. I will do it; I have never in my life neglected a matter that concerns the Jews. Recited Kiddush and then had a long conversation with Trudi about personal matters. Trudi complained that she appears so seldom in my memoirs.

Sunday, August 3, 1941   Breslau
Tisha B'Av; actually, it was yesterday, but it was postponed to today because of Shabbat. I read the Eichahs yesterday in bed; today I will read the Kinnot! Later, I will visit the Lohestrasse cemetery.

Regarding the situation: according to the photographs and the reports, a horrific slaughter must be occurring in the East, and it doesn't look as if Germany is making much headway. The newspapers are full of obituaries. The young people of Europe are being bled in this war. The Russians are resisting the attack with the most extreme determination. The reports from the East make clear how vengeance is being taken on the Jews. In Bialystok, this vengeance has been especially violent.[8] The synagogue in Czernowitz was burned down![9]

---

8. Bialystok, in northeast Poland, was taken by the Wehrmacht on June 27, 1941. Police Battalion 309 and other units under the Wehrmacht's 221st Security Division then killed at least two thousand Jews. See Christopher R. Browning, *Origins of the Final Solution: The Evolution of Nazi Jewish Policy, September 1939–March 1942* (Lincoln/Jerusalem: University of Nebraska Press/Yad Vashem, 2004), p. 255. At the same time, they established a ghetto, whose fifty thousand inmates were, with very few exceptions, killed over the next two years.

9. In early July 1941, German troops took Czernowitz, in Bukovina. Einsatz

Monday, August 4, 1941   Breslau

Went for a walk in the evening and sat down on a bench at the terminal. I was accosted from one of the streetcars, that is, one woman said to another, "A real cutthroat people. The time will come when none of them will be walking the streets." The other woman, it should be noted, evidenced no sign of assent.

Thursday, August 7, 1941   Breslau

Yesterday morning, worked for a while on *Germania Judaica* and began the article on Dresden. Went to the post office to send a large package to Frau Kohn, in Weruschau; then to the Jewish Community to begin work on the archive.[10] Discussed everything with Dr. Tallert, the syndic; I will work there twice a week, on Tuesday and Thursday. News just arrived from Berlin that male Jews between the ages of 18 and 48 are no longer permitted to emigrate. No reason was given for this decree. Spoke with attorney Jacob and attorney Zucker, who is also helping in the archive. It is in pathetic condition, housed in the cellar, and except for the files themselves, there is nothing in the archive worthy of the name. I found my father's signature (1894) in the first file that I examined, from a representative assembly. At the time he was younger than I am today.

An old elementary school student, who is a maintenance man here, visited me yesterday. His son is also in the East. It is said to be a gruesome bloodbath; all political commissars are killed immediately upon capture.[11] The war is taking on ever more inhuman forms.

Group D moved its headquarters there. Einsatz Commando 10b, under Otto Ohlendorf, murdered several hundred Jews and burned down the large synagogue.

10. This was Willy Cohn's last important mission, to organize the now neglected Jewish Community Archive. He and his coworkers were able to salvage the archive holdings from the completely inadequate cellar rooms, which is why the archive has survived to the present day. The complete archive was found, in 1945, after the war, in a building of the Jewish cemetery, in Breslau-Cosel. Today it is housed in the Jewish Historical Institute, in Warsaw. Cohn hoped that as a result of this work, the Jewish Community might protect him from being "relocated" from Breslau.

11. Indirect confirmation that people in Breslau in effect already knew about the secret Commissar Order of June 6, 1941.

Friday, August 8, 1941   Breslau

Yesterday morning worked in the Diocese Archive; also had a brief conversation with Director Engelbert. He showed me an extraordinarily revealing sermon given by the Bishop of Munster, at St. Lambert's Church in mid-July.[12] There are still some courageous people! It was mainly directed against the system of administrative detentions.

Yesterday, more than a hundred Breslau Jews received orders to relocate to Tormersdorf. We don't yet know who is affected. A number of families living in the Roonstrasse are said to be included again. It is impossible to know what might be to the good for any individual! Today I have to report to the Gestapo; I also need to see the school administration about my teaching permit.

Saturday, August 9, 1941   Breslau

Yesterday, left relatively early. Went to the school administration about my teaching permit. I was seen by a very nice official, and I will probably have the certificate within 14 days. Then I went to see municipal secretary Spiess to find out about my so-called deductions. These are the deductions that were taken from my salary in former years. Spiess told me that refunds to Jews have been suspended. More robbery! I then had some time before my appointment with the Gestapo.

A large number of Jews again received orders to leave yesterday; it appears that the evacuation of the Breslau Jews is now being driven forward at a very high speed. Well, we simply have to take things as they come. Received news from my in-laws that they will emigrate early next week. Today is Shabbat Nachamu![13] May it console me a little, and our entire tormented people.

---

12. In his sermon of July 13, 1941, Bishop Clemens August Count von Galen (1878–1946) protested against Operation Monastery, the forced dissolution of the monasteries in Germany. Earlier, the Jesuit residence in Munster had been confiscated and its occupants evicted. In further sensational sermons, on July 20 and August 3, 1941, Galen also protested against arbitrary acts by the Gestapo, and against the Nazi euthanasia campaign.

13. "Sabbath of comforting," the first of seven haftarahs of consolation leading up to Rosh Hashanah.

Sunday, August 10, 1941   Breslau
Sat for a time with Frau Oppenheim in the summer house. A pure pleasure it was not because we kept coming back to the evacuations, and such conversations don't lead anywhere.

Tuesday, August 12, 1941   Breslau
In the evening, when I returned, I found Trudi in tears. Her parents asked her to call them again. They are leaving this evening.[14] Naturally, this was very hard for Trudi.

Wednesday, August 13, 1941   Breslau
We did some real work in the Community Archive for the first time yesterday. It is not very pleasant down in the cellar; I was forced to stand for four hours getting the files in order, but the work itself was very interesting. I learned that my grandfather had been the representative of the Breslau community. I saw his signature "Julius Hainauer" for the first time, and I also found an appreciation of my father in the files. And so I represent at least the third generation of my family serving the Jewish community. Worked together with attorney Jakob; his wife was there for a time as well. The two Ehrlichs, both master builders, are also filing their drawings. We talked about the old times. They built the Trautner building for us and the family grave site in the Lohestrasse.

Friday, August 15, 1941   Breslau
I am finding the work in the archive very strenuous, I mean the Jewish Community Archive, because I have to stand to put the files in order! But on the other hand, I am finding all sorts of things. I have now found the directory of all privileged family patriarchs and their family members, one of the most important sources for the history of the Breslau Jewish community. The condition of the cellar workspace itself is deplorable. Professor Klawitter, from Trebnitz, was here yesterday morning asking about me; he had heard about the evacuations! Very decent of him! This is not something one expects from most!

14. As of October 1, 1941, they would have been unable to leave. On that date, all Jewish emigration from the German Reich was forbidden. In his diary entry of October 27, 1941, Cohn noted that his in-laws had arrived in Buenos Aires. They later went to New York.

Apparently, the radio here made the following announcement yesterday: rumor is being spread in America that the Jews are being evacuated from Breslau. This is supposedly untrue, and the Jews are relocating to the countryside voluntarily. What utter deceit. Each and every one is being forced to sign a declaration that he is leaving Breslau voluntarily.

Saturday, August 16, 1941   Breslau
Stories are circulating that entire German regiments have deserted, and that the SS is shooting anyone who raises their arms! Can this be true? Fifty young Jews who were seized in Holland, on November 8, 1940, all died of a "heart attack" in the camp in Linz.[15] Everywhere, murder!

Sunday, August 17, 1941   Breslau
Went to the bank yesterday morning, where they wanted to convince me to buy bonds, which I declined in view of the current Jewish situation.[16] I told the deputy bank director that I bought many tens of thousands in war bonds during the previous war, and that I would do so now if our fate were not so uncertain. Went to Haupt & Hoffmann; we Jews are to get only one hundredweight of coal each month! In the afternoon completed a brief article for *Germania Judaica*.

15. The Mauthausen concentration camp, near Linz, was founded near a large granite quarry shortly after the "annexation" of Austria, in 1938. It was the only Class 3 concentration camp within the territory of the German Reich carrying out a policy of "extermination through labor." As of 1945, approximately 200,000 persons had been deported to Mauthausen and its satellite camps, of whom 120,000 died or were murdered. Cf. diary entry of August 5, 1940.

16. Cohn continued to administer both his own assets and those of his emigrated siblings. In all probability this is the money he is talking about. The difficulties that Cohn encountered in this regard are touched on in his correspondence with his sister, Erna Proskauer.

Eviction

Monday, August 18, 1941   Breslau

An incident occurred after dinner that greatly upset Susanne. It seems that an Aryan boy from the house, who has been coming to the apartment for some time, has just been using her and us. And apparently our neighbors are also upset that we are still living in the apartment. This boy told Susanne that we are spies. Some outstanding people we have here! In all probability, they are trying to force us out. If things don't change soon, it may be that our dear "national comrades" will be successful!

Wednesday, August 20, 1941   Breslau

Yesterday morning worked in the Jewish Community Archive with Herr Jakob, and we established some external order; it at least looks respectable now! As I left the archive I spoke with Herr Perle, who told me that another list of 120 persons to be sent to Tormersdorf has been drawn up, but that I am not among them. Herr Perle said he thought that the Community would lodge a protest on my behalf, but it is doubtful whether that would save our apartment.

Thursday, August 21, 1941   Breslau

A gentleman with a gold party insignia came to see the apartment in the afternoon. He seemed like a decent enough man, and he won't be taking it! But at some point someone will come and then we will be out of a home. I wrote to Professor Goerlitz yesterday evening about this matter.

Friday, August 22, 1941   Breslau

Yesterday I arrived punctually at eight o'clock at the Community Archive and worked for four hours. I concentrated on the files relating to dues to the Community, beginning with the year 1800. There, too, I found quite a few things of personal interest! Regierungsbaumeister Ehrlich has arrived with a carpenter and begun to do inspections, and I hope that the most necessary repairs will now be made in the room. We were startled after dinner when a hundredweight of coal arrived and was dumped in the kitchen.

Saturday, August 23, 1941   Breslau
Anita Lasker is now working in the Sacrau paper factory and has to wear the yellow armband.[1] I ask myself whether the Community might not have prevented such young girls from being forced to work if they had kept up the secondary school. It was already quite dark, and as we walked through the tunnel we saw a train filled with soldiers on their way to the East. The soldiers were making a commotion and singing as if trying to pump up their courage. They know what lies ahead. The deputy bank director told me yesterday that the *Schlesische Tageszeitung* is not allowed to print all of the obituaries, only a certain percentage.

The government has demanded 100,000 marks from the Reich Association, rumor has it as much as 120,000 marks, for the purpose of building barracks. In all probability, some of it will be used at Tormersdorf. A second transport will be leaving for there on Monday; Herr Saul, the leader there, is here to pick up those people.[2] One can never know what may redound to the good.

Sunday, August 24, 1941   Breslau
Grandmother Proskauer visited us; I think she is quite exhausted. Like all Breslau Jews she is thinking about the prospect of relocation to Tormersdorf.

Losses in the East must be horrific. Reports from the German military constantly speak of victories, of taking this or that place, or more precisely, heaps of rubble. But it is all meaningless. Railroad cars, and even letters from the General Government, are marked with the letter V. It is

---

1. Cf. Anita Lasker-Wallfisch, *Inherit the Truth, 1939–1945: The Documented Experiences of a Survivor of Auschwitz and Belsen* (New York: St. Martin's, 2000), pp. 40–43.

2. In the system of Jewish self-administration, Martin Saul, from Breslau, was made Judenältester, or camp leader, at Tormersdorf.

supposed to stand for Victory, but perhaps it means Verloren.[3] – Advance laurels.

Monday, August 25, 1941   Breslau
Went to the Cathedral Library this morning. Found a great deal of material for my article on Magdeburg. The newspaper continues to report uninterrupted victories in the East and the Atlantic. But the losses must be dreadful. Rumor has it that on orders of an SS-Führer, 7,532 Jews and Bolsheviks were shot behind the front in a single week. Apparently, Field Marshal Bock refused to award this SS-Führer the Iron Cross 1st Class.[4] It seems it is not yet the custom to honor murderers this way. I have no way of knowing whether these things are true! But I can well imagine them!

Wednesday, August 27, 1941   Breslau
I worked in the Community Archive yesterday morning, and as much as I enjoy the work, I regret that this material wasn't organized years ago. It is so unpleasant in this cellar. Nonetheless, it is being worked on; carpenters have been working there and so has the stove fitter.

Thursday, August 28, 1941   Breslau
I worked on files relating to the New Synagogue this morning, and in the process I happened upon traces of my father and of his benevolent spirit. Once, when a lady fainted, he proposed that a recuperation room be set up in the synagogue. An entire old world wells up from memory! The cellar looked quite presentable today; a platform has been put down so that we don't have to sit on the cold floor, and a stove has been put in so I was able to get some heat going and burn some of the old rubbish that is lying around.

Herr Perle visited me, as did Director Lasch, who made a very good impression. To him has fallen the difficult task of allocating dwellings, and many members of the community curse him, but none of them would do a better job! Three members of the board were in Berlin; we will have to tighten up even more! People are forced into close quarters

3. German for "lost."

4. Cohn seems to have gotten these precise figures at the Diocese Archive. They may refer to a massacre that took place in Borisov, in White Russia. The information about Field Marshal Bock (1880–1945) has not been confirmed.

in Tormersdorf; one house that was being used has been confiscated by the military authorities; in exchange, they provided a barracks.

Friday, August 29, 1941   Breslau
Two different people looked at the apartment yesterday, and it may well be that we will soon lose it. We certainly could never have dreamed that it would come to this, having fought so long in the war, but we just have to accept it and try not to lose our nerve. However, these nerves have been strained to the breaking point these past few years!

Saturday, August 30, 1941   Breslau
Yesterday morning dictated a good piece of my memoirs to Fräulein Cohn. I am now in the fall of 1931, and so I only have one and a half years more to do since I intended the book to cover only the period up to 1933.

The Jewish Community house was attacked by Hitler Youth at ten thirty last night. There was a big parade in the Schlossplatz, and they were probably put up to it. Pretense: supposedly, the caretaker had thrown a flower pot down onto the street! They smashed the windows in his apartment; other than that nothing happened. Naturally, the sick and the children were terrified.[5] The brutalization continues apace.

Sunday, August 31, 1941   Breslau
Read the files concerning the Industrial School and happened upon traces of some of my ancestors. Found a document written by my great-grandfather Louis Jaffé, also in the list of donors the names of two great-grandmothers and one grandmother. Went with Susannchen to the Lohestrasse cemetery, and in addition to visiting the departed members of my family, also the grave of Ferdinand Lassalle. It is the anniversary of his death today. It was sixteen years ago that the workers organized a large procession to his gravesite.

Tuesday, September 2, 1941   Breslau
Diocese Archive. Did a fair amount of excerpting. I read a sermon by Count von Galen, the Bishop of Munster, in which he condemned

---

5. After confiscation of the Jewish hospital and old-age home, the internal medicine department had, since the end of 1939, been housed in the Jewish Community building in the Wallstrasse.

the killing of human beings; he even had the courage to file criminal charges![6] Naturally, there has been no response.

In the afternoon, I went to see Professor Goerlitz, who told me about his conversation with Oberbaurat Stein. Stein said that we should emphasize all of the disadvantages of our apartment; he didn't think he would get very far, even if he discussed the matter with the gentleman from the regional administration because their position is that no matter how German a Jew may feel, he would have to be their enemy after all that had been done to them. A very logical point of view. Approximately 200 dwellings have been confiscated here. Tormersdorf is full; Leubus is occupied by Aryans.[7] The city of Breslau, Stein in particular, has been ordered to erect barracks, but the city really has no room. People seem unwilling to go along with all this! Even in Aryan circles, many are deeply concerned about the fate of the feebleminded.

Wednesday, September 3, 1941   Breslau
Air raid alarm last night at one thirty, but the enemy airplanes didn't get as far as Breslau, and the alarm was canceled relatively quickly. Even so, it makes it hard to go back to sleep. The children were fine. Nor did we have any problems with our neighbors!

Trudi went to a concert today to benefit the "Jewish Duty"![8] It is been a long time since she has gone to an event! Situation: in spite of all the surface optimism, it looks very much like *neila*. The ill-feeling toward party authorities is very great.

Thursday, September 4, 1941   Breslau
Worked in the Community Archive in the morning. It is now quite comfortable in the cellar, always nicely heated. I wish I had a secretary so that I could do a proper inventory. At the moment, I am looking

6. Cf. diary entry of August 8, 1941. In his sermon of August 3, 1941, Bishop Clemens August von Galen (1878–1946) protested against the killing of the mentally ill in hospitals and insane asylums. He filed charges with the District Court, in Munster.

7. In addition to the already existing hospital and asylum at Leubus Abbey, a field hospital had also been set up at this time. Cf. diary entry of June 2, 1941.

8. Almost certainly the Jewish Winter Relief, which was consistently described in newspaper ads as being an "absolute duty" of all Jews toward those less fortunate. It also held concerts.

at all the files to become acquainted with the holdings. Today, I inspected many files from the Old and the New Synagogue, and from the Claassenstrasse and Cosel cemeteries! Susannchen paid me a visit in the cellar! Inherited many books that are now coming in from vacated apartments.

When I arrived home, I heard that someone else had looked at our apartment, an officer who made a less than favorable impression on Trudi. He even had the landlord write down the address! I hope he didn't like the apartment. Then received a letter from the Reich Ministry for the Economy regarding securities! Trudi didn't read it right; it has nothing to do with us! Unnecessary upheaval! Overall, I'm having a bad day today. I've already broken the thermos bottle and burned my finger on the stove!

Saturday, September 6, 1941   Breslau
Yesterday, a lovely and quick letter from Wölfl dated August 20, full of warmth. He asks about each and every one of us; a boy on whom we may rely.

Sunday, September 7, 1941   Breslau
No newspaper to be had yesterday. Paper is in such short supply that newspapers are quickly sold out. A number of streetcar lines won't be running in the morning as of this Sunday. There is a shortage of personnel! I think that Germany's situation continues to be very unfavorable, even though the newspapers report victories each day.

Monday, September 8, 1941   Breslau
The day began with the barber telling me that, as of September 19, we will have to wear a badge bearing the word "Jew," even six-year-old children.[9] This won't break us either, even though life will be made more difficult. In spite of it all, we will have to try not to lose our nerve. All of these measures show how increasingly bad Germany's situation is, and how the people's rage is being vented on the most helpless part of the population! This trumps the Middle Ages! Each violation carries a fine of 500 marks or one month in jail! In addition, travel by Jews has

9. The legal basis for this was the so-called "Polizeiverordnung über die Kennzeichnung der Juden" [Police Regulation Regarding the Identification of Jews], of September 1, 1941. See *Reich Law Gazette* 1, p. 547.

been banned throughout the Reich, and the obligation to report to the Gestapo tightened.[10]

Worked in the Cathedral Archive and did some excerpting for *Germania Judaica*! Nonetheless, these matters coursed around my mind! Director Engelbert told me that I may continue to work there despite the badge. He is a man of great character, far different from Walter, the archivist, and Mother Huberta. Mother Innocentia is also a person with a large spirit.

Tuesday, September 9, 1941   Breslau
Dictated a considerable piece of my memoirs yesterday afternoon; I have now written more than 1,000 pages. I also wrote a lengthy letter to Wölfl! Given current circumstances, it is hard to find the right words. I was exhausted by evening. I went for a walk, but I am very unnerved by the decree about the yellow badge! I read it this morning!

Thursday, September 11, 1941   Breslau
Went to the Cathedral Library yesterday morning, but it was difficult for me to work with so much going through my head. I showed Walter, the archivist, the decree about the yellow badge; both he and Mother Innocentia were very upset. I also showed it to the gentleman at the bank. Did a good piece of work on my memoirs; I am almost finished with the book!

Friday, September 12, 1941   Breslau
Grandmother was here just now, quite upset. Too many things are raining down on us right now. A cultural society in Breslau has been dissolved, whether in the entire Reich, I do not know![11] They intend to vent their hatred on us until the end! Apparently, a state of siege has

---

10. The above regulation also forbade Jews to leave their place of residence without police permission. See *Reich Law Gazette* 1, p. 547.

11. The Breslauer Kulturbund [Breslau Cultural Association] was founded in 1933. Such associations, which existed throughout Germany, served as self-help organizations for Jews involved in cultural endeavors. In 1936, they amalgamated to form the Reichsverband der Jüdischen Kulturbünde in Deutschland [Reich Association of Jewish Cultural Associations in Germany]. The Jewish cultural associations were dissolved throughout Germany on November 11, 1941.

been declared in Frankfurt am Main and Cassel. The Eastern Front has apparently been retaken!

Saturday, September 13, 1941   Breslau
Grete Proskauer came by yesterday afternoon as I was preparing to leave. She is Dr. Jacobson's assistant in Berlin for the General Archive of the Jews in Germany and at the Reich Clan Office.[12] She will be our guest for several days, and I look forward to our scholarly discussions. I so seldom have the opportunity to talk with someone who understands these matters. Had a conversation with Herr Perle at the synagogue. The Jewish badges, *ordre pour le sémite*, as Jewish wit would have it, have arrived from Berlin and must be picked up next week.

Sunday, September 14, 1941   Breslau
The "Jew's star" has now been announced to the Aryan population as well. The *Schlesische Tageszeitung* purportedly wrote that this is repayment for what is happening to Germans in Russia. The ban on the cultural society is connected with the resettlement of the Volga Germans; there now isn't much left to ban.

Monday, September 15, 1941   Breslau
Went to the barber this morning. Grete Proskauer accompanied me, and then went to the Cathedral Library. During our ride, I was able to show her some of Breslau's main attractions. Politics: one of the generals has fallen; an entire German army consisting of Germans, Italians, and Romanians is said to have been cut off at Odessa! Things do not look good for Germany!

Wednesday, September 17, 1941   Breslau
Yesterday worked with Grete Proskauer in the Community Archive; she didn't find anything for her genealogical research that she didn't already know. Trudi was there as well to buy some things for Susanne at the clothing store.

12. Margarete Proskauer lost her position in Berlin soon thereafter. She went underground when the deportations began and was shot while trying to cross the border into Switzerland. Cf. Stefi Jersch-Wenzel and Thomas Jersch, "Jacob Jacobson—deutscher Jude und Archivar (1888–1968)," in *Archive und Gedächtnis. Festschrift für Botho Brachmann* (Potsdam: Verlag für Berlin-Brandenburg, 2005), pp. 547–585, esp. p. 576.

Worked in the Cathedral Library this morning and spoke with the director in his office. I also read the letter that Count Galen directed at the Reich Minister, which was aimed at the Gestapo.[13] I don't think he will be able to change the current situation. Mother Innocentia told me about Mother Huberta's intriguing. When possible, I give her the cold shoulder. Frau Jilek gave us some lovely things for Rosh Hashanah; I will repay her accordingly! Bought vegetables on the Sandinsel for the last time.

Thursday, September 18, 1941   Breslau
Machunze, our landlord, announced his visit in the afternoon; however he never came. It looks as if we will lose our apartment after all. We will just have to accept it!

Friday, September 19, 1941   Breslau
We tried to get all of our errands done yesterday because today is the first day that we are required to wear the Jew's star, and we wanted to stay off the streets as much as possible. But I am convinced that everything will go smoothly, and this morning when I went to get the milk, I saw that, if anything, the Aryans find it more awkward than we do! Dictated my memoirs yesterday afternoon; I hope that in just a few more sessions I will have arrived at the conclusion of this book, January 30, 1933. I would be very pleased if I could get it finished before the end of 5701!

Saturday, September 20, 1941   Breslau
I had such a sense of happiness yesterday at having completed my work, even though it leaves me with an empty feeling, much like saying farewell to a child! Once all of this is over, I would like to be able to write the second part, covering the period after 1933!

In the afternoon, went to the Storch Synagogue in Jew's star regalia, although I had the feeling that heart weakness was setting in, which happily did not occur. But I definitely wanted to go so that people could not later accuse me of cowardice for not being there. I walked the entire distance, and the public's behavior was irreproachable. No one harassed me; rather, I felt that people were somewhat pained by this development. At the synagogue, Eugen Perle gave me the shocking

13. In a letter to Reich Minister Hanns Kerrl (1887–1941), dated April 25, 1941, Bishop Galen stated that the practice of the Gestapo denying accused persons all means of legal defense violated "natural and Christian justice."

news that another 1,000 Jews will have to leave Breslau on the shortest of notices; the first 200 will have to clear their premises by the 25th and leave on the 30th. They are simply taking things out on us, purposely during the high holidays in order to destroy this time for us.

Tuesday, September 23, 1941   Breslau
First day of fall. Second day of Rosh Hashanah. Actually, I had intended not to write on these two days, but there is so much weighing on me that I feel I must unburden myself, and I do not believe that I am committing a serious sin. I went with Trudi and the two children to the cemetery in the Lohestrasse on the evening of the New Year's celebration. The children looked for chestnuts, and I prayed. Tomorrow is the anniversary of Mother's death according to the German calendar. If at all possible, I would like to go to the cemetery again. The behavior of the public—and there were quite a few people on the street—was correct in all respects as far as our badge was concerned. The badge has had the opposite effect that the regime had intended.

On the way home, I visited Hugo Mamlok; he and his mother-in-law, Frau Gallinek, and his daughter Ilse have been affected by the evictions. It is a great calamity; three helpless people. He himself wasn't there; we offered to let him stay with us during the transition. In the 30 years that I have known him, he has always behaved very well and properly toward me, and we cannot know whether we will not find ourselves in the same situation shortly!

I handed my memoirs, which are now finished, to Trudi, with an appropriate dedication.[14] Yesterday morning and evening I went to the Storch Synagogue. The morning service upset me, particularly the Unetanneh Tokef. I believe that I have only a short time to live. Frau Brotzen told me about the terrible policy of euthanasia under which the mentally ill are being killed, including Aryans.[15] It is said that at

---

14. Cf. Willy Cohn, *Verwehte Spuren. Erinnerungen an das Breslauer Judentum vor seinem Untergang*, ed. Norbert Conrads (Cologne: Böhlau, 1995), p. 16. On the same day, Cohn delivered his final carbon copy (pages 920–1048) to the Diocese Archive for safekeeping.

15. The Nazi euthanasia program became increasingly well known after Galen's sermon on August 3, 1941, and inspired numerous protests. As a result, Hitler officially halted the program, on August 24, 1941, although clandestine killings continued.

one Bavarian asylum, they were told that there would be a concert, and then they were brought into a magically illuminated hall, where they were gassed to death. And those were by no means all incurable cases. Murder, horrible murder instigated by the state!

Saturday, September 27, 1941   Breslau
Went to see Professor Grotte yesterday afternoon to return several books. He gave me several gifts on this occasion. I arrived just as they were in the process of moving; a melancholy affair in any case. Grotte reproached me because a few months earlier I had talked his wife out of selling some of their possessions. All those who have now been ordered to leave must have their apartments cleared out by September 30; the transport is supposed to be leaving on October 10, purportedly for Grüssau, where the Bukovina Germans had previously been accommodated.[16] Given the information that Grotte had received, he was advised to leave. He was told: the last ones out will be stuffed into barracks. Apparently, a new list of 600 persons has already been drawn up for the next transport! Grotte intended a jab at me when he said that I was still needed here!

Went to synagogue in the evening and had a conversation with Herr Foerder. He told me that I should just continue to live as I have. If need be, furniture can be sold very quickly, although if I were evacuated I would try to have everything stored with a shipper! In my opinion, it is certain that, unless there are radical changes, the Germans will continue to vent their rage on the Jews! We must be prepared for that.

Sunday, September 28, 1941   Breslau
The evening mail yesterday brought, among other things, a shocking letter from Frau Kohn, in Weruschau. A hundred Jewish families were deported at five in the morning and weren't even permitted to take anything with them. What horrible barbarism. Frau Kohn found accommodations, in Welun, with acquaintances who themselves have lost everything.[17] She had a very painful hemorrhage! Will this bill of cruelty

16. Cf. Alfred Konieczny, *Tormersdorf, Grüssau, Riebnig. Obozy przejściowe dla Żydów Dolnego Śląska z lat 1941–1943*, Acta Universitatis Wratislaviensis, 1998 (Wrocław: Wydawn. Uniw. Wrocławskiego, 1997), p. 120.

17. The Polish district town of Wieluń, in the voivodship of Łódź, was renamed Welun im Warthegau in 1941. Weruschau lay in the district of Welun.

against the Jews ever be repaid? America constantly threatens the most severe reprisals, but I don't think this makes much of an impression over here. Apparently there has been an uprising in Norway, and many people have been shot. Terror over Europe. But it, too, will one day come to an end; the question, however, is who will be left when it is over. As for myself, I have lived my life, but our young children should by rights have a happy life ahead of them!

Monday, September 29, 1941   Breslau
Yesterday went for a walk in the sun with Tamara and bought something at the automat. This is the only happiness I can provide the children, going with them to the automat in the Goethestrasse, the only one that currently has sweets. The children of today have become very modest in their wants.

At noon, we received various things from Hugo Mamlok, who must vacate his apartment. He came by himself in the afternoon. I am very sorry that he doesn't want to stay with us; I would so like to have made his life somewhat easier before his departure. But a man's mind is his kingdom. I felt very badly for the old man, having to separate from everything that he so dearly loved his entire life. It is very painful! Hugo Mamlok was always such a very discriminating and sensitive man! Hard times.

Tuesday, September 30, 1941   Breslau
The evening mail brought me, among other things, a very dear letter from the Proskauers with good news, but then I got so upset that I broke down completely and began to cry uncontrollably. I have not yet really recovered this morning, and so I decided not to go to the Community Archive. This evening is the Day of Atonement, and I will try to go to services if only I can, although I doubt I'll be able to endure the air in the Friends' Hall. My nervous reserves are at an end, and yet large reserves are what are needed to face what lies ahead of us. Sometimes I think to myself that it would be better if I no longer existed, but when you have such small children it is impermissible even to think such a thing.

On the eve of the Day of Atonement people tend to become especially introspective; I know that I have sins for which I must atone, but I hope that in some things I have walked a righteous path.

Thursday, October 2, 1941   Breslau

Yom Kippur is over now! It gave me a sense of inner exaltation, even though I was unable to fast. Trudi prepared everything beautifully! I prayed in the concert hall; Susanne was with me yesterday morning. The conservative service was conducted in the Friends' Hall, and Hamburger spoke simply and well. I hope that our next Yom Kippur will be celebrated under very different circumstances.

Friday, October 3, 1941   Breslau

Professor Hoffmann came to see me in the afternoon for coffee. It was an especially stimulating afternoon, and we looked through a number of things in my library, particularly at the Hebrew photocopies. He was very nice to the children, for whom he had brought some zwieback. I went for a short walk toward evening; now we have to be back by eight o'clock.

Saturday, October 4, 1941   Breslau

At the moment, ever more assets are being confiscated as anti-state property; this takes an ax to the root of what remains of Jewish life in Germany. These are pure acts of vengeance, and it looks as if Jewish assets in their entirety will eventually be expropriated. I heard about these things in the synagogue courtyard. Attorney Jakob informs me about what is actually going on because most of what we hear is simply rumor, and untrue. Spoke with Herr Perle after synagogue. He has to deal with all of the minor disputes within the community. And, of course, the board should be conserving its strength for more important things. Every effort should be made to get the children out of Germany.

Today we have been married for 18 years. The years have passed quickly. They have brought us joy, and they have brought us sorrows. But such is married life, and Trudi has been a very good partner in marriage. We have brought up five children who will carry on for us when we are gone.

Sunday, October 5, 1941   Breslau

Went to the bank at noon, where I had no trouble withdrawing 300 marks. One always goes there with a certain trepidation because of the asset expropriations; this fate, unfortunately, has now struck Emil Kaim. Grandmother Proskauer and the Reiters came for tea; I read them a few passages from my memoirs, which is better than conversations that always revolve around the same things.

Monday, October 6, 1941   Breslau
First evening of Sukkot. Susanne built a *sukkah* under a piece of canvas on the balcony, and she and her friend prayed. I am always so happy to see a child growing into Judaism.

Worked in the Cathedral Archive this morning and had a conversation with Professor Hoffmann. Grotte appeared suddenly, his hat hiding the Jew's star in shame. I told him exactly what I thought of such behavior! He wants to store boxes of books in the Cathedral Library. It seems that Regierungsrat Halpert's assets and pension have been expropriated! Went to the tax office in the central tax office to pick up sales tax forms, then to the bank, where the clerk asked me about these measures as well.

Thursday, October 9, 1941   Breslau
Uncle Hugo Mamlok was here to say his goodbyes before relocating to Grüssau. It was very upsetting. I always find working in the Community Archive exhausting because of all the talking, completely different from the Diocese Archive! Basically, I wish that I were working all alone; attorney Jakob likes to talk, and Zucker, who again graced us with his presence, is always insulted when we have nothing new to tell him. Then picked up Tamara at kindergarten. We are now forced to stand in the streetcar, which makes it quite a strain.[18] In the United States, Germans have been made to wear a swastika and an armband bearing the word "Nazi."[19] But in the end, it is we who will pay for it all.

Saturday, October 11, 1941   Breslau
Yesterday, the first transports to Grüssau left in vehicles. A Gestapo commissar was assigned to each one. It is said to have been a very sad

18. Jews had been forbidden to sit in the streetcar; according to the diary entry on October 27, 1941, they were also forbidden from entering the compartment.

19. The law of September 1, 1941, that decreed that all Jews in Germany had to wear the yellow star was not universally accepted. Because of this, the Nazis propagated rumors such as this one. The fact that Cohn lent it credence demonstrates just how difficult it was to separate truth from fiction.

sight, all these old people. A real *Yetsi'at mizrayim*.[20] More transports are leaving today; our Edith Rösler is among them.[21] Her father had to go get her from work yesterday; they were given travel orders for today at seven in the morning! Spoke with my colleague Freund; he has kindly offered to give Susanne violin lessons.

Situation: although the Germans are advancing in the East, one nonetheless gets the impression that the special bulletin of the day before was nothing more than advance laurels! The world still belongs to the others! But in Russia, people will vent their anger on the Jews; apparently there has been an enormous bloodbath in Kiev.[22] In Prague, the targets are Jews and Czechs; the synagogues are closed, and the Czechs aren't allowed out onto the street after eight in the evening anymore either. Many shootings. This is how they are trying to win people's favor in the occupied territories, while chattering on about the hardness of the English.

Sunday, October 12, 1941   Breslau

Yesterday morning accompanied my child to the kindergarten assembly place, then went to the bank, which one has to get to by nine o'clock. Met Paul Lyon, who will be leaving for Grüssau tomorrow.[23] Emotionally, people hope for the best in the resettlement, which I suppose is a good thing.

When I got home, I met Hugo Mamlok, who was making one final farewell visit. His attitude is very dignified and firm. He believes, I might add, that we are doomed, and as I consider our situation at this moment there is much to be said for this pessimistic outlook. We just don't want to admit it! It appears that at this moment in the war, the Germans are completely bent on our destruction. We can only hope that they will fail in this plan.

20. The departure of the Israelites from Egypt.

21. Cf. Alfred Konieczny, *Tormersdorf, Grüssau, Riebnig*, p. 134f.

22. Kiev was taken by German troops on September 19, 1941. Under the leadership of Paul Blobel, commander of so-called Sonderkommando 4a, approximately 34,000 Kiev Jews were murdered on two days (September 29 and 30, 1941) at Babi Yar, a ravine northwest of Kiev.

23. Cf. Alfred Konieczny, *Tormersdorf, Grüssau, Riebnig*, p. 128f.

Monday, October 13, 1941   Breslau
Frau Jilek, the gatekeeper at the Cathedral Archive, came by after I had left home. She brought a few good things with her; she has always been so helpful to me in every respect. We gave her the little cabinet that we got from Hugo Mamlok. The time has once again arrived when one best acquires food by barter. Encountered many of the resettlers on the streetcar early this morning; later also on the Sonnenstrasse. The mandated assembly place was the plaza in front of the Freiberger railway station; time, nine o'clock. It was a very poignant sight, watching the expulsion of these, my coreligionists. The people from better families also maintained their composure, but I saw more than a few sad figures as well.

Tuesday, October 14, 1941   Breslau
Yesterday did a few things for *Germania Judaica*. Later, I rode with the two children to the Simchat Torah service. This was the first time that Tamara was aware of being in a synagogue, and it made a big impression on her! During the procession she was jostled by the older children. I carried the 16th Torah scroll. We are now celebrating the rejoicing of the Torah for the ninth time in the Third Reich! Perhaps next time we will celebrate this day in freedom.

Thursday, October 16, 1941   Breslau
Grandmother Proskauer came yesterday afternoon; she wept. Up to now we have received only unwelcome news from Grüssau; among other things, the beds hadn't arrived yet, and people had to sleep fully clothed. A car with sick people has apparently already returned. The war of vengeance on the Jews is continuing unabated in Prague and Vienna. Soviet Russian prisoners of war are given nothing to eat; they are eating the dead! This in the twentieth century. The food situation is getting more difficult by the day here as well. I sometimes have the feeling that Europe is going under.

I did some good work in the Community Archive in the morning. I read a good deal, especially from Brann's intellectual estate, which I found especially interesting.[24] Nothing further has happened as far as

---

24. Cohn was especially interested in this material because ten years earlier he had written a biographical article about Brann, without access to his papers. Willy

the Jewish situation is concerned; the new resettlement list, which is expected soon, has not yet been published! No encouraging news coming from Grüssau.

Friday, October 17, 1941   Breslau

My colleague, Professor Freund, came by in the afternoon to discuss Susannchen's violin lessons; he will first teach her theory. We then had a very interesting conversation. He tortures himself about his own situation as a person of Jewish descent and a devout Christian, and he yearns for a synthesis between Judaism and Christianity. He simply cannot get free of the person of Jesus. I told him how I thought about these things as a Jew, and I gave him Baeck's book, *Das Evangelium als Quelle jüdischer Geschichte*.[25] In particular, I recommended the part about the doctrine of the one and only G'd! In any case, it was a stimulating hour!

Rationing office, but with negative success; my request to extend Trudi's rationing card for the corset was rejected, and I had to go again for Tamara's soap card. They are making everything as difficult as possible for us; nonetheless, we must do all we can not to get too upset!

At home again I found, to my great joy, a letter from Wölfl dated September 25 with very good news about himself. It is so touching how he describes everything! Still, there was a dram of bitterness in the letter; the censorship office forbids us to answer directly.[26] So, even this joy, getting news from one of my children, and as a result hearing something about the others, is taken away!

Saturday, October 18, 1941   Breslau

Went to the synagogue, but rode there and back. Naturally, no encouraging news to be heard in the synagogue courtyard. Another 200 Jews must leave Breslau and vacate their dwellings by October 25. They will be

---

Cohn, "Markus Brann," in Friedrich Andreae (ed.), *Schlesier des 16. bis 19. Jahrhunderts*, Schlesische Lebensbilder 4 (Breslau, 1931), pp. 410–416.

25. Leo Baeck, *Das Evangelium als Urkunde der jüdischen Glaubensgeschichte* [The Gospel as a document of the history of Jewish faith] (Berlin: Schocken, 1938).

26. They could not write to each other directly because Wölfl was in the Foreign Legion, in Algeria. All letters therefore had to go through the Rufs in neutral Switzerland.

taken to Riebnig or to a similar village near Brieg.[27] It is a scene of great lamentation, and yet none of the people leaving know whether they may not have acted wisely! And yet, if this were to happen to me, I would fight to stay because here I continue to have the opportunity to do intellectual work, which is a necessity for me, and which I hope to continue until I draw my last breath. In general, it is astonishing how we Jews bear everything. This increasing terror proves to me just how bad Germany's situation is despite all the reports of victory. But before the great reversal, many, many people will lose their lives, dying a more or less agonizing death. At night I think about the terrible catastrophe that has engulfed us Jews, without daring to attribute guilt or innocence!

Monday, October 20, 1941   Breslau
The weather was terrible all day yesterday, so none of us went out. Trudi did some organizing; after all, we have to prepare in case we are suddenly forced to leave. Elli Bendix came by at noon and asked what I planned to do with my library. Those are the questions that I so especially love. With circumstances as they are I can't give her any advice.

Tuesday, October 21, 1941   Breslau
Today was a very busy and strenuous day for me. To get to the point, when I got home I found two Red Cross letters on my desk, one each from Ruth and Ernst. Ruth's letter was from April, Ernst's from June. They have been visiting each other and like being together. Ruth is very happy being out in the countryside. This is the first news directly from Ruth since she arrived; both of them left with a goal, and they will continue to pursue that goal. In these times, such news keeps a person steady.

Rode to the cemetery in Cosel with Eugen Perle and Director Lasch. They wanted me to take a look at the many books that are located in a room off of the hall. An eastern Jew named Tykocinski is working there! I instructed that they be sorted into four groups. Books that are completely unusable are to be buried; German books, prayer books, and Bibles are to be sent to the settlements, and I plan to look through the actual scholarly works again myself! I also went to Hugo's grave and prayed!

27. Riebnig lies east of Brieg, on the right bank of the Oder River. Cf. Alfred Konieczny, *Tormersdorf, Grüssau, Riebnig*, pp. 63ff., 144ff.

Director Lasch, who is the property administrator, was outside to determine whether some of the rooms might not be freed up for storage since the shortage of space is becoming increasingly acute. The five families that are currently housed in the administration building will have to leave Breslau as well to make room for others who may remain. Up to now, the Jewish community has been able to accommodate everyone. In Breslau, transports are still taking place in a more or less orderly fashion. But in other cities, particularly Berlin, thousands of Jews have been removed; in Berlin, the authorities simply came to their apartments in the evening, gave them three hours to get ready, and deported them just like that. They were probably taken to the larger ghettos in the East, where there isn't anything to eat to begin with. In the final analysis, all of these harsh measures prove to me how badly Germany's war efforts are faring. They are trying to do everything they can to prevent contact between Jews and Aryans to avoid any possibility of sympathy. The ride to Cosel was especially strenuous because I was forced to stand both ways. Director Lasch offered his assistance if I am forced out of the apartment. He disposes over Jewish dwellings!

Had a discussion with Eugen Perle; I told him that he should propose some form of legalization of my activities as an "archivist." I will gladly continue this work for free, but I do wish to enter into a more formal arrangement with the Jewish Community so that I may better fight to stay here if it comes to that.

Wednesday, October 22, 1941   Breslau
I just managed to get to the post office before seven o'clock; very irritated by the clerk who made an anti-Semitic remark behind my back, but had been very friendly when I stood before her. Some of the girls who have gone through BDM are quite filled with hate![28] Forget about it!

Saturday, October 25, 1941   Breslau
I then went to synagogue, which began relatively on time; the Reform Jews pray in the Friends' Hall. Perle accompanied me part of the way. He has not spoken to the Community authorities about my work in

---

28. The Bund deutscher Mädel (BDM) was the section of the Hitler Youth for girls between the ages of 10 and 18. After 1936, membership was made mandatory for "Aryan" girls.

the archive. It is hard to get to the so-called "notables." Well, let no one accuse me of acting out of ulterior motives.

Sunday, October 26, 1941   Breslau
We had a nice visit today. Paul Zeitz and his wife Else, née Proskauer, came by. Theirs is a mixed marriage. I don't remember whether I might have met him decades ago, but in any case I liked him very much. He is an impressive man doing whatever is in his power to help Jews.[29] His son is interned near Melbourne, in Australia, and he is doing well. Their daughter lives with them and does excellent drawings. We heard a number of things from them about the big action that was recently conducted against the Jews of Berlin. They are going after the so-called criminal elements, usually people who had a minor traffic infraction or the like! They are sent to Litzmannstadt![30] In any case, they were dragged out of their homes under fairly horrible circumstances; there are said to have been many suicides! The two of them arrived laden with gifts, among other things wonderful apples and a bottle of wine.

Monday, October 27, 1941   Breslau
Book room in the Freundegarten, where I bought a book about Jewish-Silesian history for 10 pfennigs, and a book for Professor Hoffmann. Gestapo; at least it was well heated in the former Wochentags-synagoge. But the proceedings began with a delay of half an hour. Some, including myself, were asked where we had our b.v.S. account.[31] From there, I rode to the Cathedral Library in spite of the terrible weather because I didn't know whether Frau Jilek might not have gotten something for us. She had not, however, and I certainly didn't want to send her out in such bad weather.

29. On this visit, Cohn made arrangements with Zeitz to store his manuscripts and diaries with him should Cohn be deported. Cohn could not, of course, confide this secret to his diary.

30. Lodz.

31. According to a secret decree sent by the Reich Ministry of Economics to the hard-currency offices on August 16, 1939, all German Jews with assets greater than 5,000 Reichsmarks were required to open a so-called "security account with limited availability" (b.v.S.-Konto) at a domestic foreign-exchange bank. With the exception of certain preapproved transactions, people needed special approval from the hard-currency office for deposits and withdrawals.

It is always very unpleasant standing in the open air on the streetcar sideboard for such long stretches. Received a letter from my in-laws in Buenos Aires; my father-in-law got sick on the trip and is in the Jewish hospital. They haven't been able to proceed onward. I am very happy that Trudi has received news from her parents.

Tuesday, October 28, 1941 Breslau
Rode to Cosel with Eugen Perle. Progress has been made in organizing the books. Unfortunately, books that I would not have discarded have been, but I was able to salvage a few things, especially the books printed in Dyhernfurth, which I brought to Professor Hoffmann![32] Discussed a number of things with Perle. He is having a hard time with these people; they constantly talk around an issue, and then they come up with some sort of an answer. Perle discussed my work in the Community Archive with the chairman of the Jewish Community and told him that I am doing everything. I have the feeling that Perle is very devoted to me.

Went back to the archive, then to see Professor Hoffmann at the old-age home at the Convent of St. Elisabeth. I brought him books and received a few wonderful things in exchange, among them the first volume of the American Jewish Encyclopedia. We chatted for a good hour and exchanged thoughts about Mother Huberta, of whom he does not think highly. He also told me that she isn't properly entering into the accession register the Hebrew books that have just been given to the library. She thinks that they could hurt the library. This far exceeds her competence. I also told him about my plans for expanding the library, if I am permitted to work. I always feel very good talking with Professor Hoffmann in his room at the convent! He gave me an entire package of zwieback for the children! I was also given a few apples at the cemetery.

Friday, October 31, 1941 Breslau
The Germans are now advancing on the Crimean Peninsula, but with enormous losses. This won't change the outcome of the war at all! Tonight, railroad traffic is to be completely converted; only a few passenger trains will continue running. Doesn't affect us; we don't need to travel.

32. An important Hebrew press was located in Dyhernfurth from 1688 to 1834.

"Iron saving" is being introduced, which is nothing other than a new deduction from wages. Supposedly, the money will be returned after the war. Necessities are getting scarcer by the day. But there is no inflation in the National Socialist state, so says today's newspaper.

Final Paths

Saturday, November 1, 1941   Breslau

Comfortable Friday evening. This morning I got up early. Many errands, Dresdner Bank, where "the stars shone"; there were a lot of Jews there because today is the first. I don't usually like to go on this day, but I had two transfers to take care of.

Paid the rent to Machunze. On the way there I had a feeling that I would get bad news. He told me that my apartment had been assigned to a government inspector from Liegnitz. He would like to be moved in by December 1.[1] The slip read, "Moving date not determined." Naturally, Machunze isn't eager because he is now going to have to spend money on renovations in the winter, and he would like to keep me! But I believe that in the end the Party will prove victorious, and we will be forced to tread the same path that so many others have before us. The main thing is to do it with dignity and not to lose one's nerve. We will be up to that, but I must say that I lay awake after dinner unable to sleep, many thoughts coursing through my head.

Sunday afternoon, November 2, 1941   Breslau

Didn't leave the house yesterday as I thought over what the morning had brought us. But then after dinner I did some work on an article about Erfurt. Work is always the best distraction. In the afternoon, peace of mind eluded me in spite of a very good lunch and many pills. Just took a nice walk with Trudi; it was fairly cold, but sometimes you just have to exercise your legs. We were the only Jews out and about.

---

1. The Breslau address book for the year 1943 records the new renter at Opitz-strasse 28 as Regierungs-Oberinspektor Georg Letzner.

When two boys yelled "Jew" after us, the officer who was walking with them said, "Aren't you ashamed of yourselves?"

Monday, November 3, 1941   Breslau
All Jewish real estate has been expropriated in Slovakia; the Jews are to be concentrated at a few places.[2] We are also just now receiving news from those who were sent to Litzmannstadt. They were ushered into centrally heated rooms, and they gave them a few days to set themselves up before performing labor in the factories!

Tuesday, November 4, 1941   Breslau
Alice Oelsner committed suicide, in Havana, Cuba. This apparently had nothing to do with her emigration but with her depressive nature. It really grieved me because it brought up the fate of her sister Gertrud, a friend from my youth who took the same path. There are some Jews who simply cannot cope with the times!

As I arrived in the Community courtyard after picking up the keys, I saw that initial preparations were being made for deportation to Riebnig, district of Brieg. I had a brief conversation with Emil Kaim. The Jewish Community isn't doing anything to make this departure from their heimat emotionally any easier.

Old Director Lasch, who has always been so nice to me, came by later. He will have the cellar windows locked tight for me. I showed him the Breslau community's congratulatory address for King Friedrich Wilhelm II, which was so artfully written. He told me that Rabbi Lewin completely rejects our work in the Archive; he considers it all insignificant, equally the preservation of the printed Hebrew books in Kosel! It is sad that this should be the attitude of a man like him, but it is not possible to change people his age.

Wednesday, November 5, 1941   Breslau
Didn't go out yesterday afternoon. Spent a night exhausted by nightmares. This morning worked in the Cathedral Archive. The director told me, completely depressed, about the atrocities being committed

2. Since 1939, when Slovakia became an independent state, President Jozef Tiso, a Catholic priest, had instituted a totalitarian regime closely allied with Hitler Germany. All Jewish property was "Aryanized," and more than ten thousand businesses expropriated.

against Catholic clergy in the province of Posen. I cannot bring myself to repeat the details.

Thursday, November 6, 1941   Breslau
After dinner, I was visited by an Aryan I did not know, and at first I did not understand the purpose of his visit. He turned out to be a former student of mine, Richard Halm. He used to be with the Volksfürsorge, and he is now a farmer in Dyhernfurth.[3] He brought me a half pound of butter for which he refused payment. He told me that he had learned so much from me! Then he told me about the cemetery in Dyhernfurth, which has been destroyed. However, the stones are still there and he will make sure that the cemetery is photographed for me. Then he told me a few things about the general situation. He is not hopeful about Germany's prospects; the mood among the farmers is bad. We spent an interesting hour, and I was deeply touched.

Then a woman came by and bought Tamara's baby carriage. She even paid a decent price, fifty percent of the purchase price, and because she is an assistant at the Lukas grocery store, my wife should reap other benefits as well! The woman said, "One hand washes the other."

Saturday, November 8, 1941   Breslau
Especially intensive bombing raids must have occurred over large swaths of Germany, because even the Germans are reporting on them, except that as usual they trivialize the losses. Reports from the East sound ghastly. Hecatombs of human beings are being sacrificed. Today is the infamous eve of November 9! The synagogues were set burning three years ago! And yet, the Jewish people will survive these times!

Monday, November 10, 1941   Breslau
Went to the barber; read the speech given by the Führer on November 9. Once again, he heaped abuse on the Jews; international Jewry is behind the war. Fundamentally, he always says the same thing. The tone is appalling and unworthy of a head of state. He doesn't intend to take Leningrad; the plan is to starve the city out.

3. The Volksfürsorge, or more properly, the Nationalsozialistische Volkswohlfahrt, was a Nazi charitable organization that promoted school hygiene and welfare, and distributed among the needy Aryan population property expropriated from the Jews.

Tuesday, November 11, 1941   Breslau

Today is Ruth's birthday, and my thoughts go out to this child who at such a tender age set out on her way, goal firmly in mind, and who with the help of the Almighty will continue to make her way! I am certain that our thoughts will meet over the sea, and I know that today she fears for the home of her parents, where she spent so many lovely hours. My wife baked a small cake so that her sisters might partake of this day as well. Little Tamara is so sweet whenever she talks about "my Ruth."

Went to see Professor Hoffmann at the convent. Rode with Herr Perle to Cosel; Professor Hoffmann rode separately. I didn't want to get him into a difficult situation, and we did the same on the return trip. We looked at books at the cemetery. Tykocinski explained everything very well! Professor Hoffmann also selected a few things; Herr Perle gave his expressed consent to this. Then I went back to the Archive, where I warmed up a bit and drank some hot coffee.

The Friends' Hall has also had to be cleared on orders of the authorities, that is to say, only cleared out. The benches had to be removed. It is not exactly clear what the intention is; perhaps it will be the assembly room when Jews are deported again. Well, we have to eat the dishes as they are served. There is no help for it! Something is undoubtedly in the offing! My wife was harassed for the first time while buying groceries. In general, the public's behavior has been proper!

Wednesday, November 12, 1941   Breslau

The mail brought some welcome news: a letter from Hilde Ottenheimer with a copy of a letter from Baeck. Baeck has written to the chairman of the Jewish Community that he considers it important that I remain in Breslau.[4]

Friday, November 14, 1941   Breslau

Yesterday, we had a real air raid in the middle of the day. The newspaper

---

4. Even this word from the chief rabbi was without effect. Cohn was not among the ten people whom the Jewish Community wase able to have freed subsequent to the arrests on November 21. Thanks to Prof. Franciszek Połomski, University of Wrocław, for this information.

reports that there were seven bombs and seven deaths.[5] But in reality, the losses were probably considerably greater. Naturally, the report is "barbered" to make it look as if the attack had been on innocent civilians. In reality, the intended target was undoubtedly the main railway station, and the bombs came down very close to it. Rumor has it that freight traffic has been brought to a standstill. Mother Huberta related that a military doctor on his way to the train station to inquire about the trains arrived just as a bomb hit; another woman lost both her legs! War always hits the innocent.

Saturday, November 15, 1941   Breslau
I met the mailman when I came home. Unfortunately, the mail brought us no good news; we will have to leave the apartment on November 30, and we will presumably be deported if the Community does not lodge a protest on our behalf. Where to, etc., we do not know. It is doubly terrible in this season, now that severe cold has set in. But this, too, must be dealt with, and we must endure in the interest of the children. What I've always said to others, *chasak ve'ematz*, now holds for me as well. This is especially bad given the delicate state of the children! But G'd will help us! We have discussed everything with our neighbor.

Later, I went to see Eugen Perle, who has always given me good advice. He already knew, and he had spoken to the chairman, Dr. Kohn, who referred him to Dr. Lewin. But Perle didn't wish to discuss the matter with him. He advised me to turn to Director Lasch personally since he is in charge of housing. He also advised me to get in touch with Pakulla, which I have done. I ran into him at the Jewish Community. He told me that he would do everything he could to get me a room. Nonetheless, I am not hopeful because Lewin, the Jewish Community rabbi, is not well disposed toward me. In all, the inhabitants of 300 apartments are facing eviction, which means between 1,200 and 1,500 Jews! It is unlikely that further decisions will be made before Monday; but everything must be thought through. Naturally, I had some very bad symptoms again today, and after dinner I found only a few moments of peace.

5. An article, "Bombenabwurf auf Breslau," in the *Schlesische Volkszeitung*, no. 315, dated November 14, 1941, reported the air raid on the previous day, without mentioning casualties.

Sunday, November 16, 1941   Breslau
Yesterday afternoon was the first time in my life, or at least in the last few years, that I was not capable of working. So many things coursed through my mind. Hedwig Bermann, who had not yet heard of our fate, paid us a visit. She will do whatever she can to help us prepare. I, unfortunately, cannot be counted on for much! Lay awake at night with all manner of symptoms. Took many pills, which have left me fairly broken now. Still, in the interest of the family it is my iron determination not to slacken.

Monday, November 17, 1941   Breslau
Yesterday morning worked with Fräulein Cohn; got angry with her about a stupid expression she used. In the afternoon went for a short walk with Tamara; the sun was shining, and we went to inspect a number of places where bombs had hit. One house in the Neudorfstrasse was largely demolished. Dr. Hadda renovated the Bukesfield Sanatorium, which belongs to him, at his own cost; this in accordance with an air raid protection law! This morning, an uncomfortable walk to the Community administration; first spoke with Fräulein Silberstein, then with Director Lasch. He told me that if the board lodged a protest on my behalf, he would find an apartment for me, that is, a room. Lasch was very understanding. I also spoke with Eugen Perle, who gave me tactical advice, then with the chairman of the Community, Dr. Kohn, who was initially very unpleasant, but then when I made it clear that I wasn't simply going to accept these things, he began to come around. First he told me that there was no possibility with the Gestapo,

Afterword by the Editor

Willy Cohn's diaries end with a comma on page 100 of his last surviving "book." He had filled it up. Cohn undoubtedly continued his sentence where he had left off in his next book, and had it survived, we would almost surely know more about the immediate circumstances surrounding his final journey.

What happened over the next several days can be reconstructed only indirectly. Pleas to the Jewish Community and other authorities to allow him to remain in Breslau were unsuccessful. This meant that his family's "relocation"—to Grüssau, people would have assumed—was inevitable. Now was the time to do what had been discussed just three weeks earlier, to save his diaries and memoirs. These were taken to Berlin, to Paul Zeitz, for safekeeping. As a result, Willy Cohn's diaries survived; they can be read today because of Zeitz's act of courage.

As it happened, there was no time to lose because the Gestapo struck earlier than expected. In the early morning of November 21, 1941, a thousand Breslau Jews were dragged out of bed and brought to an assembly camp near the Odertor railway station. Willy Cohn, his wife, and both of their young daughters were among them. These unhappy people were herded into the large hall of the Schiesswerder beer garden, while the Gestapo cut off all outside communication.[1] It took the officials almost four days to process the assets of all those taken into custody. These assets were then confiscated and expropriated by the

---

1. The following details are based on various sources, chief among them an unpublished dissertation. Marcus Gryglewski, "Die Gestapoleitstelle Breslau und die Judendeportationen in Schlesien," Free University of Berlin, 1996, 62 pages. I wish to express my thanks to Herr Gryglewski for his kind consideration.

German state. The despair must have been overwhelming for many in the Schiesswerder hall, and several people took their lives. Late on the evening of November 25, the remaining people were taken to nearby train tracks, where a completely innocent-looking passenger train stood ready. No one had the slightest inkling that this train would take them to Kaunas (Kovno), in Lithuania.[2]

✳

Although mass killings of eastern European Jews had been going on for some time, this deportation of 1,000 Breslau Jews to Kaunas marked the beginning of the policy of mass murder of the German Jews, not only in Silesia but in Germany as a whole. The train probably reached Kaunas on November 27, 1941, one day after another train, again carrying 1,000 Jews, arrived from Vienna. All of them were taken from the Kaunas railway station to the Ninth Fort, located outside the city, where they were kept.[3] On the morning of November 29, these 2,000 people were herded in larger groups to take part in "calisthenics." When they reached the pits freshly dug in front of the walls of the Ninth Fort, they were mowed down by SS-men and Lithuanians lying in wait for them with machine guns. At the same time, truck engines were revved up to drown out the gun fire and screams. This was not the first mass killing supervised by SS-Standartenführer Dr. Karl Jäger, but in his written report, he felt moved to describe this one as a "shooting display." He further reported that on this day, 693 men, 1,155 women, and 152 children had been shot, all of them Jewish "resettlers."[4] Tamara Cohn, barely three years old, was undoubtedly one of the youngest victims.

2. Alfred Gottwald and Diana Schulle, *Die "Judendeportationen" aus dem deutschen Reich 1941–1945. Eine kommentierte Chronologie* (Wiesbaden: Marix, 2005), pp. 108–109.

3. At the end of the nineteenth century, Kaunas was defended by eight forts and nine gun batteries. A ninth fort was built before World War I. It came to be known simply as the Ninth Fort.

4. See Christopher R. Browning, *Origins of the Final Solution: The Evolution of Nazi Jewish Policy, September 1939–March 1942* (Lincoln / Jerusalem: University of Nebraska Press / Yad Vashem, 2004), p. 395.

✻

At first, no one in Breslau knew where this deportation of Breslau Jews had gone, nor what their end might have been. One of the first to learn more, in the spring of 1942, was Cardinal Bertram of Breslau. By May 1942, family members who remained behind in Breslau also knew that Kaunas was the end destination, without, however, knowing more than that.

In 1942, it was still possible to send Red Cross letters outside the country. They had to be very brief and were subject to strict censorship. Willy Cohn's mother-in-law from his first marriage, Selma Proskauer, sent such a letter, on May 5, 1942, to her son Curt Proskauer, who had emigrated to New York. It was signed by Willy Cohn's first wife, Ella, and her husband Günther Brienitzer. In telegraph style, the letter sought to report what was known about family members, namely that Willy had been sent to Kovno, their niece Ilse to Izbica, while her brother Hugo Mamlok and his mother-in-law were still in Grüssau. This brief letter reads as follows:

> Breslau 5/5/42. We are all healthy. Are you working? Willy Kovno, Ilse Mamlok Isbica, Hugo, Frau Gallinck Grüssau. Brienitzers working as usual. Write soon. Heartfelt greetings, kisses. Mother, Günther, Ella!

✻

Unfortunately, Selma Proskauer had less than a year remaining. On August 31, 1942, she was transported to Theresienstadt, and from there to Treblinka, on September 29, 1942, where she was murdered upon arrival. Ella Brienitzer, her daughter, did not know of her mother's fate. After early 1942, the Brienitzers were fortunate to have even a single room in a "Jew house," located at Wallstrasse 37. Here, they were arrested, on the morning of February 27, 1943, in a raid conducted by SS-Hauptsturmführer Alois Brunner. They were given a preprinted "declaration of assets"—of which there remained very few. The couple was notified the following day that they had been declared enemies of the Reich, and their remaining possessions were expropriated by the German Reich. They remained in the hall of the Freundehaus until their deportation, to Auschwitz, on March 5, 1943. When the train bearing 1,405 Jewish Breslauers pulled into Auschwitz, on the evening of the same day, 125 men and 684 women and children were immediately selected for "special treatment." The surviving daughter, in Israel, later ascertained that her parents died on March 5, 1943.

Timeline

1888	Willy Cohn born on December 12, in Breslau, the sixth of eight children, to Louis Cohn, a businessman, and his wife Margarete, née Hainauer.
1895–1906	Attended the Johannesgymnasium, in Breslau.
1901	Bar mitzvah in the New Synagogue.
1902	Construction of his father's business establishment at Ring 49.
1903	Death of his father. The family gravesite is built in the Jewish cemetery in the Lohestrasse.
1906–1909	Studies in history and German literature at the universities in Breslau and Heidelberg.
1907	Begins the diaries, which he kept throughout his life.
1910	Doctoral dissertation in history under Georg Friedrich Preuss, in Breslau, titled *Die Geschichte der normannisch-sicilischen Flotte unter der Regierung Rogers I. und Rogers II. (1060–1154)*. Published in book form.
1911	State examinations in German, history, and philosophy, in Breslau.
1912–1914	Candidate for a gymnasium teaching position.
1913	Marriage to Ella Proskauer, from Breslau; divorced 1922.
1914–1918	Soldier on the Western Front. Won the Iron Cross for bravery in the field.
1915	Birth of his first son, Wolfgang Louis, called Wölfl.
1919–1933	Teaches at the Johannesgymnasium.
1919	Birth of his second son, Ernst Abraham.
1920	Publication of *Das Zeitalter der Normannen in Sizilien*.

1921	Separation from Ella Proskauer; divorce 1922.
	Publication of *Ein Lebensbild Ferdinand Lassalles. Der Jugend erzählt.* In subsequent years Cohn publishes biographies of Karl Marx (1923), Robert Owen (1924), Friedrich Engels (1925), and August Bebel (1927).
1923	Marriage to Gertrud (Trudi) Rothmann, from Berlin.
1924	Birth of his daughter Ruth.
1925	Publication of *Das Zeitalter der Hohenstaufen in Sizilien*, Cohn's most important scholarly work.
1927	Study trip to Sicily.
1928	Applies for a position at the Prussian Historical Institute, in Rome.
1929	Involved in an exhibition titled "Jews in the History of Silesia," in Breslau.
1930	Publication of *Die Geschichte der sizilischen Flotte unter der Regierung Kaiser Friedrichs II. (1197–1250).*
1932	Birth of his daughter Susanne.
	Italian edition of his 1925 book, under the title *L'età degli Hohenstaufen in Sicilia*. At the same time, Cohn becomes a corresponding member of the Society for the History of Sicily, in Catania.
1933	National Socialist seizure of power. Wolfgang, Cohn's eldest son, forced to leave Breslau because of death threats. Now on his own, he begins his studies in Paris.
	Regime forces 44-year-old Willy Cohn into retirement "for political reasons." After that, he increases his roles as a publicist and lecturer.
1934	Move to a smaller apartment at Opitzstrasse 28. Cohn awarded Cross of Honor for his service in World War I.
1935	Cohn's second son, Ernst, leaves Germany to begin a new life on a kibbutz in Palestine.
	Becomes a board member of the Jewish Museum, in Breslau.
1936–1938	Called to the Jewish Theological Seminary, in Breslau, along with a lectureship in history.
1937	Cohn and his wife begin a six-week exploratory trip to Palestine.
1938	Birth of his daughter Tamara.
	Kristallnacht. Closure of Jewish institutions. Ban on teaching and lecturing. Start of their ultimately unsuccessful attempts to emigrate.
1939	Death of his mother.

1939–1941	Collaboration on the historical and topographical reference work *Germania Judaica* with completion of as many as 80 articles, all but two of which have disappeared.
1940	Ruth's risky emigration from occupied Denmark through Russia to Palestine.
1941	Completion of Willy Cohn's memoirs, which were begun in 1940. Informed of his imminent "relocation." Clandestine plans to save his diaries and manuscripts.
	Arrest, on November 21, and deportation from Breslau, on November 25; Willy Cohn, his wife Gertrud, and their daughters Susanne and Tamara murdered, on November 29, 1941, in Kaunas (Kovno), Lithuania.
1942	Murder of his mother-in-law Selma Proskauer, née Mamlok, in Treblinka.
1943	Murder of his first wife Ella Cohn, née Proskauer (Brienitzer by second marriage) in Auschwitz.
1945	Discovery of Willy Cohn's diaries and memoirs in their hiding place in Berlin.
1975	Excerpt from the diaries published by Joseph Walk under the title *Als Jude in Breslau, 1941* (2nd edition, 1984).
1995	Publication of Willy Cohn's memoirs, edited by Norbert Conrads. *Verwehte Spuren. Erinnerungen an das Breslauer Judentum vor seinem Untergang.*
2006	*Kein Recht, nirgends. Tagebuch vom Untergang des Breslauer Judentums 1933–1941* (3rd edition, 2007). Publication of the diaries, edited by Norbert Conrads.

A Family Overview

Willy Cohn had five children from two marriages. Of the five, three were able to get out of Germany in time. His eldest son, Louis Wölfl (1915–2009), lived in France; his brother Ernst Abraham (1919–2008), who looked after his father's intellectual estate, in Jerusalem, died in Israel. Their sister Ruth Atzmon-Cohn (born in 1924) lives in Israel. Both of Willy Cohn's youngest daughters, Susanne (1932) and Tamara (1938) were murdered, in 1941, along with their parents.

Willy Cohn married Ella Proskauer (1891–1943) in 1913; they divorced in 1922. Her extended family included the Proskauers, Mamloks, and Brienitzers. Ella's mother was Selma Proskauer, née Mamlok (1865–1942); she also had a second son, Curt Proskauer (1887–1972), who married Willy Cohn's sister Erna. After her divorce, Ella Proskauer married the teacher Günther Brienitzer (1892–1943), with whom she had two children, Hanne (1923–2005) and Stefan (Steps) Brienitzer (born in 1928). They emigrated to Israel and Scotland, respectively.

In 1923, Willy Cohn married Gertrud (Trudi) Rothmann (1901–1941). The Rothmann family, in Berlin, was quite large and included her own parents, Isidor and Margarete Rothmann, in addition to Gertrud's brothers Ernst, Julius, and Horst.

Willy Cohn's extended family in Breslau was also large, but not all members of the Cohn family are mentioned in the diaries, and by the same token, not all of the Cohns mentioned were members of his family. His siblings included the engineer Martin Cohn (1873–1922); the businessman Hugo Cohn (1877–1932); the spa physician Franz Cohn (1881–1934); Erna Cohn (1891–1964), who was married to the already mentioned dentist Curt Proskauer; and the businessman Rudolf Cohn (1896–1958). They all have descendents, who are now spread across four continents.

Glossary

Hebrew and Yiddish

Note: The Hebrew terms appear below according to their most conventional English spelling. In the actual diaries, Cohn wrote Hebrew terms as he heard them, that is in the German (Ashkenazi) pronunciation, which differs from that of modern Hebrew, which adopted the Sephardi pronunciation.

Adar   Sixth month in the Jewish calendar (February–March).

aliyah   "Ascent"; the immigration of Jews to Palestine. Also, the invitation to read the Torah in synagogue.

Apala   Actually "Ha'apala," the illegal immigration to Palestine before 1948; also called Hachshara B.

assefa   Assembly.

assefa ha-clalit   General assembly (e.g., in a kibbutz).

Av   Eleventh month in the Jewish calendar (July–August). Tisha B'Av is a fasting day on the ninth day of Av.

Avoda   Religious service.

beteavon   Bon appétit.

Beth Chalutz   House of the chalutzim (see below).

chadar ochel   Dining room.

chalutz, pl. chalutzim (fem.: chalutza, chalutzot)   Pioneers; young Zionist Jews who emigrated to Palestine to build the land.

chalutziut   Pioneering.

Chamisha asar b'Shvat   Fifteenth day of the month of Shvat; semi-holiday of the New Year of the Trees.

chasak, chasak ve'ematz   "Be strong and of good courage" (Deuteronomy 31:7).

Chassidim   Ultra-orthodox religious Jews with a mystical bent.

chaver, pl. chaverim   Member, comrade (fem.: chavera, chaverot), especially in socialist Zionist groups.

chazzan   Cantor in a synagogue.

chevrah   Group.

dreidel   Yiddish: A four-sided top used in a game played at Hanukkah.

Eichah   Song of lamentation for the destruction of Jerusalem, in 586 BCE. In the Jewish tradition, ascribed to the Prophet Jeremiah and recited in the synagogue on the ninth day of Av.

El Male Rachamim   "God full of mercy"; a prayer for the dead recited at the grave and on annual remembrance days.

Elul   Twelfth month of the Jewish calendar (August–September).

erev   Eve of, day of preparation; the day before Shabbat or before a holiday. For example, erev Rosh Hashanah or erev Yom Kippur (Rosh Hashanah eve, Yom Kippur eve).

eruv   Ritual enclosure built to permit observant Jews to carry objects between, for example, the home and the street on the Sabbath, which would otherwise be prohibited.

eshkolit (pl. eshkoliot)   Grapefruit.

galut   Exile; the life lived by Jews outside of Erez Israel, or pertaining to it.

Gemara   Term used for the Talmud; to study Gemara is to study the Talmud.

geserah   Threatening decree or persecution of the Jews; Cohn uses the word to denote the orchestrated rampage throughout Germany on November 9, 1938.

Habonim   "Builders"; a Zionist youth organization founded in England in 1929, which promoted the Hebrew language and culture, and the values of socialist Zionism.

hachshara   "Preparation"; agricultural or manual preparation for emigration to Palestine. In 1934, there were 32 hachshara centers in Germany, which prepared 3,500 young people for aliyah.

haftarah   "Farewell"; sections from the books of the prophets that are read at Shabbat services to conclude the reading of the Torah.

Hallel   "Praise, hymn"; portion of the holiday service in which God is thanked (Psalms 113–118).

Hamatchil   The beginner (also title of a grammar book).

Hanukkah   Eight-day Festival of Lights commemorating the rededication of the Holy Temple in Jerusalem.

Hechalutz   "The Pioneer"; apolitical organization that prepared young Jews to work in Palestine. The movement began in 1923, in Germany.

Histadrut   Nonpartisan union of Jewish workers in Palestine, founded in 1920.

Kaddish   "Sanctification"; prayer recited for the dead at the grave and on commemoration days.

kehilla   "Assembly"; the Jewish community or an assembly thereof.

kibbutz   A collective community established by chalutzim, traditionally based in farming.

Kiddush   "Sanctification"; consecration of Shabbat, prayer recited by the male head of the household on Friday evenings. In the synagogue, Kiddush is said at the end of Friday evening services.

Kinnot   Lamentations, particularly on the ninth day of Av.

kippah   Skullcap worn during religious services or throughout the day (by Orthodox Jews).

Kol Nidre   A ceremonial declaration, in Aramaic, that is recited before sunset on Yom Kippur. The words mean "all vows."

kwuzah, pl. kwuzot   Like a kibbutz (earlier name for cooperative agricultural settlements).

Lag BaOmer   Joyous semi-holiday, the thirty-third day after the beginning of Passover; its origin is unknown, but it is mostly celebrated by lighting fires in open spaces.

Maariv   Evening religious service; the last of the three daily prayers.

machlokes   Yiddish: differences of opinion, disputes.

machzor, pl. machzorim   Prayerbook(s) for the holidays, in contrast to the siddur, the everyday prayer book.

Ma'oz Tzur   "Stronghold of Rock," an epithet of God; an old Hanukkah song sung while lighting the Hanukkah candles. It celebrates the deliverance of Jews from their enemies.

Maskir   Prayer recited in memory of the dead in the German Jewish tradition.

matzoh   Unleavened bread prescribed for the week of Passover in remembrance of the Exodus from Egypt.

mazkirut   Leadership of a kibbutz.

megillah   "Scroll"; in particular, the so-called Five Scrolls or Five Megillot: The Song of Songs; Book of Ruth; Book of Lamentations; Ecclesiastes; and Book of Esther.

menorah   Nine-branched candelabrum used at Hanukkah.

mezuzah, pl. mezuzot   Piece of parchment inscribed with a prescribed Torah verse, enclosed in a decorative case, and attached to the doorframe.

Mincha   Afternoon religious service; second of the three daily prayers.

minyan   "Number"; the minimum number of ten males required for a community religious service.

Mitzrayim   Egypt (in Hebrew).

mitzvah   A religious requirement; a good deed.

moire   Yiddish: fear.

Moshe Rabbenu   "Our Master Moses."

Musaf   Additional prayer on Shabbat and holidays.

Neila   Last prayer or concluding religious service on Yom Kippur.

Nittel   Primarily Hassidic pejorative name for Christmas.

olim   Word derived from "aliyah" to designate Jewish immigrants to Palestine.

pardess, pl. pardessim   Orange plantings; between the 1920s and the 1940s the symbol and pride of Jewish agriculture in Palestine.

Pesach   Passover.

peyess   Yiddish: side locks or side curls worn by Orthodox Jews.

piyyut   Hebrew liturgical poem, sung or recited during religious services.

Purim   Festival celebrated on the 14th of Adar in commemoration of the deliverance of the Jewish people from Persia, a story recorded in the Book of Esther.

rav   Hebrew word for rabbi, spiritual guide.

Rosh Chodesh   First day of the month.

Rosh Hashanah   Start of the Jewish calendar year, and Jewish New Year; start of the ten days of penance before Yom Kippur.

Seder   Ritualized dinner marking the beginning of Passover.

selichot   Prayers asking for forgiveness, said in the period preceding Rosh Hashanah (New Year).

Sephira, pl. Sephirot   "Enumerations"; fifty days are counted (enumerated) from Pesach to Shavuot.

Shabbat   The Sabbath, traditionally observed from just before sunset on Friday until the appearance of three stars on Saturday evening.

Shabbat Nachamu   "Sabbath of comforting"; the haftarah said on the Shabbat following the fasting of Tisha B'Av; the first of seven haftarahs of consolation leading up to Rosh Hashanah.

Shabbat Zachor   "Sabbath of remembrance," immediately preceding Purim.

shammes   Yiddish: Caretaker of a synagogue.

Shehecheyanu   Thanksgiving prayer.

Shir HaMaalot   "Song of Ascents"; title given to Psalms 120–134. However, usually used to designate Psalm 126, which is recited on Friday evening and after the meal on Shabbat as a part of the table prayer.

shotrim   Policemen.

shtreimel   Yiddish: Fur hat worn by Hasidic men.

shul   Yiddish: synagogue.

Shvat   Fifth month of the Jewish calendar (January–February).

sicha   Discussion in the general assembly of the kibbutz.

siddur, pl. siddurim   Jewish prayer book for everyday use.

siddur avoda   A committee that assigns work rotations on a kibbutz.

Simchat Torah   "Rejoicing of the Torah"; the celebration marking the end of the annual cycle of Torah readings and a new beginning.

souk   Arabic: marketplace.

srif, pl. srifim   Wooden house, barracks.

sukkah   Temporary hut (or booth) erected to celebrate the Festival of Sukkot. The huts recall those in which the Israelites lived during the forty years they wandered in the desert before reaching the Promised Land.

Sukkot   Feast of Tabernacles, celebrated on the 15th day of Tishrei (late September–late October).

tallit / tallis   Prayer shawl.

tefillin   Phylacteries worn by observant Jews during weekday morning prayers.

Tehillim   Psalms.

teshuva   "Return"; repentance, return to religious practice.

Tisha B'Av   Ninth day of the eleventh month in the Jewish calendar. Day of fasting in memory of the destruction of both temples (the first by the Babylonian King Nebuchadnezzar II, in 586 BCE, the second by the Roman Titus, in 70).

tzitzis   Knotted ritual fringes attached to the tallit.

tzores   Yiddish: Worries, troubles.

Unetanneh Tokef   "Let us now relate the power of this day's holiness." Both the beginning and the name of a prayer in the Musaf of the celebration of Rosh Hashanah and Yom Kippur. It expresses the fear and trembling at the judgment day.

vatikim   Veterans.

yahrzeit   Yiddish: The anniversary of the death of a relative.

Yetsi'at mitzrayim   The Exodus; the departure of the Israelites from Egypt.

Yishuv   "Settlement"; the community of Jewish residents in Palestine prior to the establishment of the State of Israel.

Yiskor   "Remembrance"; prayers recited in remembrance of the dead.

Yom Hakippurim   Yom Kippur, the most important Jewish holiday.

German, primarily civil service titles

Many of these titles are approximate.

Abitur   School-leaving examination.

Amtsgerichtsrat   Officer of Inferior Court.

Baurat   Government Building Surveyor.

Bibliotheksrat   Senior Librarian.

Justizrat   Judicial Officer.

Kammergerichtsrat   Officer of Superior Court.

Kommerzienrat   Councilor of Commerce.

Konsistorialrat   Councilor of the Consistory.

Landgerichtsrat   Officer of Regional Court.

Oberbaurat   Senior Government Building Surveyor.

Oberbürgermeister   Lord Mayor.

Obermagistratsrat   Senior Councilor of Magistrate.

Oberpräsident   Provincial Prefect.

Oberpräsidium   Board of the Provincial Prefect.

Oberregierungsrat   Senior officer of a government board.

Oberschulrat   Senior Supervisor of Schools.

Regierungsbaumeister   Master Government Architect (or Builder).

Regierungs-Oberinspektor   Senior Clerk of government board.

Regierungspräsident   President of an administrative district.

Regierungsrat   Senior Administrative Officer.

Sanitätsrat   Member of a board of health.

Schulrat   School Inspector (or Supervisor).

Stadtrat   City Councilor.
Studienrat   Secondary school teacher.
Volksfest   Festival of the people.

Nazi German

Gauamtsleiter   Head of an agency of the NSDAP.
Gauleiter   Head of a district of the NSDAP; sometimes translated as "governor."
Gauleitung   Leadership of a regional NSDAP district.
Gestapo   Abbreviation of *Geheime Staatspolizei*, the Nazi secret police.
Gleichschaltung   Forced coordination of all social, political, and cultural organizations to conform with Nazi ideology.
Gruppenführer   "Group Leader"; paramilitary rank approximately equivalent to major-general or lieutenant-general in the SS, general in the SA.
NSDAP   The Nazi Party (National Socialist German Labor Party).
Oberführer   Senior leader in the Sturmabteilung.
Obergruppenführer   "Senior Group Leader"; superior in rank to the Gruppenführer. In the SS, a rank inferior only to that of Heinrich Himmler.
Reichskulturwalter   Guardian of Reich Culture.
Reichsstatthalter   Governor of a Reich district.
Schupo   Abbreviation of *Schutzpolizei*, the regular German police force.
Schutzstaffel   The SS; "Security Squad," originally formed to provide protection to Hitler. Developed into the elite of the Nazi Party under Heinrich Himmler.
SS-Hauptsturmführer   SS rank approximately equivalent to captain.
Standartenführer   Paramilitary rank used by both the SS and the SA; commander of a regiment-sized formation (Standarte = banner).
Sturmabteilung   The SA; "Storm Detachment." The Storm Troopers or Brown Shirts.
völkisch   having or pertaining to national and racial attitude.